VISCOUNT HALDANE

'The Wicked Step-father of the Canadian Constitution'

VISCOUNT HALDANE

'The Wicked Step-father of the Canadian Constitution'

FREDERICK VAUGHAN

From 1911 until his death in 1928, at least in Canadian appeals, Haldane dominated the Judicial Committee as no one had before or would afterwards. In argument and decision, he revealed that his mission was to continue to protect 'those distant Canadian provinces' from any encroachment by a marauding federal government and its Supreme Court.

– John Saywell

Published for The Osgoode Society for Canadian Legal History by

University of Toronto Press

Toronto Buffalo London

ISBN 978-1-4426-4237-9

Printed on acid-free, 100% post-consumer recycled paper
with vegetable-based inks.

Library and Archives Canada Cataloguing in Publication

Vaughan, Frederick
Viscount Haldane : the wicked step-father of the Canadian constitution /
Frederick Vaughan.

Includes bibliographical references and index.
ISBN 978-1-4426-4237-9

1. Haldane, Richard Burdon Haldane, Viscount, 1856–1928.
2. Hegel, Georg Wilhelm Friedrich, 1770–1831 – Influence.
3. Statesmen – Great Britain – Biography.   4. Constitutional law – Canada –
Philosophy.   5. Constitutional history – Canada.   6. Canada. Supreme
Court.   I. Osgoode Society for Canadian Legal History   II. Title.

DA566.9.H27V38 2010   941.082092   C2010-903629-8

University of Toronto Press acknowledges the financial assistance to its
publishing program of the Canada Council for the Arts and the
Ontario Arts Council.

 Canada Council   Conseil des Arts   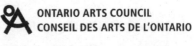 ONTARIO ARTS COUNCIL
for the Arts   du Canada   CONSEIL DES ARTS DE L'ONTARIO

University of Toronto Press acknowledges the financial support of the
Government of Canada through the Canada Book Fund for its
publishing activities.

To the memory of
Dr Eugene Forsey,
who famously called
Viscount Haldane
'The Wicked Step-father
of the Canadian Constitution'

Contents

Foreword

THE OSGOODE SOCIETY
FOR CANADIAN LEGAL HISTORY

Lord Haldane is well known to historians of Canadian constitutional law as one of the Privy Council judges most responsible for reshaping the division of powers in the direction of greater provincial power after the First World War. In this deeply researched biography, Frederick Vaughan, author of a biography of Emmett Hall published by the Osgoode Society in 2004, puts Haldane's Canadian decisions in the context both of Haldane's life and thought and of prior Canadian jurisprudence. Haldane's education, his devotion to Hegelian philosophy, his work as a leading barrister, his various causes, especially educational reform, and his service in the War Cabinet are all analysed, as are some intriguing personality quirks. What emerges is a picture of a complex and deeply principled jurist, and a better understanding of the constitutional division of powers between the federal and provincial governments.

The purpose of the Osgoode Society for Canadian Legal History is to encourage research and writing in the history of Canadian law. The Society, which was incorporated in 1979 and is registered as a charity, was founded at the initiative of the Honourable R. Roy McMurtry, formerly attorney general for Ontario and chief justice of the province, and officials of the Law Society of Upper Canada. The Society seeks to stimulate the study of legal history in Canada by supporting researchers, collecting oral histories, and publishing volumes that contribute to legal-historical scholarship in Canada. It has published eighty-two books on the courts, the judiciary, and the legal profession, as well as on the history of crime and punishment, women and law, law and economy, the legal treatment of ethnic minorities, and famous cases and significant trials in all areas of the law.

Current directors of the Osgoode Society for Canadian Legal History are Robert Armstrong, Christopher Bentley, Kenneth Binks, Patrick Brode, Brian Bucknall, David Chernos, Kirby Chown, J. Douglas Ewart, Martin Friedland, John Honsberger, Horace Krever, C. Ian Kyer, Virginia MacLean, Patricia McMahon, R. Roy McMurtry, W.A. Derry Millar, Jim Phillips, Paul Reinhardt, Joel Richler, William Ross, Paul Schabas, Robert Sharpe, James Spence, Richard Tinsley, and Michael Tulloch.

The annual report and information about membership may be obtained by writing to the Osgoode Society for Canadian Legal History, Osgoode Hall, 130 Queen Street West, Toronto, Ontario, M5H 2N6. Telephone: 416-947-3321. E-mail: mmacfarl@lsuc.on.ca. Website: www. osgoodesociety.ca.

R. Roy McMurtry
President

Jim Phillips
Editor-in-Chief

Preface

R.F.V. Heuston, in his celebrated *Lives of the Lord Chancellors*, wrote that the plaque placed by the London County Council on the wall of 28 Queen Anne's Gate – Viscount Haldane's London home – commemorating his life as a 'Statesman, Lawyer, Philosopher ... [ranked] his achievements in the correct order.'[1] By this remark, Heuston intended to suggest that, however distinguished Haldane's life was as a philosopher or as a judge, his principal achievement was the role he played as a statesman in the life of the nation and of the Empire. No one seriously challenges Haldane's contribution to these spheres of activity, but to consign his dedication to philosophy to the third rank of his achievements is to misunderstand the man and the very grounds of those achievements, especially as a lawyer and as a judge, for Haldane was first and foremost a philosopher whose love of philosophy – of German philosophy in particular – permeated all of his undertakings whether in law or statecraft.

It is not uncommon in Britain, even to this day, to hear people exclaim at the mention of Haldane's name that he was 'the best Secretary of State for War this country ever had.'[2] Some in the academic field of public administration remember him for his contribution as lord chancellor and for his efforts to reform the administrative processes of ministerial departments. Those in the legal profession remember him as a judge of the Judicial Committee of the Privy Council. Still others insist on emphasizing his contribution to the rise of 'red brick' universities throughout Britain. In Canada, by contrast, few people know that he was secretary of state for war in the years leading up to the outbreak of the First World War. Yet, while not exactly a household name throughout Canada, there is no question that Viscount Haldane is deeply etched in the collective memory of the constitutional history and law of this country. As with most prominent people, Haldane has had his supporters and his detractors. Eugene Forsey, one of Canada's leading constitutional authorities for most of the last century, referred to him as 'the wicked step-father of the Canadian Constitution.' Forsey and other Canadian constitutional authorities – including W.P.M. Kennedy, Frank Scott, and Bora Laskin – as well as a long list of historians, such as Donald Creighton, have long pilloried the name and reputation of Viscount Haldane precisely for the way he tortured the terms of the British North America Act, 1867 in order to reduce the authority of the national Parliament and to increase the legislative powers of the provinces. Even the recent new-found friends of the judicial activism of the Privy Council, such as historian John T. Saywell, have referred to Haldane's 'constitutional absurdities.'[3] But no matter how one views the development of Canadian constitutional history, there is no doubt that Viscount Haldane had an enormous impact on the course of that development.

This book emphasizes the role played by Viscount Haldane in this constitutional drama by showing how the philosophy of the nineteenth-century German philosopher G.W.F. Hegel (1770–1831) shaped Haldane's constitutional jurisprudence. It has been prompted, to some extent, by Saywell's dismissal of Haldane's Hegelianism as so much 'Teutonic metaphysics.' As a student of Canadian constitutional history and political philosophy, I have long been intrigued by the brooding presence of this Scottish philosopher-jurist in the shadows of our legal history. The only explicit treatment, until now, of the influence of Hegel's philosophy on Haldane's constitutionalism is an article by Jonathan Robinson.[4] Such neglect is unfortunate, for, in my view, Hegel's impact on Viscount Haldane is a small but important part of that great German philosopher's pervasive influence on the course of Western thought generally. This book, therefore, is in every sense an intellectual biography showing how one man, Hegel, influenced the thinking of a Scottish lawyer and how the new German philosophy of historicism entered into the legal life of Canada by way of his Scottish pupil's conscious appropriation of his 'philosophy of Right' and history. Haldane's contributions to the life of Britain as secretary of state for war and his work with Beatrice and Sidney Webb in the area of education will be treated only to the extent that they add to our understanding of the man and his life as a philosophic lawyer and judge who made a major contribution to the constitutional life of Canada and the Empire.

There have been three previous general biographies of Viscount Haldane. The first, *Haldane: 1856–1915*, by Major-General Sir Frederick Maurice, was published in 1937 and is especially valuable for aspects of Haldane's life as secretary of state for war; it ends a decade and a half before Haldane's death. The second, and most complete, account of Haldane's life is Dudley Sommer's *Haldane of Cloan: His Life and Times, 1856–1928*, which appeared in 1960. Despite its comprehensive treatment of other subjects, this biography pays little attention to how Hegel shaped his jurisprudence and is especially silent on Haldane's jurisprudence in Canadian cases. The third account of Viscount Haldane's life, Jean Graham Hall and Douglas F. Martin's *Haldane: Statesman, Lawyer, Philosopher*, appeared in 1996. This book is the least satisfactory of the existing works on Haldane. It is almost completely devoid of attention to Haldane's Canadian constitutional cases and treats unsatisfactorily the Hegelian influence on Haldane. All three biographies shy away – in varying degrees – from Hegel's philosophy. They all appear, understandably, uncomfortable entering the rarified atmosphere of Hegelian philosophy and unprepared to relate Hegel to Haldane's constitutional jurisprudence.

In addition to the three general biographies, there are a number of specialized books on Haldane relating to his work at the War Office and in the cause of education. For accounts of Haldane's War Office experience, see Edward M. Spiers, *Haldane: An Army Reformer* (1980), and Ernest M. Teagarden, *Haldane at the War Office* (1976). On his contribution to education, E. Ashby and M. Anderson, *Portrait of Haldane at Work on Education* (1974), and John F. Lockwood, *Haldane and the University of London* (1960), are valuable. On Haldane's political philosophy, there is Stephen E. Koss, *Lord Haldane: Scapegoat for Liberalism* (1969).

I would like to express my gratitude to the librarians at the National Library of Scotland, Edinburgh, for guiding me through the Haldane Papers, and to Richard High, special collections librarian at the Brotherton Library, University of Leeds, for making the Gosse Papers available to me. The librarians at the University of Edinburgh library were also very helpful in providing me with archival material relating to the teaching of philosophy at the university in the nineteenth century. The manuscript librarians at the University Library, Cambridge University, gave invaluable assistance in uncovering material pertinent to this book. I am indebted, too, to Elaine Bird, The Signet Library, Edinburgh, for her help in understanding the history and practice of that unique Scottish legal body called Writers to the Signet. I owe Neville Schaffer, QC, Glasgow, my gratitude for his assistance in matters relating to Scottish law and for putting me in touch with important library gatekeepers without whose help I would not have been able to get a foot in the door. I also wish to thank the staff of the Killam Library, Dalhousie University, Halifax, and the librarians at the Sir James Dunn Law Library at Dalhousie Law School. As well, I want to thank the staff at Library and Archives Canada, Ottawa, for their assistance; the librarians of the Royal Canadian Military Institute, Toronto, Ontario, who provided a treasure trove of books relating to the First World War; and Melissa Atkinson, National Portrait Gallery, for her assistance in acquiring several pictures for the book. As is increasingly more the case, I acknowledge my debt to many online library resources, such as the Oxford Dictionary of Biography. Also deserving of special recognition is Peter Cobbold, president of the Athenaeum Society of Nova Scotia, for giving me an opportunity to present a talk on Viscount Haldane at the Society's inaugural meeting at Northwest Cove in February 2007.

Once again, I am grateful to my former colleague, Patrick Kyba, the University of Guelph, for commenting on the first draft and for offering many helpful suggestions. I owe a special debt of gratitude to Justice Horace Krever for his painstaking review of the manuscript and for his helpful comments, all of which I have tried to incorporate. His sage advice has made it a much better book than it would otherwise have been. I am also grateful to the anonymous readers who gave the manuscript careful attention and made helpful comments, all of which improved the final version.

As in the case of other books I have written, I am deeply grateful to my wife, Carol, for her encouragement and assistance at every stage of the process leading up to the completion of the manuscript. We will always remember with affection the time we spent in Edinburgh and Leeds searching the archival sources.

Introduction

The inscription on the headstone erected in the chapel of Gleneagles reads: 'Richard Burdon, Viscount Haldane of Cloan, K.T., O.M., Born July 30th 1856, Died August 19th 1928. Secretary of State for War 1905–1912. Lord High Chancellor 1912–1915 and 1924. A great servant of the State who devoted his life to the advancement and application of knowledge. Through his work in fashioning her army he rendered invaluable aid to his country in her time of direst need.' Missing from that encomium was the enormous role he played in shaping the constitution of Canada in the critical early years of our country's life. For Canadians, his principal claim to notoriety was his efforts as a member of the Judicial Committee to pare down the legislative powers of the Canadian Parliament contained in the terms of the British North America Act, 1867 and to increase the 'autonomy' of the provinces by refining the terms of the allegedly 'misshapen federal system' he found there.

Regardless of where one looks in the history books, the name of Viscount Haldane – usually in tandem with his Scottish judicial predecessor, Lord Watson – is criticized for the way he interpreted the terms of the Canadian constitution of 1867. Eugene Forsey, a legendary force in Canadian constitutional history, criticized him for riding roughshod over the centralizing terms of 'Macdonald's constitution.' It is fair to say that no jurist in our history has received as much learned abuse as Viscount Haldane of Cloan. Twenty years after his death, he received a scholarly tongue-lashing from the late chief justice Bora Laskin, who, at the time of his writing, was Canada's leading constitutional lawyer. Laskin criticized Haldane for confining the 'Peace, Order, and good Government' clause of the constitution of 1867 to times of national emergency.[1] The criticisms of Haldane's work on the Judicial Committee have continued to run deep throughout the literature and lingered for decades. When Laskin was appointed to the Supreme Court of Canada in March 1970, Frank Scott, an old friend of many years and at the time dean of law at McGill, wrote to the new judge and said that his appointment was the 'best news since [he learned of] the death of Lord Haldane.'[2] Since Haldane had died in 1928, forty-two years before Laskin's appointment, Scott, clearly, had waited a long time for good news. In his response to Scott's congratulatory note, Laskin reminded him that 'Haldane's legacy need not imprison Canadians forever.' The clear implication was that, since the Privy Council itself had declared eight years earlier that it no longer felt bound by its past judgments, Canadian courts, especially the Supreme Court of Canada, was likewise not bound by the past judgments of the Judicial Committee.[3]

Despite Laskin's optimism, however, to this day the constitutional directions set down by both Lord Watson and Viscount Haldane have never been seriously reversed. Canadian constitutional law is still locked in the twisted brambles of the Watson-Haldane jurisprudence. 'Peace, Order, and good Government' continued for many years to be restricted to times of national importance, although the Supreme Court of Canada has affirmed more recently that the clause may be properly used in other circumstances.[4] And the main decentralizing influence of Viscount Haldane remains firmly in place. The truth of the matter is that the Canadian federal system functions today more according to Haldane's (and Watson's) way of thinking than that of Macdonald's and most of his colleagues, our constitutional framers.[5]

Richard Burden Haldane, despite his reputation in the pages of Canadian history, was by any standard of measurement an extraordinary man noted for his aloof and determined demeanour and his prodigious work ethic. He participated at the highest cabinet levels in the major affairs of the British nation as a member of Parliament from 1885 through the years leading up to and immediately following the First World War. He was on intimate terms with all the leading politicians of the day, including Herbert Henry Asquith, David Lloyd-George, and Ramsay MacDonald – all three of whom became prime minister. He served in the Liberal cabinet of Asquith as well as in Ramsay Mac-

Donald's first Labour cabinet, and was to return to the 'woolsack' (the Speaker's throne) as the first Labour lord chancellor in 1924. As a cabinet minister, he instituted major reforms in the British Army and took a leading role – with George Bernard Shaw, Sidney and Beatrice Webb, and Harold Laski, among others – in the extension of university education throughout England and Wales. As well, he attempted major domestic judicial reforms while serving as lord chancellor. Above all, he presided over a number of important Canadian cases as a judge in the House of Lords and as a member of the Judicial Committee.

My first objective in this book is to explicate Haldane's intellectual debt to the nineteenth-century German philosopher G.W.F. Hegel, whom Haldane read for fifty years and acknowledged as his mentor. Then I propose to show how this serious, life-long student of philosophy brought his abstract philosophical knowledge to bear upon all aspects of his practical life, whether in military affairs, in education, or in the law. By far his most enduring contribution was in the area of the law and judging, especially in Canadian constitutional cases in which he took a special interest. His training in modern German philosophy made him, in a sense, an outsider, an alien both to the British bar and to the public at large. An aura of the loner dogged him throughout his long career in politics and on the bench. And not a few in Canada and in the United Kingdom viewed him with suspicion for introducing a foreign influence into the constitutional law of the Empire.

Owing to the daily drumming in the Northcliffe press, the question of Haldane's patriotism grew and reached a crescendo when it was uncovered that he had once publicly called Germany his 'spiritual home.' The repeated taunts in the daily newspapers eventually led to his resignation from the cabinet in 1915. This man, thundered Viscount Northcliffe's newspapers, was too 'pro-German' to be trusted with a seat at the cabinet table of a nation at war with Germany. And so his friend Prime Minister Asquith – to his lasting shame – acquiesced in Haldane's resignation from the cabinet.

Haldane was also an outsider among many of his contemporaries because he was not an Oxford or a Cambridge man. His elementary and university education took place almost exclusively in Scotland. Rather than proceed to Oxford, as many expected he would, he elected to go to Germany to study under one of the leading scholars of the day, Hermann Lotze at the University of Göttingen. He set out to become a philosopher and graduated with an MA in philosophy from the University of Edinburgh. Such was his reputation in academic circles that at one point, early in his career, he was offered a chair in moral philosophy at the University of St Andrew's. But, by long family tradition on both sides, his roots were deeply sunk in the law. The more he reflected the more he was drawn to the Inns of Court and a life at the bar. For Haldane, however, the new direction did not mean that he would jettison his love of philosophy. He saw the practice of law as the perfect way by which to bring philosophy to bear upon the important matters of state, just as Hegel had intimated. He became an acknowledged Hegelian scholar in his own right and, through his writings, openly strove to introduce the great German's philosophy into everything he did. As Dudley Sommer has written: 'Any account of the life and work of Richard Burdon Haldane would be pitifully incomplete unless due regard were paid to his philosophical thought. It was indeed the impelling power of his life.'[6] Another of my objectives in writing this book is to shed a searching light on the current role and authority of the Supreme Court of Canada. In other words, it is critical to see how the Hegelian legacy is operating under the 'living tree' jurisprudence that has taken hold in the Supreme Court of Canada since the adoption of the Charter of Rights and Freedoms. Modern rights jurisprudence owes much to Hegel and that influence has entered into the lifeblood of Western law generally and into Canadian law by way of Viscount Haldane. The heart of the story is how nineteenth-century legal pragmatism – prudence tempered by deference to the will of Parliament – was overborne by German idealism inspired by G.W.F. Hegel. Richard Haldane gave the back of his hand to the best efforts of our colonial constitutional framers and early Supreme Court of Canada judges. Running throughout this story is the forbidding presence of Hegel and sheer Scottish pigheadedness; it is a story of how a Scottish law lord, armed with German idealism, set out to make Canada into a 'genuine federal state.'

In a Postscript I will show how Hegelian historicism, masquerading as 'progressivism,' lies at the heart of the emerging Charter jurisprudence in the Supreme Court of Canada. The Postscript is a necessary part of Haldane's story because it is the nature of philosophers that their influence extends beyond their times. Who would deny that the reclusive Immanuel Kant – who never left his native Königsberg – has had a profound influence through his writings on the course of Western philosophy? Haldane died in August 1928, but his life's work did not end at that time. We shall see that he saw himself as a leader, even one of greatness, who sowed the seeds that would shape future generations. Seven years before he died, he wrote that 'the influence of such leaders may be confined at first to a few. It may never permeate newspapers or be displayed in the limelight. But nonetheless it will be great if, filling at first the minds of only a comparatively small band of disciples who have accepted it, that influence gradually shapes to begin with, general opinion, and in the end the institutions which are responsive to that great opinion.'[7] He never wavered from the conviction that 'ideas when great enough, have a penetrative power which extends beyond the boundaries of nations and across oceans ... The gift with which a really dominant personality is endowed almost always extends in some way beyond its sphere.'[8] It is imperative for those concerned with the public law of Canada to understand that what Haldane has bequeathed to us contains critical *problems* stemming from his commitment to Hegelian historicism.

Viscount Haldane bequeathed to posterity a voluminous correspondence with leading politicians and intellectuals of the day, as well as a large body of documents relating to his education and to his life in politics and on the bench. He also wrote a dozen books on education, law, and philosophy. Before entering politics and the law, he wrote articles on Goethe and Hegel and translated the principal text of Schopenhauer. His letters written to his mother and to his closest friend, Sir Edmund Gosse, librarian of the House of Lords, contain a plethora of acute observations on the leading figures and issues of the day and especially on his legal work, both on and off the bench. Applauded or reviled, Richard Burdon Haldane was unquestionably a 'step-father of the Canadian Constitution.' And the philosophical foundations of his contribution to the continuing life of Canada – however controversial – deserve to be better understood and acknowledged.

VISCOUNT HALDANE

'The Wicked Step-father of the Canadian Constitution'

Göttingen, 1874

The streets are filled with noisy revellers boistrously singing ancient songs to Bacchus as, preceded by a band with tuba and horns, they snake their way in procession to the beer halls. It is Sunday noon and this medieval German university town is celebrating as it has every Sunday for generations. Even preachers, hurriedly completing their sacred duties and quickly changing into festive garb, rush to join the procession. Missing from the sea of cheering students and townsfolk is a solitary figure walking along the unkempt battlements which surround the town, remnants of medieval fortifications that are today deserted by the Germans for the beer-hall concerts. Few bother to notice him; those who do dismiss him as likely a foreign student as yet uncomfortable with their beer-stained pagan celebrations. This son of devout Scottish Baptists is contemplating the sermons of Dr Robert Smith Caudlish rather than going to church because the English services had ceased for want of a preacher and a congregation. No one could then guess that this solitary pensive figure clad in his native Scottish broad tweed would one day be responsible for putting into the field of battle against Germany an efficient English fighting force which would crush the ambitions of the kaiser. Certainly, no one in Göttingen that Sunday morning in April 1874 was apt to identify the man who would turn the Canadian constitution upside down as a judge of the Judicial Committee of the Privy Council. 'Tomorrow is Sunday,' the young man wrote forlornly to his mother the next Saturday, 'which is the most uncomfortable day in the week on account of the noise and number of people in the streets on that day.'

1

Home and School for the Mind

For the first time in my life I have heard of a prominent public man who converses by letter every day with his mother.
– Albert Einstein to Elizabeth Haldane, 15 June 1921

After loading the coach with crates of personal belongings – securing them tightly on the roof racks – Richard Burdon harnessed up the four stately brown horses for the long trip from Rotherhurst in Kent to West Jesmond near Newcastle in Northumberland. The year was 1826.

A week before, he had received word that his father, Sir Thomas Burdon, was not well and he worried that he might not be able to get to see him before matters worsened.[1] He bundled up his wife and two young daughters and set out by coach road for Newcastle. The road, which scarcely deserved the name, had begun to witness the results of neglect since the train had arrived on the scene little more than a decade earlier. The shift in emphasis away from horse-drawn means of transportation towards railway travel had started to show in the rutted throughways and ill-maintained roads. Richard Burdon wanted to arrive at his destination with his horses in good condition; he had groomed and taken excellent care of the beasts and intended to make further use of them in the north. He rested, watered, and fed his horses regularly en route, stopping every twenty miles to do so. The trip to Jesmond, at times over treacherous terrain, took the young family ten days to complete.

The ardour of the trip north, in fact, exacted its toll in the death not long after their arrival of one of the great horses for whose heart the strain was simply too much.

Family Background

Richard Burdon was the youngest of four sons of Sir Thomas Burdon, owner of a successful colliery in Jesmond near Newcastle-upon-Tyne; two of his brothers had died early and his only surviving brother fell out of favour with his father 'for not helping him in his office in Newcastle and going to live in London.'[2] The elder brother was provided for in his father's will but the thriving family colliery business in Jesmond was left to the younger son.[3] Upon graduating from Oxford, Richard did not join his father's business but, after becoming a solicitor, became a commissioner in bankruptcy. He was appointed by his uncle, Lord Eldon, to the post of secretary for presentations, in which office the young man oversaw the appointment of Church of England 'livings' to successful applicants. His daughter Mary Elizabeth was to relate in her memoirs that 'as Secretary of Presentations to his uncle certain pertinent questions of right and wrong came up acutely before him, and he asked himself how could it be that the Church which he loved as the Church of Christ could give away livings to the highest bidder and the care of souls into the bargain which were precious in the sight of the Lord?'[4] Those seeking these preferments frequently made 'presents of different sorts' in order to secure the goodwill of his uncle. Qualms of conscience led the young man to resign his position and leave Lord Eldon's service. His abrupt departure left a little bitterness on the part of his uncle, who considered Richard as the son he was deprived of with the death of his own son, John Scott, a decade earlier. Richard left London and settled with his wife and young daughters in Rotherhurst, Kent, with a view to establishing himself as a lawyer. Within a year of settling in Kent, Richard received word that his father was gravely ill and was summoned home.

The Burdons arrived at their destination in mid-July when the country was experiencing one of the hottest summers on record. They were greeted with the news that Sir Thomas had died a few days before their arrival. After presiding over the funeral and settling his father's estate, Richard assumed ownership of the Wallsend Colliery; he set about immediately building a new house since the foundations of the old family home had begun to weaken as a result of the mining operations of the colliery. Mary Elizabeth recorded years later that her father had been 'startled by finding the responsibilities that my grandfather's will had laid upon him and the changed life it entailed.'[5]

Mary Elizabeth – the elder daughter of Richard Burdon and the future mother of Richard Burdon Haldane – and her sister were raised according to what she called a 'Spartan' regimen: 'The day commenced by our being wakened by our nurses, taken by the two, and plunged over head in a deep bath of cold water.'[6] The sisters were placed under a governess, Miss Taylor, who was a strict disciplinarian quick to punish violations of the schoolroom. The two girls spent 'twelve hours of every day there under her supervision.'[7] 'The system of the day,' Mary Elizabeth later recorded, 'was to administer corporal punishment. We, or rather I, as my sister escaped from having had scarlet fever and being pronounced delicate, was shut up for a day at a time and fed only on bread and water.'[8] In addition to careful study of the Bible, the young girls received formal academic instruction in Greek, Latin, and French. The instruction must have been agreeable, for Mary Elizabeth, at least, never lost her deep devotion to learning.

Mary Elizabeth Burdon's mother, Elizabeth Sanderson-Burdon, was the only child of Sir James Sanderson from York. Sir James was a hop merchant and banker and was high sheriff and twice lord mayor of London. He died at the age of fifty-two, just two years after Elizabeth was born. He had wanted a son and, while disappointed at having a daughter, left instructions in his will that his daughter and only child was to be educated as a boy, 'and a very valuable library was left for her use.'[9] Upon marriage, this only child was also obliged by terms of the will to assume the name of 'Sanderson' along with Burdon. Those instructions clearly set down that the child was not to be taught music or any of the usual accomplishments of a young lady. Instead, she was to be tutored in Latin, Greek, and other subjects suitable for a 'masculine mind.'

Elizabeth's mother was uncharacteristically – given the age – free of the religious oppressiveness that characterized her own parents. And, having been educated 'as a boy,' she was free to roam and explore a non-religious literature beyond the range of most girls of her generation. Despite the want of formal instruction in music, she became proficient at the piano and taught herself to read and compose music. She also passed on to her daughters her love of learning and a spirit of intellectual independence. At times she would take the girls away from their governess and in the privacy of her boudoir read from Voltaire's

History of Louis XIV, Charles XII, and *Peter the Great,* thereby not only introducing the girls to a world of court splendour beyond England but also exposing them to the mind of one of the most daring iconoclasts of the age. These moments were to leave their mark on the inquisitive daughters. Little wonder that Mary Elizabeth would bring these same talents into her own home and shape her children as independent thinkers.

Besides formal academic instruction, Elizabeth taught her daughters to become engaged in the life of the community. When, for example, the cholera epidemic struck the British Isles in 1832, Elizabeth became actively involved in helping the sick and dying and she made sure that her children knew of the suffering around them. Nor were politics excluded from the education of this household; the parents began to show their preference for Liberal politics early in their life and communicated their views by discussing the political issues of the day with their children. Elizabeth even provided a governess to teach the children of the pitmen who worked in the family colliery. The Burdons were in every sense enlightened entrepreneurs, especially by standards of the day, when colliery owners in some parts of the country – noticeably in Wales – took little care of their workers. The children were not isolated from the harsh realities of city life, particularly the lot of young working boys. 'In those days the line of demarcation between classes was very strong. But though our hearts were touched by hearing of the boys who were sent up chimneys to sweep them and who often stuck fast with disastrous results, and of those who were laid hold of and made to serve aboard ship, in our neighbourhood conditions were fairly good.'[10]

The year 1832 was memorable not only for the dreadful cholera epidemic but also for the famous Reform Act. Even though she was a child at the time, Mary Elizabeth later remembered the excitement it caused when the family learned of the passage of this landmark bill. The news was conveyed to them by the driver of the Chevy Chase coach which ran between Newcastle and Edinburgh. 'The coach passed over our own gate and at the foot of the avenue leading to Overacres the horn blew as it stopped to give it. People collected at the gate to hear the wonderful news, and, as we were fortunately without a governess at the time I was present, though only a child of seven.'[11]

If there was one aspect of Mary Elizabeth's childhood that came under critical scrutiny in later years, it was the atmosphere of, what she called, 'introspective religion.' Ten years after the family moved to West Jesmond, the Burdon parents fell under the spell of Paul Methuen, a member of the Plymouth Brethren, who succeeded in leading them out of the established Church of England and into the rigid embrace of evangelical Christianity. As a result, Mary Elizabeth's life was not to remain as agreeable as it had been for so many years as a child. The religious intensity of her home at length threw a pall over her life. Her parents imposed a routine of unrelenting Christian witness; there was very little childhood play that did not fall under the disapproval of some form of religious discipline, and Sundays, of course, were play-less and of unending religious observance. Strict oppressive Calvinism instilled in Mary Elizabeth the belief that she was a hopeless sinner incapable of ever pleasing God: 'My [youthful] happiness,' she later wrote, 'was only marred by the thought of my own sinfulness, which never left me.' Her home experience would prompt her to conclude that religion is 'too often ... the wedge of torture, and to sensitive natures an engine of cruelty.' This religious background led her to resolve to bring up her own children 'in the light of day with the full glare of public opinion blazing on the work of their education. It is their own fault if they are not independent thinkers.'[12]

Years later Mary Elizabeth described her home life in those early formative years: 'My father now retired much into a contemplative life, busying himself with writing and reading. Our lives hence went on in an even flow, studying French, Italian and German with our governess and masters when they could be got. In the afternoon we read history aloud, and were questioned upon it. In this way we studied the histories of Hume, Smollett, Russell, Buchanan, Rollin, and Crevier, besides Mitford's *Greece* and other similar books. In the evening my father read to us *Paradise Lost*, Cowper's *Task*, Dryden's works, and Pope's *Homer*. With our Italian master we read Tasso and Metastasio.'[13] In this mixed crucible of strict Christian piety and secular education, Mary Elizabeth's character was formed and it served her and her children well throughout her long life. She became not only the mother of five talented children but the guiding presence in all their accomplishments. She never ceased to educate herself. As her eldest son, Richard, recorded: 'She read extensively, in various languages, and her reading included difficult philosophical books, as well as memoirs and histories.'[14] She loved nothing more than to converse with the steady parade of learned in her home. 'She conveyed the sense that she was genuinely looking at things from a high point of view, which reached not only to the things set down but over them. Her mental activity was great and its range was wide.'[15] She was in every sense the polar star which guided her children by gently prodding them to reach higher and higher intellectual heights by demanding of ·herself what she expected of her children.

The Burdon children were, through their grandmother, Lady Burdon, great-nieces of Lord Chancellor Eldon and of the renowned jurist and judge Lord Stowell, both owners of large properties in Northumberland. Through these contacts with such distinguished lawyers and judges, the children became consciously proud of their maternal ancestors. Their grandmother saw to it that they became steeped in the folklore of this part of their family history. Mary Elizabeth, especially, became deeply conscious of the law and the legal history of the realm and she transmitted her pride and enthusiasm to her children from their earliest years.

In the midst of days of stifling religious severity – and much to her delight – Mary Elizabeth met a young man and fell deeply in love for the first, and perhaps the only, time in her life. The young man was not only handsome but adventurous; she found that being with him filled her days with laughter and life in general took on a wonderful new excitement, full of joy and free of the clouds of Calvinist oppression. But her new-found joy was soon suddenly to come crashing down. When it became clear that she was ready to marry the young man – she never confided his name to her diary – her parents objected that he was insufficiently religious for their daughter and forbade the relationship to continue; marriage to such a man was out of the question. In her brief autobiographical account of this period of her life, Mary Elizabeth recorded that she never got over the loss of her first love. For the remainder of her days, she kept the memories of his joyful presence in the privacy of her heart and revealed them in secret accounts many years later only to her daughter, Elizabeth.

Having acquiesced in the judgment of her parents, Mary Elizabeth resolved to go abroad as a Christian missionary when her anonymous first suitor was sent packing. But her parents also prevented this adventure and encouraged her, instead, to marry the widower Robert Haldane, a friend of her father's. 'In my youth,' she explained in her diary, 'a married woman had no more position than a cat, and it was my intention to be a missionary and devote my life to the care of the heathen. But when Mr. Haldane wished to marry me I felt it was my duty to obey the nearer call and devote my life to him and his six motherless children.'[16] Little did she realize at the time that she would herself become a mother of five intelligent and ambitious children. Few children have been born to a mother as broadly educated as she or as determined to raise her children in the life of the mind.

Mary Elizabeth brought with her into her marriage to Robert Haldane a resolve to supervise closely the education of her children and to assist the cause of women, especially those who had 'fallen by the way.'[17] As her daughter Elizabeth was to record, 'I think it was partly her feeling for the unfortunate of her sex that made her sensitive to the position of women generally and anxious that their interests should be guarded by law; she felt very keenly about the inequalities that then existed, and she was a supporter of granting the suffrage to women very much for that reason.'[18] A friend would write at the end of her life: 'Instead of leading a forlorn existence defending some untenable position behind a sandbag on a barricade, she came into step with her children and adventured with them whole-heartedly in the treasure rooms of the new knowledge and new ideas of our time.'[19] But, despite her intellectual curiosity with things philosophical and scientific, Mary Elizabeth Haldane remained, as Sir Edmund Gosse noted in his *Times* obituary upon her death, 'profoundly religious, and to the end delighted to discuss, but no longer with any hardness, the strenuous tenets of her youth.'[20]

The widower Robert Haldane, father of Richard Burdon Haldane, was born in Edinburgh on 27 January 1805, the third son of James Alexander Haldane, father of fifteen children – having married twice – and a fierce evangelical Christian. As boys, both Robert and his elder brother James came under the influence of the fiery brand of Christian evangelicalism unleashed by the Plymouth Brethren then gathering momentum throughout England and parts of Scotland. Robert was educated at Edinburgh High School and later in Geneva where the red flames of Calvinism, carefully cultivated at home, were – to the delight of his father – fanned into a life-long missionary fervour. After returning from Switzerland to his native city, he undertook the study of law at the university and on 5 March 1829 became a 'writer to the signet' – a unique Scottish legal office reaching back to the fourteenth century. ('Writer,' as used here, is old Scots for lawyer or attorney. Today writers to the signet are required to be Scottish solicitors.[21]) Robert married Janet Makgill of Kemback in the County of Fife in 1841. But his life was to suffer a severe blow with the death in childbirth of his beloved wife in February 1851. Her death left him to raise on his own six healthy children.

Robert had absorbed his father's religious passion and had nurtured a rigid Calvinistic theology; in his early life he had dreamed of leading a missionary expedition to the West Indies but family circumstances prevented him from realizing this ambition. He never abandoned his evangelical crusade, however, and when he became established at Cloan in Auchterarder, Perthshire, in 1851, he built an addition on the barn and held religious services for the local people for many years. He was an industrious man and prospered in his profession as a writer to the signet, acquiring many trusteeships and the management of numerous estates, and secured a lucrative practice by which to support his large family. By every account he was a devoted and solicitous father of what became a family of eleven children, six from his first marriage and five from his second.

Robert introduced Mary Elizabeth into the elegance of her new home at 17 Charlotte Square, Edinburgh, immediately after the wedding. Charlotte Square, the architectural achievement of the eighteenth-century architect Robert Adam, was – and remains to this day – renowned for its beauty. The stone row house at number 17 consisted of three floors with eighteen rooms. The children's nursery and school rooms were located on the third floor. As was the custom in those Victorian days, the Haldane children spent most of their days with their governesses and tutors; they took their evening meal with their parents, at which time they were expected to give an account of the day's efforts at both games and schooling.

The Age of Victoria

Richard Burdon Haldane, the eldest son of Robert and Mary Elizabeth, was born on 30 July 1856 into this distinguished Scottish family whose ancestry has been traced back for more than 700 years without a break in the male line. He was also born into the heart of Victorian Britain. Queen Victoria had reigned for nineteen years when Richard was born. It was a time when the industrial wonders of Britain were bursting with energy and unleashing an unbounded entrepreneurial enthusiasm accompanied by unspeakable urban squalor; it was the age of the rise of large manufacturing cities complete with clouds of coal-dust smog that was to give London and other large cities such as Birmingham and Manchester their reputation for unhealthiness. Had he been born twenty years earlier, however, during the passage of the Reform Act of 1832, Richard would have breathed in an atmosphere of cynicism and irresolution as well as the industrial smog. In those days, one historian has noted: 'Statesmen were without ideals, the Church without vision, the Crown without honour, and the common people without hope.'[22] It was the age that brought forth Charles Dickens and the unforgettable characters of his beautifully acerbic prose. 'What was the atmosphere which surrounded the most successful age in Britain's history?' asks one recent observer of things Victorian. 'It was the fog that spreads through the pages of *Bleak House*, choking, blinding, befuddling. It was the dark crimes and prison stenches in *Oliver Twist, Little Dorrit,* and *Great Expectations.*'[23] By good fortune, however, in 1856, Britain was on the steep rise of industrial expansion unequalled in her past history. And it was driven by the noisy steam locomotive that changed the life of Britain forever. A generation earlier, Edmund Burke had lamented the emerging political and economic reforms as the end of the age of chivalry: 'That of sophisters, economists and calculators has succeeded; and the glory of England is extinguished for ever.'[24] But those who harboured such regrets were lost in the excitement of this rising generation of Victorian merchants and entrepreneurs.

Just five years before Richard's birth, the Great London Exhibition of 1851 opened in Hyde Park. The opposition to this event – fierce, protracted, and led in Parliament by Colonel Charles de Laet Waldo Sibthorp – was overcome by the enthusiastic endorsement of the prince consort, who was president of the Royal Society of Arts. Inspired by the great success of the Paris Exhibition of 1840, and not to be outdone by the French, Albert and his cohorts succeeded in winning the approval and funding of Parliament. The first great hurdle for the royal commission responsible for the exhibition was to build a suitable structure to house the wares of 14,000 exhibitors without doing violence to the Hyde Park property. After reviewing and rejecting 240 proposals, the commission adopted the design submitted late in the process by Joseph Paxton, chief gardener to the Duke of Devonshire. 'What Paxton had designed was nothing more than a gigantic greenhouse, 1,848 feet in length, 408 feet in breadth.'[25] *Punch*, which had joined with *The Times* to ridicule the whole project, dubbed the design 'The Crystal Palace.' And the name stuck.

And so, on 1 May, Queen Victoria came down for the opening of the Exhibition. She endorsed the venture with the claim that the event constituted nothing short of 'a peace festival, which unites the industry of all the nations of the earth.'[26] The sights before her were like a hymn of praise to the infinite resourcefulness of the human mind. Raw materials, machinery, manufactures, and fine arts all had their place. As one British historian writes:

The British and Colonial section, one half of the whole exhibition, included Nasmyth's steam hammer, the hydraulic press used for the construction of the Britannia bridge over the Manai Straits, manufacturing machines and railway equipment, the Ross telescope and photographic apparatus. Then came every variety of textiles, precious metals, Wedgwood pottery, and even a mediaeval court designed by Augustus Pugin. Seven whole sections were given up to produce from the Empire. Then there were the foreign displays from almost every country in Europe – as well as from the United States, whose exhibits included the first trays from the Californian gold-fields, Colt's revolver, and McCormick's reaping machine. One exhibit not within the Crystal Palace was Prince Albert's Model Lodging-house, built near the Knightsbridge Barracks, designed to accommodate two working-class families.[27]

No one could have known at the time that the atmosphere of peace the queen celebrated was to be shattered less than three years later when the entire nation almost to a man was clamouring for war against Russia in the Crimea.

To the delight of its supporters and the chagrin of its detractors, the Exhibition was a resounding success, with a profit of £186,000 gleaned from the pockets of an astonishing six million visitors. Henceforth the Great Exhibition would be billed as 'a symbol of a staggering prosperity and of a still greater prosperity to come. The fruits of Free Trade, the thought of constitutional reform achieved without violent revolution, nearly forty years of peace and a growing Empire overseas, all combined to give the Victorian a sense of optimism and a certain self-satisfaction.'[28]

It was just the boost to morale the country needed, or so said the emerging industrial class. But London in 1851 was not all glitter and glass. It was a city that had seen its ranks swell over the previous fifty years from 850,000 inhabitants to two and a half million, straining the housing and sewage resources of the city to the breaking point. John Phillips, chief surveyor for the Westminster Court of Sewers, related in one report that 'I have seen in such places human beings living and sleeping in sunk rooms, with filth from overflowing cesspools exuding through and running down the walls and over the floors ... I should be ashamed to keep pigs in so much filth as I have seen human beings living amongst.'[29] Dickens more famously chronicled the life of the London poor in 1852 in *Bleak House*, where he painted a portrait of the city in the grip of winter: 'smoke lowering down from chimney pots making a soft black drizzle with flakes of soot in it as big as full grown snowflakes.' The previous year, the year of the Great Exhibition, Henry Mayhew published his *London Labour and the London Poor*, in which he exposed the raw underbelly of the poor sections of the city. The picture was not pretty: squalor, poverty, sickness, disease, and starvation. It was not the picture the country wanted the world to see. But it was an integral part of the city's life and it would enter Richard Haldane's line of vision through the insistence of his mother and sister, Elizabeth, and, later, of Beatrice and Sidney Webb.

No one was to embrace the modern industrial inventions more warmly than Richard Haldane, who had been born in Edinburgh at a safe distance from the sulphurous smog of the industrial heartland. He especially embraced the railway locomotive for it permitted him in the heyday of his achievements to hasten off from London to Bristol for a lecture on the need for greater education for the working class and then to return the same day to London, where, after midnight, he would complete the writing of a judicial opinion for the Privy Council. By the happenstance of birth, Richard Haldane missed the painful adjustments necessitated by the rapid expansion of the railway system. He missed the great outcry, led by Thomas Creevey in the House of Commons, against the 'railway dragon' which, belching smoke and sulphur, brought the unhealthy atmosphere of London, Birmingham, and Manchester uncomfortably close to the genteel squires of rural England. Matters were made worse by the return trains from Bristol, Liverpool, and other industrial centres, from which uncouth and unskilled young men disembarked to swell the ranks of the poor in the city of London.

It would have helped him little to know that the impetus behind these modern mechanical inventions came chiefly from Scotsmen such as 'the insane [George] Ferguson who frothed with rage at the mouth' over the great commercial prospects that railway expansion promised. This 'Scottish infatuation' was well in place and its early days were but a faded memory when Richard Haldane entered the world in the congenial and comfortable home in Charlotte Square, Edinburgh. His mother, however, never forgot her own excitement upon the arrival of the new railway. 'The first locomotive was,' she described in her memoirs, 'a curious grasshopper-looking machine that made a tremendous noise, and if our ponies came anywhere near it they at once made off in terror.'[30] But it meant travelling in record time between Edinburgh and London; the dreaded horse-drawn coaches were uncomfortable and unsafe and the travelling public welcomed their replacement by the more comfortable railway trains.

However comfortable life was for the Haldane family, it was not so good for the average Scot. Living conditions for most people in Scotland during these Victorian years were a far cry from idyllic.[31] As bad as housing conditions were in England, they were far worse in Scotland. Six years after Richard Haldane's birth, the census of 1861 revealed that 34 per cent of all Scottish houses had only one room; 37 per cent had two rooms; and 1 per cent of the population lived in houses without windows. A half-century later, in 1911, 7 per cent of England's population lived in one- or two-room houses; in Scotland, by contrast, 50 per cent of the population lived in such restricted quarters. To make matters worse, there were no poor laws at this time for relief of the indigent. The cities of Glasgow and Edinburgh were rampant with disease and poverty. Adding to the problem was the dramatic rise in population of the two principal cities between 1841 and 1911. During this period, Glasgow's population tripled, putting a strain on public-health services. Tuberculosis accounted for 13 per cent of all deaths in the 1870s, which was an improvement over previous years when the country suffered 361 deaths from tuberculosis per 100,000 of population. All of this occurred at a time when Edinburgh boasted the most advanced medical profession in the English-speaking world. The benefits of this medical expertise were slow to filter down to the average Scot.

Edinburgh, the capital of Scotland, dominated by the great castle, has been for centuries the putative seat of government. It was also, in the eighteenth century, the location of the open sewer, the Nor Loch, below the castle – running parallel with what is Princes Street today – where the stench was so powerful that the city became known as 'Auld Reekie.'[32] The sewer was later drained and transformed into a beautiful park dominated by an enormous statue of Sir Walter Scott, and farther along, the National Portrait Gallery.

Life in rural Scotland was perhaps even worse than it was in the villages and cities. Communicable diseases were not as rampant in the countryside owing to the distances that separated people, but even this benefit became a thing of the past as migration to the villages and cities spread the latter's germs beyond their boundaries. In 1851, 30 per cent of all males were employed in agriculture; fifty years later, that number had decreased to 14 per cent. The draw of the cities and the unavailability of farm land forced young men and their families into larger urban settlements. With the rise of the factories and mining industries, young men and boys found employment in dreadful conditions equal to those chronicled so vividly in England by Dickens.

While Scotland could boast of four universities in the nineteenth century, access to higher education was restricted – though not as restricted as it was in England, where there were only two universities, Oxford and Cambridge. In Scotland in the 1860s, there was one university place available per 1,000 population; by contrast, in England there was one place per 5,800. Scotland's universities took great pride in their famous sons, such as Adam Smith and David Hume and the bevy of philosophers who called forth the 'Scottish Enlightenment.'[33] No part of the United Kingdom regarded education more seriously or made a greater effort to ensure that working-class children should learn to read, write, and do simple sums than Scotland. Literacy was prompted – as much else in eighteenth-century Scotland – by the demands of evangelical Christianity. Since reading the Bible was the central part of Christian life, the working poor were taught to read and write. As a result, Scotland's lower class was far ahead of England's. Every parish in the Lowlands had its parochial school funded partly by a tax on landowners and partly by the pupils themselves. By 1872, Scotland had adopted compulsory education for children from age five to thirteen. The cause of educational reform of the lower classes spread throughout the United Kingdom from Scotland, especially through the *Edinburgh Review*, founded in 1803, which soon became the most influential journal in Britain and beyond.

The Haldanes were sufficiently affluent to escape the harshest features of Scottish life but they were not unaware of the plight of the poor; Mary Elizabeth, while providing a comfortable life for her family, saw so it that her children knew of the dreadful conditions of the poor and turned their heads in the direction of reform. Thanks to her efforts, they grew up in a home that supported liberal social and political reforms. The warmth of that home was to embrace Richard throughout his early childhood, especially when each spring the entire family retreated to Cloan, the small family estate in rural Perthshire where the Haldanes spent the long warm summers.

A Comfortable Home

Richard's father, as writer to the signet, spent most of his time in conveyancing and estate matters and related work in the Court of Sessions. He was also a devout Baptist who hoped to pass on his religious convictions to his children. However, given the formidable presence of his mother, Richard's father tended to drop into the background whenever his wife entered the conversation. He never appeared to resent this overshadowing, for he took great pride in the intellectual – if not religious – development of his children. In his own words, Richard related that his father 'was not literary or political, being interested mainly in religious matters outside his own work as a lawyer.'[34] Of his half-brothers and sisters, Richard says very little. In his *Autobiography*, he simply noted that the 'differences in years resulted in most of the elder ones marrying and having families of their own, and in us younger ones being mainly those at home. Affectionate as were their relations to each other, the two sets of children did not come into constant contact.'[35] From all accounts it appears that Mary Elizabeth was warmly received by her step-children and she enjoyed for the rest of her life the affection of her adopted family and their children. Strangely, however, she makes no reference to any of her adopted children in her memoirs. Once having done her Christian duty to raise her step-children, Mary Elizabeth gave over the major portion of her mature life to raising and educating her own.

The Haldane home in Edinburgh, however formal and highly charged with intellectual preoccupations, contained, according to the eldest son, 'an affectionate family.' Robert and Mary Elizabeth were eventually to have a family of four sons, Richard (1856), George (1858), John (1860), and William (1864), and one daughter, Elizabeth (1862). George, or 'Geordie' as he was known, was a favourite of his siblings. The home was a happy one in which Richard and his brothers and sister enjoyed the affection and encouragement of their parents. It was miles away, literally and figuratively, from the dysfunctional home of his exact contemporary and later friend, George Bernard Shaw. Shaw's home in Ireland was marked by social snobbery in the midst of grinding poverty, a drunken father, and a cold, neglectful mother. His childhood was poles away from that of the young Scotsman who was to join forces with GBS – the Bohemian without the Bohemian vices – in later life in the pursuit of educational and social reforms.

The house in Charlotte Square was comfortable, 'well-furnished with good rosewood and Utrecht velvet furniture in the drawing room and rather beautiful marble mantel-pieces and glass-drop chandeliers.'[36] Upstairs, however, where the schoolroom was located and where the children spent most of their time, was decidedly ugly. 'The carpet was of a dim crimson and the one armchair for our tutor of a sort of crimson rep.'[37] And, besides, it smelled of the cardboard used to support chalkboards. On the other hand, the family's summer home, named

Cloanden by Mary Elizabeth Haldane, was 'simple but sweet and fresh ... clean chintzes covered the chairs and we had home-made scones instead of baker's bread and plenty of milk in old-fashioned white jugs adorned with raised ferns.'[38] Both homes shared one thing in common: an atmosphere charged with the excitement of education. Mrs Haldane was the constant encouraging force behind what would appear to many people as an obsession with learning. Not one of her children, however, appears to have resented the atmosphere. And every one of them became distinguished in his or her own chosen field of endeavour. Contrary to the times, instruction was available to daughter Elizabeth as well as to Richard and his younger brothers. Elizabeth became a noted authority on the great French philosopher René Descartes. She wrote an impressive biography of the philosopher and translated French and German philosophical works into English – including Hegel's *Philosophy of History* – and became the first woman justice of the peace in Scotland. Not surprisingly, she also became deeply involved with the struggle of women to take their place in the professions, such as medicine. She took an active part in soliciting votes for women candidates for the local school boards that emerged throughout Scotland with the passage of the Scottish Education Act of 1872.[39]

Information on Richard Haldane's early formal education, outside the home, is sparse and incomplete. He himself recounted in his *Autobiography* simply how he was not impressed with his formal elementary education but that he had the great good fortune to come under the care and direction of Dr James Clyde at the Edinburgh Academy. Clyde was a teacher whom Haldane called a 'remarkable personality.' His abiding legacy to the young Haldane was 'always to seek for truth in the first place.'[40] But it was this same teacher who first led him away from the religious faith of his father by raising serious doubts about many of biblical teachings. As one biographer has related: 'Dr Clyde was a Stoic and a passionate seeker after truth, two qualities which were to appear in marked degree in his young pupil's character in later life. One of Dr Clyde's duties was to read the Old Testament with his class and, while setting himself to avoid disturbing the faith of his pupils, he could not help letting them see that he himself did not accept what the Old Testament narratives recorded. This was not lost on Richard Haldane and ere long he was seeking an answer to the persistent questions which his parents' theology did nothing to explain.'[41] Clyde succeeded in planting the seeds of agnosticism which were to blossom later when the young pupil turned eighteen and his father insisted that his son become baptized by total emersion. Until then, however, Richard was ever careful to conceal his growing agnosticism from his parents and other members of his family.

After two years at the feet of Dr Clyde and upon completion of his course of studies at the Edinburgh Academy, Richard, with a mixture of fear and anticipation, enrolled in the University of Edinburgh in the fall of 1872 at the age of sixteen. In its old lecture halls, he was to find a new world more conducive to his enquiring mind and devoid of religious restrictions, a world where great ideas were being framed and discussed under the tutelage of some of Scotland's most famous philosopher-scientists, whom he had earlier known only by reputation. The experience was to be a transformative one.

2

The University of Edinburgh and the Seeds of German Philosophy

Here for the first time in British academic philosophy, the new German thinkers were seriously studied, and here too began the inner dissolution of the Scottish school and the transition to other lines of thought.

– James Bradley, 'Hegel in Britain'

The towering presence at the University of Edinburgh of Sir William Hamilton, professor of logic and metaphysics and 'the last great leader of the Common Sense school,'[1] turned heads in the direction of the philosophy of Immanuel Kant. Unlike most of his English contemporaries, Hamilton possessed a knowledge of German. He challenged the traditional Scottish orientation towards France with a call for more German philosophy in a provocative article in the *Edinburgh Review* for 1829, entitled 'The Philosophy of the Unconditioned.' Hamilton put his considerable presence behind the turn towards German philosophy; he helped to prepare the ground for that German-oriented renaissance of philosophy which took place throughout Scotland in the twenty years before Haldane's birth in 1856.

Hegel in Scotland

The step from Kant to Hegel proved a short one. By 1846, ten years before Haldane's birth, J.D. Morell had published in two volumes his

Historical and Critical View of the Speculative Philosophy of Europe in the Nineteenth Century. This book not only contained a serious study of Kant but also introduced readers to the writings of Hegel. And, despite Morell's contention that Hegel's teachings led to the denial of freedom and the diminution of religion, his teachings began to attract the attention of even theologians like Thomas Chalmers, principal of the Free Church's New College.

By the time the young Haldane arrived at the University of Edinburgh in 1872, serious teachers of German philosophy were well entrenched. Professors David Masson and W.Y. Sellar were both, he said, 'what Professors ought to be,' and they introduced him to the great debate over the importation of German philosophy into Scotland. Masson, in particular, sided with the brilliant J.F. Ferrier, professor of moral philosophy and political economy at nearby St Andrew's University. Ferrier had ignited a storm of debate with a strong attack on Sir William Hamilton in the *Imperial Dictionary of Universal Biography* (1856–63). But it was 'the sense of awe and excitement communicated by his remarks on Hegel in the *Institutes* [that] really whetted the appetites of his readers. Ranking him with Plato, Leibnitz and Spinoza, Ferrier was in fact the first British philosopher to elevate Hegel above Kant and Schelling and to present him as a thinker of unique wonder and promise.'[2]

But Hegel's presence in Scotland was not a calming influence. Rather, it ignited a long and often acrimonious debate especially among the philosophers closest to Richard Haldane. Over the ensuing decades, we find friends such as Andrew Seth Pringle-Pattison and Thomas Hill Green locked in disagreement over the correct understanding of Hegel's ontology. And both quarrelled vigorously with F.H. Bradley, the Oxford don. Pringle-Pattison and Bradley were, years later, frequent visitors to 28 Queen Anne's Gate, Haldane's London home, for long and protracted discussions that would continue to the end of their lives. Thus, Haldane's education in the arcane philosophy of Hegel was formed in the turbulent sea of ongoing debate. It should come as no surprise that his own view of Hegel was somewhat eclectic.

In addition to Masson and Sellar, Haldane fell under the spell of John Stuart Blackie, of whom he wrote in his later years: 'Though always interesting, he was too erratic in his methods to be an adequate teacher.'[3] There is no question about it, Blackie was an eccentric teacher, but the former student writing in his old age did not give him the credit he was clearly due. For Blackie was an imposing figure throughout Scotland during the early years of Haldane's life and education. He was a popular public figure who spoke widely throughout the country urging the resurgence of Scottish pride through educational reforms. But he was theologically a non-conformist and his theological heterodoxy came to public attention when he was appointed professor of Latin at Marischal College, Aberdeen. The college requirement was that a new professor sign the Westminster Confession affirming the Presbyterian orthodoxy. Blackie objected to such 'creeds and tests.' His views on such matters should not have surprised the citizens of Aberdeen, for Blackie had spoken on the subject of 'liberty of thought' at a Whig banquet there three years earlier. He was not about to change his mind on such important issues for the sake of an appointment to the chair of Latin. But he clearly needed the job and, hence, signed the confession. He explained his action, however, in a public declaration: 'I have signed not as my private confession of faith, nor as a churchman learned in theology, but in my public profession and capacity, and in reference to university offices and duties merely. I am a warm friend of the Church of Scotland, and I have been accustomed to worship according to the Presbyterian form, and will continue to do so; but I am not sufficiently learned in theology to be able to decide on many articles of the confession of faith.'[4] Not only did he issue the clarification, he sent a copy to a local newspaper with a note saying: 'I hold that in law a non-theological professor is not subject to the spiritual jurisdiction of the Church. He signs the articles as articles of peace only.'[5] The Aberdeen Presbytery was not amused at Blackie's mental reservations; it saw them as a repudiation of the spirit of the confession and held up his appointment for two years in protest. In the end, Blackie took the chair and proceeded to teach Latin and Greek.

Without question, this professor was a flamboyant presence throughout Scotland and it was not the last time he would make his strongly held views known by way of the press. But he was determined to make his thoughts on other subjects, touching the national life of Scotland, known as well. For John Stuart Blackie spoke widely and provocatively in public about the need for Scots to preserve and promote their Gaelic heritage. Though other professors and some students thought of him as a scatterbrain professor in the classroom, Blackie was a popular force widely admired by the general public. He was nothing less than a tireless itinerant prophet who, complete with fierce countenance, a long mane of white hair, and an elaborate plaid cloak draped over his shoulders, stalked the Scottish landscape. And the daily press revelled in reporting his every word. In 1830 he along with two other young

Scots went to Göttingen and studied philology and the German language. The most important impression he came away with was that German university education was superior to that available in Scotland. 'The German universities are the model institutions of the kind ... [a] bazaar of universal knowledge, while the Scottish Universities, except in the medical department in Edinburgh, are mere shops for retail trade in certain useful articles.'[6] Blackie sent his thoughts home and they were duly published in the *Edinburgh Literary Journal* and received with not a little annoyance by Scottish professors. But that reaction only contributed to steel Blackie's resolve to continue to send back to Edinburgh glowing accounts of German higher education complete with the suggestion that Scotland had much to learn from the Germans. In 1873 he toured Germany and sent back lengthy accounts of his travels praising German culture and especially its higher education. *The Scotsman* ran these articles and they were read avidly by the public.

Richard Haldane could not have missed, now in his second year at the University of Edinburgh, these pieces nor could he have been left unimpressed or unaware of how they prompted spirited discussions on campus. As well, they appeared at a time when he was being urged by a few of his professors at Edinburgh University to pursue further philosophical studies in Germany, not at Oxford or Cambridge where his parents were initially bent on sending him. His strict Calvinist parents worried, however, that their gifted son might fall under the lax influence of the Anglican Church at Oxford, which at the time was flirting with the trappings of Roman ritual under the Tractarians, so they were easily persuaded to send him elsewhere.[7] It was, indeed, the voluble Blackie who convinced Haldane's parents to send their son to Germany for higher studies.

Yet it was not just the opportunity to study Hegel drew Haldane to Germany for graduate studies, for he could have come in contact with Hegel's philosophy by going to Oxford or Cambridge. This powerful German philosopher had made his presence known in Britain years before Haldane set out for Göttingen. T.C. Sandars, a fellow at Oriel College, Oxford, for example, was a noted Hegel scholar and produced a volume titled *Oxford Essays* in 1855 which contained a penetrating essay on Hegel's 'philosophy of Right.' But Germany possessed something more than merely the formal study of Hegel; like no other country, it offered an atmosphere pulsing with the excitement of an emerging modern philosophy. Immanuel Kant's philosophy of critique inflamed the minds of disciples who quickly became locked in combat with the upstart younger disciples of Hegel, providing the world with a clash of intellectual giants which has continued to the present day. Haldane felt this excitement and throughout his life, whenever the opportunity arose, expounded to academic audiences on the stimulation of studying in Germany. It was the place to be for the serious student of philosophy.

In addition to his love of German philosophy, Haldane quickly acquired a deep admiration for German military discipline and for German literature generally, especially Goethe. It led him to acknowledge, publicly, Germany as his 'spiritual home' and developed into a passion which he was ever ready to share with young students of philosophy. These attachments to the German way of thinking and culture became so deeply rooted in him that, many years later, he travelled to Oxford and spoke to students of the need for British students, statesmen, and businessmen to learn and appreciate more deeply German philosophical, educational, and scientific achievements. But, above all, he told his young Oxford audience in 1911: 'The practical life of the Germany of to-day rests, far more than does that of Great Britain, on abstract and theoretical foundations. To understand it we must examine its intellectual development.'[8]

His central focus in this lengthy address was on the 'German habit of mind.' Four years earlier, in an address to students at the University of Edinburgh, Haldane had praised German education, claiming that 'as a triumph of the spirit of organisation it is unrivalled except by that wonderful outcome of scientific arrangement – the German Army. And the means by which all these things were called into existence and brought about was chiefly the co-operation of the University with the State in producing the men who were to lead and to develop the organisation.'[9] It was the German 'spirit of organisation' and 'systematic thinking' that he admired. As if laying bare his own soul, he announced that the 'student of philosophy must live for and think of little else before he can get rid of the habit of unconsciously applying in his inquiries categories which are inapplicable to their subject matter. For he has to learn that it is not only in practical life that the abstract and narrow mind is a hindrance to progress, and an obstacle in the way to reality.'[10]

True to his Hegelian mentor, Haldane told his audience that the study of philosophy was intended to serve as the theoretical foundation of service to the state with a view to ensuring progress. This determination to awaken British education to the high possibilities prompted by modern philosophy and science was to be promoted by the life of the mind in quest of the spirit of progress that moved the world. Richard Haldane began to absorb this fundamental disposition reading Hegel at Edinburgh, and it was sharpened and developed during his brief formal study in Germany. 'The abstract formulas of the old metaphysics no longer interest the general student. But he has begun to realize once more the splendid and convincing power with which the great German thinkers disentangled from a mass of historical material the permanent basis of moral and intellectual values, and brought to the general consciousness a significance in these values that is beyond the level of what is transitory formerly utilitarian.' Chief among those 'great German thinkers,' of course, was Hegel, who set his sights on a return to philosophical idealism with the goal of improving the 'inner life' of the individual and through that transformation to propel the state to higher achievements in science and culture. This, Haldane learned as a young man in Göttingen, was the true meaning of *progress*. And at the forefront of his admiration was the energetic Prussia. 'Now German policy is largely influenced by Prussia. It is the habit of mind of Prussians to begin by defining a principle and then to test everything by it.'[11]

Not only must the student come to understand this Prussian trait, he must also begin to assimilate it into his own habit of mind. 'German habits of thinking in abstract terms, even when dealing with the most immediate and practical affairs, and of looking for principles everywhere, make things at time trying for those who have not this useful if difficult habit of mind in the same degree.'[12] It was this 'useful if difficult habit of mind' that Haldane himself had acquired through the study of modern German philosophy. Few people have revealed more about their own habits of mind through their lectures than Richard Haldane. The more he spoke about his intellectual life, the more he showed that he was not an ideologue but a true philosopher. He viewed the ideologue as a captive of a simplistic formula with which he approached all theoretical and practical problems and judged them in terms of their compliance or non-compliance. Such, indeed, was the tendency demonstrated repeatedly by his compatriot Fabians. These are the 'intellectuals who produce the intellectual's *ideologies*, which they take for philosophy and pass off as such.'[13] Haldane was a philosopher prepared to listen to other points of view and comfortable with but non-committal to people like Sidney and Beatrice Webb as well as G.B. Shaw and Harold Laski. By definition, as Haldane understood philosophy, one must resist the simplistic application of inappropriate categories to urgent social and political problems, as he cautioned his Oxford undergraduates. Above all, he said, 'there is no more fertile source of error than the application of principles that properly belong to another.'

It was widely believed throughout the English-speaking world – in the United States as well as in Britain – that Germany's secondary and post-secondary education was second to none, and that its universities were producing graduates of superior quality. Lord Bryce wrote: 'There is no people which has given so much thought and pains to the development of its university system as the Germans have done – none where they play so large a part in the national life.'[14] It is ironic that, at the very time Haldane was entering the German academic milieu looking for guidance, Germans themselves were arguing over the sorry state of education. Schopenhauer and Nietzsche were both critical of German higher education in the decades just prior to his arrival in Germany. Two years before Haldane reached Göttingen, Nietzsche delivered a lecture in Basel 'On the Future of Our Educational Institutions,' in which he announced that Germany was beginning to neglect its traditional humanistic education by a turn to commercial and scientific applications of knowledge.[15] This was exactly what Hegel had proposed and what excited the young Haldane fresh from Scotland.

Among the Scots intellectuals who were fervent admirers of Germany, the most prominent was the indomitable Thomas Carlyle, who captured the attention of an entire generation of scholars and, indeed, of the general public, first with his *Life of Schiller* (1823–4) and then with a translation the following year of Goethe's *Wilhelm Meister*. Carlyle introduced his readers to the delights of serious German romantic fiction. As if this were not sufficient, he inflicted upon the world an eight-volume biography of Frederick the Great in which he championed the thesis that the people could be rescued from their misfortunes through the actions of great men. The rational, idealist Haldane never succumbed to Carlyle's blandishments or to his rhetorical tone. Yet he was nevertheless attacked for his praise of German political and educational practices.

This was the period when Prussian and much of European affairs were dominated by Otto von Bismarck, the domineering chancellor of Prussia who had cast an aggressive shadow over the affairs of Europe for the first forty-two years of Haldane's life. 'Bismarck [was],' Edward Crankshaw has written, 'a naturally dictatorial figure, manipulating with extreme skill the spirit of nationalism, which in Germany was stronger than in any other land for the simple reason that it first had to create a nation. Bismarck created that nation – and in his own image.'[16]

But it was the emerging united Germany's currents of thoughts, not its politics, that captivated Haldane. He looked beneath the surface of events and saw forces operating that excited him: the new historical scholarship sewn a generation earlier by Johann Gottfried von Herder, who developed a philosophy of history showing the course of man's progress, and later, the cause of cultural history championed by Jacob Christoph Burckhardt. Herder taught that 'the proper subject of the historical sciences is the life of communities and not the exploits of individuals.'[17] It should also be noted that the historical scholarship that dominated German university education in philosophy prepared Germans for the advent of Charles Darwin, whose theory of natural selection fit so perfectly with the emerging philosophical historicism. As Fritz Stern has observed, 'the truth of Darwin ... had swept aside the moral truths of earlier times and thus prepared the way for the triumph of relativism.'[18] Not surprisingly, Darwin was more immediately embraced with enthusiasm in Germany than in England when he crashed upon the scene in 1859 with *The Origin of Species*.

One other Scottish intellectual influence entered Haldane's life at the University of Edinburgh during the years prior to his departure for Germany. The self-taught James Hutchinson Stirling, eight years his senior, and author of a popular book on Hegel, did much to inspire the young student to look more deeply into the German philosopher. Stirling was the son of William Stirling, a wealthy Glasgow textile manufacturer, and Elizabeth Christie Stirling, both of whom were widely read and encouraged their son to become a student of learning in general and medicine in particular. James became a physician and practised his profession for a decade in Pontypool, Monmouthshire. When not tending to the sick, the young doctor applied himself to serious philosophical reading and study. He became absorbed by philosophy and devoted a great deal of his free time to reading continental philosophy, especially Hegel. When his entrepreneur father died in 1851, leaving him a wealthy man and free to pursue full time his love of philosophy, Stirling abandoned his medical practice. He moved his family first to France, where he learned French and absorbed a good deal of Voltaire and Rousseau, and then to Germany, where he became steeped in German philosophy. But in neither France nor Germany did he enrol in a university academic program leading to a degree. When he eventually returned to live permanently in Edinburgh in 1860, intent on achieving an academic position from which to propound his knowledge of modern continental philosophy, he found the doors of academia closed to him. His failure to acquire the formal university graduate credentials haunted him throughout his life and prevented him from ever achieving his ambition to obtain a university chair in philosophy. Nevertheless, he was sufficiently secure financially to proceed freely as he wished.

Stirling's failure to obtain an advanced academic degree did not deter him from writing. In fact, he assaulted the academy in 1865 with a two-volume study of Hegel published under the alluring title *The Secret of Hegel*. It was, as Kirk Willis has noted, 'the first comprehensive treatment of Hegel in Britain at a time when his thought was attracting great interest.'[19] The academy was not impressed with this dilettante's efforts, but students of philosophy in the universities devoured the book. Haldane confessed in his *Autobiography*, written at the end of his life, that he came to know this book intimately and read it many times. Stirling's style attempted to mirror the bombast of Carlyle, which did more to offend than to impress the learned professors. One reviewer consigned the book to oblivion with the remark that Stirling had succeeded in one thing: keeping Hegel's secret securely intact. But Richard Haldane knew the book thoroughly and it succeeded in deepening his interest in Hegel.

However repudiated by the academy – he was twice nominated unsuccessfully to chairs in moral philosophy at both Glasgow and Edinburgh – Stirling was much admired by young students of philosophy. Despite the wall of opposition that confronted him, he continued to write and to translate works on philosophy from German into English, thus making contemporary German philosophy more readily accessible to English-speaking students, especially in Scotland. In addition to a series of articles on philosophic matters in *Mind* and the *Journal of Speculative Philosophy*, he wrote a textbook on Kant and translated into English F.C.A. Schwegler's *Handbook of the History of Philosophy*. These, along with other books on Huxley and Darwin, became popular with undergraduate students of philosophy throughout Scotland and had much to do with the young Haldane's early formation. But still, the doors of the academy remained shut. Eventually, however, Edinburgh University relented and appointed Stirling to the post of Gifford Lecturer in 1889–90 at the age of sixty-nine. His inaugural Gifford Lecture on the relation of philosophy and theology did little to improve his reputation. But, to their credit, both Glasgow and Edinburgh conferred

upon him an honorary LLD. He died on 19 March 1909 at the age of
eighty-nine, 'a forgotten figure who had outlived his family, friends,
and fame.'[20]

German University Life

After farewells to his mother and his old nurse, Betsy Ferguson, who
accompanied him to the ship, Richard Haldane, aged seventeen, sailed
from Leith for Hamburg in April 1874 at the end of his second year
of philosophical studies at the University of Edinburgh. Much to his
delight, the young philosophy scholar met on board ship a fellow Scot
named William Rogers from Dundee. He was a few years older than
Haldane and had already completed a year studying chemistry at Göttingen. Rogers was returning to his studies in Germany after a holiday
at home. He talked at great length with enthusiasm of Germany in general and of Göttingen in particular and prepared Haldane for what he
was to experience in the celebrated German university town.

Upon arrival at Hamburg, Haldane spent the day sightseeing. The
next day he left by train for Göttingen, where he arrived at four the
following morning. The University of Göttingen was founded in 1737
by King George II of England in his capacity as elector of Hanover, an
office also held by his predecessor, George I. To the chagrin of their
English subjects, the Georges spent considerable time in Hanover, preferring to reign over England at a distance.[21] But Göttingen, nevertheless, became a centre of English cultural influence through the writings
of Friedrich Christoph Dahlmann, who taught English constitutional
history. Dahlmann openly applauded, with the approval of the English
kings, the liberal character of the English constitution, particularly its
constitutional monarchy, trial by jury, and freedom of speech and the
press. But Dahlmann was not alone in his admiration of the English
constitution and its liberal constitutional protection of individual freedoms. He was soon joined by other like-minded professors, especially
in the northern German areas.[22] The young Haldane thus entered into
an atmosphere steeped in English constitutional history, all of which
served to buttress the values and attitudes acquired in his early Scottish
life and education.

Immediately upon settling himself in Göttingen, Haldane began to
study the German language under the tutelage of Fraulein Schlote, who
fast became a cherished friend; long after he left Göttingen, Haldane
continued to write his old language teacher and made a point of visit-

ing her many years later on trips to Germany as lord chancellor. She did much to introduce the young Scottish student to German literature on his way to becoming fluent in the language. But, before consigning himself to the care of Scholte, the young scholar wrote a lengthy letter to his mother, a habit that was to end only upon her death at the age of 100 in 1925. In this first letter home, Haldane announced: 'Here I am at last at my destination.' He then proceeded to give a detailed account of his rooms in Lindel Strasse no.1 which he shared with several German students.[23]

Armed with a letter of introduction from John Stuart Blackie, Haldane called the next day on Professor Lotze, whom he recalled later as a 'quiet, reserved old man.'[24] In a letter to his mother the following day, he wrote about this initial meeting: 'I called yesterday on Lotze, the professor of metaphysics who is delighted to hear of his dear friend professor Blackie, whose Greek letter of introduction puzzled him to make out at first, the writing being rather indistinct.'[25]

The eighteen-year-old Scot related in a letter home his first impressions of his German fellow students. 'The Germans, I have met with study well, but not so much as they get credit for with us; but everyone is well-educated even several of the soldiers having occasionally a stripe on their shoulders to indicate that they have passed an exam in Greek and Latin which exempts them from 2 years service.'[26] He returned to this theme three days later, observing that 'the students, however, do not work nearly as much as I expected, some of them avoid going to lectures, and drinking beer and smoking all day. However, the most of them have learned a great deal at the Gymnasium (or school) where they always stay till they are twenty-one, and where they learn far more than we do at our universities. Even an ordinary student laughs at 4 out of 5 of the working students who come from Oxford or Cambridge.'[27] He noted, especially, the absence of examinations and prizes: 'There are no such things as examinations in the classes, and much less any thing so contemptible, in the German Eye, as prizes, a great improvement on us, and which I think accounts for the fact that the Germans arc so much better informed, since they do not cram things as with us, but really learn them.'[28]

As for his new professors, the young scholar was clearly unimpressed. At least he was not impressed with the way they dressed. 'The professors for the most part,' he continued in this letter home, 'look as if they had seen more books than soap and tailor's shop, for most of them are men of about 60 wearing coloured spectacles broad Tyrole hats, with dirty badly shaven faces and their clothes almost tumbling off. They sometimes lecture in Latin, some times in German, it being much the same to them and the students.'[29] In light of his subsequent religious scepticism, it is interesting to note that in these early letters from Göttingen, Haldane told his mother that he had kept up his religious practices. On one occasion, he was unable to attend church, he told her, for 'want of a preacher and a congregation.' So he stayed 'at home and read Dr Caudlish's sermons.' He was more than a little scandalized at the behaviour of the German pastors. 'For example, yesterday, the pastor having got through with his service in an hour, went straight-off to a beer-concert at a sort of public house outside of town.' Sunday was, to his surprise, a day for great beer parties and concerts in Göttingen. The contrast with his native Scotland could not have been more stark. While the German students were carousing at concerts and drinking beer on Sunday, Haldane told his mother that he 'took a solitary walk on the ramparts which were deserted by the Germans for the concerts.'[30] Even the occasional church sermon by one of the pastors did not escape his critical eye. One pastor 'was pulled up for heresy, which must be something very bad for the Germans would not pull him up; one can go to hear the professors of Dogmatic Theology deliver a lecture in the University Church, but he is also exceedingly unorthodox.'[31] Haldane returned to this theme five days later in a letter home. 'Tomorrow is Sunday,' he wrote somewhat dejected, 'which is the most uncomfortable day in the week on account of the noise and number of people in the streets on this day. I do not know whether there is to be a preacher worth hearing or not, so I must inquire. If there is not I will take a walk right into the country as far from the town as possible, as the noise and number of bands playing etc is very great.'[32]

But every day was not Sunday and he soon settled down to learn philosophy under Lotze's guidance. When he first met with his new mentor, he gave an account of his philosophic confusions – the 'crisis of my mind,' he called them – and Lotze advised him 'to read Fichte's popular works, and particularly the *Vocation of Man*.' 'With the aid of Berkeley,' Haldane later recorded, 'I began to work myself out of my mood and, under the stimulus of Lotze's teaching, to acquire a wider point of view.'[33] The young student quickly became very fond of his gentle tutor and remembered him ever after as 'one of the greatest and most spiritual of modern German thinkers.'[34]

But Richard Haldane went to Göttingen with a firm foundation in Hegel's teaching and knew what he wanted: more Hegel. Before leav-

ing Edinburgh he had become familiar with the writings and trans-
lations of James Hutchinson Stirling whose translation of Schwegler's
Handbook of the History of Philosophy contained a stimulating chapter
on Hegel which the young aspiring philosopher could not have read
without becoming excited. It constituted a brilliant challenge to the
selfish individualism which had been unleashed by the Industrial
Revolution and had reduced life to the acquisition of more and more
material things. The serious young Scot read with increasing enthusiasm Schwegler's account of Hegel's conception of the state and the
prospects of public service which it opened up to him. 'The state to
him [Hegel],' wrote Schwegler, 'is the rational ethical substance within
which the life of the individual must find itself – it is existent reason
to which the subject must with free vision adapt himself.'[35] And what
must he have thought when he read that for Hegel the best constitution
was a 'limited monarchy ... as exemplified in the English constitution?'
How could the young student of philosophy not be enflamed with enthusiasm when he read that the 'evolution of universal history is usually connected with a dominant people, in whom dwells the universal
spirit, correspondingly developed, and as against which the spirits of
the other peoples are without right?'[36] He must surely have seen that
Hegel was speaking to the monarchical core of the British Empire, a
truly 'dominant people,' providentially entrusted with the great mission of fulfilling the Absolute Spirit of freedom. It was as if Hegel were
urging young British philosophers to comprehend their role in the uni-
versalizing of the spirit of freedom portrayed throughout the British
Empire.

Thus imbued with enthusiasm for Hegel, Richard Haldane reported
in his early letters home that he was spending a lot of time with his
German mentor.[37] 'I spent a very pleasant afternoon with Prof. Lotze
on Monday. I had a long conversation with him on the relations of philosophy to religion, on Materialism, the Immortality of the soul and so
on.'[38] At this stage of his study of philosophy, Haldane was clearly interested in theological matters and Lotze's Christian orthodoxy must have
come as a surprise to him. He took delight in reporting to his mother
that Lotze 'said a life time's reflexion on these subjects (he is a man of
about 65 and is about my father's build and like him very active) had
convinced him that no ascertained truth in philosophy clashed with religion. Speculations might, but time had shown that speculations were
untrustworthy till proved in accordance with facts, and that he was
convinced that no one of the schools even of Mill or Bain had ever suc-

ceeded in bringing a single *fact* forward against Christianity.'[39] Such comments must have been reassuring to the arch-Calvinists back in Edinburgh, especially his father. He went on to elaborate on Lotze's view of the relation of philosophy to religion. 'He did not believe that religion and philosophy had much in common, they were not necessary to each other's existence, but the reason of this was that their spheres were different. Philosophy could never perform the function of religion and as an example Mill might be cited.' He appears to have taken pleasure in telling his parents that 'the Baptists are esteemed here more than any other British denomination.' And then he added the curious note that 'the Church of England ... [is] considered unlikely to last.'[40] He must have been playing to his father's prejudices with such a comment.

On this occasion, the young Haldane offered a few more observations about his esteemed teacher. Lotze was considered by his peers at the university to be reclusive and unsociable. Available accounts of the man portray him as rather frail and suffering from rheumatism. At least once, Haldane reported that his teacher was unable to lecture because of poor health.

These early letters home reveal a serious young student wrestling with his religious faith, which had been severely tested by Dr Clyde at Edinburgh Academy. But they also reveal that his German mentor was secure in his own Christian orthodoxy. In early July 1874 Haldane wrote to his mother about a long conversation he had had with Lotze. 'I have just returned from a visit from Lotze who invited me to come and sit with him. I had an exceedingly pleasant time, a long talk in which he expounded the nature of Faith and pointed out the relationship between it and positive knowledge, at the bottom of which it lies ... I told him that philosophy was my "hertz-studium" but that I felt it to be very insufficient unless it culminated in Faith. That, he said, rejoiced him to hear, for he felt himself convinced that without Faith all fell to the ground.'[41] This reported conversation is striking for two reasons. First, it tells a great deal about the state of mind of the young philosopher who was eventually to abandon his Christian faith for agnosticism not long after his return home. And, second, it tells more about Hermann Lotze, who in the maturity of his philosophic life sounded much more like an orthodox Augustinian theologian than a German idealist philosopher. He certainly was not a disciple of Hegel. Nor does his principal work, *Microcosmus*, read as compatible with Hegel's radical historicism. His philosophy tended to have more in common with

Kant, whom he cited with approval. He frequently recited the 'golden saying of Kant, *If Law ceases, all worth of human life on earth ceases too.*'[42] One can only guess what impression this 'golden saying' made upon a young man who would devote so much of his life to the law.

In this letter Haldane also observed that Lotze looked unwell and was not likely to live much longer. 'His body looks quite washed away and inadequate to the support of his gigantic head,' he related. 'When he goes all scientific Germany will be Materialistic with the exception of one or two second-rate men.'[43] Three weeks before, he had told his mother that he was reading Kant, having finished his assigned readings of Fichte. After Fichte he planned to get 'to work systematically upon Hegel, who however is a hard nut to crack.' This implies that his time under Lotze was spent in preparation for Hegel rather than in devoting his full attention to the great philosopher. All in all, it seems that he spent only three weeks formally studying Hegel under Lotze's supervision, during the course of which, in light of his earlier accounts of his conversations with his mentor, Hegel must have been presented as a Christian. This was not that unusual, for Hegel was interpreted by a few contemporary Christian writers as a crypto-Christian; not a few Christian writers attempted to explain Hegel's *Weltgeist* as an extension of Christian providence into the philosophy of history. But in this they were clearly mistaken, as Hegel was later to demonstrate. Certainly, nothing the young Haldane appears to have learned from Lotze would have contributed to undermining his Christian faith. But he does add in this letter that 'when I finish these [authors] I can think of coming home with a clean conscience, but it will take a good deal of time to digest them.'[44] One thing is clear: Haldane did devote a 'good deal of time' thinking over his reading of Hegel and, from what he tells us later, came to conclusions radically different from those of his old mentor.

If there is one other thing that the young Scottish student revealed in these letters home from Göttingen, it is that he was honing his skills with a habit of hard work. 'I have been very busy lately getting up between 5 and 6 to read metaphysics which is dreadfully hard work as the matter is very abstruse.' In this last letter from Göttingen, Haldane announced that on 'Thursday morning at 4:45 I am to start by the night-mail for Cologne and on Saturday morning am to leave Rotterdam for Leith.' Thus did the summer semester of 1874 at the University of Göttingen pass and shape forever the mind of this young Scottish philosophy student. He never forgot those happy days and spent the rest of his life building on the foundations laid there. But, in light of his later writings, Haldane seems to have absorbed little of Hermann Lotze's gentle Christian philosophy. Haldane himself would, in short order, abandon his Christian faith but continue to wrestle with the relation of reason and revelation. The one thing he conceded to Lotze was the uncompromising quest for the truth, no matter where it led. This fixation Haldane was to demonstrate years later in his Gifford Lectures on faith and reason.

Master of Arts

Upon returning home in late July 1874, Richard Haldane resumed his study of philosophy at the University of Edinburgh. For the next two years, he studied under the inspiring direction of professor Campbell Fraser, the university professor of logic and metaphysics. According to his sister Elizabeth, shortly after his return to Scotland, Richard accepted an invitation to give a series of twelve lectures on philosophy to the Young Men's Institute.[45] The young scholar kept the notes to these lectures and they reveal a philosophical maturity beyond the author's years.[46] Beginning with the question 'What is Philosophy?' Haldane guided his students – principally gathered from the trades – through a series of tightly constructed lectures on the nature of philosophy as science. From there he moved systematically through the 'progress of Moral Philosophy,' drawing on Aristotle and modern authorities, especially German authors such as Kant and Hegel. His lectures consisted of dialogues with the authorities which demanded considerable concentrated attention on the part of his students. He clearly did not talk down to them, and many must have been left in a cloud of confusion as he trekked through the dense material promising to 'inquire into the value and origin of knowledge.' Night after night for twelve weeks, he would ask such questions as: 'What are the peculiar features of moral actions?' After leading his students through the labyrinth of moral reasoning, he took aim at the prevailing moral theories put forward by the increasingly influential Utilitarians; he would explain how 'moral judgment' was different from 'intuition' and then 'attempt to prove that Justice is right.'[47] In one lecture, he formally addressed James Mill and his utilitarian theory of the moral law. 'Mill says that we must wait till the moral character is sufficiently formed. But this is not enough[:] if a sanction is rational at all it must be so always.'[48] From there Haldane went on to explain Kant's notion of absolute good. 'Here all thought of happiness as the end of human life is discarded. The explanation of all is to be found in the notion of Duty. This notion comprehends under it that of good will. This involves the acknowledgement that the will is affected by certain inward hindrances.'[49] At one point he suggested that, for the student caught in the conflict between Hegel and Hume, the via media was Kant.

The one overriding feature of these lectures is that Haldane did not force his students to adopt one philosophical perspective to the exclusion of any other. His style of pedagogy was to lay before his students the variety of alternative explanations or propositions and urge them to choose and defend their selection. It was an approach to learning that he himself adopted and it is why he could later consort with intellectuals who were diametrically opposed to his own chosen perspective. He thought that an active open mind was the one essential characteristic of the philosopher. He understood philosophy as it was originally formulated by Socrates, as the never-ending *quest* for wisdom, not possessed as a mountain climbed once for all time.

His lectures to the Young Men's Institute clearly portrayed a mind that was wrestling with the innovations in philosophy that had characterized the early modern period initiated by Descartes and Bacon. In his lectures on 'Logic and Metaphysics,' he introduced his students to Descartes, Bacon, Hobbes, Locke, Schwegler, and Stewart. And, while he demanded much of his students, he appears to have demanded more of himself.

Haldane's notes also contain a list of the authors he was expected to read for his master's degree at Edinburgh University. The list is long and comprehensive. He was obliged to read, in addition to the principal works of Hegel, 'all Berkeley's works; Hume's Essays and Human Nature; Kant's Kritik Vernunft.' The only ancient works he was required to read were Plato's *Republic*, books 1–4 and 7, the *Theatetus*, and *Parmenides*. In Aristotle he was required to read *The Ethics* and the *De Anima*. The emphasis, however, was on modern European philosophy including Kant's metaphysics and ethics. According to his notes, he prepared for his senior examination, set for 11 February 1875, by reviewing not only the subjects suggested in the lectures but readings from Aristotle's *De Anima*, Locke's *Essay Concerning Human Understanding*, and Liebnitz's and Cousin's critiques of Locke's epistemology. The essay topic assigned was: 'Is Metaphysics an inductive and progressive science?' To no one's surprise, Richard Haldane passed his course of studies with distinction.

In outward appearance, people noticed that the young man had changed considerably during his five-month sojourn in Germany; he was much thinner than when he left for Göttingen and now sported long hair and a moustache. But he was as earnest and determined to study philosophy as he had ever been. In a letter to a German friend written from Edinburgh over Christmas 1875, he outlined the course of study he had set for himself:

I am very busy just now with the study of the work of your great and too-little recognised countryman Hegel. The extreme difficulty of this study makes one get on very slowly even with the help of a great number of commentaries. I have also been busy with Wundt's *Physiologische Psychologie* and Fechner's *Elemente der Psychophysick*, books, the former of which at least, you have no doubt heard of ... Have the German apostles of *Naturwissenschaft* as great a horror of metaphysics as our English men of science? ... I wish we could meet again and drink a few *Schoppen* in the Ratskeller. I have just been reading the scene in *Faust* at Auerbech's Keller and it reminded me very much of our old times.[50]

In the spring of 1875, these philosophical ruminations were abruptly interrupted when disaster struck the happy Haldane home in Edinburgh. Richard's younger brother, George, died suddenly of diphtheria. The family was devastated by the death of 'Geordie' and Richard never forgot to note the anniversary of his passing for years to come. The young philosophy scholar grieved and found escape by immersing himself in his studies. In April 1876 he graduated from the University of Edinburgh with first-class honours. He was awarded, in addition to the Grangehill medal for philosophy, the Gray scholarship and the Ferguson scholarship in philosophy open to the four Scottish universities.

Soon after the death of his brother, Richard was confronted with a major religious crisis within his family. It was understood throughout the family that, upon reaching the age of eighteen, the children would be baptized by immersion. Richard, by now steeped in Ernest Renan and David Friedrich Strauss – leading anti-Christian authors – in addition to German philosophy, resisted the wishes of both parents. Upon the persistent pleadings of his father, Richard consented but only after explaining that he would undergo the ceremony with a clear understanding. Just as John Stuart Blackie had done years before in comparable circumstances at Aberdeen, Richard announced that he did not believe in the efficacy of Christian baptism and that he would formally disavow it upon ascending from the baptismal font. He gave an account of the incident in his *Autobiography*.

My father did not, I think, realise in the least how far away from each other our minds were on foundational questions. He proposed that the ceremony should be gone through quite privately at the church to which the family went when in Edinburgh, and that no one should be present excepting those immediately concerned. I do not think that he had taken in the importance which I attached to this undertaking. Anyhow, he seemed to have let the appointment be known, for, when I got to the church, there were present not only the minister, but a crowd of deacons and other onlookers. My mind was at once made up. To begin with, I told them all openly that I would not refuse to go through the ceremony, but that I should make a definite explanation the moment it was over. I rose dripping from the font, and, facing the congregation, announced to them that I had consented to go through what had taken place only to allay the anxiety of my parents, but that, now, as those present might have misunderstood, I must say something to them. It was that I could not accept their doctrines: that I regarded what had taken place as the merest external ceremony; and that for the future I had no connection with the church, or its teaching, or with any other church. I then changed my clothes and walked away from the building. There was much consternation, but nothing was said, probably because there was nothing to say. My cousin, the late Bishop of Argyll, who was present, walked after me and was very kind and sympathetic. But the incident was a closed one. It was never alluded to afterwards, and silence was preserved in our household on the subject.[51]

It is difficult to believe that the young man's resistance to baptism came as a surprise to his father, for Robert Haldane was well aware of what his son was reading. On one occasion, Haldane relates in his *Autobiography* how his father was determined to burn George Elliot's translation of Strauss's *Life of Jesus* because it contained anti-Christian sentiments which would do his son great harm. The son was able to salvage the book only by claiming – falsely – that it was a library book and had to be returned.[52] His baptism was one of the few occasions when Richard Haldane defied the wishes of his father. As he understood it, he had no choice in the matter since his convictions led him to break with his father's rigid orthodoxy. Richard's disavowal was not the show of a youthful petulance or simply a desire to strike out in independence; he loved his father, whom he claimed was devoted and affectionate. He made his public disavowal because he was philosophically convinced that he was right. The event signalled a turning point in his intellectual development, marking him out as both determined and single-minded. Emerging from the waters of baptism, the boy was left behind and the mature, independent young philosopher emerged,

whatever the condition of his soul. He could not and never would hereafter allow any man, not even his beloved father, to compromise his
deepest principles. But Haldane did not cease to think seriously about
matters of faith. He understood that the relation of faith and reason
was important and he continued to wrestle with the enduring issues
involved for the rest of his life.

Shortly upon graduating, Richard Haldane 'set himself seriously to
the study of law.'[53] Why did this young scholar whose abiding interest
lay in philosophy not chart a career in university teaching? Most of his
friends who shared his love of philosophy became dons or professors
of philosophy. To some of his friends, his turn to the profession of law
constituted a new course away from philosophy towards a career at the
bar and, perhaps, a life in politics. But nothing was further from Haldane's mind. For him, the turn to the study of law was a direct outcome
of his Hegelian philosophy. For Hegel, the true life of the philosopher
was a practical one: to participate in establishing the rational character
of the state; and the heart of Hegelian statecraft was constitutional law,
the very speciality Haldane was to embrace. But he never abandoned
the serious study of philosophy. The two were inextricably intertwined
in his view. Indeed, philosophy became the driving force – the central
source of inspiration – of his life both in court and in Parliament.

The Affairs of Empire

This young law student, fresh from Scotland and new to the Inns of
Court, could not, of course, have had even an inkling that he was destined to bring both law and philosophy to the service of an expanding British Empire. Even more remote from his consciousness, surely,
was the central role he would play in shaping the constitutional life of
Canada.

The years immediately preceding the birth of Richard Haldane saw
the British Army extending the boundaries of the Empire into south
Africa and India. It was the decade of imperial expansion. Great Britain
had already staked a claim in North America but had lost the American colonies a century before; it was left with the northern half of the
continent, including a large French-speaking population of more than
100,000 people whose loyalties were naturally with France. On 30
March 1856, exactly four months before Richard was born, the war in
the Crimea ended with the Treaty of Paris. Great Britain – ever concerned about challenges to its dominance of the seas – was fearful of

the emerging Russian fleet and had joined with France and Sardinia to check the expansion of Russia into the Black Sea. Russia had invaded Turkey in 1853 demanding free passage for its warships through the Dardanelles Strait, which was controlled by Turkey.

In far-off India, a year later, the Indian Mutiny erupted in Bengal and was put down in a bloody confrontation with the native sepoy troops. The following year, 1858, Parliament passed the India Act, under which Britain assumed sovereignty over India from the East India Company and thereby extended the limits of the Empire to which Haldane was to become deeply devoted. But it was an Empire that would soon begin to carry great costs. Events leading up to the general election of 1880 revealed a British Empire 'embroiled in the takeover of the Transvaal in 1877, the invasion of Afghanistan in 1878 and the war against the Zulu kingdom which began in 1879 ... Matters were made worse by the near annihilation of a British column at Isandlwana in Zululand in the first month of the war, and there were some near-run things in Afghanistan.'[54] The horrors of these escapades brought the aged Gladstone out of retirement once again, and, filled with an uncommon energy, he stumped the country during the general election of 1880. He railed against 'Beaconsfieldism' and denounced the atrocities of imperial misadventure as a stain on the reputation of Britain as the dispenser of fair play and justice. 'Ten thousand Zulus had died,' he told a Glaswegian audience, 'for no other offence than their attempt to defend against your artillery their homes and families.'[55] Gladstone and his Liberal colleagues were returned to office with a comfortable majority. And Richard Haldane began to take an interest in politics.

Unknown to Haldane, however, during these days of expanding Empire, affairs across the vast expanse of ocean in British North America were taking on critical dimensions. The British North American colonies, both French and English components, were working their way through a series of internal political and economic adjustments on the way to nationhood with an uncommon determination to cement their ties with the Empire. The distinguished Canadian historian W.L. Morton has designated the period between 1857 and 1873 'The Critical Years.' They were the years during which the leading politicians in Canada were beginning to see more clearly the need for a united country, rather than five squabbling colonies and a vast unsettled western territory threatened by American manifest destiny. The bloody skirmishes of 1837–8 in both Upper and Lower Canada were well behind them and the long campaign for colonial self-government had been achieved by the date of Haldane's birth. But much more had yet to be done. Both the imperial government and the leading politicians of the day were in agreement that the colonies should be united into one country. Imperial trade preference had been cancelled and trade reciprocity with the United States had been repealed, developments that together tended to give impetus to the dream of many for a new united British nationality in the northern half of the American continent. All this was reinforced by the rumblings of protectionism throughout the neighbouring republic. Many manufacturers pined for the glory days of reciprocity when 'American goods and capital flowed into Canada in ever-increasing volume. The north-south flow of trade exceeded the east-west.'[56] Those were profitable years, especially for the producers of raw materials, such as lumber, and manufactured goods in the Maritime colonies. But nationhood beckoned and the process towards achieving it was fraught with difficulties, not the least of which was the defiant determination of many of the leading politicians, such as John A. Macdonald, to remain faithful to their British heritage.[57] They were suspicious of any attempts of those who would weaken the ties with the mother country with the promise of closer integration with the neighbouring republic.

Having completed his formal education at the University of Edinburgh and having chosen to pursue a career at the bar, Richard Burdon Haldane now entered a new phase of his life. Over the years ahead, he would forge a long and distinguished career as a jurist and in Parliament, one that would have important consequences for all of the Empire, including Canada.

3

The Practice of Law and Life in Parliament

Jessel, when he had caught the point, began to play with me as a cat does with a mouse. But I had the authorities even more at my fingers' ends than he had, the consequence of portentous study.

– R.B. Haldane, *Autobiography*

Richard Haldane began the formal study of law as a 'junior legal counsel' or 'devil' in the well-known firm of Tods, Murray and Jamieson. There he immersed himself in conveyancing and Scottish feudal law. He also served for a brief period in the fall of 1876 and winter of 1877 as devil in the Drummond and Reid firm doing mercantile and other legal business prior to leaving for London and Lincoln's Inn the following spring.

From the earliest days of his legal education to the end of his life, London was to be his home. It was there, in the course of his early years of practice, that he encountered some of the leading legal practitioners of the day, such as Horace Davey and Ferrar Herschell, and pleaded in the House of Lords before celebrated judges such as Sir George Jessel. It was Horace Davey who introduced Haldane to Canadian constitutional appeals in which he quickly acquired a reputation as an authority. More important, his early career in London opened up to him a life in politics alongside aspiring young barristers such as H.H. Asquith and Edward Grey. London also provided him with access to an expanded social life which included the theatre, as well as offering an entrée into the social activism of the times through association with Beatrice and Sidney Webb and other Fabians. Thanks to the Webbs, Richard Haldane developed an interest in educational reform which became a secondary passion to the end of his life. But privately throughout those years he nurtured his love of German philosophy and it soon became clear that his approach to law was to be fully informed by his readings in the philosophy of Hegel.

By going to the English bar, Haldane departed from his father's career focus, which was exclusively on Scottish law. Richard referred to 'the tradition, derived from a sort of family agreement on the subject, that I should ultimately go to the English Bar.'[1] This tradition, he further explained, came from his mother's, the Burdon-Sanderson,[2] side of the family not the Haldane. 'One of my great grand-uncles, John Scott, Lord Eldon, had been Lord Chancellor, and another, his brother, William Scott, Lord Stowell, had been a great jurist and judge.'[3] He then recounted the family folklore that when he was a young boy and the family visited the London home of his maternal grandfather, Richard Burdon Sanderson (after whom the boy was named), his nurse, the ever doting Betsy Ferguson, took him to the House of Lords, then in recess. The prescient nurse seated the boy upon the woolsack and exclaimed in the broadest of Scots to the empty chamber: '"The bairn will sit there some day as of right."'[4] 'At all events,' he concluded in his account of the occasion, 'for the English Bar I was destined by general family acclamation, and into the spirit of the decision I entered early.'[5] He quickly impressed everyone with whom he came in contact with two traits that were to characterize him throughout his life in court, on the bench, and as a minister of the crown: the capacity for hard work and an extraordinary memory. He thought nothing of working far into the night without interruption, and rising the next morning after a few hours' sleep fresh and ready for the day's business.

When he was devil for Horace Davey, he quickly impressed the distinguished barrister – and later law lord – with his thorough command of the material and his ability to recall instantly a required point of law or a controlling precedent in common law. He had the good fortune to meet Davey early in his career in London; until this point he knew the man only by his great reputation and had admired him at a distance for many years. He was soon to find in the distinguished lawyer a soulmate in the law. 'It suited him [Davey] when I had taken enough trouble, for I devoted myself, as he did, to unravelling first principles of law.'[6] Haldane showed that he had a unique ability to penetrate cases and emerge with the central principle upon which to hang a formidable array of supporting arguments. He demonstrated his grasp of the Hegelian injunction to uncover the 'spirit' of the law. It was a talent he was to demonstrate later in his career in Canadian constitutional cases in which he took special pride, to the annoyance of many lawyers and politicians back in Canada.

Student-at-Law

Richard Haldane arrived in London in April 1877 at a time when there was much social unrest, both politically and intellectually. It was a time that would culminate in what has been called 'the decade of a thousand movements.'[7] Societies and associations championing the poor and disadvantaged sprung up like mushrooms; socialist meetings of every stripe arose clamouring for major changes in the commercial and political structure of the state. London was then the largest city in the world; its population exploded between 1831 and 1851 by over 700,000 people.[8] When the young aspiring lawyer arrived from Scotland, the city boasted a population of 2,362,000 people. The density of population, to say nothing of the poor state of medical knowledge, led to the spread of deadly diseases such as diphtheria, tuberculosis, typhus, smallpox, and rabies throughout the 1880s and to the end of the century.[9] While Haldane was acutely aware of the plight of the poor, he travelled in the better circles of society thanks in part to his family connections and his friends at the bar.

The young Scot could not have failed to notice the prevalence of the Scottish imprint on London life. Scottish bakers dominated Bread Street, while Clyde-trained iron-shipbuilders were so common on the Isle of Dogs at Millwall that 'the Scottish dialect and Christian names' were prevalent, pubs had signs like Burns and Highland Mary, and other spirits were accommodated at 'the kirk.'[10] It is estimated that about 50,000 Scots lived in London at this time and they founded such institutions as the Scottish Hospital off Fleet Street and the Caledonian Asylum for orphans of Scottish soldiers, sailors, and marines. 'By the end of the century they also had their highland games, annual dinner, Scottish dancing gala and a London Scottish golf club.'[11] Richard Haldane, however, seems not to have attempted to attach himself to any specific Scottish group or association. What new friends he made came from his contacts in the law and through association with the likes of

Beatrice and Sidney Webb who were active in accumulating 'scientific' data relating to the problems emerging with the voracious expansion of the sprawling new London.

It was the intellectual atmosphere of London that appealed most to Richard Haldane, and while sceptical in some measure about the role of the new 'social science,' he cultivated attachments in those circles. It was a time, Beatrice Webb recorded in her diary, dominated by

the naive belief of the most original and vigorous minds of the 'seventies and eighties' that it was by science, and by science alone, that all human misery would be ultimately swept away. This almost fanatical faith was perhaps partly due to hero-worship. For who will deny that the men of science were the leading British intellectuals of that period; that it was they who stood out as men of genius with international reputations; that it was they who were the self-confident militants of the period; that it was they who were routing the theologians, confounding the mystics, imposing their theories on philosophers, their inventions on capitalists, and their discoveries on medical men; whilst they were at the same time snubbing the artists, ignoring the poets and even casting doubts on the capacity of the politicians?[12]

Added to the 'cult of science,' as she called it, was the growing contempt among historians of philosophy for metaphysics. Intellectual historians such as George Henry Lewes dismissed metaphysics 'as condemned, by the very nature of its method, to wander forever in one tortuous labyrinth, within whose circumscribed and winding spaces weary seekers are continually finding themselves in the trodden tracks of predecessors who could find no exit.'[13]

The young law student was fully aware of these currents of thought but paid them only passing attention, so busy was he in locating lodgings and making contacts and preparing himself for the bar. Five years before his arrival at the Inns of Court, the benchers had adopted a more rigorous scheme of legal education. In the old days, a student-at-law simply attached himself to an established barrister and read law in his chambers and devilled for his senior until such time – usually after three years – the young man applied for admission to the practice of law. (The legal profession was then closed to women and not destined to be opened to them for several decades after Haldane's death.[14]) Criticisms of the haphazard character of legal education had circulated among the profession for many years, but without result. In due course, however, the benchers of the Inns of Court succumbed to the growing chorus of criticism from within the profession and instituted reforms in 1872. The reforms made it a firm rule that no student would be called to the bar until he had passed examinations in Roman law and in the leading branches of English law. Formal lectures in law were instituted and, after paying ten guineas, law students were admitted to the lectures. The examinations were compulsory but attendance at the lectures was voluntary. The lectures were scheduled to coincide with the academic terms at the universities in an effort to give them a measure of academic respectability. Those who succeeded in passing the examinations were acknowledged in a list published by the benchers.[15] It was under this reformed regime that Richard Haldane became a student-at-law at Lincoln's Inn.

In addition to knowing few people in London, Haldane had very little money, but his resources were sufficient to secure rooms off the Bayswater Road. He financed those early months in London by borrowing against the inheritance he was destined to receive upon the death of his mother. He had to borrow £100 in order to purchase a set of required law books.[16] It was a good thing for him that he became self-supporting relatively quickly because his mother was destined to live until a few weeks beyond her one hundredth birthday. Mary Elizabeth Haldane died in May 1925, by which time the gifted son had become comfortably well-off from the practice of law and his lord chancellor's pension and was no longer in need of an inheritance income.

The young Haldane shrewdly took advantage of his family contacts, which were, once again, on his mother's side. Upon the recommendation of Farrer Herschell, who was later to serve as lord chancellor and participate in several important Canadian cases as a member of the Judicial Committee, he became a pupil in the firm of William Barber. Barber had a large practice at the Chancery bar and quickly sized up the mental capacity of the young Scottish student and engaged him in writing drafts of pleadings and deeds. As Haldane related in his *Autobiography*, this work – in 'Equity drafting and conveyancing' – was relatively easy when compared to 'sifting the books of the German metaphysicians.'[17] It was during this initial period in Barber's chambers that Haldane demonstrated his work habits. 'Not only did I work all day, excepting when in Court watching cases and the way in which the great leaders opened them before great judges like James and Jessel, but I read law almost continuously.'[18] He also 'began to feel something like a passion for law,' which was to remain with him to the end of his life. 'At night in my rooms,' he wrote later of this period of his life, 'and

often in my bed, I used to read law books. The original editions, uncor-
rupted by the commentators who had half obliterated the substance by
bring it up to date in new editions, especially fascinated me.' As well,
he immersed himself in the library of Lincoln's Inn and committed to
memory a long series of cases which he was able to dredge up years
later, citing the precise locations in the sources. On his own admission,
he was blessed with an 'exceptionally good memory.' Barber began to
steer the more difficult cases to the young student, who was excited
by the confidence shown in him by his legal superior and proceeded
to produce drafts of these cases which Barber invariably used in court.

In order to broaden his instruction in English law, and with Barber's
encouragement, Haldane quit the Barber firm and entered the chambers of Lumley Smith, a renowned common law practitioner. 'There,'
he recorded, 'I began to learn a good deal of common law.'[19] Barber had
passed on to Lumley Smith his high opinion of the young Scot, who
quickly became responsible for Smith's 'more difficult cases.'

Owing to the lack of personal contacts – compounded by his native
shyness – Haldane's social life was severely restricted; most of his fellow students-at-law were classmates from either Oxford or Cambridge
and hence a part of a network of old friendships. The Scottish student,
shy and somewhat lacking in social graces, found it difficult at first but
soon escaped the deficiencies of a limited social life by immersing himself in the business of law. What little social life he had in these early
years as devil arose out of his visits to the home of William Barber,
where he met many members of the Chancery bar. In addition to those
contacts, Haldane was taken under the wing of his uncle John Burdon
Sanderson and his wife. They introduced him to friends and tried to
broaden his circle of acquaintances. Under their influence, he even persuaded himself to take dancing lessons. During these lessons he met
Mrs Elizabeth Garrett Anderson, who used to hold evening classes at
her home.[20] 'At her house I began to go to dances, and to dances I was
invited out, an experience which was rather new to me.'[21]

At this juncture in his *Autobiography*, Haldane brings the matter to an
abrupt close with the statement: 'However, this inclination was of brief
duration.' Clearly, something happened during these dancing soirées
which caused the young man, who on his own admission demonstrated
'deficiencies of a somewhat restricted upbringing,' to reconsider his attendance. Almost certainly dancing was not part of the Calvinist home
in Edinburgh or at Cloanden but he appears to have enjoyed the company of the young women he was meeting at these dances. The account

of this uncharacteristic episode in his early life is followed coldly in his *Autobiography* by the observation: 'The passion for reading law continued. I moved into rooms in Bruton Street, and there pursued it. Philosophy still continued to interest me much, but law became predominant, and I was also taken up with Political Economy.'[22]

Bruton Street was a short street off Berkley Square, Mayfair, about five minutes' walk from Hyde Park and not far from the centre of London society of the day. 'How well I recollect those first days of my early London seasons' in the 1870s, Beatrice Webb recorded ruefully: 'the pleasurable but somewhat feverish anticipation of endless distractions, a dissipation of mental and physical energy which filled up all the hours of the day and lasted far into the night; the ritual to be observed; the presentation at Court, the riding in the Row, the calls, the lunches and dinners, the dances and crushes, Hurlingham and Ascot, not to mention amateur theatricals and other sham philanthropic excrescences.'[23] It was a life that held no attraction for the dour Scot bent on a career at the bar and showing no inclination to acquiring the necessary social graces.

Whether Haldane saw these social diversions as impediments to the serious pursuit of law, we can only surmise. One thing is clear: he was struck by the lack of seriousness shown by his fellow pupils in Barber's chambers, as he had been with his Göttingen fellow students a few years earlier. They were 'fond of sport and not very industrious.' Small wonder that he was rarely invited into their social circles. The future lord chancellor showed to the end of his life no interest in any sport and was ever industrious. If there was one thing he knew about himself, it was that he could outwork his contemporaries. And he did. He had no time (or money) for wining and dining, though he attended the required dinners at the Inns of Court. A more active social life would have to wait until he had established himself as a successful barrister.

In the midst of his legal preoccupations, Richard Haldane's father died in Edinburgh in 1877 at the age of seventy-two, two years before his son was called to the bar. The account of his father's passing given in the *Autobiography* confirms what we learned earlier about the distance of the man from the life of his children. After noting the death of his father, and the fact that with his death 'a good deal devolved on me at first, as the oldest of his second family,' Haldane commented: 'He passed away as he had lived, full of faith in what for him were eternal verities.' '*For him*,' but clearly not for the son. And then he said of his father: 'He had been throughout too far away from the subjects that were interesting us who were his younger children ever to enter much into our inner lives. But,' the son concluded, 'he was full of affection, and when we succeeded in anything he took pride in our success.'[24]

These rather cold recollections of his father stand out in contrast to the son's expansive eulogy of his mother almost half a century later. There, the son recorded: 'To me the striking feature through the dozen [last] years of which I write was my mother's steady growth in mental stature ... her outlook and mental grasp were widening to the end steadily. She read extensively, in various languages, and her reading included difficult philosophical books, as well as memoirs and histories.'[25] He commented on his mother's deep religious convictions but noted that 'what she sought for was rather to hold fast to the highest quality in this [life], where the human and the divine were never for her shut off from each other.'[26] It is difficult to read these comments without believing that his mother's character was meant to be understood in contrast with the more rigid piety of his father. 'Thus she was intensely religious, with expressions for her religion that were characteristic of her mind ... But her views were never thrust on [her children]. She claimed liberty of thought, and she accorded it equally freely.'[27] It would be difficult to imagine the son writing in these terms of his father, who had forced him to submit against his will to baptismal immersion. Haldane's sister, Elizabeth, summarized the strictness of the Calvinist religious atmosphere in which she and her brothers grew up. 'We learned the doctrines of Calvinism from our father: the distinction between Sanctification and Justification, between Free Will and Predestination, but even we children came soon to know that these doctrines that meant so much to our forefathers, who had indeed spent their birthright in maintaining them, were to us empty words.'[28] Surely it was their mother – 'the truly religious, but far from Calvinist, English mother' – who steered them through the forbidding shoals of their father's Calvinism.[29] There is scarcely a word to be found in all the children's memoirs and recollections about the funeral of their father, in great contrast with the lengthy accounts of their mother's life and death.

Not long after the father died, the widow Haldane took her daughter to Paris where they visited the opera and the many galleries of the famous city. It would be impossible to conceive of a city that contrasted more starkly with that of staid Presbyterian Edinburgh than Paris, with its Catholic cathedrals and reputation for moral laxity. Clearly, it was a trip she had not able to make while her husband was alive. One can only guess at how long she must have wanted to make it. We know that she was a woman with an intellectually curious mind and this trip reveals a great deal about her. She seemed unconcerned that it would expose her children to unwholesome religious and moral influences. 'We never went to the theatre,' Elizabeth was quick to reassure her diary. 'Sarah Bernhardt seemed to dominate the scene, and we came into touch with a side of life we never knew before.' But, when her brothers visited, they 'did not have the same scruples' and took their sister to the Grand Opera where they enjoyed a performance of Goethe's *Faust*, 'an occasion never to be forgotten,' Elizabeth noted. The young woman later confessed: 'This winter in Paris did a great deal for us as a family in liberating us from the shackles of Scottish Victorian and Puritan propriety.'[30] Of whether their father would have disapproved of this liberation, there can be no doubt. Nor can there be any doubt that Mary Elizabeth Haldane shared the sense of liberation, if not, perhaps, to the same degree as her daughter and sons. The eldest son, however, while too busy in London trying to establish himself, heartily approved of his mother's excursions into the lighter side of French society.

As the eldest son, Richard assisted his mother in selling the Edinburgh home in Charlotte Square, and after purchasing the Perthshire property from his father's estate, he helped her to relocate to Cloan. She must have foreseen the eventuality of leaving Edinburgh and the move to Cloan because several years before her husband's death she persuaded him to enlarge and modernize the Perthshire estate. It had served as the summer retreat for the family for many years and was loved by all members of the family. With the move from Edinburgh, Cloanden became for many decades the family home, a place where Richard took refuge from time to time for the rest of his life, frequently accompanied by friends such as H.H. Asquith and Edward Grey. Cloanden was a large three-storey building erected a century before. Its most notable feature is the tall, thin, round four-storey medieval-looking stone turret, capped with a tall conical slate roof and a Maltese cross. Connected to the turret by a four-storey link is a three-storey rectangular stone edifice, rather tall for its footprint but very elegant in its proportions. This main building has a steep-pitched, slate mansard roof, topped with a cast iron rail enclosing a 'widow's walk.' The medieval turret on the northwest corner is balanced by a rectangular turret, corbelled out from the third floor of the southwest corner of the main building. The elegant proportions of the estate are enhanced by a two-storey bay window facing west, framed by the turrets. A central dormer on the main building roof completes the composition of the west facade. The southeast corner of the main building is accentuated by a tall, thin stone chimney projecting out from the second storey. Flanking the manor house are a glass conservatory on the south face and a two-storey entrance wing to the north. An assembly of coach houses and other outbuildings were located to the east. The locally quarried stone, accentuated by dressed stone corner quoins and dressed stone door and window trims, gives an air of permanence and prosperity.[31]

The Haldane children loved every square inch of the house. Several years before moving into the house, Robert Haldane had, at his wife's insistence, added a large wing to the left of the main entrance; it was architecturally compatible with the principal part of the house and constructed of the same locally quarried stone. At the time when Mrs Haldane relocated her family to Cloanden, there were no electric lights, but as soon as Richard was able to afford it he installed electric lights and heating. No one was more pleased with this improvement than Elizabeth, who became fascinated with electric lights when she and her mother had visited Paris. 'While in Paris in 1879–80,' Elizabeth wrote in her memoirs, 'we had seen some arc electric lamps as a wonderful new development.' Before the installation of electricity, however, Cloanden enjoyed 'the general improvement of gas lighting with the aid of incandescent burners.'[32]

While these events were unfolding in Edinburgh and Perthshire following the death of his father, the young student-at-law's reputation was beginning to make the rounds of the London professional circles. In June 1878, while still a student, he was retained in an appeal before the House of Lords when James Traynor, a leading Scottish advocate, could not come up to London to argue the case. 'The Parliamentary agent, who knew about me and that I understood Scotch law, asked me to take his place. Unfortunately, not having been called I could not accept a Brief before the House (and so cannot address it) nor can I accept a fee in the case, as I am not a barrister yet, but it is a very satisfactory introduction.'[33] The best his position permitted him was to consult with the Scottish and English barristers 'to discuss the Scotch law with them, they knowing nothing of it. I am also to have a private consultation with the Solicitors before hand tomorrow morning.'[34] Clearly, the young man was making a name for himself even before he was admitted to the bar.

Two days later he reported to his mother that he had received 'a letter this morning from the Parliamentary Agent asking me to meet Mr. Bristowe, Q.C., for a second consultation this afternoon at 5. None of their Counsel understand the Scotch law and I am preparing an argument for them. The Lord Advocate [Maurice] Kay, Q.C., and John McLaren are on the other side and there is great anxiety as to the results, as I found a weak point in our case which had not been noticed by the English lawyers.' He then added, understandably in mild frustration, 'I wish only that I had been called.'[35] It must surely have been heady stuff for a young student-at-law to be associating with such distinguished members of the bar and being in a position to instruct them at such a high level. It did much to steel his confidence in his own judgment. His ego must have been further stroked when the next day he was approached by J.P.B. Robertson, a leading 'Parliamentary and Scotch agent' who counselled him to become 'thoroughly *au fait* in Scotch Feudal Law so as to be able to advise upon and settle Scotch Conveyancing Questions, I would get a large practice there in London, and a very lucrative one as well.'[36] Robertson, a celebrated Scottish advocate, pressed the young man, telling him that 'since the retirement from practice of the last Scotch Counsel here the London Agents and Solicitors were in great difficulty, and had asked him to recommend some one who was equal to the work, to qualify himself.'[37] The young man listened politely but refused to commit himself. He gave every impression in a letter to his mother that he was busy making contacts and that his vision of his career was broader than the one outlined by Robertson. 'I met Herschell this morning at Westminster,' he concluded one letter, 'who was most pleasant and offered to get me into the chambers of any Common Law Counsel I wished. So I am going to ask him to get me into one of his Chambers in January, so that I can stay in Edinburgh until Christmas to work there.'[38]

His advice continued to be sought in the case before the House of Lords, which concerned an inheritance of a young widow who 'will lose heavily unless this appeal succeeds.'[39] He took great pride in finding a mistake in the argument prepared by 'the two QCs who had advised in the case and by the Scotch Counsel who drew it.'[40] He happily reported two weeks later when the court rendered judgment: 'The widow who brought the appeal has succeeded on every point. She gets about 10,000 pounds clear which is very satisfactory.'[41]

Barrister

Richard Haldane was called to the bar at the end of 1879 at the age of twenty-three and opened his own chambers in a garret in New Square, near Lincoln's Inn, where he waited impatiently for briefs. In October 1880 he wrote to his mother: 'No briefs yet. One's time is well filled up with reading however ... Since coming up one has been getting through between 11 and 12 hours' reading a day and I intend to keep on doing so.'[42] As one might expect for a new barrister, these early days were financially bleak. The fact that he 'knew almost no London solicitors' put him at a distinct disadvantage.[43] His fee book for 1880 showed that he earned £31,10s.[44] And, while this was a sum above that earned by barmaids who earned about £20 per year for eighty-hour weeks, it was considerably less than the £150 pounds a clerk with ten years' experience in the Gas Light and Coke Company earned.[45] Haldane's income was to improve considerably, in part because William Barber kept a close eye on him. In addition to inviting the new barrister to his home to meet people prominent in the law, he asked Haldane to revise Dart's *Vendors and Purchasers* for a new edition.

It was not uncommon at this time for aspiring but brief-less English barristers to turn to writing in their lean early years in practice. When Judah Benjamin, for example, escaped from the United States following the Civil War – he had served as attorney general as well as secretary of war under Jefferson Davies – he wrote a major book on the comparative law of sales while waiting for briefs to come his way. It is known to this day as *Benjamin on Sales*.[46] Haldane thought for a time about trying his hand at journalism in order to make ends meet. But he soon found that journalism was frowned upon by the legal profession. Generally speaking, the benchers looked unkindly on those who attempted to augment their livelihoods by writing for newspapers.[47] The benchers of Lincoln's Inn, for example, in the early years of the nineteenth century, attempted to block admission to practice of those who were paid for writing for newspapers. This did not prevent several famous writers from emerging from stints in legal chambers. Charles Dickens, for example, spent a year and a half in Gray's Inn. Even Thackeray (Middle Temple) and Wilkie Collins (Lincoln's Inn) served some time honing their skills among barristers at the Inns of Court. One of the most famous authors of his age, Walter Scott, apprenticed in the law offices of his father and was admitted to the Scottish bar in 1799. He became sheriff-dupute of Selkirkshire and in 1806 was made clerk of the Court of Session, holding the latter post for twenty-five years.[48]

In the early years of his practice, Haldane began to realize that he did not have the talent to become a trial lawyer. In July 1882, for example, he wrote home telling of a successful trial in the county court at Marylebone in which he broke the testimony of the plaintiff's solicitor on cross-examination. While he was able to report that he 'was highly complimented by the Judge and my clients were much pleased as they thought they had no case,' he was uncomfortable in the thrust and parry of the trial. 'I do not think,' he wrote to his mother, 'that for the ordinary work of a barrister I was at all exceptionally qualified. For example I was never good in handling witnesses or the rough and tumble of *nisi prius* work. But in the Supreme Tribunals where the facts have to be marshalled, brought under principle, and exhibited in the light of varying judicial systems, I think I possessed some advantages which were not common, due to philosophical studies and familiarity with difficult phrases of logical systems. It was easy for me to pass from one system of law to another wholly different, grasping what was distinctive of the spirit of the jurisprudence with which I was dealing.'[49] The decision that followed upon this self-assessment was a wise one, for Richard Haldane became in time an outstanding advocate before the House of Lords and the Judicial Committee of the Privy Council.

By 1882, with his earnings beginning to rise, Haldane had moved to Down Street, Piccadilly, not many blocks southwest of Bruton Street. His new rooms, located just off Piccadilly and across from Green Park, were a convenient walk to Hyde Park Corner, which had by this time attained fame as a location for 'unfettered freedom of speech'; there is no record, however, of the shy Scottish lawyer venting forth to the spot. He also joined at this time the Junior Athenaeum Club and frequently wrote home from there. He happily related that, in about the fourth year of practice, his reputation for being 'an energetic and pretty ingenious Junior' began to draw the attention of solicitors and his billings started 'to shoot up.'[50] His good fortune was to improve permanently owing, once again, to the vigilance of his early mentor, William Barber. Through his impeccable contacts, Barber was informed that Horace Davey was in need of a devil. Barber recommended Haldane, who jumped at the opportunity. 'I now became immersed in Davey's cases,' he recorded in his *Autobiography*. 'I used to read them carefully, make out what I thought to be his real points, and hunt out the authorities. Davey was, I think, the finest advocate on pure points of law that I have ever seen. In legal matters he had a mind like a razor, and he was accurate to the last degree.'[51] In describing Davey's mind, Haldane was describing his own. The two men, though separated by age and years of experience, developed a genuine respect and affection for one another.

Horace Davey was twenty-three years older than Haldane and had been educated at Rugby and University College, Oxford, where he distinguished himself as a student. He took a double first class in classics and mathematics; he was, for a time, senior mathematical scholar and Eldon law scholar and was elected a fellow of his college. He was called to the bar at Lincoln's Inn in 1861 at the age of twenty-eight. He became a Queen's Counsel in 1875 and developed an extensive Chancery practice. He showed an interest in politics and entered Parliament in 1880 as member for Christchurch, Hants, but he lost the seat at the next general election. His efforts to return to Parliament in 1886 on Gladstone's coattails were unsuccessful. While he found a seat two years later, in Stockton-on-Tees, he lost it in the election of 1892. Thus ended his political career. But he was appointed by Gladstone a lord justice of appeal in 1893 and, the following year, a lord of appeal in ordinary, having been created a life peer with the title of Lord Davey of Fernhurst. He died in London on 20 February 1907 at the age of seventy-four. He was one of the most distinguished judges of his generation and his death was a great loss to the bar and bench of England. During his years in practice, Davey demonstrated a fine intellect and few of his contemporaries appeared before the courts with a more formidable presence than he. 'Sir Horace Davey,' one observer noted, 'ranked among the finest intellects and the most subtle pleaders ever known to the English Bar.'[52] By the early 1880s, when Haldane came in contact with Davey, the celebrated barrister was earning £25,000 per year; by contrast, Haldane's fee book showed a princely income of £1,000 for the year, which he considered fairly good.

One of the very first cases in which Haldane assisted Davey was an application for leave to appeal from the government of Quebec. The solicitor general of Quebec was under strict instructions to have Davey represent them before the Judicial Committee. Davey had accepted the brief and was prepared to argue the matter, but the night before he was due to appear in court he received word that he was to appear in the House of Lords to continue an argument in a past-heard appeal. It was 'a summons which took precedence of that to the Privy Council.' Davey was caught off guard and attempted to find a suitable replacement for his Quebec client, but 'no other leader of eminence could be got to take a brief at very short notice in a case involving a complicated question of Canadian constitutional law.'[53]

Davey sent his clerk to Haldane's rooms at eight that evening to inform his junior that he would have to open the case in Davey's stead.

Undoubtedly taken aback by such a task, Haldane nevertheless accepted the challenge at once, much to the chagrin of the Quebec solicitor general and Freshfields Solicitors, who were aghast at the prospect of this young barely fledged barrister standing in for the great Horace Davey. 'I sat up through much of the night,' Haldane recalled later, 'and mastered the real point.' Davey, at the first meeting with his Canadian clients, had suggested that the Quebec solicitor general open the petition. The poor man demurred with the explanation that he was explicitly instructed by his superiors not to do so. If he did, he explained, and the application was refused, 'the responsibility would be such that the Government of Quebec might fall.'[54] There was nothing Davey could do under the circumstances but leave the matter to his junior, Richard Haldane. And so, having announced that his junior would lead, the eminent barrister seized his hat and disappeared. 'This did not comfort the unhappy clients,' Haldane recorded. 'Old Mr. Wiseman, the well-known Privy Council Clerk of Freshfields, rose from his seat and said in high dudgeon: "The House of Freshfield has briefed Sir Richard Bethel, Sir Hugh Cairns, Sir Roundell Palmer, and other great men, and none of them every treated the firm as Mr. Davey has to-day."'[55] And he promptly stormed out of the room.

There was nothing the startled litigants could do but assent to this outrageous change of plans. Haldane took charge and the next morning appeared before the lords of the Judicial Committee, whose members were surprised that they were to be addressed by such a young barrister and not the illustrious Davey. 'I opened my argument as shortly and moderately as possible, and stated the point on the constitution of Canada concisely.' Haldane reasoned that, while the monetary amount in the appeal was very small, 'it might lead to real injustice ... if we were not allowed to bring a question that was of far-reaching public importance before the Supreme Tribunal of the Empire.'[56] After deliberating over the matter, the law lords returned. 'They did not know my name,' the young barrister later recorded, 'but they said that what had been stated had satisfied them that we ought to have leave to appeal.' His clients, while delighted with the decision, were not pleased. 'Neither the Solicitor-General nor Freshfields said a word of thanks to me. They went away as persons aggrieved,' he later recorded, somewhat amused.[57]

Richard Haldane savoured this first victory throughout his long years at the bar. In fact, his first case before the Privy Council and his first Canadian case was the beginning of a series of such cases that earned for him a reputation for expertise in Canadian constitutional law and launched him on a lucrative career at the bar. As luck would have it, Davey's late-night summons to appear in the House of Lords triggered a series of events that led to Haldane becoming, in his own mind at least, a repository 'of the learning about the Canadian constitution.'[58]

As he was enjoying the afterglow of his first major court victory in the privacy of his garret, who should climb the narrow staircase leading to his chambers but the venerable Freshfields solicitor Mr John Wiseman himself. 'He said that the partners had read the shorthand note of the brief argument at the Privy Council and now sent me a brief for the Province of Ontario in a great case ... This particular brief was marked 150 guineas, and it introduced me to many Canadian cases over here.'[59] Unfortunately, there is no record in the law reports of Richard Haldane conducting an Ontario case before the Judicial Committee during these early years at the bar.

With respect to Haldane's assessment of his own reputation as an authority on Canadian law, the one man who deserved such a reputation was surely Horace Davey. He appeared in most Canadian cases during the late 1880s, usually in tandem with Oliver Mowat, Ontario's attorney general. The law reports show that Davey, Farrer Herschell, Lumley Smith, and J.P.B. Robertson – who had encouraged Haldane to specialize in Scottish law – appeared frequently before the Privy Council in Canadian cases, but never do they list Haldane as a participant. The reported cases, also, show that he did not participate in important Scottish cases of the day. This is especially curious in light of his boast that he was becoming known as one versed in Scottish law. In a House of Lords case, *Ewing v. Orr Ewing* (1885), for example, in which both Davey and Robertson appear before Lord Watson and other law lords, there is no mention of Haldane. Nor is he present in the celebrated *The Lauderdale Peerage Case* (1885), where one might surely have expected to find him. In this case both Herschell and Davey appear, but not Haldane.

Davey retired from practice eight years later when he was appointed to the bench. Few people admired him more than Richard Haldane and Davey appears to have reciprocated by demanding more and more of his young friend. In 1883, for example, Haldane recorded in his *Autobiography* that Davey found himself in the thick of an impossible case. The Scottish Petroleum case[60] was brought on appeal from the Chancery Court judgment of Justice Kay who had dismissed Davey's effort 'rather contemptuously.'[61] Although Davey thought the appeal was hopeless, the young Scot doggedly, and to the annoyance of his senior, kept digging away into the authorities. But he failed to penetrate the convictions of the great Davey, who 'brushed all my suggestions aside, and said that when the case was reached he should discover an engagement in another Court and leave me to open our appeal, of which he was sure he could make nothing.'[62]

When the case was called, Haldane found himself before the great Sir George Jessel, master of the rolls, and two lords of appeal. Jessel toyed with the young barrister, whom he was seeing before the court for the first time, 'as a cat does with a mouse.' As Haldane confided to his *Autobiography*, he and Jessel sparred back and forth. 'But I had the authorities even more at my fingers' ends than he had, the consequence of portentous study. He could not break me down, for I would not yield an inch. He began to get excited and to throw the power of his personality into the struggle with me, while his colleagues remained silent.'[63] The case was adjourned for the day. The next day Haldane found himself before the two lords of appeal but no Jessel. The court announced that the master of the rolls was gravely ill and that the case would have to be opened afresh on a subsequent date. Jessel was never to return to court for he died of Bright's disease a few days later. Haldane's younger colleagues at the bar chided him for weeks after for having killed the great jurist with the power of his arguments at his initial and only encounter with the man.

But Jessel was to have the last laugh, for when the case was reheard before three different lords justices, Davey once again allowed the ever confident young Haldane to conduct the case alone. When he apologized somewhat diffidently to the court for the absence of his senior colleague, Lord Justice Nathaniel Lindley interrupted with the comment: 'Mr Haldane, the Court of Appeal is of the opinion that your clients have no need to regret the absence of your leader.'[64] The young man graciously accepted the compliment and proceeded to present his case systematically, buttressing it with a wall of learned authorities. But, despite his best efforts, Haldane lost the case after trying manfully to wring gold from a handful of legal dross for several hours. As Davey had correctly surmised, the case was hopeless but the tenacious young barrister would not concede until he heard the verdict from the court itself. Despite the negative outcome, Richard Haldane had clearly impressed three solicitors who were in court awaiting their own cases to be called. Within a few days of the Scottish Petroleum case, Haldane began to receive briefs from the solicitors who had witnessed his defeat in the Court of Appeal. Without doubt, he showed himself to be a determined and skilful advocate who would go to the wall for his clients in defiance of overwhelming objections. Not unexpectedly, therefore, his fee book for 1884 showed an income of £2,000 for the year. He had turned one defeat into several triumphs. His career began to improve rapidly from that moment on.

Letters home during the period following his admission to the bar indicate that Richard had become attracted to a woman he does not name.[65] It was a totally new experience for the young Scottish bachelor, as he related to his mother. 'Forces have taken possession of my life,' he wrote, 'forces of which I knew nothing until now.'[66] The stirrings of romantic emotion appear to have caught this ultra-rationalist completely off guard. After several more letters to and from his mother, the matter seems to have petered out. The romantic interlude ended as mysteriously as it began but it left him vulnerable in a way he had not previously thought possible. In due course the 'forces' were to enter his life again, as we shall see.

The young barrister began gradually to feel that he had made a name for himself at the bar and thought sufficiently of his achievements and his place in the legal fraternity to apply in 1887 to the lord chancellor for the Queen's Counsel designation, or for 'silk,' as it is called in the profession. He was thirty-one at the time. He was, not surprisingly, rebuffed on this occasion but wrote again two years later, having persuaded his new friend H.H. Asquith to join him in the application. This time the two young barristers were successful. They were both named in the list of new Queen's Counsel announced by Lord Halsbury in February 1890. At the young age of thirty-three with but a short career at the bar, Haldane became the youngest QC to have been appointed for over fifty years. He wrote his mother to share his good news: 'My youth as a QC is the subject of much gossip in the press and about legal circles and is an advertisement in itself. A silk gown seems to be regarded as something very wonderful by the public.'[67] Not to mention how wonderful it was regarded by himself. He was clearly thrilled at the social impact the gown also made: 'It is quite curious to see what social importance even people like Lady Roseberry and the Spencers attach to it. I think it must be the lace ruffles, which, by the way, I have declined to wear.'[68]

In 1886, while awaiting briefs to come in and convalescing from rheumatic fever, Haldane became active in teaching at the Working Men's College in London. This college had been founded by Major-General

Frederick Denison Maurice, who later became Haldane's first biographer and a reader at Lincoln's Inn.[69] Maurice frequently enlisted the assistance of younger members of the bar and Haldane was persuaded to give a series of lectures on 'What is Philosophy?' This experience, which was very successful and which he enjoyed greatly, was the beginning of a long interest in adult education. It would eventually lead him to become active with the Webbs and others in the cause of educational reform. It was during this early period that Haldane found the time to devote to a translation of Schopenhauer's *The World as Will and Idea*, which he eventually completed in 1886 with the aid of John Kemp, a man who would make his own reputation as a philosopher.

During this period of his life, Haldane also began to taste the theatre life of London; accompanied by his sister, Elizabeth, he frequently attended musical concerts and stage performances in the west end. The young barrister enjoyed these social occasions immensely, but his interest in music performance and live theatre did not sink deep roots. The strong pull of philosophy, however, drew him back to books on the subject and, more important, to lengthy conversations and correspondence with those of like mind. He soon developed a reputation among his peers for being more fond of ideas than of men; it was a reputation that was to dog him to the end of his public life.[70] As his closest friend, Sir Edmund Gosse, confided to his diary: 'He seems like thought itself made flesh, pale, ponderous, bland. The more I see of him in delightful intimacy, the more he seems to me our one great intelligence in public life.'[71]

Hall and Martin have speculated that 'Haldane philosophized to satisfy a religious need.'[72] Nothing could be further from the truth. To say, as these authors do, that Haldane harboured a 'sense of guilt [for allowing his religious faith to lapse] and a feeling that he was offending his parents' by substituting philosophy for theology is not supported by the facts and is, more to the point, to misunderstand the man profoundly. Haldane never exhibited a sense of guilt in these matters. At no place in his voluminous correspondence with his mother and other members of his family and friends does one find anything remotely approaching a sense of guilt. Neither can one find that his mother ever reproached her son for his turn away from theology towards philosophy. Furthermore, he never abandoned his religious practices entirely. After he moved to London to study law, and, therefore, after his rift with his father over baptism, we find Richard Haldane writing to his mother about attending church.[73] And on several occasions he confessed to having heard sermons of various clergymen while a student in London. Years later, when he gave the Gifford Lectures at the University of Edinburgh, he explicitly addressed the relationship of philosophy and theology. There is not a whiff of guilt or regret in these closely reasoned lectures.

It is likewise incorrect to say or intimate that, by undertaking the study and practice of law, Haldane was abandoning philosophy. He understood the practice of law – armed with philosophy – as the one sure avenue into the life of the state, indeed the only dependable way by which one could make a difference in the conduct of state affairs. As Hegel had taught, philosophy's principal function is not to construct in theoretical abstractions an ideal state but to elicit the positive truth with which reality is already formed. The philosopher's task is to understand that reason and history are not inseparable. The central motive force of state life is the rational force of law. Reason unfolds through the process of universal history, of the rise and decline of nations. The world spirit – the *Weltgeist* – unfolds through the history of individual nations and is the source of art, religion, and philosophy. History is one great freight train, each boxcar representing succeeding epochs hurtling forward to an ever receding horizon.

The true student of Hegel understood that philosophy makes its entry into the lifeblood of the state by way of the law. The law was for Hegel the very foundation of the state and lawyers and judges had special responsibilities towards the state by virtue of their legal calling. There is no question that Hegel's theory of the state (a word he always capitalized) has led many to conclude that he robed the state with a greater measure of authority than it should enjoy, that he lionized it. But Haldane understood his conception of law and its role in the state as an instrument of freedom. In this matter Hegel drew upon Immanuel Kant, who wrote that 'a constitution allowing the greatest possible human freedom in accordance with laws by which the freedom of each is made to be consistent with that of all others – I do not speak of the greatest happiness, for this will follow of itself – it is at any rate a necessary idea, which must be taken as fundamental not only in first projecting a constitution but in all its laws.'[74] Haldane, the life-long student of Hegel, appears to have known better than his detractors what the role of law is in Hegel's state. As we shall see, he took the extraordinary step of addressing the American Bar Association meeting in Montreal in September 1913 explicitly to inform this great gathering of the Hegelian duties and opportunities open to them as Anglo-Saxon lawyers riding, as it were, in the lead boxcar of history.

There can be little doubt that Hegel's philosophy of the state troubled many people, especially in Britain where the sounds of Prussian jack-boots tended to echo in the recitation of his philosophy. Not surprisingly, Hegel quickly attracted a large body of critics who took special aim at his teaching on the nature of the state. The most common charge levelled against him was that he was teaching a doctrine of totalitarianism. Hegel's state was perceived as a political condition where the individual is subservient to the state. 'All the worth which the human being possesses – all spiritual reality, he possesses through the State,' wrote the master. And again, 'since the State is mind objectified, it is only as one of its members that the individual himself has objectivity, genuine individuality and an ethical life.'[75] Richard Haldane revelled in the heady obscurities of this Germanic challenge to the romantic and utopian view of the state which had begun to take root in modern Europe and – however more slowly – in Britain.

Parliament and Club Life

Shortly after being called to the bar, Richard Haldane became involved in several clubs, one of which, soon to be dubbed the 'Eighty Club,' was devoted to finding liberal-minded candidates for Parliament. This informal group of young lawyers began its life at Haldane's home on Bruton Street, London. It has been described as a group of itinerant missionaries who in later years gained distinction in the House of Commons.[76] The club attracted the likes of H.H. Asquith, Lord Dalhousie, John Morley, Lord Spencer, and Sir Charles Russell. The group met for dinner annually at the Blue Posts, Cork Street, Piccadilly.

To no one's surprise, the rising Scottish barrister began to feel the pull of Parliament; it was one of the most natural steps in the direction of an assured success at the bar. After sounding out unsuccessfully – despite the formidable efforts of his mother – the electoral waters of West Perthshire where the family home of Cloanden was located, Richard Haldane turned his attention to East Lothian, which was virtually the pocket borough of the Conservative Wemyss family. Haldane was a Liberal and was invited to stand for Gladstone's party in the upcoming election of 1886.

In accepting the invitation to be the Liberal candidate for East Lothian, Haldane set out his political credo and linked arms with the venerable William Gladstone, long-time leader of the Liberal Party. 'I feel that Mr. Gladstone has made possible for the Liberal Party higher and purer principles than those of the past, and the belief that we are on the eve of a period in which we may set an example of unselfishness in Europe, both in domestic and foreign affairs, has for some time past increased my desire ultimately to take part in the work of the House of Commons.'[77] This proved to be an auspicious time for the young barrister to break into politics. It was only the second general election following upon the Reform Act of 1867 which did much to extend the franchise. It was also the first election since the passage of the Franchise Act, which had initially been rejected by the House of Lords but eventually passed in 1884. This act extended the vote to workers and was nowhere more popular than in Scotland. 'East Lothian was then to a large extent a constituency of big properties and lairds who followed the general practice of the time in seeing to it that their tenants were of their political colour,' wrote one historian.[78]

The notoriously shy Haldane, to the surprise of his friends, girded himself for the battle and set out to win the votes of the newly enfranchised farmworkers and small artisans of the constituency. He noticed that he was able to draw to general meetings only a few people of sterner stuff who were prepared to challenge the lairds. He saw also that he would have to conduct a campaign that was foreign to his reserved nature. But he was determined to give his first venture into politics his best effort; accordingly he 'spent much of his time tramping up and down the constituency and talking to the farm labourers and working men.'[79] This type of campaigning had never been done before; certainly he had never done it before.

Much to his own surprise, and the delight of his family, Richard Haldane was elected to Parliament by a large majority. His brother John related to him in a letter the jubilation those close to him shared upon news of his electoral victory. 'Last night there was a bonfire on the hill, a thousand people came up with torches and a band, and there were fire works afterwards. The people were immensely enthusiastic.'[80] Little could Richard have known at the time that he had won the loyalty of East Lothian voters for the next twenty-five years.

Despite, however, his long years in the House of Commons, Haldane was never to take a leading role in the life of Parliament. He and others recognized quickly that he lacked the forceful speaking talents required for star performers in that august legislative body. Along with Edward Grey and others, Haldane was quite willing to let Herbert Asquith assume the role of point man in the House debates, a role he assumed with distinction. As a good Gladstone Liberal, Haldane was a firm supporter of Irish Home Rule but his name is not attached to any significant legislation during those long years in Parliament, except for the Army reform bills of which he was immensely proud. But the House of Commons was a platform from which he would pursue extra-parliamentary objectives, such as reforms in education, one of his passions. He would also distinguish himself as a member of Asquith's cabinet in his role of secretary of state for war. But he was no House of Commons man as were Churchill and Asquith.

Gladstone's success in this election of 1886 was a fragile one; he won by a majority of eighty-six seats; Parnell led to Westminster a bloc of eighty-four Irish Nationalists, adding to Gladstone's discomfort. Many Liberals urged that under the circumstances the Salisbury administration should stay in place. Unfortunately, the government was defeated on an amendment to the Speech from the Throne. Gladstone, at the age of seventy-seven, formed his third administration. Haldane joined the ranks of the government under Gladstone with Lord Herschell as the lord chancellor and Horace Davey as solicitor general. He knew he was no orator and did not even attempt the customary maiden speech; he understood that he was destined to play a minor role in the daily life of Parliament and he willingly accepted this role; his strength, he recognized, was in his ability to function behind the scenes where he might influence the course of others.

A seat in the House of Commons served to reinforce the bonds of friendship between the three young Liberals, Grey, Asquith, and Haldane; it brought the three together almost daily and a bond quickly began to form between them. Grey and Haldane, especially, became more acutely aware of their mutual intellectual strengths; both were idealists and both demanded the highest from themselves. Grey's biographer, G.M. Trevelyan, wrote that 'Grey, always primarily interested in the perfection of character and personality, was never contented either with himself or others ... among public men his own intimate friend, Haldane, ere long came nearest to his ideal.'[81] Grey acknowledged his admiration of Haldane in a letter of 1890. Wrote Grey: 'Your influence will always be greatly indirect, and it will be your privilege never to be able to measure it. If it were not for you I do not think I should have even the hold on public life which I have now. There are others too more worth influencing. I should say, for instance, that Asquith owed some of the very best of himself to you; in knowing you both I feel as if it was so.'[82] The three friendships deepened into closeness and led Grey, Asquith, and Haldane to visit one another's family homes. All three appear to have shared a personal trait of reserve in expressing their deepest emotions; all three bore personal setbacks with equanimity and reserve.

Asquith was by far the most politically successful and acknowledged by almost everyone as a man born to succeed. He was highly intelligent, having excelled at Oxford as a classics scholar, and good looking, with a powerful voice and flawless diction. He could hold the House of Commons in thrall and often did so. Haldane became a frequent guest at Asquith's home, especially after the death of his beloved first wife, Helen. Asquith's second wife was the effervescent Margot Tennant, youngest daughter of Sir Charles Tennant, MP, one of the richest men in Victorian England. He had met her in the spring of 1891 at a large dinner party at the House of Commons. Asquith was immediately smitten and so, too, was this vivacious twenty-seven-year-old woman, who sized up the young widower as 'the man who could help me and who would understand everything.'[83] For she, too, had her ambitions and this 'Cromwellian figure' suited her just fine.

Asquith's second marriage brought the bachelor Haldane into the cauldron of a life he knew nothing of. He became Asquith's best man at the wedding, on 10 May 1894, and was a frequent visitor at the new home presided over by the fiery young bride who could give vent to a hot temper and a sharp tongue when the occasion prompted. At first Haldane did not know what to make of his friend's new wife, but he soon learned that she had plans to be a dominant influence in the life of her talented husband. It would be impossible to conceive of a woman more different from Asquith's first wife, Helen, who had remained at home, rarely ever accompanying her husband to dinners or state functions. Margot Asquith, in contrast, became an important influence behind the scenes – and at times, to Herbert's chagrin, at centre stage – from the moment she came into her husband's life. Her first challenge was a domestic one: to establish herself in the minds of Asquith's children, especially the eldest son, Raymond, as the mistress of the household.[84] It was no easy task, but she prevailed and in short order won the affection of her step-children. Raymond's death in France in 1916 was a tragedy full of mixed emotions for Margot; for no one, she feared – not even she herself – occupied a place in the heart of Herbert Asquith equal to that of his handsome, talented eldest son. When the tragic news of Raymond's death arrived, Margot did not intrude upon the grieving father's privacy and allowed him to mourn alone in silence for three days. Slowly she then began to take charge; the first change she made was how she would address her new husband. She disliked the name Herbert, as everyone called Asquith, and became the only one to address him as 'Henry.' Unlike Haldane or Grey, however, the debonair Asquith had an eye for the women and it took all of Margot's talents to keep him from wandering.

Haldane's first of very few speeches in Parliament was delivered in March 1887, when he spoke on the Criminal Law Amendment Bill; he deplored the continued attempts to rule Ireland by force. As far as he was concerned, Home Rule was the only reasonable solution to this intractable domestic problem. But his mind was made up only after he and Asquith had visited Ireland to examine conditions for themselves; what they saw affected them profoundly. As Colin Clifford has noted: 'In 1886 [Haldane] and Asquith had gone to Ireland together and had spent much time cross-examining both landlords and tenants. They had also been present at the eviction on the Kenmare estate of the chief local Land Leaguer, which took place under the protection of seventy police. All they saw and heard only strengthened their conviction that Home Rule was the only answer.'[85] But Gladstone's vision of self-government for Ireland died in the early hours of 7 June 1887, when Parliament defeated the bill by a vote of 343 to 313. Gladstone asked the queen for a dissolution and it was granted. He charged about the country in the ensuing election haranguing his audiences, assured that 'the hand of the Lord was upon me.' Unfortunately for the aging prime minister, the good Lord did not have a vote. The results were decisive but a bitter disappointment. Gladstone and his Liberals were sent into opposition with 191 members along with 85 Irish Nationalists. The Conservatives had won a commanding majority with 316 seats and the support of 78 Liberal Unionists.[86] Haldane had won re-election but found himself in opposition more quickly than he had anticipated.

Yet these were good days for the young Scot, for they gave him time to spend on his rapidly increasing legal practice. They also gave him the opportunity to cement ties with like-minded parliamentary colleagues, such as Asquith and Grey, and, above all, to consolidate his home in Whitehall Court, overlooking the Thames, where he treated his friends to exquisite dinners for several years before moving to his permanent home at 28 Queen Anne's Gate, near St James Park. There he began to acquire one of the finest wine cellars in London. People rarely declined an invitation to dine at the Haldane table, which quickly became famous for its outstanding cuisine, thanks to the culinary skills of Mrs Pinnie who prepared his meals for many years.[87] But not everybody

was impressed with Haldane's meals. His new friends Sidney and Beatrice Webb, for example, looked askance at the expense that went into
the meals; there was far too much poverty and hunger throughout London's east end for them to enjoy such lavish events. As R.H. Tawney
was to note, there was no rich food or memorable wine at the Webbs's
table. To partake of what Mrs Webb called 'dinners,' he wrote, was better identified as 'a participation in [an] exercise in asceticism.'[88] Small
wonder that Beatrice Webb ended her life as anorexic. Despite her affection for Haldane the man, she would always be a critic of his eating
habits and his girth.

Impervious to open or implied criticism from his new socialist
friends, Richard Haldane soldiered onward into the social and intellectual life of London. His dinners were frequented by such struggling
notables as George Bernard Shaw, Sydney Olivier, Graham Wallas, and
a long list of social reformers. And he was clearly intellectually excited
by the Webbs and their circle. The Webbs brought together a coterie of
people – irrespective of their political party affiliation – willing to work
to spread the new gospel of the welfare state. The dinner conversations
were intense and stimulating to the Scots barrister and for all who attended. This group around the Webbs, who soon became known as the
Fabians, preached a gentle form of socialism, one that would come by
small steps rather than by violence or revolution. Haldane hovered on
the fringes of this group without ever formally becoming a member
because he enjoyed the stimulation of their conversation.

Despite his proximity to the Webbs, Haldane did not become a socialist. Socialism in its many guises – including its radical version in
the form of communism – was then all the rage. But Haldane never
succumbed to its allure. The philosopher was ever suspicious of the
inducements of ideology; he understood the fundamental incompat-
ibility between Hegel and Marx, especially the latter's misplaced faith
in 'the people' and violence as a political tactic of redress. He saw
Marxists as the direct descendants of the Jacobins and the terror that
followed the French Revolution of 1789. He liked the 'inevitability of
gradualism' proposed by the Fabians but his sights were on the Empire
and the need to strengthen it through law and political organization,
not through the social reconstruction so dear to the Webbs.

Richard Haldane liked being a member of Parliament, for the position afforded him an entrée into inner circles of several clubs and associations. In addition to the National Liberal Club and the 'Eighty Club,'
Haldane was a member of the 'Co-Efficients.' H.G. Wells described

the latter group as a 'curious little talking and dining club.' But it was more than that. It was there that Haldane joined the Webbs along with others, such as G.B. Shaw and Harold Laski, as comrades-in-arms in the cause of education for the working classes.

The Co-Efficients were more formally organized than some of the other clubs to which Haldane belonged. This club contained a roster of offices with members designated as experts. Haldane represented law, Bertrand Russell, science, Sir Edward Grey, foreign policy, Sidney Webb, municipal affairs, W. Pember Reeves, the colonies, Sir Clinton Dawkings, public finance, H.G. Wells, literature. Carlyon Bellairs, Leopold Amery, and Leo Maxse represented journalism. Arthur Balfour, G.B. Shaw, Lord Alfred Milner, Lord Robert Cecil, Henry Newbolt, and Josiah Wedgwood were to join the group at a later date. One can only imagine the level of discussion prompted by the strong opinions of such an assembly and Haldane played a prominent role. The aim of the club was, in the words of Sidney Webb, to debate 'the aims, policy and methods of imperial efficiency at home and abroad.' And it was to be unconnected with any political party.

Perhaps this last stipulation was the reason the club did not survive. As Hall and Martin have written: 'Joseph Chamberlain's policy of tariff reform divided the "Co-Efficients" more and more. Gradually the belief in the possible world leadership of England was deflated, by the economic development of America and the militant boldness of Germany.'[89] These developments may well have dissuaded some members of the club but they did not make a dent in the imperial resolve of Richard Haldane. He never wavered from the conviction that the Anglo-Saxon political tradition was the one sure promise of world stability under the rule of law. He would return to this theme in his many speeches on the subject over many years.

It was out of such rather casual groups as the Co-Efficients and the Eighty Club that eventually emerged the 'Synthetic Society.' Through membership in the 'Synthetic Society,' the young member of Parliament met a miscellany of thoughtful people who would convene on the last Friday of each month from January to May to discuss after dinner a short paper on a theistic topic presented by one of the members. The club consisted of fifty-four people including Arthur Balfour, Wilfred Ward, later editor of the *Dublin Review*, Lord Hugh Cecil, Lord Rayleigh, Baron von Hugel, Professor Andrew Seth Pringle-Pattison, William Temple, and G.K. Chesterton. Haldane found these gatherings stimulating and the friendships formed invaluable.

About 1888, shortly after the Gladstone electoral defeat, a small group of young Liberal members, led by Haldane, Grey, and Asquith, began to hold dinners at the National Liberal Club and, occasionally, at the Savoy Hotel. The dinner guests were by invitation and consisted principally of political figures to whom the members wished to discuss a given topic of political interest. The leadership of the Liberal Party was still, nominally at least, in the hands of the elder statesman, Gladstone, but Sir William Harcourt undertook the day-to-day work of the party. He had the reputation for being indefatigable and an impatient House leader. And he was not a little critical of the young Turks for not giving more time and attention to parliamentary affairs. Haldane, especially, was a puzzle to Harcourt because he was not sufficiently partisan. Haldane's genuine willingness to consider the other side of an issue, his willingness to concede that a member opposite had a good point, his reluctance to become partisan – all of this troubled the uncompromisingly partisan Harcourt. As Sommer has written, Harcourt 'would naturally have liked to harness the outstanding ability of Haldane and his friends to the Party machine. Haldane, on the other hand, apart from his deep interest in educational and social questions, was finding his work at the Bar as a prominent Junior more and more exacting.'[90]

Haldane and Education

Party politics were never Haldane's consuming ambition. He was more interested in ideas than in men – or at least in those ideas that would be used to improve the lot of men. In a letter to Ronald Ferguson, Haldane wrote: 'What we have to do at home is to try to gain the confidence of the electors and to mould their opinions. To my dying day, I think I shall maintain the proposition based on the analogy of my own mind, that a democracy has not got, as is assumed in practice, a body of definite opinion, for the expression of which in Parliament it seeks delegates, but that it is an assembly of human beings earnestly seeking guidance from those of whose sympathies it is sure.'[91] Moulding men's opinions by helping to shape the course of events became the preoccupation of Richard Haldane for the remainder of his life. Armed with a deepening appreciation of German literature, especially of Goethe, Haldane turned to the bar and the law, where he was able to bring his considerable analytical skills to the task of shaping opinions in important areas of public life.

However much Richard Haldane was deeply engrossed in the practice of law and in parliamentary affairs, he had time for a cause very close to his heart: higher education for the working people. Having seen first hand in Germany the impressive results of university education, he was easily drawn into the movement spearheaded by the Webbs and their circle of friends such as Laski. Haldane had been drawn to educational reforms because of his experience in Germany as a young student; he came to agree with his old sponsor, John Stuart Blackie, that Britain generally, and Scotland in particular, lagged far behind the educational developments in Germany. Blackie had written that 'the German universities are the model institutions of the kind, the real *panepistemion*, as the Greeks phrase it, or bazaar of universal knowledge, while the Scottish Universities except in the medical department in Edinburgh, are mere shops for retail trade in certain useful articles; and the English universities are shops of a higher order and more gentlemanly appearance, dealing only in a few select articles sought after by persons of much money and great leisure, more from a certain aristocratic tradition and respectable show than from any practical fruits which they are destined to bear.'[92]

Richard Haldane fell under the spell of German education and culture early in his career and remained so throughout his life. Years later, in a prize address to the students of Birkbeck College, London, on 26 October 1906, he told his audience that when the Prussians were defeated by Napoleon in 1806 they did not brood over their losses but turned inward and began to see that their weakness in battle came from their weakness in education. As a result, the Prussians set out to reform their universities, pressing into service, especially, the brains of the greatest teachers of science. When time came to go to war again, as it did in 1870, the Prussian army excelled as a united fighting force skilled in the art of warfare and aided by the latest weapon technology; the improvements in education had begun to percolate throughout the emerging nation. By the time Haldane visited Germany, three years after the German victory in 1871 in the Franco-Prussian War, Bismarck's social and educational reforms had taken hold. But what impressed the young Scot most was the rigour of the post-secondary education. The German universities were light years ahead of the British universities. In science, for example, the German universities virtually invented chemistry, which was to play a critical role in the First World War as well as the Second. He was immensely impressed with the state-supported polytechnic institutes that dotted Germany, in which young men and women were trained in the application of technology to the benefit of industry and commerce. Haldane wanted nothing less than to mobilize the educational forces of Britain exactly as the Germans had done under Bismarck. But Haldane's educational reforms were to be accomplished within the British democratic tradition. In his *Autobiography* he wrote:

Our common principle was one of faith in the effect of higher education on democracy. We did not indeed think that such education was everything. There were other phases of mental activity, such as religion and the love of the beautiful, which were no less important. But we thought that people whose minds were freed from the fetters of ignorance would develop these other phases more readily. We also thought that the student would feel that he had been assisted towards equality with his fellow citizen, not absolute equality – for nature and circumstance would preclude that – but in the sense of having something more like even chances with his fellow creatures. The universities were under existing circumstances too frequently preserves for the sons and daughters of the rich. Our plans, if they could be carried into effect, would at least diminish for a large number the exclusion from the chance of self-development.[93]

Haldane and his cohorts, such as the Webbs, were respectful of the efforts of the Workers' Educational Association and did not wish in any way to trespass on its territory. Instead, they formed the British Institute of Adult Education.[94]

But there was another force operating on the young Scots barrister and that one came from home. His mother showed him from his earliest years how important education was to his own life and to that of his brothers and sister. He believed, therefore, in educating women and was convinced that the time had come for women to take their place in the professions. He watched as his sister, Elizabeth, and his mother encouraged women in Scotland to seek positions in the local school boards established under the Education Act of 1872. The great liberating results of education – classical as well as scientific – were immediately a part of his own experience and he wished to extend them to others less fortunate than himself. Drawing on his own home life, he believed that when you educated a woman you educated a family. In his travels throughout England and Scotland on behalf of educational reform, Haldane claimed that he frequently found a more receptive audience among women, who showed a distinct desire 'for better chances of mental emancipation for their children than they themselves had had.'[95]

One of the few speeches Richard Haldane made in the House of Commons was in 1889 in support of the bill to reform Scottish universities. This initial interest in education quickly brought him to the attention of those who were attempting to reform London University. He wanted to progress slowly by instituting a solid on-site teaching program which would allow students to relate easily with their professors. The faculty of the university, however, were far more ambitious and far more impatient. They wanted nothing less than a fully fledged degree-granting university as quickly as possible. With the aid of the Webbs, Haldane was able to contain the impatience of the faculty and began the work of establishing the institutional foundations of the university.

Haldane's interest in London University bound him even more closely to the indefatigable Sidney Webb, who was chief of the Technical Education Board of the London County Council. He worked his negotiation skills behind the scenes and was able to convince the Conservative Arthur Balfour, a philosophical scholar of distinction, to adopt the London University cause. This allowed the resourceful Webbs to bring pressure on members of the Conservative Party, especially Sir John Gorst, who introduced a bill in Parliament and was immediately attacked by Sir John Lubbock, member of Parliament for the university. Haldane relates his sudden intervention in the heated parliamentary debate in his *Autobiography*, describing himself as 'for once like one inspired.' He pressed upon the House the urgency of having a university in the heart of the Empire to which students 'from distant regions might come as the centre for them of that Empire.'[96] As a result of his efforts, Haldane records, the bill passed on second reading without a division.

But the government and soon found itself in hot water with the Irish members of Parliament who demanded a charter for a Catholic university in Dublin. Arthur Balfour asked Haldane to explore the issue with the Catholic hierarchy in Ireland. After securing the consent of the hierarchy, the Irish University Bill was passed on second reading. But the bill was defeated at a later stage and the establishment of Irish universities was not to become a reality for another ten years. In due course, Parliament granted charters to two universities, one predominantly Catholic in Dublin and the other Protestant in Belfast.

However important Richard Haldane's contributions were to the cause of education throughout Britain, he was quick to make it known that there were many others who assisted the cause and played critical roles. Their combined efforts resulted in the emergence of new universities such as those at Bristol, where Haldane was to become chancellor, and at Nottingham, Liverpool, Manchester, and Birmingham. His work in bringing higher education to Birmingham was aided by its debonair mayor, Joseph Chamberlain, who saw the prospects of a university for his city as a matter of civic pride. His enthusiasm was quickly taken up by other mayors throughout Britain and resulted in the spread of post-secondary education throughout the kingdom.[97] As was his habit, Haldane insisted on giving credit to a list of men who had worked tirelessly for educational reforms, people like G.D.H. Cole, Harold Laski, Robert Peers of Nottingham, and R.H. Tawney, as well as a host of others who played an important role in Parliament, such as Oliver Stanley. Not to be overlooked in this matter is Haldane's indefatigable fundraising efforts on behalf of university education. He related in his *Autobiography* how he persuaded Sir Ernest Cassel to direct a donation of half a million pounds to 'higher education for the working classes.'[98] He took special satisfaction in working with the Webbs in establishing the London School of Economics and Political Science, which became famous the world over for its influential graduates. As Hall and Martin have concluded: 'During his time no single person had a greater influence on public educational policy than Haldane.'[99]

But Haldane's contributions to educational reforms pale by contrast with his impact on reform of the British Army. Strains were beginning to develop in the old alliances between European nations; France and Germany had barely papered over their differences since the Franco-Prussian War of 1871 but the glue was starting to come unstuck. Bismarck's enormous new army was flexing its muscles and, tired of ceremonial drilling, was eager to demonstrate its superiority on the field of battle. Meanwhile, the British Army was in tatters, nursing its embarrassment over unsuccessful ventures into the Crimea and South Africa, episodes that had exposed a tattered leadership at the top and a massive need for a more efficient battlefield ordnance capability. And, despite the best efforts of several secretaries of state for war, no one seemed capable of bring in the necessary reforms. No one, that is until Richard Haldane appeared on the scene. Having achieved a comfortable position at the bar and having been elected to Parliament, Haldane was ready to take on greater challenges, guided, as we shall now see, by his deep commitment to Hegelian philosophy.

4

From the Inns of Court to the War Office

Richard Haldane is the greatest philosopher and the greatest politician now alive, though he is only now beginning to come before the public, being very modest by nature.

– Herbert Henry Asquith, 1901

Shortly after taking silk in January 1890, Richard Haldane's personal life underwent a decisive change of direction: that old 'force' that had blindsided him several years before struck once again. In the spring of that year he became engaged to Valentine Munro Ferguson, a young woman he had known for many years. She was of a distinguished Scottish family. Her brother, Ronald Crauford Munro Ferguson, was four years younger than Richard Haldane. They both entered Parliament the same year as Liberals. Ferguson served as member for Leith from 1886 to 1914, and he was elevated to the rank of viscount and left the House of Commons at the outbreak of the First World War to become governor general of Australia.

Richard was clearly excited about the prospects of his upcoming wedding and visited London and Devonshire with his prospective bride to scout out a place to live. At this time he was making a comfortable income and the future looked bright and profitable; he was earning about £2,100 a year and was ready to settle down. As well, he was beginning to enjoy the social life of London, especially the music. 'He delighted in the opportunities London afforded for hearing good music and was an enthusiastic Wagnerite long before London society turned to Wagner. He attended the Richter concerts whenever he could spare the time and wrote to his sister, "I have joined Mrs. Garrett Anderson's *Quartette Association*. We have a series of concerts in private houses with first-class artists. They don't, however, lean much to Wagner."[1] Wagner was far too Germanic for the more sedate London music lovers. The personal life of the German composer combined with the puritan tastes of his English audience tended to mute the impact of this new and brilliant composer's music. It was to take London some time before it could warm to Wagner. Elizabeth Haldane recorded her own and her brother's embrace of the composer: 'Gradually my brother and I awoke to the delights of music, and especially of what was then called "The Music of the Future," meaning by that, Wagner in particular. That was a real awakening, quite separate from anything we were taught – a sort of revelation of what music could mean. And also a sort of protest, such as youth loves, for the older generation called it loud and meaningless sound.'[2] This new German music ran headlong into the 'Puritan dread of pleasure – even artistic pleasure – unless it were to lead to something useful to mankind.'[3] Richard Haldane, however, having been schooled in the richness of the Germanic culture, took to Wagner with deep and permanent attachment.

Haldane was at this time more excited about his future than he had ever been: he was making a name for himself at the bar and in politics. But, besides and above all this, he had found the one woman he wanted most to spend his life with. On 14 March 1890 he wrote to his mother: 'The sun is shining brightly and nature seems to be equally bright. I was never so happy ... It will be a perfect marriage of affection.'[4] Congratulations from his friends flooded in along with wedding gifts while preparations for the big event began to take shape. But these days of delightful euphoria were to come abruptly to a crashing halt. His betrothed wrote him unexpectedly from Scotland announcing the termination of their engagement. The news struck him like a thunderbolt. From all available accounts he was completely unprepared for this blow. For a time the jilt threw him into confusion: gifts had to be returned and invitations rescinded while everyone around him searched for explanations. Like a philosopher, he tried to understand the event in rational terms, writing to his mother that 'I am convinced that there came a sudden break down of feeling due simply to some physical cause ...These things are not after all so very difficult to understand if you take them as external misfortunes like death or a severe illness.'[5] Only one steeped in the cold waters of Germanic philosophy could offer this kind of explanation for such a deep emotional tragedy. Why Valentine Munro Ferguson called off the wedding, no one will ever know. She left no record of the event nor did she appear to have confided in anyone. Perhaps, as he hinted in his letter, there was 'some physical cause' to which only Valentine was privy. In any event, she died unmarried seven years later. Haldane recalled vividly this rejection at the end of his life. In his *Autobiography*, written three years before he died, he explained the matter this way:

I had fallen deeply in love with a remarkable girl of distinguished quality and of good position. The response to me on her side came slowly, but when it did come it seemed to have come very surely. We had many tastes in common and much the same outlook on life and affairs. We became engaged in March, 1890, and there followed some weeks of unbroken happiness. Towards the end of April I had left her, in order to return to my duties, after a visit we made together in Devonshire. Suddenly, without previous warning, and as a bolt from an unclouded sky, there came to me in London a note saying that all was over. She felt that she had misunderstood herself, and her decision to break the engagement must be taken as final. I could not realize what had happened. Our friends urged on her that the original decision, working out admirably as it appeared to be doing, was right and this second and sudden decision was a mistake. Her family, who were intimate friends of mine, and some of her friends asked whether she was sure of her new declaration. The attempt to shake her resolution proved to be useless. The decision was as irrevocable as it was rapid, and she would not go back by a hair's breadth on what she had intimated to me in writing. Only once or twice again in the course of my life did I see her, and then only momentarily and casually. After five weeks of uninterrupted happiness, happiness, to the best of my judgment then and now, for her as well as for me, all was changed and at an end.[6]

In contrast to the cool, philosophic explanation he had offered in his letter to his mother, the young barrister confessed in his *Autobiography* that he fell into depression and had trouble sleeping. 'My feeling was that somehow I had failed ... to this hour I treasure the memory of these five happy weeks, and bless her name for the return she made in them to my devotion to her, and for the feeling inspired apparently in both of us. I came to realize afterwards, when the pain was past, that my love for her, though it failed, had brought to me not loss but a great gain.'[7]

The break-up must have seared the heart of his mother, who herself had never forgotten her own romantic disappointment many decades before. In this instance, moreover, the young Munro Ferguson woman was a close friend of Richard's sister but appears not even to have confided in her. She faded into the background of Haldane's life, but, writing about the event in his *Autobiography* late in life, he clearly continued to feel the sting of this youthful rejection. Two things are clear: he never forgot Valentine and he never married.

In an effort to put this crushing emotional event behind him, Richard Haldane, accompanied by his brother John, went two months to Germany for a working holiday. They both wanted to re-establish contact with developments in German philosophy. John Scott Haldane was to become a distinguished Oxford physiologist and was a fitting companion on this occasion. In a long letter written from Freiburg to Mrs Humphry Ward, a novelist, Richard indicated what the two men were up to on this 'part holiday, part work' trip to Germany in the summer of 1890. 'There are several people in the University here whom we wanted to see,' he related. They were attempting to go beyond a book Richard Haldane and his friend Pringle-Pattison had published earlier entitled *Essays in Philosophical Criticism*, in which the Haldane brothers had explored 'the relation of the organic world, in which life and God and psychical phenomena are the distinguishing conceptions, to the sphere of pure mechanism.'[8] By soaring high into the arcane abstractions of German philosophy, he attempted to overcome the hurt in his heart. He continued in the letter: 'Prof. Weissmann is the chief apostle of the reduction of the former to the latter, and we are spending a good deal of time with him. It is really the same problem as the one in which you are so much engrossed, that of the possibility of lifting up Christianity from the region of *Vorstellung* [theatre] into that of *Begriff* [concept]. Weissmann is analogous to those who would make the whole truth depend on an historical "yes" or "no." So it is, too, with Hegelianism.'[9] The trip, clearly, was a heady bromide destined to clear any man's heart of an emotional hit as strong as a jilt; he literally found safe harbour in the quiet waters of philosophy during his recovery. But it indicated demonstrably how deeply philosophy was part of the man at this early age and stage of his legal career. It was a core component of his character, not a casual cloak put on and put off as an occasion might demand. The man was a philosopher to the core of his being and he brought philosophy to bear upon everything he did in life, especially in the law.

In this same letter to Mrs Humphry Ward, Haldane expressed uncharacteristically a frustration with his life. 'To an English politician, one of the regrets of whose life is the difficulty of stirring the working classes in a free country into action, it would be amusing were it not pathetic to observe the terror of the educational classes at the Social-Democratic movement in Germany. The University has no notion, apparently, of throwing itself on to the forward movement with the hope of winning the confidence of the people and so guiding them aright.'[10] Guiding the people 'aright' was one of Haldane's abiding commitments, as we have seen earlier. He cautiously praised the interest being shown in Karl Marx and Ferdinand Lassalle, both dedicated to guiding the people. 'The names of Marx and Lasalle occasioned a little torrent of feeling from a quiet-going professor this morning. Yet after all, what is the good of our reading to us, who are in public life, if we cannot use it in the effort, with all the strength we possess, to guide the current of opinion among our constituents?'[11] In this letter the young man showed that he was still grieving over the loss of his great love. 'This is a long letter on one subject,' he concluded, 'but when a soul has missed the goal towards which it was striving, and is still staggering, it naturally, in recovering its balance, seeks to restore the prop which it knows of old and has never found to fail. It is more relief to me than I can express to find myself again engrossed in the old searchings, and to be able to believe that they will mean, even in a practical life where they are supposed to be remote, an amply sufficient future to me.'[12] The 'old searchings' could help heal the wound but it would clearly take time.

Richard and John Haldane returned to England at the end of the summer, John to Oxford to pursue his life's work in science and Richard to his work as a barrister. The freshly minted QC began in the court of Justice Kay, and shortly after in Justice Robert Romer's court when Kay was elevated to the Court of Appeal. By temperament and bent of mind, he was especially suited to the Court of Appeal, where the clash of ideas was at stake, where the philosopher could get his teeth into the 'underlying principle' of the case at hand.[13] In addition to the mental energy expended, he asserted a prodigious physical capacity. In a letter to his mother he outlined to her a single day in his early life at the bar. 'Life is rather a racket, but it is good to be busy. I had a night of it last night. Left Court at 1 pm., when I had spoken for two hours. Read a brief and prepared my speech and addressed 3,000 people at Bradford. 7:30 p.m. Caught the 9.45 train, read two briefs with the aid of a candle. Reached my chambers at 3.30 a.m. to find an earnest intimation that I must read a brief which had been sent down to meet me. Got up at 7.30, read the brief, and was in court at 9.45 a.m. and was on my feet at 10.30 to deliver an elaborate argument. Not a bit tired, only hustled a little.'

The Turbulence of Politics

The closing decades of the nineteenth century were turbulent political times: Gladstone in, Gladstone out; Salisbury in, general election; Gladstone back with greatly reduced majority. In 1892 Gladstone, prime minister for the fourth time at the age of eighty-two, chose a cabinet that included Asquith as home secretary and Grey as under-secretary at the Foreign Office. But no place was found for their friend, Haldane. However disappointed Asquith and Grey were at Haldane's failure to make the cabinet, the disappointment was not shared by the man himself, who was content to concentrate on his career at the bar. Rather than attempting to secure a place for himself, Haldane was lobbying for others to make the cabinet.

In a letter to Gladstone's chief whip, Sir Algernon West, we find him pressing the name of Arthur Acland for a position in the cabinet. His chief concern was to tap into 'the nascent body of opinion in the constituencies which care little for any Irish policy and concentrates itself on social questions.'[14] By this Haldane was referring to the emerging power of the working class or 'the labour party, using the term in the widest sense.' He was convinced that the Liberal Party had to recognize and begin to lead the new voters who had come into politics with the Reform Act of 1867. He worried that, having championed the cause of electoral reform and having extended the franchise to include working men, the Liberal Party ran the risk of failing to reap the benefits. And Acland was the ideal candidate to do the job. His 'experience in settling industrial disputes and getting at the minds of the working people would enable him to develop the function of his office from the very first.'[15] 'I believe that I am expressing the sentiments of the bulk of the rank and file in the House when I say that it will be a deep disappointment if he is not placed in a position under Mr. Gladstone where he may exercise real influence and attract to us still more of that confidence of the industrial classes on which we greatly depend to-day for our future.'[16] Not content to leave the matter there, he went on to suggest that the Board of Trade, 'not a very important office at present,' be reformed 'with the announcement that the labour department was to be extended and annexed to it.'[17] Haldane's advocacy was only partially successful. Acland went into the cabinet but as the minister responsible for education. The ministry of labour was not to become a reality for another thirty years.

Haldane's efforts to secure Acland a place was characteristic of the man; he looked for the best man for the job and bent every effort to see that he was appointed. He rarely sought or accepted preferment. He was, accordingly, not disappointed in being passed over by Gladstone. On the contrary, Haldane believed that he was free from the burdens of cabinet responsibilities to pursue his chief ambitions, which were education and social reforms. He lacked the enthusiasm for cabinet politics but he never lost his enthusiasm for these two causes. As Sommer has written, 'it is sometimes suggested that Haldane "turned to Labour" only at the close of his life. In one sense, of course, this is true, but it is evident from the very beginning of his political career that he embraced many of the ideals of the early Labour movement and his whole outlook was a good deal nearer to the Webbs' than to that of Harcourt ... Throughout his life the Cause was always more important to Haldane than the Party.'[18] This was because the cause was the embodiment of his idealism while the party was an expedient. Above all, his idealism was to be found in his pursuit of the law. There was a cause at the heart of his lawyering and, later, of his judging. That cause was the formation and consolidation of the law of the Empire as an instrument of 'progressive evolution.'[19]

The conviction that there was a 'progressive evolution' behind events was inspired by his study of Hegelian philosophy. For his great German authority, human events are moved by the 'Spirit of freedom.' It is the task of the statesman to perceive that spirit and to guide the people with an eye on the progressive embodiment of freedom. Hegel had taught him that 'the principle of freedom' was the 'proper basis of the State.'[20] It is for this reason that Haldane took to the law and pursued its 'progressive' development in the 'great tribunal of the Empire,' the Judicial Committee of the Privy Council. Haldane was to appear increasingly more frequently before this high judicial body now that he was freed from the constraints of cabinet politics. For all these reasons, the young barrister – he was only thirty-seven – took the risky step of 'going special.' That is to say, he would specialize as an appeal barrister, accepting only those briefs that were to be argued before the House of Lords or the Judicial Committee of the Privy Council. 'I was largely influenced in deciding to do this by Mr Hill of Collyer Bristow and Co. One of the ablest men in the profession. When I went special, following his advice, he began to employ me greatly. He took me in for the appeal to the House of Lords in the Great Real Property case of *Ffoxwell v. Van Gruthen* [1897] AC 658 where I won a complete victory for him.'[21] The move was a profitable one also because it 'meant that I would not appear in any court at first instance without a special fee of 50 guineas in addition to that marked on the brief.'[22]

Haldane's talents for impartiality – he was on friendly terms with members from all parties in the House of Commons – did not go unnoticed by the senior members of the government. In 1895 he declined an offer of the Speakership of the House of Commons. In a letter to his mother, he explained: 'Yesterday I received an unexpected approach from Lord Rosebery and the Cabinet that I should take the Speakership. I refused quietly but firmly. I think I was right, though the position of first commoner is a great one. But I felt that the life would be artificial and a complete break with my work.'[23] It was pressed upon him that he was widely acceptable to both sides of the aisle; he was flattered but unmoved. He refused even though his close friend Herbert Asquith had urged him to take the position, insisting that it would be a 'dereliction of duty' for him to turn it down. But Haldane knew himself better than his friends knew him. He would have chafed at being cribbed, cabined, and confined by the demands of the Speaker's duties and restricted by his non-partisan responsibilities from involvement in his other causes, such as education. The Speakership, too, would have restricted his income, although the office commanded a comfortable £10,000 annual stipend. He knew he could obtain at least as much financial security practising law. And so he gratefully declined the honour.

While a young member of Parliament, Haldane argued cases before the House of Lords. One case, *Nobel Explosives Co. Ltd. v. Anderson* (1894), showed his strengths when technical or scientific issues were at issue in law.[24] This case, involving the founder of the Nobel Prize, concerned a patent for a slow-burning propellant made from nitroglycerine and nitro-cellulose. Alfred Nobel made a fortune by inventing what became known as dynamite. Until this time, the highly sensitive nitroglycerine was all but unmanageable. Nobel made it manageable by causing it to be absorbed in porous unexplosive substances whereby it was converted into a powder called 'dynamite' – or 'Nobel's safety powder.' More important, he also made it a main component in military firepower. Haldane studied carefully the chemistry and the military implications of the case with the able assistance of his brother John and steeled himself for his appearance in the high court against the crown.

The appellant company, Nobel's Explosives, sued William Anderson, the director general of the Government Ordnance Factories, for an alleged infringement of Nobel's patent awarded in 1888. Nobel had tamed the fury of nitroglycerine by the use of 'cordite' or smokeless powder. The trial judge had ruled that there was no patent infringement because, at the date of the patent, soluble nitro-cellulose and insoluble nitro-cellulose were known as different substances – that they were formally distinguished by chemists. The House of Lords concurred in the trial judge's decision and dismissed the appeal. But this was not to be the end of Haldane's affair with dynamite.

In typical fashion, Haldane had prepared for the case by studying the material relating to the manufacture of explosives and, especially, its potential for military application. Little did he know at the time that such knowledge would come in handy beyond this court case. In the early days of the South African War, for example, while travelling by train back to London from a visit to the Horners[25] at Mells in Somerset, he encountered the secretary of state for war, Lord Lansdowne. The two men began discussing the war and, to Lansdowne's surprise, his young companion showed a remarkable knowledge of matters relating to gunpowder and propellants. Haldane proceeded to tell the secretary for war that the British propellants were defective and were, in fact, ruining the army rifles. Lansdowne, much impressed by his young companion, responded by suggesting that Haldane chair a parliamentary committee to look into the matter. Haldane declined the chairmanship with the argument that the committee should be presided over by a scientist in order to give it the necessary credibility. Lansdowne agreed and appointed Lord Rayleigh, an eminent scientist as chair, but insisted that Haldane join the committee as a member, which he did willingly now that the chairmanship was settled on a highly respected scientist.

Haldane enjoyed the work of the explosives committee to such an extent that he convinced his brother John, with his background in science, to join with him in delivering a public address in order to educate the general public in the matter of military firepower. The brothers announced a 'Public Lecture on Explosives by R.B. Haldane, MP', with illustrations to be conducted by Professor John Haldane.' The event was to take place in Scotland at Auchterarder, not far from the family home at Cloan. The police, however, having seen the advertisement, arrived at the hall and cleared the first three rows and placed a constable in charge. Elizabeth Haldane attended the event and wrote of it: 'There were minor explosions. Richard did the talking and John acted as the laboratory boy ... afterwards we duly burnt a stick of cordie on the lawn at Cloan; but some of the rest of the explosive powder was given by me to the butler to bury carefully, and he and a stable boy thought they would try it out, just to see what would happen. The result was that their faces were badly burned. The man indeed was nearly blinded.'[26] This ended Richard's and his brother's public scientific performances.

Secretary of War

In the midst of his busy career at the bar and his preoccupation with parliamentary affairs, Richard Haldane found that his reputation as a skilful negotiator had drawn the attention of Henry Campbell-Bannerman, who succeeded Arthur Balfour as prime minister in 1905. Campbell-Bannerman, unlike Balfour, was no intellectual and was suspicious of Haldane because of his reputation as a philosopher. He used to refer to his younger parliamentary colleague behind his back with a tinge of sarcasm as 'Old Schopenhauer.' Still, aware of Haldane's organizational talents, the prime minister, somewhat reluctantly but upon the urgings of Herbert Asquith and Edward Grey, appointed him to the War Office as secretary of state in his first cabinet. It was an appointment he did not make lightly because he himself had served twice under Gladstone in the same post. In his *Autobiography*, Haldane said of his appointment: 'Myself he did not like at first, and this was hardly to be wondered at, knowing what the war Office was, he was said to have observed, "We shall now see how Schopenhauer gets on in the Kailyard."'[27] Haldane's friends Asquith and Grey became chancellor of the exchequer and foreign secretary, respectively.

Richard's mother urged her son not to accept the appointment to cabinet unless the terms were satisfactory; she and her daughter felt that Richard was better suited to the Colonial Office, where 'he felt that there was interesting work to be done.'[28] But they both acknowledged that he had developed an interest in military affairs and would be happy at the War Office. Beatrice Webb described in her diary Haldane's excitement at going to the War Office: 'Haldane came in. He also was in a state of exuberant delight over this new task. "I chose the War Office out of three offices. Asquith, Grey and I stood together, they were forced to take us on our own terms. We were really very indifferent," he added sublimely. "Asquith gave up a brief of £10,000 to defend the Khedive's property that very week; I was throwing away an income of £15,000 or £20,000 a year; and Grey had no ambition and was sacrificing his fish-ing ... The King signified that he would like me to take the War Office; it is exactly what I myself longed for. I have never been so happy in my life" and he beamed all over.'[29] Haldane described the day of his appointment in his *Autobiography* in starker detail:

It was a day of the blackest fog that I remember. When the ceremony was over we set off with our Seals to our respective offices. I had a hired brougham, and Grey and Fowler left in it with me. We stuck in the darkness of the Mall. I got out to see where we were and could not find the carriage again. Fowler got back to the Palace. Grey, after a long wandering round and round eventually reached the Foreign Office. By trudging through the mud and feeling among the horses' heads I at last got to the War Office, then in Pall Mall. Fortunately I had kept hold of my Seals. I was a little exhausted when I arrived. I handed the Seals to the Permanent Under-Secretary to take charge of, and asked the tall ex-Guards soldier in attendance for a glass of water. 'Certainly Sir: Irish or Scotch?'[30]

Major-General Sir Frederick Maurice wrote that Haldane was, like many people of the day, unimpressed with the way the British Army had 'muddled through' the South African War. 'It was this [embarrassment] that first turned his mind to the task of applying general principles to our military organization and made him jump at the chance of going to the War Office.'[31] Campbell-Bannerman had good reason to believe that the task was one few people would touch; not only was morale low but public opinion of the army was even lower. Everyone was aware of the criticisms that had come out of Lord Esher's royal commission on the South African War. Haldane certainly was, and when stumping for Parliament in 1900 he emphasized the need for army reform. 'Speaking at Tranent, he condemned the government for its lack of military preparations, for entering the war without sufficient men, horses and guns.'[32] It was an issue ready-made for the liberal imperialism of which Richard Haldane was a leading proponent. Campbell-Bannerman, of course, knew this and in fact sent Haldane to the War Office fully convinced that he would stumble in unfamiliar territory.

The first decision Haldane made upon assuming office was to consult with Lord Esher as to staffing. Esher enthusiastically recommended Colonel Gerald Ellison as the new minister's principal military secretary; Ellison had been secretary of the Esher commission and impressed everyone with his knowledge and administrative skills. Haldane took a liking to the colonel immediately and soon found that the two con-

stituted an ideal working combination. It certainly helped that Ellison
'had been trained in part in German military surroundings and had
studied military history and organisation.'[33]

After a few months of intense consultation with senior military officers and a thorough review of the many previous proposals for army
reform, Haldane introduced into Parliament the Army Reform Bill,
which proposed the establishment of a general staff of seventy-two
officers along the lines of the German general staff. This was the first
opportunity he had to put into practice what he had so long admired
about the German military high command. The purpose of this innovation was to make the senior military staff more professional and proficient and beyond the reach of purchase.[34] As Lord Carver has written:
'The example of the professionals in the Prussian army in the Franco-
Prussian war was a major factor in persuading the House of Commons
of the need to make the British army professional, both by the abolition
of purchase and by the creation and training of a general staff.'[35]

The practice of purchasing commissions had been formally discon-
tinued in 1871. The repeated efforts of the House of Commons to repeal
the practice met with resistance in the House of Lords where members
jealously protected the privilege of purchasing commissions for their
sons and friends; they rejected all attempts to abolish it by legislation.
Since the practice had been instituted by royal warrant, Gladstone persuaded Queen Victoria to abolish it by warrant. But, as Lord Carver
was quick to note, the abolition of purchase 'did not have as great an
effect on the type of officer commissioned into the army as its sponsors
had hoped. A high proportion continued to be sons of the aristocracy,
of landed gentry and of former army officers, products of the burgeon-
ing public schools with their concentration on a classical education,
their emphasis on the importance of character rather than knowledge,
and their neglect of the sciences.'[36] Despite his own formal education
in the liberal arts, Haldane shared the growing enthusiasm for a more
scientific approach to military training and he encouraged the generals
to explore the study and application of science to military strategy. Haldane half-jokingly said that he wanted to post a sign at the War Office
reading: 'Thinking Costs Nothing.'[37]

In addition to reforms of the general staff, Haldane created an expeditionary force of six infantry divisions and a cavalry division organized for the purpose of deployment overseas when required. The
defence of the United Kingdom was entrusted to a territorial army
of part-time volunteers consisting of fourteen divisions and fourteen

mounted brigades. Needless to say, not all these reforms were greeted with enthusiasm by the senior military, especially among those career officers who suddenly found themselves replaced. Writing home in December 1905, shortly after taking office, Haldane wrote: 'We had our first Cabinet this morning – most harmonious. I took a fair share in it. I had been having the disagreeable task of getting rid of incompetent persons of high standing. However, this has been done and I have this afternoon sent a letter in a red box to the King telling him of my arrangements. It is all becoming easy and familiar now, for the first two days the technique was difficult.'[38]

For the next few years, Haldane worked away at the institutional and attitudinal barriers to military reform he met around every corner. He knew he was handicapped by not having the slightest military experience from which to command respect of his ministry subordinates – all of whom were career soldiers – but he gradually won them over by ensuring that they received due recognition for their efforts and that all commendations were recorded on their records. It was a highly unusual combination of civilian and military talent sharing a high-level ministerial position. Regular forces were, of course, suspicious of the use of volunteers. But as Field Marshal Viscount John French of Ypres wrote after the First World War: 'Backed up by the opinion and advice of a very few soldiers of experience, the Secretary of State for War [Haldane] cast all this prejudice to the winds and determined upon a regular and complete divisional organization for the Territorials. It was a great and courageous decision.'[39] In the face of repeated objections from military officers, Haldane remained, wrote French, 'steadfast.' At the war's end, it was clear that the territorial divisions performed magnificently and Haldane received his 'reward.' 'When I say, he "got his reward," I may well be misunderstood. He got nothing but calumny and grossly unjust abuse; but the "reward" to such a man does not come in the ordinary way. He had proved the value of his great work and that is all the reward he ever wanted.'[40]

It is widely acknowledged that Haldane's reforms made it easier for the British Army to respond promptly and efficiently to the war that erupted on the continent in August 1914. With the death in battle of so many young subalterns, Haldane's decision to transform picked territorial battalions into an Officer Training Corps proved especially prescient. But Britain as a whole, unlike either France or Germany, was, in fact, pitifully unprepared for war. In May 1915, after being at war since the previous August, Britain's armament production was less than adequate. The country was 'signally lacking in the basic industries and techniques necessary for full war production – to such an extent that while the Germans were making 250,000 high-explosive shells daily and the French nearly as many, British production was only 700.'[41] Only after Lloyd-George had been appointed minister of munitions and saw through Parliament the Munitions War Act, which centralized the production of armaments, was the workforce mobilized in the cause of war. Prior to this act, weapons production was in the hands of the purchasing departments of the War Office and the Admiralty. Haldane did not baulk at this diminution of his ministerial power; quite the contrary, he welcomed the move, which allowed him to focus his energies on the task of reorganizing the army. Still, the prime minister had to contend with the flight of workers from the essential factories into the ranks of the military. After much cajoling and arm-twisting, Lloyd-George was able to wrest from Haldane's army some 40,000 men and send them back to munitions factories.[42]

There is no question that Haldane was invigorated by the organizational challenges at the War Office. He was acutely aware that the British Army had succumbed to amateurism with inadequate tactics and outmoded strategies. Above all, as Sommer has remarked: 'The South African War had disclosed not only serious weaknesses in our military preparedness to wage war effectively in South Africa, but, what was more potentially dangerous, our incapacity to meet a threat from the continent of Europe.'[43] Haldane's predecessor, Hugh Oakeley Arnold-Forster, was well intentioned but lacked the requisite strength of personality and vision to effect reforms; he was impetuous and demonstrably incapable of getting along with the generals. Lord Esher's committee was established following the South African War to bring about changes in the War Office and it quickly became obvious that Arnold-Foster had to go. Fortunately, Esher was an admirer of Haldane as well as a confidant of King Edward. Both men welcomed the appointment of Haldane to the post and were confident that he would bring about the desired reforms. And their confidence was not misplaced.

Though physically similar in build to Churchill, Haldane was temperamentally vastly different. The Scottish lawyer never aspired to be prime minister or to be at the centre of political events. In a letter to Lord Milner, he admitted to having 'no gift of expression and no real capacity for managing men – much less leading them.'[44] Churchill never entertained doubts on these matters and actively sought to lead men and, of course, to become prime minister. Haldane respected Churchill's ability to get things done but had doubts about his fitness for 'planning out the solution that was necessary' at critical moments.[45] Haldane was recognized, however, as a competent administrator, which explains his selection as secretary of state for war first under Campbell-Bannerman and then under his friend Herbert Henry Asquith's prime minister-ship. Campbell-Bannerman never did warm to Haldane; the prime minister thought Haldane was conspiring behind his back to have him removed to the House of Lords in order that Asquith could become prime minister. All of which was, of course, true since there was just such a plot cooked up by Grey, Asquith, and Haldane at Relugas House and known ever since as the 'Relugas Compact.' Campbell-Bannerman refused to accede to the pressure but eventually resigned in April 1908, making way for Asquith to succeed him. But Haldane did not harbour a grudge against Campbell-Bannerman and eventually came to like him, admitting that he found him to be a congenial superior.

Field Marshal Sir William Robertson wrote in *Soldiers and States-man, 1914–1918* that Haldane 'did not, as some of his predecessors had done, enter the War Office with his mind made up and a scheme in his pocket for putting his ideas into practice, but he tried first to as-certain what was wrong by enquiry from those who were qualified to enlighten him.'[46] He thus became popular with his senior military of-ficials – much to Campbell-Bannerman's surprise – and subtly co-opted them into his reform schemes, some of which they initially resisted. But he didn't simply depend on his subordinates. He diligently prepared himself for his new task by studying 'the great principles on which continental military organisations had been founded, as set forth by Clausewitz, Bronsart von Schellendorff, and Von der Goltz, with the description of Napoleon's mind in Yorck von Wartenburg's book, writ-ten from the standpoint of the German General Staff. From the French point of view I was much influenced by a volume which is too little known today, Colonel Ardant du Picq on *The Moral Factor in War*.'[47] He also made himself familiar with the works of previous British reform proposals. Esher's committee had produced a plan for the reorganiza-tion of the army staff which Arthur Balfour had implemented in part before leaving office. When asked by the Army Council upon assuming office what kind of army he had in mind, Haldane answered without hesitating: 'a Hegelian army.' At this response, he recorded in his *Auto-biography*, 'the conversation then fell off.'[48] But he was not toying with his audience; he meant it. In a memorandum prepared for the Army Council, Haldane spelled out what he meant by his puzzling repartee to the bewildered generals:

As regards the purpose of the Army, what is obviously required is a highly organized and well equipped striking force which can be transported, with the least possible delay to any part of the world where it is required. Its possible work may vary between the defence of India, against a Russian invasion, to some small war in a Crown Colony. It must be ready for any effort great or small. Behind it, there must be a sufficient supply of troops to maintain it 'undiminished in numbers and efficiency' and home defence must be adequately provided for ... The command and all training will be in the hands of the General Officer Commander-in-Chief. The schemes which will form the basis of their organization in peace, and of their allotment in wars, will be prepared by the General Staff.[49]

In brief, the army would be reconstituted in a rational manner with clearly articulated objectives and supported by a rational, hierarchical command structure. Or, as Haldane was to put the case himself: 'Germany had organised a national Army to as near perfection as possible, and at a cost proportionately much less than ours. I felt that I would much like to see the German organisation at work. I had been doing what I could to improve the feeling of the public here towards Germany.'[50] He was convinced that the English 'were worse at organising for the fulfilment of definite ends beyond those of the moment, than almost any of their rivals.' But he added: 'Give him [the Englishman] a few years and he has not only taken care of himself in the meantime, but is generally leading.'[51] Whether this could be called *Hegelian* is a moot question. What is beyond dispute, however, is that Haldane structured the military organization according to a formal plan designed to achieve a rational objective suited to the emerging new conditions. The capricious or arbitrary was to be bleached out by the cool water of pure reason, prompted by the need to respond to new circumstances and new weapons of warfare. What could be more Hegelian than that?

The new secretary of state for war read, especially, the report of the royal commission which had been struck by prime minister Arthur Balfour to look into the South African War and presided over by Lord Esher.[52] To his credit, Balfour adopted immediately one of the major reform recommendations suggested by the commission and abolished the office of commander-in-chief and placed the army under the control of an Army Council with the chief of the general staff as the principal military member. But this put in place the mere skeleton of a general staff; it was left to Haldane to flesh out the structure of high command.

One of the peculiar aspects of Haldane's tenure at the War Office was the fact that, to the chagrin of many in the military, he never argued for a large army. Rather, he spoke on the hustings in favour of a small but efficient army: 'one extremely efficacious and capable for foreign service which would be mobile for service at home, but which need not compete with the enormous armaments of Europe that fought under totally different conditions.'[53] He was never to depart from this view. Despite being secretary of state for war, Haldane did not press for large budgetary estimates, to the annoyance of some of his imperialistic colleagues. He always believed that a strong navy was necessary for defence of the island kingdom and he skilfully avoided falling into the trap of militarism by not proposing a policy of 'fortress Britain' impenetrable to foreign military assault. He was the quintessential realist who reasoned deeply and consulted widely before coming to a decision.

The secretary of state for war technically had responsibility for the navy, but in practice he did not. The Admiralty was subject to 'the near-monopoly of the navy's officer corps by the aristocracy and gentry. For the navy was no longer a deadly functional instrument of policy: it was an exclusive yacht club.'[54] Undoubtedly, this was a harsh judgment, but one not far off the mark and shared by many people. However, by the outbreak of the First World War, the Royal Navy had been dragooned into the modern age by the sheer brilliance and determination of Haldane's old friend, Admiral of the Fleet Sir John Fisher, who served as first sea lord from 1904 to 1910. Haldane got along well with the acerbic and driven admiral; he liked his concentration on redesigning the imperial fleet to serve as an effective fighting force against an emerging German navy. Under Fisher's leadership, the navy had been brought back from the Mediterranean and the far reaches of the Empire and redeployed and outfitted to meet new more demanding combat standards. He equipped the Royal Navy with new ships and saw the education of naval officers greatly improved.[55]

Like Haldane, Fisher was ever on the lookout for talented men to occupy important posts. He had become impressed in 1889, when he was director of naval ordnance, with a young officer, Lieutenant John Jellicoe. Jellicoe came from a marine family and took intense pride in his naval career. Eschewing the social life that characterized the peace-time navy, he studied and made himself familiar with gunnery and the advances in ammunition. Along with Sir John Fisher, Jellicoe became a champion of big guns and this led him to be appointed to the committee that drew up the plans for *Dreadnought*, the first of the all-big-gun capital ships. This ship, completed in 1906, made all its predecessors obsolete. Fisher engaged his young protégé as naval controller responsible for ship design, armour, guns, and shells. After serving as second-in-command of the Channel Fleet, Fisher expressed the intention in 1911 to make Jellicoe commander-in-chief of the Home Fleet. Next year, Fisher defined Jellicoe's role in his new navy even more closely. He wrote on 2 April 1912: 'If war comes before 1914 then Jellicoe will be Nelson at the Battle of St. Vincent. If it comes in 1915 he will be Nelson at Trafalgar.'[56]

War came to Europe in August 1914 with the assassination of the Archduke Ferdinand in Sarajevo. Germany declared war on 10 August to the almost universal approval of the German people. As Max Weber wrote to Ferdinand Tonnies: 'This war with all its ghastliness is nevertheless grand and wonderful. It is worth experiencing.'[57] In England, King George V issued a proclamation on 4 August when Belgium's neutrality was breached by German forces. The Parliament of the United Kingdom did not give its assent to the proclamation until two days later, when voting a credit of £100 million in support of the war effort.[58] The response on the streets of both Germany and Britain was overwhelming jubilation. Crowds gathered in the principal cities of each country shouting enthusiastic slogans of support for the war. Many Germans saw the event as a return to the great heroic tradition of German arms. The people of Britain saw it as a occasion to put an end to war once and for all by crushing the kaiser's armed forces. As everyone now knows, this war became one of the bloodiest in history, with thousands of combatants on both sides thrown into the path of certain death by bumbling commanders in the field and inadequate equipment and resources. As Douglas Haig, who replaced Field Marshal French in December 1915, after the failure at Loos, wrote: 'The British Expeditionary Force in August 1914 did not possess the heavy guns and howitzers, the high explosive shells, or even the machine guns of the German Army.'[59]

But bumbling was also rampant in the higher reaches of politics. Ernest D. Swinton, later major-general, provided a candid account of the comic opera that passed for high-level preparations at the senior committee level.[60] Many among the political elite could not countenance the prospects of war and urged restraint. Leading military men such as General William Robertson complained of the view held by politicians such as Lloyd-George that visible military preparations would only incur 'the displeasure of Germany.'[61] As late as January

1914, Lloyd-George 'derided the possibility of war and urged that the season was "the most favourable moment for twenty years" for cutting down expenditure on armaments.'[62] He repeated these same sentiments on 23 July 1914, adding that the 'industrial classes' were being over alarmed.[63] Small wonder that John Buchan was to write of him: 'Mr. L[loyd] G[eorge]'s imagination, vivid and notable as it was, was essentially short range; his mind was wholly uninstructed in the problems of international policy.' Swinton, as well, paints a portrait of military and political leaders on the Committee of Imperial Defence running in circles over whether to develop the tank; several old cavalry officers adamantly argued that they would never replace the horse by machines that would break down. As if horses didn't 'break down.' To no one's surprise, the British Expeditionary Force transported 170,000 horses to the battlefields of Europe during the first years of the war. Tanks came later, after the German Army tank corps arrived on the scene, putting the lie once and for all to the indispensability of horses. It is difficult for us today to learn that high-ranking military officers clung resolutely to outdated military tactics. According to Field Marshal Lord Carver, Douglas Haig, 'in spite of his experience in South Africa ... could not bring himself to abandon the concept of a cavalry charge as the ultimate aim of cavalry training.'[64] He was soon to learn otherwise but not before the blood of thousands of Britain's most promising sons, including Raymond Asquith, son of the prime minister, stained with their blood the muddy fields of France.

However much Haldane contributed to preparing the nation for war by reforming the army, he gave a great deal of credit to Winston Churchill as first sea lord for bringing scientific principles to the Admiralty. 'Churchill did fine work in strengthening the Fleet up to the high level in numbers which it reached just before 1914,' Haldane later wrote in his *Autobiography*.[65] He also noted that 'not only did he [Churchill] agree about the necessity of a scientific War Staff for the Navy, a Staff which would study battle plans and also the types of ships and guns, but he made me a proposition. If I would withdraw my insistence on going to the Admiralty to fashion the War Staff there on the lines which had been followed in the Army, he declared himself prepared to ask me to come over to the Admiralty and to sit with him and the Admirals and fashion the new Staff with them. With this proposal I closed.'[66] He thought that what he could not do by the front door he was content to do by the back door. But the wily Churchill rarely ever consulted Haldane about internal Admiralty affairs; on this occasion, the Hegelian philosopher was outmanoeuvred by the artifices of the non-philosopher. Nevertheless, Haldane had a decisive colleague in Churchill and one fully in sympathy with his desire to devise new weapons and strategies. He especially approved of Churchill's insistence that the newest ships convert from coal- to oil-fired engines, the implications of which went far beyond the capacity of the ships to engage the enemy in future conflicts. This single move rendered more important than ever British control over the Suez Canal and access to the oil-rich Gulf states. Britain, along with the western industrial world, was rapidly developing an industry and military uniquely dependent upon oil, most of which resided beneath the sands of Iraq and Saudi Arabia. Churchill, a student of political and military history more than Haldane, the student of the Hegelian *Weltgeist*, began to see the enormous geopolitical importance of the Arab states and the implications that the need for oil held for the Royal Navy. Haldane was content to leave such matters and concerns in the hands of Winston Churchill.

Admiral Sir John Jellicoe was instructed by Churchill early in 1914 to replace Admiral Sir George Callaghan and take command of the Grand Fleet at Scapa Flow on the eve of the Great War. The Imperial Fleet was the great pride of Lord Fisher; it was now time for his protégé to assume command and wield it effectively in a new kind of war against an enemy navy fast becoming well equipped with battleships and gunpowder but also with submarines and other innovations. Despite the numerical superiority of British ships over Germany's – twenty-four to sixteen – the circumstances required new strategies and untried manoeuvres. As Correlli Barnett has written: 'Until 1912 there had been no Admiralty staff and no naval staff college, there had been no systematic study of strategy in the Royal Navy, and in 1914 there was thus no operational war plan. Instead there were the personal and vehement prejudices of the men at the top.'[67] The matter was urgent in view of the fact that the island kingdom depended upon its navy both to defend its coastline and to provide logistical resources to the army in the field overseas and to maintain secure the commercial sea lanes by which Britain fed itself. 'The fact that the Royal Navy had no corporate brain meant that its training, equipment and technical design were unrelated to one another or to coherent basic principles. Admiral Lord Charles Beresford had quarrelled violently and publicly with Fisher over the questions of war plans and naval staff in 1910.'[68]

Despite Churchill's enthusiasm for many of the reorganizations Haldane was making in the army, equivalent reforms were being resisted at the Admiralty. Several senior admirals were simply incapable of making the suggested reforms. Jellicoe, whatever his other qualities, was pre-eminently unqualified to reorganize and command a navy as a part of the fighting force of the Empire. 'Jellicoe had not been principally trained or enjoyed experience as a strategist.' One historian has noted, 'except as an officer at sea, his career had been entirely concerned with material equipment and administrative detail. Neither he nor any senior officer of the fleet had received any staff training or a high education in strategic studies; he had never served on a proper professional staff and never made use of one. Jellicoe himself had never had an advanced general education.'[69] It troubled Haldane to see the internal squabbling taking place at the Admiralty but there was nothing he could do. 'I was myself taken up almost entirely with the large task of reorganising the Army for possible war. I should have liked to have extended that work to the Navy, and did the best I could, but the Government was not really interested in those things, and the result was that there was very little opportunity for this sort of scientific consideration in Cabinet deliberations.'[70] It helped little that Lord Fisher was against the establishment of a naval general staff, partly because he was a 'prisoner of the navy's tradition and believed that admirals, by themselves, did all the thinking necessary in the fleet, and partly because a corporate brain like a general staff would curb his personal rule.'[71] These matters were left to the Sandhurst-trained Winston Churchill, who, like Haldane, relished the challenge but ran into far greater opposition from his naval superior officers.

True to form, Haldane looked for competent men to place in control. He surrounded himself at the War Office with individuals of proven talent such as '[Gerald] Ellison, [Charles] Harris, [Douglas] Haig, [Spencer] Ewart, and [Harold] Nicholson.'[72] These men, in concert with the adjutant-general, General Charles Douglas, saw to it that army reforms were undertaken. At the end of the war, when Haig returned to London at the head of a victorious British Army – a ceremony to which Richard Haldane was not invited – he made a special detour to 28 Queen Anne's Gate to see Viscount Haldane and, after expressing his personal gratitude to the former secretary of state for war, left him a copy of his despatches as a token of appreciation for the former war minister's unflagging support during the war. Haig wrote on the overleaf of the despatches: 'To Viscount Haldane of Cloan – the greatest Secretary of State for War England has ever had. In grateful remembrance of his successful efforts in organising the Military Forces for a War on the

Continent, notwithstanding much opposition from the Army council and the half-hearted support of his Parliamentary friends.'[73]

Haldane's army reforms won for him a permanent place in the annals of British military history. To this day, Haig's assessment of him as the greatest secretary of war in British history is widely shared. The secret of Haldane's administrative success resided in the fact that he buried his own ego and shared the credit of his successes with his subordinates, such as Colonel Ellison, his principal secretary. Unlike his predecessor, Campbell-Bannerman, Haldane genuinely admired military men and treated them with respect and demanded much of them. Those who showed themselves capable were promoted, those who didn't perform did not survive. He trusted his military advisers and prodded them to greater achievements. Besides, he worked harder than anyone else and never asked a subordinate to do more than he was himself prepared to do. And never did he seek the credit for the achievements of other men.

Resignation

Haldane's outspoken admiration for German culture, including philosophy and military organization, earned for him the enmity of a few powerful people, such as Leo Maxse of the *National Review* and Lord Northcliffe, proprietor of *The Times*. This enmity would lead to the dismissal of Haldane from the cabinet in 1915. Haldane's pro-German leanings were well known, especially to the press lords of the day. But a mission he made to Germany in 1912 sowed the seeds of his undoing as a minister of the crown, at least for a time.

In January of that year, Sir Ernest Cassel, a prominent British financier and long-time friend of King Edward's and also well-known to the kaiser and other German officers of state, went to Berlin with a memorandum for the kaiser allegedly approved by at least several members of the British cabinet.[74] The memorandum outlined a proposal that would bring a halt to the arms race that had come to strain the relations between Germany and Britain. It suggested, for example, that if Germany were prepared to cut back its naval program, Britain would be prepared to discuss colonial compensation and even to consider a non-aggression pact between the two countries. The kaiser and Chancellor Theobald von Bethmann Hollweg agreed to receive a British cabinet minister to pursue the terms of the memorandum officially. Cassell reported that Winston Churchill, first sea lord, and Edward Grey, foreign secretary, would be most welcome to come to Germany to discuss the proposals further. These were times when German-British relations on both sides were marked by suspicion and misunderstanding: 'It seemed to public opinion in Germany that England ... had been anxious to encourage a quarrel between Germany and France, in which she could join. On the other hand, the English people were convinced that Germany intended to make war on England.'[75]

Churchill wanted no part of the venture and neither did Grey, who had trouble understanding the German view of the world at the best of times. Grey persuaded Richard Haldane – who had just moved from the War Office to the lord chancellorship – to make the trip. Haldane agreed to go but under the umbrella of strict secrecy. He left for Germany with his brother John and let it be known privately to a number of his friends that he was going in connection with the work of the royal commission on the University of London in which he was known to be actively involved. He also instructed his staff to say – if word of his trip became public knowledge – that the purpose of the trip was to investigate developments in technical education in German universities.[76] That pretext had plausibility because Haldane had long worried that there had been too little attention given to the advancement of science in British universities. 'Science had been developed and applied in Germany as it had not been with us, and it was very difficult to get my colleagues to realise this, and to avoid, when I approached it, being put down as a pro-German enthusiast.'[77] Despite Haldane's efforts, Britain was slow to embrace the cause of science and was to reap the consequences of this neglect throughout most of both world wars, when it was always one step behind Germany in technological advances. German chemistry, at the beginning of the Second World War, was far superior to that of the allied countries and as a result the German Army almost won the war with superior rocket power and air power with jet propulsion. No greater contrast could be found between Richard Haldane and Winston Churchill as in these matters, notwithstanding Churchill's fascination with firepower and explosive devices. While Haldane was urging scientific reforms upon the universities, Churchill was strutting the landscape sounding warnings of the 'Teuton and of all that the Teutonic system meant.'[78]

The Northcliffe press, however, got wind of the 'secret mission' and matters were made worse when it became known that Ernest Cassel, a German by birth but now a naturalized citizen upon marriage to an English woman in 1878, was behind the scheme. What could have been more repugnant to British interests than these two men – one a native-born German, the other a Germanophile by conviction – covertly meeting with the German political and military high command? As soon as war between Germany and Britain had been declared in August 1914, criticisms of Haldane began to be voiced publicly. A report from London that appeared in the *Vancouver Daily Province* for 5 January 1915, under the headline 'Haldane Accused of Favouring Germans,' read:

The Unionist rump, including *The Daily Express*, the Duke of Somerset and L.J. Maxse, editor of *The National Review*, are endeavouring to break the political truce by attacking Lord Haldane and some of the recent attacks have been incredibly vindictive. The anti-Haldane campaign centres round the charges that Lord Haldane reduced the regular army when he was at the War Office and that he is really sympathetic with Germany and a warm admirer of the German Emperor. Mr. Maxse in the current number of *The National Review* declared that it was intended to appoint Lord Haldane Secretary for War when war became imminent and in that event Lord Reading would become Lord Chancellor. The alarm those changes aroused crystallized so rapidly that, within 48 hours, Lord Haldane, who was known to be actively opposed to the dispatch of a British Expeditionary Force, deemed it advisable to beat a retreat ... 'Lord Haldane wisely bowed before the storm' says Mr. Maxse, 'It was about the only wise thing that he had done in nine years official life.'[79]

Letters to the editor of the *National Review* calling Haldane 'the member for Germany' showed that the campaign of vilification was beginning to take hold in the public mind. 'I am now reading the February number of the *Review*,' wrote another correspondent, 'and I am glad you are still dealing with Lord Haldane in a manner that ought to carry conviction to readers of the shameful scandal of his presence in the British Government.'[80]

What Maxse started the ebullient press lord, Lord Northcliffe, finished.

No one encouraged the attacks on Haldane more than he and the newspapers he controlled. His power was immense. He was not concerned with dispassionate judgment – on the contrary he was the instigator of violence, in thought and propaganda. No politician was safe against his attack and he was hated and feared in consequence. His newspapers told the people (working on the lowest denominator) what they wanted to hear in time of war, which, as Dr Johnson has rightly said, is good of themselves and evil of their enemies. Haldane could in Northcliffe's eyes be judged an enemy – he talked German, he had visited Germany many times and he had even had the effrontery to speak well of the Germans on occasion![81]

But few members of Parliament fanned the flames of anti-Haldane sentiment more than the Canadian-born Andrew Bonar Law, leader of the Conservative Party. He pointedly assaulted the competence and achievements of the secretary of state for war in the House of Commons where he challenged the very stuff of the army reforms. He attempted to diminish the advances in firepower initiated under Haldane's leadership. Bonar Law's attack on Haldane 'killed all hope of the bipartisan approach to Army affairs which Haldane had so constantly sought to achieve and with some small measure of success while Balfour led the Opposition.'[82] Haldane had taken steps to prevent this kind of partisanship in the run-up to war by keeping Arthur Balfour, the Conservative opposition leader, informed on all matters relating to army reforms. Bonar Law's ambitions shattered all those efforts. His volatile anti-Haldane speeches fed the press provided by Maxse and Northcliffe. Partisan attacks on Haldane erupted even in the House of Lords, where rumours of Haldane's 'giveaway' circulated amid the brandy and cigar smoke. The absurdity that Haldane had proposed to give away a part of the Empire for unspecified concessions from Germany made the rounds and increased the press hostility towards this 'pro-German' minister of the crown. Haldane, to the annoyance of his friends and the consternation of his enemies, showed his contempt for these allegations by maintaining an impenetrable silence.

But 'the vile Press campaign,' as Churchill later called it, was successful and Haldane resigned from cabinet. His friend Earl Grey wrote to Prime Minister Asquith deploring the vilification and lamented the loss of Haldane from the counsels of the government. In response, Asquith, while agreeing completely as to the viciousness of the press campaign to unseat Haldane, did not insist that Haldane remain in the government. Haldane's account of events leading up to his leaving the government is characteristically devoid of any resentment or recrimination. He offered his resignation in order to take pressure off the Asquith government in the time of war.

I liked to study what other nations had accomplished and to appreciate sympathetically the reasons why they had accomplished it. I am not sure that this spirit, good as it is for tolerance, is equally good as a training ground for getting the confidence of the British public. I had gone to Germany too often, and had read her literature too much, not to give ground to narrow-minded people to say that Germany was my 'spiritual home.'

Anyhow, in August 1914 a formidable section of the public here had turned against me. I did not think that this was good for the Government, and in the autumn of 1914 I felt bound to go to the Prime Minister and to say that, as the attacks on me must obviously affect the general position, it would probably be better that I should not remain in office. He laughed at the idea of this, but I took a more serious view of it. If my full story could had been made public I think that the attacks would have been destroyed. But both Asquith and Grey were averse to making public the details of previous negotiations with Germany while the War was going on. I had therefore to remain unshielded, and I had no illusion as to what in the end the result was likely to be. The public aspect of these attacks demanded consideration. In my own view, as things stood, my work, such as it was, had been finished, and I felt that I was no longer contributing strength to the Government. As time went on, and the storm raised against me increased, I saw that the Prime Minister was not likely to be able to form a Coalition Ministry if I remained as Lord Chancellor and I wrote to him to say so. Nor did I greatly care. Strategical questions had passed into other hands, and I was no longer really needed.[83]

Haldane then related how Asquith circulated a letter asking all members of cabinet to resign in order to free him to reconstitute the government anew for the war. Haldane immediately sent his resignation. Grey and others were stunned to learn that his old friend was not to be included on the new government benches when Asquith had reconstituted his cabinet. No one was less surprised than Richard Haldane, as his own account of the matter testifies. He sincerely believed that he had done his work and that he was prepared to go into retirement. Haldane's account of these events is confirmed by Asquith's son Herbert, who wrote about the events in his *Moments of Memory*.[84]

Haldane's retirement was not to be a brooding retreat where he licked his wounds and pondered over what might have been had the press treated him more favourably. He retreated to Cloan and began immediately to write a book on philosophy which had been percolating within him for a long time. The result was *The Reign of Relativity*, a dense but important work of philosophy that quickly went into five printings. Yet, despite his best efforts to conceal the hurt, as Edward Spires has noted, there is little question that Richard Haldane felt the sting of the press attacks as well as the desertion of his former parliamentary friends. 'The ordeal ... had left its scar. It was evident to friends and family that Haldane had suffered. "Richard," observed his sister, had "really felt those attacks more even then he should."'[85] He would not have been human had he not felt to some extent the vicious attacks upon his patriotism and integrity. However much Haldane insisted that he had offered his resignation to the prime minister in order to take the heat off the government when the country was at war, many people thought that Asquith had treated his old friend shabbily by not resisting the calls for his resignation. The whole affair put a strain on their friendship which lasted for a long time. As late as 1921 Harold Laski was writing to Justice Oliver Wendell Holmes in Washington about his efforts to repair the rift: 'With the Asquiths (this *entre nous*) I have been engaged in a pretty little intrigue to get Haldane back to a basis of friendship with them. Ever since L[loyd] G[eorge] became Prime Minister Haldane has gravitated towards him. Not I think on intellectual grounds, but just because Asquith was morbidly conscious of unfairness in dropping Haldane in 1915.'[86]

But, while some of his political colleagues may have distanced themselves from their old friend during this period, the king did not do so. On 26 May 1915 King George, on his own initiative, pointedly conferred upon the beleaguered faithful servant the Order of Merit. The gesture touched the loyal Scot deeply as he headed home to Cloan.

No one was more upset by the vitriol being heaped upon Richard Haldane than his closest personal friend, Edmund Gosse, who was equally exasperated with Haldane's refusal to reply to his detractors as he was with the attacks themselves.[87] He collected newspaper accounts of the anti-Haldane sentiment and fulminated in private over the dreadful injustice being done to his friend. One clipping denounced Haldane as 'a man whose material home is in Germany and one whose spiritual home is there. Send Haldane to his spiritual home. Out you go you blackguard and scoundrel.'[88] This was too much for Gosse, who wrote a blistering letter to the *Morning Post* on 8 January 1915, addressing especially the 'spiritual home' theme. While his friends were defending him in letters to the press, Haldane was comfortably settled in at Cloan; he had paid for the electrification of the home ten years earlier so that now he could work with the benefit of electric lights and central heating. 'I am very happy here,' he wrote to the exasperated Gosse, 'I have finished 5 chapters of "Philosophy After the War."'[89] In addition to doing philosophy he was also 'reading Roman law and physical chemistry to fill in interstices.'[90] 'Oh the peace and comfort of being free to live in this atmosphere rather than that of the colleagues of L.George! It would take a very strong call to duty to make me go to that atmosphere, were I summoned. I rejoice that British Philistinism forbids it.'[91]

And so 'Old Schopenhauer,' at the age of fifty-nine, settled in with his books at Cloanden and immersed himself in Hegelian philosophy while the war raged around him at a safe distance. In addition to his extensive library, he had the stimulating company of his beloved mother and his sister, Elizabeth, both of whom engaged him in his philosophical efforts. He also had his dog, 'Bruce,' to accompany him on his long pensive daily walks through rural Perthshire.

5

Haldane in the School of the Master

Thought is not a fixed state of being, [Hegel] maintains, but a restless activity, a process of development from the indeterminate to the determinate, from the vague to the clear, from the abstract to the concrete.

– Frederick C. Beiser, 'Hegel's Historicism'

In adopting Hegel as his guide, Haldane must surely have known that he was entering a deeply divided fraternity of scholars. German philosophers had become the centre of serious attention throughout the Western academic world. For a time it appeared that Immanuel Kant, the reclusive Königsberg professor, would prevail unchallenged for the foreseeable future. That ended with the arrival of Hegel armed with a sweeping new historical philosophy of state. He soon accumulated almost as many enemies as friends when he burst upon the European philosophical scene in the middle of the nineteenth century. Any attempt to distil or summarize his thought invariably elicits strong critical reaction. Our task, however, is not to distil the whole of Hegel but to attempt to understand what Richard Burdon Haldane found so compelling in his philosophy of state. After all, it was Haldane himself who said he was influenced by the philosophy of Hegel. Whether he understood Hegel as well as subsequent generations of Hegel scholars is not for us to decide. That subject is destined to remain an in-house matter of debate among struggling students of nineteenth-century German philosophers. 'What Hegel really meant' is the abiding focus of the learned literature on Hegel and Hegelianism. The 'young Hegel' is pitted against the 'mature Hegel' throughout this literature and there appears to be no end of the debate in sight. Haldane never became engaged in that debate; he took what he wanted from the master and ignored the squabbles of the academy even when they involved the heated contributions of his friends such as Pringle-Pattison and Bernard Bosanquet.

What Haldane Learned from Hegel

Initially, Hegel was not well received in his native land. He was attacked immediately upon entering the scene by those who saw his radical historicism and statism as inherently incompatible with Protestant Christian orthodoxy, to say nothing of Catholic orthodoxy. Even Haldane's old teacher, Hermann Lotze, viewed Hegel as a serious threat to orthodox religion. But this was not Lotze's primary objection to Hegel. He viewed Hegelian philosophy as an invitation to ponder the fate of mankind in the great chain of history as a form of fatalism; human beings in this view of history become the unconscious participants under the sway of the World Spirit towards ends unknown and unwilled by them. Lotze worried about the loss of the place of the freely willing individual in the great Hegelian sweep of the historic process towards freedom. He never lost sight of the important role played by the individual in shaping a life of joy and happiness.[1] Haldane's old teacher wrote about the need to understand how the state 'which has grown up historically can be transformed so as to harmonize better with the growing need which men feel for freedom of development.'[2] Lotze was more concerned with the substantive ends of national life than Hegel appeared to be and the role to be played by individuals – especially leaders – in the articulation and achievement of those ends. Above all, Lotze urged his readers to turn back to classical Greece for guidance. 'Human life properly so called had its beginning in leisure, and to learn how to occupy and enjoy leisure in a way worthy of humanity was the business of Greek education, which, in order to attain this end, not only did not shun the labour of severe and long-continued discipline, but even undertook it with eagerness.'[3]

By all accounts, Hegel was not an easy man to defend on the personal level. According to Haldane himself, 'Hegel does not appear to have been a particularly pleasant person in controversy. He indulged at times in diatribes against his opponents, and he has paid the usual penalty of being miscalled and misrepresented.'[4] Miscalled and misrepresented, indeed. Haldane's distinguished contemporary, Bertrand Russell, summed up his view of Hegel with the comment: 'It follows from his metaphysics that true liberty consists in obedience to an arbitrary authority, that free speech is an evil, that absolute monarchy is good, that the Prussian state was the best existing at the time when he wrote, that war is good, and that an international organization for the peaceful settlement of disputes would be a misfortune ... What he admired were ... order, system, regulation and intensity of governmental control.'[5] It would be difficult to find a greater caricature of Hegel than that found in these acerbic lines from Russell. But it was, nevertheless, a commonly held view in British intellectual circles, owing, in no small part, to Russell's powerful pen.

Haldane was fully aware of this view of his master and gave his own account of Hegel's philosophy in 1895 in an article for the *Contemporary Review* in which he attempted to portray Hegel more favourably. The article began with a lengthy encomium on the great German poet Goethe, who was reasonably well known to British audiences through the works of Thomas Carlyle. Haldane there acknowledged that 'among English-speaking people the influence of Goethe has probably been the greatest force of the century.'[6] But, Haldane continued, his principal objective on this occasion was 'to consider ... another great personality of the Jena-Weimar circle.' That man was Hegel, who, said Haldane, 'has to-day but few professing adherents in his own country, but his power is not dead or even dormant. It has only been transferred from Germany to Great Britain and America.'[7] Not sufficient to leave it at that, the young philosophy student – he was thirty-nine years of age at the time he wrote this piece – went on to say: 'In the Scottish universities the younger professors of philosophy are mostly Hegelian. Even in Cambridge, never prone to speculative tendencies, there exists to-day the germ of an Hegelian centre. Oxford has been the cradle of an Hegelian movement, the greatest and farthest-reaching since the days of the philosopher himself, for it is hardly necessary to remind you how profound is still the influence of Thomas Hill Green, alike in our philosophy and our theology.'[8]

Haldane himself read deeply in the primary Hegelian sources in German. He confessed to Professor J.H. Morgan that he had read Hegel's *Phenomenology of Spirit* nineteen times. This may not be the exaggeration it appears. For anyone who has ever studied Hegel's writings knows that one must read and reread his works many times before they reluctantly surrender up their deepest thoughts. Haldane's good friend Pringle-Pattison once recalled that 'whenever we met I was sure to find that he had just been re-reading one or other of the master's works, perhaps the *Phaenomenologie* most frequently of all. It is hardly out of place to speak of them as his bedside companions; they were certainly the books to which he most frequently turned for relaxation, if one may so speak, at the close of a busy day.' It is perhaps too unkind to suggest that reading Hegel at bedtime would quickly induce sleep, even for Richard Haldane. Hegel's philosophy, he explained, 'is not like that of Kant, a theory of knowledge, for his Idealism is not subjective Idealism. It is a system in which both subject and object appear as themselves "moments" in that ultimate reality which we may call experience, or knowledge, or as Hegel himself does, thought, a final activity which is subject and not substance, and which embraces in its movement all those distinctions which appear as ultimate from the psychological standpoint.'[9] Hegel, Haldane insisted, presented a 'new German lamp' by which philosophers were obliged to re-examine 'the old results.' 'One of the most fertile sources of error,' he announced, 'lies in the application of the categories of one science to the subject matter of another.'[10]

Echoing Hegel, Haldane insisted that 'our business is to take the world as we find it, and when we want to increase our knowledge of the phases of it on which we concentrate our attention, to remember that, legitimate as it is, every such process involves abstraction from other facts and phases which are equally real.'[11] Taking the world as we find it meant understanding that history is the rational unfolding of the spirit of freedom. Contrary to a dominant theme in modern philosophy which disparaged the idea of nature as the guide in human affairs, Hegel, said Haldane, urged a return to nature: 'Back to nature was his [Hegel's] cry: back to the world of phenomena, which is not to be thought of as though there were some noumenal world behind it, but is to be taken as the supreme and ultimate fact. The world is there, and it is only our tendency to be run away with by metaphors which causes any difficulty.'[12] At one point, conceding that perhaps Hegel had not pronounced 'the last word,' Haldane went on to conclude that 'when we turn to Hegel himself, and find how he has revolutionised the study of history, what new light he has thrown upon the development of the world of events as well as of the world of thought, what a power he was in practical affairs, in influencing not only the speculative thought, but the Prussian Government of his day, we ask whether in his writings we have not a mine which for all that has been done remains even now unexhausted.'[13] Those who take up the great invitation announced by Hegel, Haldane promised, would find the great truth of historical relativism: 'They will see that the truth may be ever developing, and that what is true for one generation is not true for that which succeeds it.'[14] Hegel was the true revolutionary, said Haldane, who, in 'giving up the individual self with its ends for the sake of the family or the public interest ... would have us believe that we find that self again, and not less real because it is now seen to be part of a larger whole, by membership of which it is enriched.'[15] It was an invitation to a new kind of citizenship, a citizenship where the citizen would give up his or her selfish wills in exchange for the general will of the community, a proposition that finds resonance among democratic liberals to the present day. So far has the Hegelian invitation to historicism taken root in Western nations today that most people take for granted that 'times change,' by which they mean to echo Hegel's teaching that 'values' change with the passing of time, or, as Hegel would say, with the progressive 'immanentization' of the *Weltgeist* as 'freedom.'

The major political event in the life of this great German philosopher was the French Revolution of 1789, which erupted when he was a young student of philosophy and theology in Tübingen. This earthshattering event inspired by the revolutionary teachings of the French *philosophes* transfixed the imagination of many young German and French philosophy students, Hegel and his close friend F.W.J. Schelling among them, and radically unhinged the times. It was and remains one of the most important political events in modern history; the face of Europe was reshaped and the course of all European nations was subsequently changed as never before. Some nations, like France, have never come out from under the revolution's destabilizing influence. It led Hegel to brood over the course of human history from the earliest of times. 'History' became his abiding preoccupation or intellectual passion. Not the study of the past but the *meaning* of history enticed him. As Peter Preuss has written:

The nineteenth century had discovered history and all subsequent inquiry and education bore the stamp of this discovery. This was not simply the discovery of a set of facts about the past but the discovery of the historicity of man: man, unlike the animal, is a historical being. Man is not wholly the product of an alien act, either natural or divine but in part produces his own being. The task of existing is a task precisely because it is not a case of acting according to a permanent nature or essence but rather or producing that nature within the limitations of a situation. History is the record of this self-production; it is the activity of a historical being recovering the past into a present which anticipates the future.[16]

He might have added that no one contributed to that discovery more than Hegel. As Stanley Rosen has noted, 'Hegel conceives of history as the process whereby man's spirit comes to a progressively more complete understanding of itself, through a progressive understanding of the world.'[17] Human progress was no longer looked upon as the progression from lower mechanical devices to higher ones, from a lower standard of living to a higher one; it became understood as the rational unfolding of the spirit of freedom. Man was henceforth viewed not as the product of history but as the maker of history.

Germany was the venue of this quintessentially modern philosophical perspective. German philosophy since the time of Hegel 'may be characterized as the attempt to combine Greek thought and Christian practice in the form of the philosophy of history ... man is no longer defined as subject to a transcendental moral law, nor as absolute ego or Geist. Instead he is understood as the creator of God and the potential free master of nature and history through creative work in accordance with the laws of nature and history.'[18] Hegel played a critical role in the 'liberation' of modern man from the shackles of pre-modern philosophy and theology. Prompted by his great predecessor, Jean-Jacques Rousseau, Hegel understood modern man as infinitely flexible, without a predetermined and limiting nature. Nietzsche, Hegel's great historicist successor, took this one important step further with the 'death of God'; under his historicist refinements, all men become godlets, 'creating' their own moral standards through the release of their own creative energies unencumbered from below by a static moral nature or from above by a divine or transcendent imperative. It was an inspiring message served up to young minds throughout Europe and one of those minds belonged to Richard Burdon Haldane.

The French Revolution threw all of Europe – especially intellectual Europe – into a tailspin. The violence with which the old order was savagely swept away terrified the people as well as popes and potentates. While critical of the brutal excesses that followed the storming of the Bastille, Hegel nevertheless saw the event as the unleashing of a pent-up yearning of the spirit for human freedom. He began to ask himself whether history was a record of disconnected events without rhyme or reason – as the prevailing histories taught – or whether there was a pattern that revealed a rational process beneath the rubble. Until this time, the study of history was dominated by the likes of Carlyle in Britain, who taught the 'great man' theory of history: all human events were the products of a single man at some point in history. The study of history, therefore, became the study of great political and military leaders such as Frederick the Great. Hegel replaced this school of thought by bringing philosophy to bear upon the task of understanding the entire record of past history – from antiquity to modern times – as it had been passed down over the many centuries. And he began to see a pattern, a 'rational order' in the train of past events. With this was born what Voltaire had called the 'philosophy of history.'

Hegel revisited the great historians of the past, from antiquity to the present. He did not progress very far before he encountered the Christian understanding of a providential history which held that, with the coming of Christ, history was the record of the unfolding of the providential order to an end time with the second coming of Christ. In the Christian view, history did, indeed, have a meaning because it had a divine purpose: salvation history. Hegel embraced the paradigm but translated 'the language of religion into that of philosophy.'[19] Indeed, he secularized Christian history by 'the transformation of Christian eschatology into the philosophy of history, culminating in the teaching ... that the human mind is essentially identical with the rational order of history, and so with God.'[20] In doing so, he revealed the influence of Giambattista Vico, who in his *New Science* liberated the unfolding of history from the embrace of Hebrew and Christian history.[21] Hegel's musings set him on a collision course with the Christian church – both Protestant and Catholic – which he only compounded in his *Phenomenology of Spirit* where he interpreted the incarnation of Christ as teaching that 'the divine nature is the same as the human,' so that he could conclude the book with human self-consciousness divinizing itself as 'absolute knowledge.'[22] 'World history is,' he announced, 'the progress of the consciousness of freedom.' Thus history assumed a new meaning, a messianic meaning linking progress and freedom, the two themes that would guide Richard Haldane especially as a judge. As Haldane said in his Creighton Lecture in 1914: 'It is only by tracing the genesis not merely of culminating events but of national institutions and by exhibiting them as the outcome and embodiment of the genius of the people to whom they belong, that in many cases they can be made intelligible. This principle is the foundation of the historical method.'[23]

Hegel arrived upon the European intellectual scene at a time when the strongest currents of philosophy were running in the direction of individualism as enunciated by Kant and by the Enlightenment philosophers; economic and political liberalism was the rising state philosophy, promising individual progress out of a free market controlled by Adam Smith's invisible hand. Hegel dared to challenge this with a philosophy of state. For Hegel, the state is the paramount institution to be established among men; it provides the total context for all social relations including justice, friendship, political authority, patriotism, and, above all, individual freedom. The state must, accordingly, be nurtured and jealously preserved as the only human institution that would ensure a progressive survival of mankind. The political state, according to Hegel, is the instrument through which spirit (*Geist*) guides the human condition. 'The main agent of true or rational freedom in Hegel's social philosophy,' one recent student of Hegel has explained, 'is not the individual human being but cosmic spirit.'[24] Individual human beings participate in this cosmic spirit by participating in the *Sittlichkeit* of the particular community. Not surprisingly, Haldane considered constitutional law as the most rewarding study and practice of law. Few men attempted to comprehend these matters more fully than he. This is why he read and reread his master's principal writings over and over again. In his Gifford Lectures, where he dismissed William James's dependence on sentiment, Haldane was following Hegel's repudiation of the romantic movement, based as it was on feeling rather than on the rational understanding of human life, both social and individual. He would continue to cite Goethe, Haldane's one constant poetic companion, frequently joining with Hegel in citing Goethe's *Faust* where the great German poet has Mephistopheles say: 'Despise the mind and scientific work, the highest gifts of all mankind, and you have surrendered to the Devil and must go to destruction.'

'As for the individual,' Hegel wrote, 'everyone is the son of his time, and therefore philosophy is its time comprehended in thought. It is as silly to imagine that any philosophy could transcend its own time as that an individual could jump out of his time.'[25] In this way Hegel introduced the concept of radical historicism by which ethical stands, or 'values' as they have come to be called, develop over time. As political freedom develops ever more broadly through the course of history from the few to the many to all human beings, so too do the ethical standards of right and wrong, good and evil, just and unjust progress over the course of time. This is why the state is critical for Hegel, for it is the state that provides the incubator for the ever emerging ethical and political forces; it also provides the agency of private and political restraint. It is why he could say that 'the ethical truth exists as law.'[26] And this is exactly what Haldane said in his Montreal address; he told his audience that much of his speech would appear to them as belonging more properly to ethics than to law. But the truth of the matter, he argued, is that ethics and law are mutually interdependent. And, above all, they are of human construct, not of divine origin as Hebrew and Christian revelation taught or inbred by nature as the ancients had taught. The work of the universal *Weltgeist*, the new secular providence, is to guide the human condition ever upwards towards the end of history conceived as universal moral and political freedom.

By identifying the state as the highest human achievement, Hegel was accused of raising the state to an idolatrous level, as Bertrand Russell had asserted, and of encouraging an aggressive nationalism that made war between competing states inevitable. It is little wonder that he has been accused of infusing nineteenth-century Europe with a belligerent nationalism which was put to music, in Germany, as 'Deutschland über alles.' Haldane rejected this criticism with the explanation that 'it was not Hegelianism ... but the violent reaction against idealism which set in throughout Germany soon after Hegel's death, that gave rise to the dominance of militarism.'[27] 'The state,' he insisted, 'is an individuality, an exclusive single entity which is related to others through this individuality.'[28] International relations take on the character of the relation between individuals. The constitution of the state, is 'rational in as much as the state differentiates its operation according to the nature of the concept and likewise determines it.'[29] The state is a human rational concept to the extent that it is 'a reflection or image of the eternal reason.'[30] Hegel's rejection of the unity of church and state only served to gain for him the hostility of the European Christian church. But he defended himself with the claim that only by such separation can the state fulfil its function above the churches and represent the generality of thought. 'It is therefore very wrong to say that the separation of state and church is a misfortune,' he exclaimed. 'Only through this separation has the state been able to become what it was intended to be: the self-conscious rationality and ethics. Likewise it is the most fortunate thing that could have happened to the churches.'[31] It was exactly this line of reasoning that led the young Scottish philosophy student to walk away from the practice of the institutional church.

As it did for Hegel, law became Haldane's central focus. But it is law understood differently from the previous understanding as the will of the legislature expressing the will of the people. The new modern state armed with the uncovering of the meaning of history would take its bearing from the *general will*, which Hegel adopted from Jean-Jacques Rousseau. The general will is not to be understood as the sum total of popular will and it is most emphatically not simply the majority will, though it could be both. It is the will revealed to the philosophic judge within the emerging *Sittlichkeit*, the spirit of the people at a given historic moment in the cause of freedom. That, indeed, is how progress becomes defined and it is a measure of Hegel's enduring influence that this is the dominant understanding of modern progress into the present century.

Hegel and the Reform Bill of 1831

Hegel intruded himself uninvited into the domestic politics of Great Britain by commenting on one occasion only: during the early debates on the Reform Bill in 1831.[32] He admired many aspects of the British constitution because it had evolved gradually like a healthy organism. After noting that England 'with great exertions, maintained itself on its old foundations' and had survived the 'general convulsion' caused by the French Revolution, Hegel stated that the country 'seemed so much the more liable to be affected by it, as a public Parliament, that habit of assembling in public meeting which was common to all orders of the state, and a free press, offered singular facilities for introducing the French principles of Liberty and Equality among all classes of the people.'[33] Hegel identified 'the leading feature of what the Englishmen call their Liberty' as the decentralized community structure of the English constitution. 'In England,' he observed, 'every parish, every subordinate division and association has a part of its own to perform. Thus the common interest is concrete, and particular interests are taken cognizance of and determined in view of that common interest.'[34] He contrasted the English constitution in this respect with the French, where 'down to the least village the Maire is named by the Ministry or their agents.'[35] (Hence Mary P. Follett's statement that 'true Hegelianism finds its actualized form in federalism.'[36]) These remarks on the virtue of decentralization in the English constitution must have found favour with the Scottish lawyer and judge.

Hegel was, however, suspicious of recent proposals to change the English constitution. The debates surrounding the Reform Bill of 1831 troubled him; he feared that, by extending the voting franchise, the British state would succumb to popular sentiment and not rational deliberation; sentiment must never oust reason from its proper role or function in the state. 'In the English constitution,' he wrote, 'the democratic element plays an important part through the participation of the people in the election of the members of the Commons – the statesmen who have the largest share in the power of deciding upon general matters. It is a nearly general opinion among historians that when private interest and dirty monetary advantage interfere in the election of the key men of the state, such a state of affairs must be considered a precursor to the loss of political freedom, of the collapse of its constitution and of the state itself.'[37] He feared the Reform Act for those very reasons.

In constitutional terms, it is interesting to note that Hegel was disdainful of the notion of the separation of powers in the state because it introduced an element of competition into the constitution.[38] According to Hegel, the state is an organism and the constitution is the central ordering principle of that organism. It is the means by which the rights, duties, and activities of citizens are designated and preserved in the interest of both private and public freedom. Under the well-ordered, *rational*, state, Hegel identified three powers: '(a) the power to determine and establish the universal laws – the Legislature; (b) the power to subsume single cases and the spheres of particularity under the universal – the Executive; (c) the power of subjectivity, as the will with the power of ultimate decision – the Crown.'[39] These powers can be conceptually distinguished but they must not be separate so as to be in competition. The state is a single organism and must function in a unified manner as a living organism. This is why, for Hegel, the test of a nation's constitution is whether that constitution facilitates its own realization in the life of its citizens, thereby ensuring the enjoyment of freedom. In this matter he was repeating what Montesquieu had said: that the nation at first forms its constitution but in time the constitution forms its citizens.[40] But he rejects Montesquieu's endorsement of the constitutional separation of powers. For Hegel, a constitution acquires the character of rationality if it meets certain conditions. Its laws should express the concrete will of the people – their changing values, interests, ideas, and customs. The transformation of the general will (properly understood) into a concrete way of life prompted him to insist that the state is ethical in character: 'the state is the actuality of the ethical Idea. It is ethical mind *qua* the substantial will manifest and revealed to itself, knowing and thinking itself, accomplishing what it knows and insofar as it knows it.'[41] By virtue of his or her rationality, a person is a free ethical entity and the state exists to serve their highest ends. 'A man counts as a man in virtue of his manhood alone, not because he is a Jew, Catholic, Protestant, German, Italian, etc.'[42] But the question that is begged here is: How is the state to know the general will and how is it to ensure institutionally the conditions of freedom? The election of representatives to legislative bodies ensures that the aspirations of the people are taken into account in the formulation of laws. But there is, Hegel insists, a special place for those who possess the wisdom as to what constitutes the *Sittlichkeit* of the state. These men of wisdom are to be found, Haldane later affirmed in Montreal, among those learned in the laws of the state: lawyers and judges. They are privileged advisers to the state. This is why Hegel urged that the best and the brightest seek positions in the civil service of the nation. There was no higher calling for a man of talent.

Finally, for Hegel, constitutions or statutes must never be viewed as fixed and inflexible; they must constantly be subject to rational reform in light of the most recent aspirations towards freedom. All laws, including the constitutional law of the state, are children of their times and must constantly be adapted to the demands placed upon them by the emerging new aspirations of the times. Haldane understood this task to be the core of the judicial function: to bring the constitution in line with the rising expectations of the people. This is precisely how he saw his duty as a member of the Judicial Committee of the Privy Council. It is why he could say that Lord Watson put 'flesh and bone upon the constitution of Canada,' and why he felt no compunction in doing the same. The Canadian provinces were chafing under a constitution that imposed an unduly strong central government. The principal task before the Judicial Committee was to reshape the British North America Act, 1867 into a genuine federal constitution where the aspirations of the provinces would be recognized better than were by the framers of the act in 1867.

Haldane and the Art of Statecraft

The most explicit account of Haldane's statecraft in his own words is found in his lengthy introduction to Mary Follett's *The New State*, first published in 1918. Early in the essay he said that had Hegel 'lived in Boston in 1920, instead of in Germany a century earlier, he would probably, as far as I can judge from his writings, have said something not very different from what Miss Follett says.'[43] It was the highest praise he could have bestowed upon her.

Haldane's friend and Oxford professor of philosophy, Bernard Bosanquet, had acquired a copy of Follett's book and became excited about it; he paid a visit to Haldane in London and loaned it to him, saying that it was 'the most sane and brilliant of recent works on political theory.'[44] Haldane liked the book so much he wrote the author and offered to write an introduction to the next edition; he thought it might help her reach a wider audience in Britain. Follett was, of course, delighted with the suggestion and published Haldane's introduction in the third impression, September 1920.

Haldane noted in his introduction that the 'cardinal doctrine of her book is that the state is what its members make it to be. Sovereignty is a relative notion. The individual is sovereign over himself in so far as he can develop, control and unify his manifold nature.'[45] What followed is little short of a paraphrase of what Hegel had said in the *Philosophy of Right*. 'The form of the state,' he continued, 'and the meaning of the resulting sovereignty may vary, following general opinion at different periods and under different conditions, and so may the mode of expressing the imperative. But all ultimately comes back to the will of the people of the state.'[46] These sentiments can be found in Haldane's attitude towards the aspirations of the fathers of Canadian Confederation and explain why he was so dismissive in his Judicial Committee judgments of the reasoning in the Supreme Court of Canada. Following Hegel, Haldane would not be prevented from developing the constitution of Canada by an act of the imperial Parliament; neither parchments nor the intelligence of the Canadian framers held a persuasive appeal or binding authority for him because they contained no enduring wisdom – there simply was no such thing as an enduring wisdom. He viewed reason as progressive, as an expression of the ongoing spirit of a given people, the *Volkgeist*; it could never be arrested at any given historic moment nor could it appeal to an enduring wisdom. The written expression at any given moment, however authoritatively expressed, reflected only that given moment. Succeeding generations were at liberty to jettison the wisdom of the past in favour of newer expressions of freedom inspired by the emerging new *Geist*.

To Haldane's Hegelian mind, by according a permanence to the parchment wisdom, the judge was betraying his or her responsibility to work with the trends and aspirations of the times. What mattered was, as we shall see, how forceful advocates such as Oliver Mowat of Ontario would argue before the Judicial Committee in defence of evolving provincial autonomy. Those authorities, such as Mowat and Mercier, advocates of life in the provinces at the time, were the ones who had clout, not a dead parchment or colonial framers from a by-gone era. The will of the people at the moment is what counted. 'The will is not a static thing but is a form of the dynamic activity characteristic of mind.'[47] The state is not governed by 'abstract principles' allegedly enunciated in a written document. 'It is a process: a continual self-modification to express its different stages of growth in which each and all must be so flexible that continual change of form is twin-fellow of continual growth ... The state is made, not by external acts, but by the continuous thought and action of the people who live its life. In this sense it is never perfect for it is a process that remains always unbroken in creative activity.'[48] He concluded his introduction to Follett's book with the remark: 'In reform there is no finality no more than there is in truth in general, of which reform is only an example. It is the quality reached in the striving itself, and not in a result, apparently but not really to be attained once for all, that we may profitably seek to satisfy our desire for the sense of something accomplished.'[49] Under this way of thinking, constitutions – such as the constitution of the United States – are not enduring documents meant to give indefinite guidance to states; they are suggestive guidelines which all subsequent generations are at liberty to bend, follow, or ignore. Or they were, to use the terrible image of the Judicial Committee, skeletons in need of 'flesh and blood.'

Haldane brought this line of thinking to the Judicial Committee and accordingly took little or no notice of the intentions of the fathers of Canadian Confederation or, indeed, of the imperial Parliament; those intentions were subordinate to the task at hand, which was to bring the *practice* of the constitution in line with the aspirations of the given historic moment. 'I am a lawyer whose almost daily duty,' he wrote, 'it is to ascertain the reasons why the law has become what it is, because unless I can do so, I am bound to fail in the interpretation of its scope and authority.'[50] The task of the lawyer and, by extension, the judge is to uncover the context, which includes the 'spirit of the times.' In his eulogy of Lord Watson in 1899, Haldane revealed explicitly his own conception of the judicial function and attributed it to his predecessor. 'He was an Imperial judge of the very first order. The function of such a judge, sitting in the supreme tribunal of the Empire, is to do more than decide what abstract and familiar legal conceptions should be applied to particular cases. His function is to be a statesman as well as a jurist, to fill in the gaps which Parliament has deliberately left in the skeleton constitutions and laws that it has provided for the British Colonies. The Imperial legislature has taken the view that these constitutions and laws must, if they are to be acceptable, be in a large measure unwritten, elastic and capable of being silently developed and even altered as the Colony develops and alters.'

No one could have presented Hegel's thoughts on these matters more precisely. The Canadian constitution, the British North America Act, 1867, was a skeleton in need of clothing with living flesh and blood. It should come as no surprise that Viscount Haldane brought these sentiments to bear in Canadian constitutional cases. Armed with the teachings of his philosophical mentor, Haldane, the statesman and jurist, set out to uncover the *Sittlichkeit* of the Canadian nation by way of uncovering and enforcing the *Sittlichkeiten* of the several provinces. We must turn now to see how this important predecessor jurist-statesman uncovered the *Sittlichkeit* of the Canadian nation and gave it formal legal recognition, the internal logic of the British North America Act, 1867 notwithstanding

6

Haldane in the Shadow of
Lord Watson

Lord Watson put clothing upon the bones of the [Canadian] Constitution, and so covered them over with living flesh that the constitution of Canada took a new form ... A long series of decisions were given by him which solved many problems and produced a new contentment in Canada with the constitution they had got in 1867.

– R.B. Haldane, 'Work of the Judicial Committee'

At the height of his busy life at the War Office – with occasional side ventures into higher education in the company of the Webbs – it looked to Richard Haldane, in the first decade of the twentieth century, as if the remainder of his life was destined to be spent in such ministerial matters, far away from his profession as a barrister. And while he remained actively involved in the pursuit of philosophy and kept close contact with professional philosophers such as Bosanquet and Pringle-Pattison, and men of science such as Einstein, these associations remained on the periphery of his formal life as a minister of the crown. Little did he know that damp spring morning in March 1911, when Herbert Henry Asquith, who had succeeded Campbell-Bannerman as prime minister upon his death in office in 1908, summoned him to Number 10 Downing Street, that his life was about to change suddenly and dramatically. To his surprise, Asquith, calling on Haldane's sense of duty to the Liberal reform agenda, offered his friend a peerage and the leadership of the Liberal Party in the House of Lords.[1] This, he knew in a flash, meant that he would be returning full time to the law at the highest level of the profession; as a barrister he would now sit as a law lord.

The appointment to the House of Lords in March 1911, while he was still secretary of state for war, appealed to him greatly even though he knew he would miss the excitement of ministerial politics at the War Office. But not even he could have known then that, one year after his ascension to the Upper House, that he would become lord chancellor. As lord chancellor he would preside over the House of Lords and be responsible for the administration of justice throughout the kingdom; he would serve as president of the Judicial Committee of the Privy Council, the highest court of appeal for the British Empire; and he would occupy a senior position in the cabinet and become the highest-ranking member of the legal profession in the United Kingdom. Clearly, the events of that March morning were to change the direction of Richard Haldane's life forever and alter the course of the law throughout the dominions and colonies of the British Empire profoundly.

To the Woolsack

After breathing new life into the army by a host of major reforms, and after assisting in the initiation of new universities throughout the provinces, Richard Haldane replaced the ailing Lord Crewe as leader of the Liberal Party in the House of Lords and assumed a lead role in advancing the cause of liberal reforms. The Liberal Party at this period was attempting to consolidate its position as the progressive party of the working class. Leading Liberals from Campbell-Bannerman through Asquith and Lloyd-George knew that the working class, which had been enfranchised beginning in 1867, would one day demand social legislation aimed at relieving the plight of the poor. The party responded with a series of progressive social measures including free school meals for children of large families followed in short order by schemes designed to alleviate the plight of the elderly through old age pensions as well as unemployment and health insurance program for workers. Asquith knew that Haldane wholeheartedly supported these Liberal reforms and would mount a strong defence in the Lords where there lingered a resistance to such social programs. Indeed, almost immediately upon taking his seat in the House of Lords, Haldane became an active participant in the debates surrounding the National Insurance Bill.[2]

Appointment to the House of Lords also brought with it the appointment as a lord of appeal at the age of fifty-five. This was, as Sommer has noted, 'a most unusual promotion for one who had never before held high judicial office.'[3] But the appointment was greeted with enthusiasm throughout the bar, such was Richard Haldane's reputation among his legal peers. And it was a reputation that would only grow, for, while Haldane's contributions to the reform of the British Army and to extension of university education throughout England were formidable and enduring, they pale by contrast with his influence on the development of the constitutional law of the British dominions and colonies. The law was his life or, as he called it, 'my old Mistress.'[4] A year after his elevation to the peerage and upon the resignation of Lord Loreburn, Haldane was elevated to the woolsack as lord chancellor.

As much as he was for the remainder of his life to enjoy his work on the Judicial Committee of the Privy Council, appointment to the House of Lords was not an honour he sought. In fact, at first he baulked at the suggestion; he enjoyed his work at the War Office and was revelling in the praises his reforms were garnering. Accepting the peerage was made more difficult by his mother's advice that he not go to the House of Lords but stay in the Commons and at the War Office. In response to her claim that she disliked the idea, Haldane explained somewhat impatiently: 'I don't much like it [either], but it is not a question of liking but of duty. It appears unlikely that Crewe will be able for some time to come to stand any great strain of work and Morley is 73. Asquith feels that he must have someone in the Lords on whom he can rely. So I have agreed and I am to be Viscount Haldane of Cloan.'[5] He remained active as a lord of appeal in ordinary and as a member of the Judicial Committee to the end of his life. And, while many occupants of the highest legal office in the realm considered it an honour, Haldane considered it as a platform from which he could and did bring about changes in the life of the law of the United Kingdom. During those years he presided over many domestic cases but – as we shall see in due course – his Hegelian interests in the constitution of nations led him to focus his attention on the constitutional law of the British Empire which he viewed as the accumulation of Anglo-Saxon political wisdom and the greatest gift to the civilized world. For this reason, the new lord chancellor took special delight in his major responsibility to preside over the Judicial Committee, the highest court of appeal for the far-flung colonial possessions of the Empire.

The origins of this venerable institution lie back before the fifteenth century in the ashes of the Court of the Star Chamber.[6] After a series of changes over the ensuing three centuries, it took on its modern form with the reforms recommended by Lord Brougham in 1833. Prior to that date, none of the three privy councillors who constituted the committee was required to have judicial experience. After Lord Brougham's reforms, however, the Judicial Committee took on a formal judicial character. The Judicial Committee Act of 1833 required at least three qualified judges but they were to remain unpaid. In 1871 the government decided that judges of the Judicial Committee should be paid and members of the newly constituted court were drawn from those members of the House of Lords who were barristers. Haldane earned a sizeable £10,000 stipend per annum as lord chancellor; however generous for a public servant at the time, this was half of what he could have earned in private practice.

By the time of Haldane's appointment to the House of Lords, the appeal jurisdiction of the Judicial Committee covered more than a quarter of the earth's population. In addition to entertaining appeals from the dominions and the colonies, the Judicial Committee had jurisdiction over consular courts in China and in the dominions of the Ottoman Empire. The only domestic jurisdiction the Judicial Committee possessed, at the time, was over ecclesiastical causes arising from the Church of England.[7] 'Haldane made a point of presiding over the Judicial Committee in every important constitutional appeal whenever he could,' one authority has noted. 'He had a profound influence on the constitutional law of Canada. He sat on 32 appeals concerning the validity of Canadian legislation and gave judgement in 19 of them.'[8]

Viscount Haldane believed that the Judicial Committee played an essential role in cementing the bonds of the Empire. 'We sit there to administer Buddhist Law, or Hindu law or Mohammedan Law, one after the other,' he explained in a lecture to the University of Edinburgh Law Society during his first year as lord chancellor.[9] 'We administer Roman-Dutch law from South Africa or from Ceylon, French law from Quebec, or the common law of England for Ontario, or curious mixtures of law which prevail in various colonies, sometimes Italian Law, sometimes Roman.'[10] The Judicial Committee was the highest court of appeal for Canada as well as for Australia and New Zealand and other colonies and possessions of the Empire. In 1949 Canada ended appeals to the Judicial Committee, making its own Supreme Court the final court of appeal.[11] Appeals in criminal cases from Canada were terminated in 1935.[12] Most of the important disputes, however, between the provincial governments and the central government of Canada relating to the division powers under the British North America Act, 1867 were decided in the Judicial Committee well before 1949. Not infrequently Judicial Committee rulings reversed judgments of the Supreme Court of Canada or a provincial court of appeal.[13] It is no exaggeration to say that, in the important areas of the constitutional life of Canada, the law was made in the Judicial Committee. And no one made a greater contribution to the development of that law than Viscount Haldane sitting as a judge on that unique judicial body, where, he claimed, he showed 'a personal interest in Canadian appeals.'[14]

Just as he found when he went to the War Office, in the lord chancellor's office he inherited procedures and processes which had been in place for many years, and many of them were not to his liking. The office was, in fact, notoriously inefficient.[15] Some of the administrative procedures he found easy to reform but as a judge the one thing he could not change single-handed was the large body of judicial precedent by which he was bound. Technically speaking, judgments of the Judicial Committee constituted advice to the queen, which meant that only one decision was announced without a hint of disagreement or dissent among the other four members of the committee. Needless to say, there were no concurring decisions, either. The practice of issuing a single judgment frequently concealed from the formal record the dissenting reasons of other members of the board, thus giving a false sense of unanimity. The practice endured, however, until 1966, when the Judicial Committee announced that it would issue dissenting opinions whenever they arose; the new practice reveals more fully the interior dynamics of the proceedings and provides better guidance for future litigants.[16]

The work of sorting out the tangled clauses of the British North America Act, 1867 had begun before Haldane went to the Lords in 1911. Appeals from Canada began not many years after royal assent had been given to the terms of Confederation. More important, the new lord chancellor inherited the past decisions relating to Canada enunciated principally by his great Scottish predecessor, Lord Watson. Watson had presided over several important Canadian cases during his tenure on the bench – from 1888 to 1899 – and had begun to give a definite shape to the federal character of the Canadian constitution before Haldane arrived on the scene. The demands on this unique judicial body required that succeeding bancs of law lords – and occasionally senior judges from the dominion and colonies[17] – give due deference to the accumulated body of precedent enunciated by their predecessors. As the title suggests, the Judicial Committee is a committee of Her Majesty's Privy Council, the formal advisory body to the sovereign. To overrule past Judicial Committee precedents would be tantamount to repudiating the previous advice to the monarch as incorrect. Obviously, these demands placed members of the committee in a peculiar position – unlike any other judicial body – and severely restricted their freedom to develop the law in ways that departed from those of their predecessors. The wall of decisions left by Lord Watson in Canadian cases, in particular, constituted a serious challenge to Lord Chancellor Haldane, who had his own ideas as to how the constitution of the North American Dominion ought to be developed.

Lord Chancellor Haldane's predecessors, Lord Watson and other law lords of the Judicial Committee, struggled in a series of cases to make sense of the federal design ambiguously contained in the language of the British North America Act, 1867. Watson began the process of restricting the legislative intrusion of the Canadian Parliament and government into the legislative jurisdiction of the provinces by reducing the scope of several provisions of the constitution and by expanding others. During his tenure on the Judicial Committee, Watson undertook to rewrite the constitution in order to bring it into line with his views on what constituted a *federal* constitution. The British North America Act, 1867 simply stated that the Canadian provinces that were parties to the constitutional arrangement desired 'to be federally united in a Constitution similar in principle to that of the United Kingdom.' It then divided the legislative powers between the federal and provincial levels of government in two sections of the document, section 91 and section 92. But in doing so the act, while appearing to give each level of government 'exclusive' legislative jurisdiction in carefully enumerated 'classes of subjects,' incorporated a powerful tilt in favour of the central Parliament in several important areas of legislation, including taxation. The law lords of the Judicial Committee were called upon to resolve disputes arising under these ambiguous terms of the Canadian constitution. Viscount Haldane inherited the efforts of Lord Watson to resolve appeals from the Canadian provinces protesting against the intrusion into their 'exclusive' areas of legislative jurisdiction by the new national Parliament led by Sir John A. Macdonald. Watson's decisions in Canadian constitutional cases stood as a solid wall of precedents permitting room for few end runs. Haldane, however, found himself in fundamental agreement with the direction his predecessor had charted. It is no coincidence that the two names – Watson and Haldane – are almost always bound together in the annals of Canadian constitutional history. Haldane's views of the Canadian constitution were intimately tied to – if not restrained by – those of Lord Watson. To understand Haldane's impact on the Canadian constitution, therefore, it becomes necessary to understand the extent to which Watson influenced the course of Canadian constitutional jurisprudence throughout the years preceding Haldane's arrival on the Judicial Committee.

Lord Watson and Canadian Federalism

In many respects, Lord Watson's role in interpreting the British North America Act, 1867 requires an explanation more than Viscount Haldane's. Watson, almost singlehanded, chartered the course that Haldane and others followed. And that course was not only at variance with the course being taken in Canada by the Supreme Court of Canada; it was also at variance with the traditional deference to the legislature that had come to characterize judicial interpretation of statutes in British courts of law. Why did Watson give judicial sanction to the Canadian advocates of decentralization such as Oliver Mowat, aided by the forensic talents of Edward Blake? The Supreme Court of Canada had resisted these advocates. Why did this Scottish law lord champion the provincial autonomy movement in defiance of the language of the new constitution – a statute of the imperial Parliament – and of the emerging jurisprudence of the young Supreme Court of Canada? The answers lie in part in Watson's temperament and in his Scottish heritage. And, while Haldane did not share his temperament, he did share his Scottish heritage.[18]

William Watson (1827–99) was born the elder son of Thomas Watson, a minister of the Church of Scotland, and was educated at Glasgow and Edinburgh. Rather than follow his father into the ministry, Watson chose to pursue a career in law and was called to the bar of Scotland as an advocate (the Scottish equivalent of barrister) in 1851. Tracking his career and inner life as a lawyer and judge has been seriously restricted by the fact that he studiously avoided a paper trail. Except for the decisions he rendered as a judge, Lord Watson left very little else in writing. There are no Watson papers of any significance: no letters, no diaries, no drafts of judgments, no bench notes, no clippings chronicling his life and achievements. This is a great pity, for the surviving fragmentary accounts of his life and career make clear that he was a colourful character, and, as late as 1963, it was said that he had 'the mind of a master and the hand of a great craftsman.'[19]

The few short accounts of Watson's life that survive are expressed in general terms and written by former acquaintances upon his death in 1899. From these sources Watson emerges as a respected but unloved judge. The anonymous author of the tribute in the *Scottish Law Review* upon Watson's death, for example, is anything but flattering.[20] The photograph of the full-length portrait of Watson that accompanied the article shows him as a tall erect man of late middle years. He has a full head of unruly gray hair cut short with a full, closely cropped, grey beard. He has a strong face offset with a deep frown that betrays a man of impatience, as if ordering the portrait artist to hurry up. And impatient he surely was if the *Scottish Review* tribute is to be believed. He possessed, the author acknowledged, a 'voice of thunder for he became somewhat dull of hearing and was not aware of his tone.' 'His voice and figure and indeed his accent were unmistakably, but not offensively, Scotch.'[21] The author of the tribute, obviously an English barrister who had appeared before the judge, could not resist letting posterity know that Watson 'was no grammarian or philosopher: No one accustomed to listen to him could ever predict how any sentence was to end; and we are quite sure that many of his propositions ended in an entirely different manner from what their author intended or the listener expected.'[22] Pity the poor court stenographer, the author opined, who had to transcribe his oral arguments. The unidentified author of this tribute summed up Watson before his appointment to the bench as a 'plodding advocate and an indifferent politician' who won 'real fame in the House of Lords.' But, once on the bench of the House of Lords and the Judicial Committee, this 'plodding advocate' performed with the best of his colleagues. 'His opinions are in the books, and no one can read them without being struck by Watson's erudition and mastery of principles, and also by his luminous power of exposition.'[23]

This encomium strikes every student of the Canadian constitution who has had to follow Watson's line of reasoning in the *St. Catherine's Milling and Lumber Company* (1889) case with puzzlement. In that case Watson ruled that the federal government of Canada could legislate in aboriginal matters in 'unsurrendered lands it did not own' and the provincial governments 'could not legislate for or secure a surrender of lands it would own.'[24] Sidney L. Harring, author of *White Man's Law*, has observed that 'almost no part of its analysis, taken element by element, is good law.'[25] As late as 1997, the Supreme Court of Canada was still trying to make sense of Watson's judgment. In *Delgamuukw v. British Columbia*, Chief Justice Antonio Lamer ruled that Watson's definition of aboriginal land tenure in *St. Catherine's Milling and Lumber* was not helpful: 'The subsequent jurisprudence has attempted to grapple with this definition and has in the process demonstrated that the Privy Council choice of terminology is not particularly helpful to explain the various dimensions of Indian title.'[26] This hardly constituted a ringing endorsement of the precedent.

But, whatever his personal idiosyncrasies, Lord Watson played a major role 'in determining that the policy and practice of the privy council in Canadian appeals was of capital constitutional importance and his mastery of English law, if less conspicuous, was hardly less consummate; the English bench and bar came to look on him as one of their own.'[27] Thus, the *Oxford Dictionary of Biography* concluded its account of Lord Watson's life with this final glance back at the judge – replete with tantalizing qualifiers.

Upon the death of Lord Gordon in 1879 Watson had been appointed by Disraeli a Lord of Appeal in Ordinary. In May, 1880, he was created a life peer with the title of Baron Watson of Thankerton. From that date until his death nineteen years later in 1899 Watson was a formidable presence in the judicial proceedings of the House of Lords and before the Judicial Committee especially in Canadian appeals. Upon Watson's death at the age of 72, in 1899, Viscount Haldane paid formal tribute to his predecessor praising him for rendering:

> an enormous service to the Empire and to the Dominion of Canada by developing the Dominion constitution. At one time, after the BNA Act of 1867 was passed, the conception took hold of the Canadian courts that what was intended was to make the Dominion the centre of government in Canada, so that its statutes and its position should be superior to the statutes and position of the Provincial Legislatures. That went so far that there rose a great fight, and as the result of a long series of decisions Lord Watson put clothing upon the bones of the Constitution, and so covered them over with living flesh that the constitution of Canada took a new form. The provinces were recognized as an equal authority coordinate with the Dominion, and a long series of decisions were given by him which solved many problems and produced a new contentment in Canada with the constitution they had got in 1867.[28]

This fulsome assessment of Lord Watson's contribution to the constitutional life of Canada was received in some quarters of the young Dominion with a mixture of disbelief and outrage. The legacy of the Canadian fathers of Confederation was still fresh in the minds of most Canadians living at this time and they bristled at the suggestion that the Canadian constitution required 'clothing' let alone 'living flesh.' They thought that the 'clothing' and 'living flesh' had been quite satisfactorily provided in 1867. What is striking here is the fact that Haldane's language is almost verbatim the language used by Edward Blake before the Judicial Committee in the *St. Catherine's Milling and Lumber* case. Haldane appeared in this case as Horace Davey's junior and heard Edward Blake describe the British North America Act as 'in many points little more than a skeleton, which is to be clothed with flesh and muscle, nerve and sinew, into which the breath of life is to be breathed by interpretation.'[29]

But, since the Judicial Committee was the highest court of appeal for Canada, the development of the Canadian constitution was, ultimately, in the hands of law lords, such as William Watson, sitting at 11 Downing Street, London. This is not to overlook the fact that the Supreme Court of Canada wrestled seriously with major constitutional issues before they went on appeal to the Judicial Committee. Many of those early Canadian decisions, as Richard Risk has noted, 'tended to favour the Dominion.'[30] Canada's highest court was beginning, throughout the latter half of the nineteenth century, to enunciate a body of constitutional law arising out of its own experiences and history. But those efforts were to be set aside or ignored by the Judicial Committee, especially under Watson and Haldane.

The principal task that faced the judges of the Judicial Committee in the early litigation coming on appeal from Canada was to respond to the emerging provincial claims to greater legislative authority and protection against the central Parliament's legislative intrusions. The political life of the new Dominion was characterized by squabbling between the provincial politicians and their federal counterparts in Ottawa sitting in the new capital complete with an impressive and massive Parliament building. Both levels of government pointed to the terms of the constitution, which tended on its face to give overriding authority to the central Parliament and government, reducing the provincial governments and legislatures to subordinate bodies. To rub salt in the provincial wounds, the constitution armed the federal government with the powers of 'reservation and disallowance' whereby the national government could set aside any item of provincial legislation and, if it so wished, disallow it. The provisions tended to make a mockery of the constitution's pretence to be a federal constitution. The provinces argued that the terms as understood by the central government were not consistent with their understanding of the federal character of the new constitution. In short, the crucial question quickly became: To what extent was the constitution of Canada truly a *federal* constitution where the two levels of government possessed exclusive legislative jurisdiction immune from the interference of the other level?

When one looks carefully at the wording of the British North America Act, 1867, where both levels of government are granted 'exclusive' legislative authority, it comes as no surprise that the new constitution gave rise to a great deal of litigation concerning areas of overlap (such as taxation). But the framers at Quebec knew this and were confident that any judicial resolution of conflicting claims would result in a victory for the central Parliament and government.[31] Disputes between the federal and provincial governments erupted almost immediately after Confederation, leading to litigation before the highest courts of Canada and the Judicial Committee. In the minds of the early authoritative commentators on the British North America Act, 1867, such as Robert MacGregor Dawson, there was no disputing that the intention in 1867 'was to create a strongly centralized federation, and to that end the Dominion was endowed with very substantial authority.'[32] 'For over twenty years after Confederation,' Dawson went on to say, 'these parts of the British North America Act [sections 91 and 92] were interpreted in accord with the original intentions [of those who wrote the constitution].'[33] 'But the Judicial Committee through a long series of decisions has succeeded in substantially frustrating this intention and supplying an interpretation of its own which seems far removed from the text.'[34] There is little doubt in anyone's mind that, whether one agrees or disagrees with the jurisprudence of the Judicial Committee of the Privy Council, Lord Watson and his successor, Viscount Haldane, interpreted the terms of the original constitution to produce a more 'workable federal' constitution for Canada.[35]

Neither Watson nor Haldane were working from an a priori abstraction of an 'ideal' federal state or constitution. No such thing existed then or today. In the nineteenth century, the leading example of a federal constitution was the United States. But even that state was required to correct the earlier attempt to establish a federal constitution under the Articles of Confederation, which broke down for want of 'energy in the executive' power at the national level.[36] The constitution that emerged from the convention in Philadelphia in 1787 states that 'the People of the United States, in order to form a more perfect Union, establish Justice, insure domestic Tranquility, provide for the common defence, promote the general Welfare and secure the Blessing of Liberty to ourselves and our Posterity, do ordain and establish this Constitution for the United States of America.' We have no way of knowing whether Watson or Haldane had ever read the *Federalist Papers* or any British authority on the American federal system, such as Edward Freeman's *History of the Federal Government, from the Foundations of the Achaian League to the Disruption of the United States,* published in 1863.[37] There is little or no evidence that British judges, including law lords, read such material. Nevertheless, for whatever reason, 'by the end of the [nineteenth] century, the Judicial Committee had imposed a radically different template on sections 91 and 92, and [had] authoritatively asserted the independent status of the lieutenant governor as the representative of the crown for all purposes of provincial government. However mysterious the inner workings of the committee, the author of the decisions embodying the new doctrines was William Watson.'[38] This 'new doctrine,' beginning with the reduction of the force of the 'Peace, Order, and good Government clause' at the head of section 91 which began principally under Watson's guidance, makes it necessary to understand clearly the extent of his impact on the critical terms of the constitution. Watson set down how the courts should interpret the terms of the British North America Act, 1867, so as to reduce the legislative authority of the federal Parliament and increase the legislative authority of the provinces. And Viscount Haldane built upon that legacy.

The major constitutional question that dominated constitutional litigation during Watson's tenure on the Judicial Committee was, in a nutshell, this: How could the courts – the Supreme Court of Canada and the Judicial Committee – enforce the terms of the constitution of 1867, which, on its face, gave the Parliament of Canada a dominant jurisdiction over the provinces in apparent defiance of the minimum conditions of a federal constitution where the component parts, the provinces, are granted certain legislative powers beyond the reach of the federal Parliament or government.

The conflicts that emerged over the proper construction of the division of legislative powers between the federal Parliament and the provincial legislatures dominated most of the litigation. Section 91, which outlined the legislative powers of the federal Parliament, gave the central government the broad power 'to make laws for the Peace, Order, and good Government of Canada' and then listed twenty-nine areas of legislation that belonged 'exclusively' to the federal Parliament. But that listing was grammatically governed by the words: 'and for greater Certainty, but not so as to restrict the Generality of the foregoing Terms [POGG] of this Section.' Among other matters, the enumerated powers contained authority over 'any mode or system of taxation' and 'the regulation of trade and commerce' as well as the criminal law of the country. Unlike the constitution of the United States, where authority of the Congress is restricted in these matters, the language of the new Canadian constitution contained no such restrictions. The section concluded with the rider: 'And any matter coming within any of the Classes of Subjects enumerated in this Section shall not be deemed to come within the Class of Matters of a local or private Nature comprised in the Enumeration of Classes of Subjects by this Act assigned exclusively to the Legislatures of the Provinces.'[39] The legislative powers of the federal Parliament could hardly have been more precisely enunciated. By contrast, the section outlining the legislative powers of the provinces could hardly have been more confusing. Section 92 simply stated: 'In each Province the Legislature may exclusively make Laws in relation to Matters coming within the Classes of Subjects next hereinafter enumerated.' In the previous section, the federal Parliament was given general taxing power covering 'any Mode or System of Taxation' and for unspecified general purposes. The provincial legislatures were restricted to 'Direct Taxation within the Province in order to the raising of a Revenue for Provincial Purposes.' These provisions of the British North America Act, 1867 prompted most of the litigation during the early years of the country's history.

The history of litigation between the federal government and the provinces shows, without question, that there was a serious conflict between the highest Canadian courts and the Judicial Committee. By following the long-established British practice, the Supreme Court attempted to resolve the jurisdictional conflicts between the levels of government on the basis of the written language of the document; it understood its responsibility as being to give force and effect to the intention of the legislature, the Parliament of Great Britain, as expressed in the language of the act, to provide Canada with a strong central Parliament. As Sir John A. Macdonald said in explaining the proposed constitution for a united Canada: 'Here we have adopted a different system [from the United States]. We have strengthened the

Central Government. We have given the General Legislature all the great subjects of legislation. We have conferred on them, not only specifically and in detail, all the powers which are incident to sovereignty, but we have expressly declared that the subjects of general interest not distinctly and exclusively conferred upon the local governments, and local legislatures, shall be conferred upon the General Government and Legislature.'[40] And Macdonald added in order to emphasize the distinctive character of the proposed union: 'We have thus avoided that great source of weakness which has been the cause of the disruption of the United States. We have avoided all conflict of jurisdiction and authority.'[41]

The Supreme Court of Canada, established by federal legislation in 1875,[42] had to wait only two years before being required to settle a conflict over the taxing power of the provinces. In *Severn v. The Queen*, (1877),[43] the court was obliged to pass on the constitutionality of an Ontario law requiring brewers to take out a licence for selling fermented or malt liquors at wholesale. A divided court decided against the government of Ontario and in favour of the federal Parliament's jurisdiction to level taxes in an area where the federal Parliament had already legislated. The question not only was whether the licence was a tax but whether it fell within the legislative authority of the Ontario legislature to pass the legislation given its restricted taxing powers. The court majority, led by the chief justice, Sir William Buell Richards, argued that the court was obliged to look at the intention of the framers and not merely at the language of the act. Above all, the chief justice contended, the court must bear in mind the overall intention of the Canadian fathers of Confederation to avoid 'the difficulties which had arisen in the great Federal Republic.'[44] Richards and the court majority insisted that the new Canadian constitution was intended to prevent the possibility of strong provinces arising; the provinces were, hence, to be restricted to very limited and specified powers. The United States offered a recent history of what happened when provinces or states became strong in a federation. Richard accordingly ruled that the intention of the framers of the act with respect to taxation was obvious 'beyond all doubt.'[45]

In this very first important constitutional case, the court majority set down its canons of judicial construction before the Judicial Committee imposed its own as a 'corrective.' The Supreme Court of Canada clearly attempted to follow the rule that judges take into account 'the position of those who framed the Laws and give assistance in interpreting the words used and the object to which they are directed.'[46]

Chief Justice Richards concluded: 'I consider the power now claimed to interfere in the paramount authority of the Dominion Parliament in matters of trade and commerce and indirect taxation so pregnant with evil, and so contrary to what was intended by the framers of the British North America Act, that I cannot come to the conclusion it is conferred by the language cited as giving that power.'[47] The central issue before the Canadian courts, not just the Supreme Court of Canada, was the appropriate canons of judicial construction.

The results of *Severn* were scarcely in print before the Supreme Court of Canada found itself faced with a series of cases involving other major constitutional issues. Beginning with *Valin v. Langlois*[48] and *Lenoir v. Ritchie*,[49] both in 1879, the Supreme Court of Canada interpreted the constitution as Chief Justice Richards had done in *Severn*. The court made it clear in *Valin* that the 'Peace, Order, and good Government' clause of the constitution authorized the federal Parliament to enter areas of provincial jurisdiction. The proper approach to judicial construction was by way of the plain words of the act in concert with the intention of Parliament. The court also intimated that it was willing to take into consideration the views of the Canadian legislators who took part in the Confederation conferences leading up to the drafting and adoption of the constitution.

By setting out the proper terms of judicial construction of the British North America Act, 1867, the Supreme Court hoped that it would guide the law lords on the Judicial Committee. As we shall see, this hope was not to be realized. For a time, in the early cases before the Judicial Committee, the law lords followed the traditional British rules of statutory construction as the Supreme Court of Canada had done. Prior to Lord Watson assuming his place on the Judicial Committee, the law lords tended to favour the federal government and viewed the emerging Canadian constitutional jurisprudence with a measure of deference. In the Canada Temperance Act case of 1882, for example, the Judicial Committee sided with the Supreme Court of Canada and held the federal act valid under the 'Peace, Order, and good Government' powers of the Parliament of Canada.

This initial support of the Judicial Committee for Canadian court rulings in constitutional cases was to change permanently and dramatically with the arrival of Lord Watson in 1888. He showed almost immediately that he was resistant to colonial instruction and was demonstrably more sympathetic to provincial legislative ambitions. According to John T. Saywell, who has written the most exhaustive account of Watson's impact on the constitutional jurisprudence of Canada, Watson unabashedly reshaped the constitution of Canada through a series of decisions where he interpreted the terms of the constitutional text of 1867 beyond recognition. In the final analysis, Watson, Saywell records, did nothing less than 'reconstruct Canadian federalism to his own satisfaction';[50] he virtually wrote 'the text for symmetrical federalism.' And so the victory for the federal Parliament in the Canada Temperance Act case was to be short-lived.

The great constitutional debate between the federal Parliament and the provincial legislatures over the division of powers did not take place exclusively in the judicial forum. These were turbulent political times throughout the new Dominion when the provinces were beginning to exercise their legislative powers and serve notice that they were not going to take an overbearing federal government – even aided by the Supreme Court – sitting down. Strong provincial leaders such as Oliver Mowat in Ontario and Honoré Mercier in Quebec made it indelibly clear that, no matter how the act of Confederation was worded, they were going to exercise their provincial strength.

Lord Watson was not one to allow an inconvenient precedent to get in his way; neither was he reluctant to give the back of his hand to a fellow judge.[51] In one of his most important cases dealing with the Canadian constitution, *Attorney General for Ontario v. Attorney General for the Dominion* (1896),[52] Watson dismissed the opinion of Sir Montague Smith, issued in *Citizens' Insurance v. Parsons*,[53] fourteen years before, when he restricted the reach of the 'Peace, Order, and good Government' clause. 'The observation was,' Watson said in passing, 'not material to the question arising in that case, and it does not appear to their Lordships to be strictly accurate.'[54] This was typical of 'Old Bluster,' as Watson was known by some, dismissing the arguments of an opponent rather than engaging them on their merits. Sir Montague Smith was a wise and learned judge and deserved greater respect. But that was not Watson's style. After appearing to agree with the previous decisions of the Supreme Court of Canada that the 'Peace, Order, and good Government' clause of the constitution was meant to be read broadly as the wording of the section appeared to imply, Watson ruled in the local prohibition case that the clause should be restricted to 'exceptional circumstances.' And in this case he also restricted the authority of the federal Parliament to incorporate companies to 'dominion companies' only, formally excluding the federal government from intruding into provincial powers of incorporation.

In addition to restricting the scope of 'Peace, Order, and good Government' and emasculating the trade and commerce clause in the local prohibition case, Watson made several attempts to narrow the federal powers and expand the provincial powers. He ruled, for example, that the provincial jurisdiction over 'property and civil rights' in the provinces was an area in which the federal government could not enter easily, if at all, not even armed with 'Peace, Order, and good Government,' unless in 'exceptional circumstances.' It is also worth noting that Watson introduced into the constitutional debate the notion of 'provincial autonomy.' Nowhere in the constitutional act of 1867 is there to be found anything remotely suggestive of 'provincial autonomy.' Indeed, it can be argued from the debates that took place at the Quebec Conference in 1865 that the leading constitutional framers – such as Macdonald, George Brown, and Charles Tupper[55] – took pains to ensure that 'autonomous' provinces would not emerge. It was their view that 'states rights' contributed much to sparking the American Civil War. They took steps to prevent this occurring in Canada by avoiding anything like 'provincial rights' or 'provincial autonomy.'

The question that nags at the student of Watson's rulings on the Canadian constitution is: Why did he depart so significantly from the more moderate previous judgments of the Judicial Committee which tended to respect the intentions of the Canadian framers of the constitution? What drove him, or, better still, who influenced him? Watson came to the highest courts in the land, the House of Lords and the Judicial Committee, as Viscount Haldane acknowledged, 'knowing nothing [and] became a great English lawyer.'[56] How did this narrowly trained Scottish advocate presume to treat the terms of the constitution of Canada in such a cavalier manner? As a partial answer to all these questions, it has been suggested that, as a Scot and sensitive to Scottish nationalist aspirations, Watson naturally gravitated towards 'provincial autonomy.' His Scottish roots led him to be distrustful of a centralized control of local matters. The Scots had resented the inability to administer their own local affairs since the Act of Union in 1707. There is considerable merit to this proposition; it explains the passion with which Watson pursued the cause of 'autonomy' for the Canadian provinces in defiance of the terms of the Confederation act.

But another factor may have been at work too. Watson grew up in a Scotland at a time when Scots had begun to reassert their Celtic pride and demand more local control. Did his Scottish background push him in this direction? Or did some one pull him in the direction of autonomous provinces? Perhaps someone who appeared before him impressed him with arguments in favour of greater Canadian provincial autonomy. One of the obituary notices remarked that he delighted in sparring with counsel and who among the outstanding 'silks' who appeared before him could have withstood the verbal badgering of this brusque Scot? There is no record of any of the leading barristers openly standing up to Watson in court. So who among the leading counsel of the day could have presumed to instruct Lord Watson on the nature of federal constitutions? All reasonable suspicions point to one man, someone who knew a great deal about federal constitutions – far more than any other English barrister – and was persuasive before the bench. That man was Judah Benjamin, an outstanding barrister who appeared frequently before the House of Lords and the Judicial Committee. Benjamin had participated in nine Canadian constitutional cases between 1874 and 1882.[57]

As the attorney general and secretary of war in the government of Jefferson Davis during the American Civil War, Benjamin had clear views on federalism and was a strong proponent of state autonomy. The fact that he appeared as frequently on behalf of the federal government in these cases as he did for the provinces does not diminish the likely impact of his views on the federal character of the new constitution for Canada. That constitution formally announced that the parties to the Confederation desired 'to be federally united.' The issue became: How can the terms of the entire act be construed in the light of that overarching objective? In only one of these cases, *Dobie v. The Temporalities Board*, did Benjamin appear before Watson. In this, his first Canadian constitutional case, Watson upheld the federal Parliament's power to create a corporation which operated in the provinces of Ontario and Quebec. In addition, the board ruled that the Quebec Act, which presumed to repeal and amend the federal act and to destroy the corporation created by federal statute and replace it with a new one, was ultra vires the Quebec legislature. Watson also wrote that it was beyond the powers of the provincial legislatures to alter materially the class of persons interested in the corporate funds. Benjamin had argued that the provincial acts in dispute were valid and binding. 'It is not the case,' he reasoned, 'that the powers of the dominion and provincial Legislature are mutually exclusive.'[58] Watson countered this line of reasoning with the comment that

the general scheme of the British North America Act, 1867, and in particular the general scope and effect of sections 91 and 92 have been so fully commented upon by this Board in the recent cases of the *Citizen Insurance Company of Canada v. Parsons*, and the *Queen Insurance Company v. Parsons* that it is unnecessary to say anything further upon that subject. Their Lordships see no reason to modify in any respect the principles of law upon which they proceeded in deciding those cases; but in determining how far these principles apply to the present case it is necessary to consider to what extent the circumstances of each case are identical or similar.[59]

Watson went on to explain the controlling precedents by stating that there are two steps to reaching the conclusion as to identity or similarity. The first thing a judge must do in determining whether an act of a provincial legislature is intra vires is to see if it is authorized by the terms in section 92 of the act, not by first viewing it through the terms of section 91. 'If it does not then the Act is of no validity. If it does then these further questions may arise, viz., "whether notwithstanding that it is so the subject of the Act does not also fall within one of the enumerated classes of subjects in sect. 91, and whether the power of the provincial Legislature is or is not thereby overborne."'[60] In *Dobie*, the court adopted a reverse two-step approach in resolving disputes between the federal government and the province. It is passing coincidence that this was precisely the approach recommended by Benjamin. Such an approach gives an undue weight to the provinces because the constitution act states that the provincial powers are 'exclusive,' which implied that they were *in some sense* beyond the reach of central government jurisdiction. And Judah Benjamin knew that better, perhaps, than members of the Judicial Committee. In the *Dobie* case Benjamin lost. But did he win in the sense that he sowed the seeds for the reverse two-step approach noted by Watson? In due course this approach would lead to provincial autonomy and the reduction of the scope of the 'Peace, Order, and good Government' clause of section 91, and towards a more fully 'federal' constitution for Canada. It should be noted that Judah Benjamin appeared before Watson in the House of Lords several times in Watson's first years on the high bench, and Watson must surely have known of Benjamin's reputation as a lawyer of extraordinary ability.[61] But Benjamin had only two years before Watson to make his mark on the man, for in late December 1882 he suffered a severe heart attack that forced him into retirement. He died at his home in Paris on 6 May 1884 at the age of seventy-three.[62]

There is no intention here to suggest that Judah Benjamin taught

Watson all he knew about 'federalism.' Watson had not time for theoretical abstractions; he was no philosopher, as his obituary notices insist. In fact, Watson never talks about federalism in his judgments or elsewhere, as Haldane was later to do. As well, there was very little literature available on the subject of federalism for any British judge to consider even if he wished to do so. The leading authorities on federalism at the time that were consulted by the Canadian fathers of Confederation were, as we have seen, the American *Federalist Papers* and Edward A. Freeman, an Oxford history don, who wrote *History of Federal Government*.[63]

One thing is certain: Watson's clear departure from the line of reasoning of his predecessors requires an explanation, especially in light of Lord Hobhouse's decision in *Bank of Toronto v. Lambe* (1887), one year before Watson went to the House of Lords.[64] In that case, involving the power of the provinces to levy taxes on companies carrying on business within the province, Hobhouse ruled that 'questions of this class have been left for the decision of the ordinary Courts of law, which must treat the provisions of the Act in question by the same methods of construction and exposition which they apply to other statutes.'[65] As Saywell has observed, the *Lambe* decision made it clear that the law lords implied that 'cases arising under the BNA Act would be determined "by the same methods of construction and exposition" applied to any other case, pleading strict rules of statutory construction and refusing to examine extrinsic aids or Canadian context.'[66] Lord Watson clearly departed from this approach by first restricting the power of the federal Parliament to legislate for the 'Peace, Order, and good Government' of Canada when the act explicitly draws attention to its scope by stating 'notwithstanding anything in this Act.' But he gave the coup de grâce to Macdonald's constitution in *Liquidators of the Maritime Bank v. The Receiver General of New Brunswick*.[67] There, Watson ruled that 'a Lieutenant-Governor, when appointed, is as much the representative of Her Majesty for all purposes of provincial government as the Governor-General himself is for all purposes of Dominion governments.'[68]

This was a critical judgment, for once the crown was located in the provinces it was an easy step to talk about 'autonomy' of the provinces.[69] Watson claimed that 'it would require very express language, such as is not to be found in the Act of 1867, to warrant the inference that the Imperial Legislature meant to vest in the provinces of Canada the right of exercising supreme legislative powers in which the British Sovereign was to have no share.'[70] In brief, he argued that such an important constitutional proposition could not have been intended without explicit instructions, or 'express language,' to do so. And no express language abolishing the place of the queen in the legislative life of the provinces could be found. No one can fault Watson in this matter. For it was perfectly reasonable for him to require explicit provision for the extinguishment of the formal relation of the crown with the colonies, now called provinces. The Confederation debates in all the colonial legislatures debated this point extensively and the grand centralizers, such as Macdonald, Tupper, and Cartier, all responded to this issue by saying that the new constitution created anew – 'de novo' was the expression used – the relationship of the British North American colonies with the mother country. The four parts or provinces were to come together to form one, single constitutional entity with one formal tie to the British crown through the governor general of Canada. In the view of the centralizers, Part III of the Confederation act titled 'Executive Power' had done this. That part reads:

All Powers, Authorities, and Functions which under any Act of the Parliament of Great Britain, or of the Parliament of the United Kingdom of Great Britain and Ireland, or of the Legislature of Upper Canada, Lower Canada, Canada, Nova Scotia, or New Brunswick, are at the Union vested in or exerciseable by the respective Governors or Lieutenant Governors of those Provinces, with the Advice, or with the Advice and Consent, of their respective Executive Councils thereof, or in conjunction with those Councils, or with any Number of Members thereof, or by those Governors or Lieutenant Governors individually, shall, as far as the same continue in existence and capable of being exercised after the Union in relation to the Government of Canada, be vested in and exerciseable by the Governor General.

The language of this provision was not sufficiently precise or explicit for Watson. He ruled that the framers of the act failed to bring about the extinguishment of the direct relation of the crown to the provinces in a specific manner. This failure left the provinces with the perfect right to petition the imperial courts to have their long-established direct relationship with the crown – which prevailed in each province at the time of union – be recognized in law, so that that the lieutenant governor would be recognized as the direct representative of the crown.

But how can one say that section 12, cited above, did not make the extinguishment clear? Lord Watson never answered this question because he did not take it into account. He implied strongly that the termination of the direct provincial tie to the crown could be accomplished only by an explicit statement to that effect. He could find no such statement.

However important this step was in the constitutional development of the Canadian provinces, it was only the beginning of the provincial trek towards a fully fledged autonomous legislative status. More remained to be done, especially with respect to the clarification as to the scope of provincial legislative powers in light of the 'Peace, Order, and good Government' clause at the head of section 91. On its face the act seemed to imply a strong national government with clearly subordinate provinces.

Had Watson consulted the available legislative history, that is, the account of the debates in the Parliament of Canada which took place in 1865 as well as the record of the debates that took place in the other colonial legislatures when this subject was discussed at great length, he might have come away with a different understanding of the issues. But he did not consult those discussions and rejected every effort of counsel to bring them to bear on the issues; he looked for a clear statement terminating the office of the crown in the provinces and studiously avoided legislative history.

Clearly, Watson's rulings were more in keeping with the basic features of a federal constitution where the two orders of government – the central or federal legislature and the provincial legislatures – are assigned autonomous legislative powers. The fundamental principle of a federal constitution is that one level of government may not invade the other level's assigned legislative jurisdiction. The British North America Act, 1867 permitted the federal Parliament to invade and regulate provincial areas of jurisdiction by way of 'reservation' and 'disallowance.' In short, the Canadian constitution did not meet the basic requirements of a workable federal constitution where the central government may not invade the jurisdiction of the component parts. But it reflected the wishes of the Canadian fathers of Confederation to provide a constitution with a strong central government. Someone had to have instructed this aggressive judge and it is not likely that it was another judge on the bench with him. We do not even know whether they ever circulated their reasons for judgment before they were published. As shocking as this sounds, we have it on the testimony of Viscount Haldane himself that he published judgments before showing them to his colleagues. On one occasion he sent a draft copy of a Judicial Committee judgment to his closest personal friend, Sir Edmund Gosse, librarian of the House of Lords, asking for his comments.[71] On another occasion, in an unnamed

Quebec case, Haldane explicitly told Gosse that he planned to publish the decision without showing his colleagues. 'My colleagues will probably argue when they read it in print, but it has gone to press.'[72] So much for collegiality.

The few times the record provides a transcript of what took place in the course of a case before the Judicial Committee, as in *Local Prohibition*, historians get an entirely different picture of the intensity of the debate among members of the board during contentious cases. The *Local Prohibition* case is especially important because the major players in the court drama included Edward Blake, one of Canada's most distinguished lawyers, famous for his eloquence and leader of the Liberal Party between 1880 and 1887; he was also a relentless critic of the chief architect of Confederation and its first prime minister, John A. Macdonald, who championed the cause of a strong central government. Serving with Blake in this case was none other than E.L. Newcombe, the federal deputy minister of justice who brought with him years of experience in framing legislation and appearing before the Supreme Court of Canada in constitutional cases; he was elevated to the Supreme Court of Canada as a puisne judge in 1924. On the other side of the case, for the distillers and brewers of Ontario, were Richard Haldane, who was in mid-career as a member of Parliament and as a barrister, and Wallace Nesbitt, a man with an outstanding reputation throughout Canada as a lawyer. It was a clash of titans by every measure and the judges before whom this great contest took place included Lord Ferrar Herschell, Lord Horace Davey (in whose chambers Haldane served as a junior), and, on the board, Lord Watson. The Judicial Committee was presided over by Lord Halsbury as lord chancellor, before whom Haldane had appeared several times; it was Lord Chancellor Halsbury, indeed, who handed Haldane his patent when he took silk in 1890.

The Ontario Liquor Licence Act was a clever attempt to reach back into pre-Confederation provincial law and resurrect provincial legislative authority over the sale and consumption of alcohol, a subject that the federal Parliament had already legislated upon in the Canada Temperance Act. The government of Ontario argued that municipalities should have the powers by them formerly possessed and declared:

The council of every township, city, town, and incorporated village may pass by-laws for prohibiting the sale by retail of spirituous, fermented, or other manufactured liquors in any tavern, inn, or other house or place of public entertainment, and for prohibiting altogether the sale thereof in shops and places

Viscount Haldane of Cloan, lord chancellor.
(Henry Walter ['H. Walter'] Barnett, National Portrait Gallery, London)

Herbert Henry Asquith, Earl of Asquith and Oxford.
(André Cluysenaar, National Portrait Gallery, London)

Edward, Earl Grey of Fallodon.
(Harold Speed, National Portrait Gallery, London)

Haldane in Berlin, 1906.
(*Haldane: 1856–1915* by Sir Frederick Maurice, Faber and Faber, 1937)

Sir George Jessel, master of the rolls, Professor Hermann Lotze of Göttingen, Horace Davey. (*Richard Burdon Haldane: An Autobiography* by Richard Haldane, Hodder and Stoughton, 1929)

Haldane family home, Perthshire.

(Richard Burdon Haldane: An Autobiography by Richard Haldane, Hodder and Stoughton, 1929)

Lord Haldane and Professor Albert Einstein at Queen Anne's Gate, 1921.

(*Richard Burdon Haldane: An Autobiography* by Richard Haldane, Hodder and Stoughton, 1929)

Mary Elizabeth Haldane, mother of Richard Burdon Haldane.
(*Mary Elizabeth Haldane: A Record of a Hundred Years*, edited by her daughter,
Hodder and Stoughton, 1925)

other than houses of public entertainment ... nothing in this section contained shall be construed into an exercise of jurisdiction by the Legislature of the province of Ontario beyond the *revival of provisions of law which were in force at the date of the passing of the British North America Act,* and which the subsequent legislation of this province purported to repeal.[73]

The Ontario act was a direct challenge to the view of the constitutional framers that the Confederation act of union had the legal effect of an entirely new beginning, that the provinces did not bring with them into Confederation a residue of former colonial powers. The radical reformulation of legislative powers, both at the national level and at the provincial level, was at the heart of the national-provincial disputes that led to so much litigation. To Watson, the Scot who chafed under the centralization of Scottish affairs in London, this must have been grist to his mill. How could he not have seen that the national government of the new Canada was centralizing powers over local affairs – the regulation of liquor – that properly and formerly belonged to the provinces? After much convoluted and tortuous debate before the Judicial Committee, where Watson repeatedly interrupted Canadian counsel, 'Old Bluster' ruled that 'the exercise of legislative power by the Parliament of Canada, in regard to all matters not enumerated in s.91, ought to be strictly confined to such matters as are unquestionably of Canadian interest and importance, and ought not to trench upon provincial legislation with respect to any of the classes of subjects in s.92.'[74]

Watson and Scottish Nationalism

Saywell was one of the first commentators on Watson's constitutional jurisprudence in Canadian cases to mention that Watson's Scottish nationalism was, to a considerable extent, grounds for his decentralization of the Canadian constitution. 'However much Watson may have professed to rely on the "plain meaning of the words in the constitution," in both argument and decision he enthusiastically engaged in substantive, if idiosyncratic lawmaking, which might have had roots more personal and experiential. For his comments in arguments and *dicta* in decision do reveal that he had an instinctive predisposition both to decentralization and to judicial lawmaking, which might be expected from a partially assimilated Scots lawyer trained in the civil law.'[75] This leads Saywell to acknowledge that Watson's legal training was decisively different from that of his fellow English-trained judges, for whom precedent and central government control were part and parcel of their legal upbringing, as well as judicial deference to the will of Parliament.

The Scottish Watson viewed a precedent that obstructed his line of reasoning as a challenge to be 'distinguished' out of the way, not as a binding authority pointing the way. Because of the unavailability of personal papers and letters, we may never know what motivated him to become a lawmaker determined to champion the cause of provincial autonomy. The exchange between Richard Haldane, a Scot also but trained in English law at the Inns of Court, and Lord Watson during the *Local Prohibition* case sheds a little but not a great deal of light upon the subject. Haldane appeared in this case on behalf of the province of Ontario and announced that he had it 'on high authority' how the question of alcohol regulation had come up for legislation by the province. Then he embarked on a brief history: 'The Temperance party in Parliament there, is pressing very strongly for legislation' and the government of Ontario was uncertain as to its powers to regulate the liquor trade.

This history lesson led Watson to interrupt Haldane and engage him in a conversation as to the laws regulating pubs in Scotland. They sparred back and forth for a time, convinced that there was something to be learned for the Canadian case from the fact that rural pubs in Scotland were required to close at 9:00 and 9:30 p.m. while city pubs were permitted to remain open until 11 p.m. 'The scheme of the [Ontario] Act is local,' Haldane insisted, 'and its purpose is to deal with something in the nature of a local regulation or restriction.'[76] Haldane struggled to keep *Hodge* before their lordships. The board had ruled in *Hodge* that the province of Ontario Liquor Licence Act, 1877 was a valid item of legislation in the interest of regulating a purely local matter for the good governance of taverns and pubs.[77] This exchange might not have been the deciding factor in his decision, but Watson ruled for the province of Ontario.

Watson's efforts to reduce the scope of the 'Peace, Order, and good Government' clause of section 91, to affirm the lieutenant governor as the direct representative of the queen in the provinces, and to define the powers of the provincial legislatures more precisely took hold of the fundamental law of Canada. He was never universally loved, neither at home nor in Canada. But his legacy is firmly entrenched – for better or for worse. Saywell claims that Watson's decisions and especially his obiter dicta 'reveal that he had an instinctive predisposition both to decentralization and to judicial lawmaking.' Surely, there is no question that Watson's political background and legal training placed him squarely in the midst of the life of Scotland. During his lifetime, Scottish nationalism – arising out of discontent with control from London – was gaining considerable ground, especially since Prime Minister Gladstone had supported Home Rule for the Irish.

In 1886 an Edinburgh citizen, Charles Waddie, formed what quickly became known as the Scottish Home Rule movement. Even the volatile John Stuart Blackie joined it. Blackie was elected its chairman at a meeting in Glasgow in 1888 and threw his considerable energies behind the movement. The one thing that Scots chafed under since the Act of Union was the lack of power over local matters; the prevailing political order enforced a centralization where local Scottish affairs were decided in distant London at the hands of non-Scots. Blackie, no secessionist, called for a reform that would see the Scottish members of Parliament meet for six or eight weeks in Edinburgh to decide local Scottish issues; upon completion of this part of their work, members would go to Westminster and participate in the great affairs of the larger nation. Blackie believed that 'it was desirable that as much local individuality as possible should be preserved in the component parts of a great empire – as much as was consistent with unity of action and subordination to a central authority in all matters of general concern.'[78] But Blackie saw this accommodation to local Scottish interest as a transitional move. What he urged upon his audience was a form of federal union of the three national component parts: 'I am a strong advocate for the Union of the three Kingdoms of the Empire, but this Union should be a genuine Union of the three peoples; each with its own head – a Scottish Parliament to meet in Edinburgh, an Irish Parliament in Dublin, and English Parliament in London and a British Parliament there as well. This would be a *bona fide* Union, a brotherly Union, not a swallowing up of the smaller by the one great member, by a monstrous centralisation which is the destroyer of all variety.'[79]

Blackie's sole entrance into the affairs of Canada occurred in 1884 when he wrote to an acquaintance in Montreal that 'as to the French in Canada, no doubt the government of one race by another is always a difficult problem; but it has constantly to be done, and we must make the best of it. In Ireland John Bull has made not the best but the worst of it; and when the worst is once produced it is, like a hereditary disease, very difficult, sometimes impossible to be cured.'[80]

While Blackie's views were not exactly identical to the ones later to be expressed by Richard Haldane, there are, nevertheless, remarkable similarities between them. The most significant difference between Blackie's and Haldane's plans for the Empire is contained in the role Haldane assigned for the judiciary as an instrument of unity. Central to his plan was a Supreme Court of the Empire, as we shall see.

Blackie's views were widely circulated throughout Scotland, especially in *The Scotsman*, and were greeted with considerable popular approval. The constant cry throughout the public assemblies of Scotland throughout Watson's life concerned the 'insolent centralisation' and concluded with the chant: 'Let Scottish business be transacted in Edinburgh.'[81] It would be passing strange if Watson, the deep-dyed Scot, was unaware of these sentiments and even more passing strange if he did not agree with them with a characteristic ebullience. Little wonder that he preferred to embrace the longings for local autonomy of provincial Canadians rather than the sterile language of a parliamentary act. Nothing came more easily to this 'typical and ardent Scot.' As Saywell has remarked: 'During his four years in the Commons and later in the Lords, Watson showed no interest in politics but was assiduous in protecting and promoting Scottish interests – Scots law, religion, local government, the universities. And just as he was solicitous for Scottish interest while in parliament, so too was he solicitous for minority interest in Canada.'[82]

All of Lord Watson's decisions relating to the Canadian constitution formed a central part of the legacy which Viscount Haldane inherited upon entering the House of Lords. But, as we shall now see, however much he agreed with the direction taken by his predecessor, the new Viscount struck out on his own course armed with the philosophy of Hegel and the determination to uncover and promote the *Sittlichkeit* of Canada.

7

Haldane and the Reign of *Sittlichkeit*

Ethical life [*die Sittlichkeit*] is the idea of freedom, as the living good which has its knowledge and volition in self-consciousness, and its actuality through self-conscious action.

– G.W.F. Hegel, Philosophy of Right

Few judges took as much delight in expounding publicly the philosophical foundations of their thinking as Viscount Haldane. He embraced every opportunity to speak or to write about the fundamental principles which guided his judicial reasoning. Prior to delivering the Gifford Lectures in 1902, for example, Richard Haldane published *Education and Empire* in which he set out his thoughts on university education, especially his plans for a new college of science and technology in London on the German model of 'scientific training,' as well as his musings on the 'Constitutional Development of the Empire.' This book reveals that he had cultivated a dense Germanic prose style both in his writing and in his manner of speaking; he studiously avoided imagery or metaphor, both of which he openly criticized in the philosophical writings of others. He thought that philosophical matters became unnecessarily muddled by flowery literary images. As a result, he was a difficult man to listen to and to read. He never made concessions to his audience, neither to their patience nor to their capacity. On one occasion, when he spoke at Durham before 1,300 miners on behalf of Sidney Webb's candidacy for Parliament, he was incomprehensible to the workers. Harold Laski related an account of the speech in a letter to Justice Oliver Wendell Holmes: 'Webb is standing for a miners' constituency in Durham and he asked Haldane on the score of old friendship to come and speak for him. Haldane agreed on condition that he should make only a semi-political speech. I asked Webb what he talked about. He asked me to put the question to Mrs. Webb. She didn't seem very certain and referred me to Mrs. Bertrand Russell who had been there at the time. Mrs. Russell was not quite sure but thought it was about the second part of Goethe's *Faust*. Can you imagine the spectacle of Haldane addressing thirteen hundred miners just up from the pit upon *Faust*?'[1] No one who knew Haldane was surprised to learn that, to the utter fatigue of his audience, the speaker droned on far too long.

The Gifford Lectures

Richard Haldane's reputation among serious students of philosophy was so high – despite his distance from the academy – that he was asked to give the Gifford Lectures in 1902; he was forty-seven at the time and three years before going into the cabinet. This prestigious lecture series had been inaugurated by the will of the Scottish jurist, Adam Lord Gifford, in 1887. The bequest stipulated that the lectures – to be held at the university at Edinburgh, Glasgow, Aberdeen, or St Andrew's – were to advance the cause of natural theology. Lecturers were challenged 'to promote and diffuse the study of Natural Theology in the widest sense of the term – in other words, the knowledge of God.' Haldane took that to mean that 'Lord Gifford in founding these Lectureships may be said to have been to promote a *thinking* consideration of the Nature of God and of His relation to the actual world.'[2] Lord Gifford was a devout Protestant and, like his father before him, a zealous Sunday school teacher. He was fully aware of the climate of hostility towards the Christian faith that had begun to emerge during his lifetime and so endowed in perpetuity a lecture series designed to provide serious reflection on the truths of the Christian religion. The hostility towards the Christian religion that Gifford saw hovering like a dark cloud over his beloved Scotland worked on two levels. First, among the learned, the beautifully written but scathingly anti-Christian *The Rise and Fall of the Roman Empire* by Edward Gibbon was widely popular and influential, if not read in its entirety – it appeared in six thick volumes – and its central arguments were propagated in abbreviated form by the author's anti-Christian devotees. Prominent contemporary historians such as Thomas Babington Macaulay and J.B. Bury saw to it that the monumental work was always in circulation. On the more popular level, however, the writings of William Winwood Reade, author of *The Martyrdom of Man* (1872) and an earlier book, *The Veil of Isis* (1862), constituted a violent attack on the Catholic Church, and succeeded in extending the anti-Christian polemic to the average non-academic reader.

People as notable as Winston Churchill read and were deeply affected by Reade's books. Churchill acknowledged in his *My Early Life* that Reade's *Martyrdom of Man* left him permanently sceptical toward religious matters and especially towards Christianity. 'I now began to read,' the young Churchill wrote, 'a number of books which challenged the whole religious education I had received at Harrow. The first of these books was *The Martyrdom of Man* by Winwood Reade.'[3] Upon reading Winwood Reade's book today, one is struck by the extraordinary flight of historical fancy that pervades it; the narrative sweeps through ancient and modern history with airy abandon, pretending to show how Jesus was a victim of hallucinations and how the Christian church was hi-jacked by Paul of Tarsus.[4] It is a breezy and unscholarly screed against all things Christian. It would make a contemporary militant agnostic blush to have written it. How the young Winston Churchill could have taken this book seriously speaks more to the poverty of his formal education than to the strength of the book's central argument. Churchill did acknowledge, however, that 'of course if I had been at a University my difficulties might have been resolved by the eminent professors and divines who are gathered there.'[5] On the other hand, he might not have been shaken from his scepticism had he attended university, but he at least might have been exposed to philosophy and have been able to see through the influence of superficial authorities.

Reade's book along with William Lecky's *The Rise and Influence of Rationalism*, in addition to Edward Gibbon's work, confirmed Churchill in his religious scepticism, especially towards Christianity. But, unlike Haldane, Churchill was no philosopher; he never attended a single course of philosophy in his entire education. In this respect he was a reverse image of Richard Haldane. Though one can picture Haldane comfortably in the company of Albert Einstein – who was a guest on several occasions at 28 Queen Anne's Gate – it is impossible to imagine Churchill in conversation with the great mathematical mind. Little wonder that Churchill and Haldane never became close friends, as was the case with Grey and Asquith. Not only were they 'university men,' they were deeply interested in things of the mind. Churchill's wisdom was of the practical order but, as his autobiographical writings reveal, he considered his education seriously deficient. No such doubts were present in the mind of Richard Haldane. Duff Cooper has written that Haldane was perceived by some to be an intellectual snob, that he looked down on those who were not as well educated in philosophy as he was himself.[6] This was not an uncommon view of the man and it has the tinge of truth to it. But Haldane was a deadly serious scholar and this seriousness of mind was reflected in the seriousness of his demeanour. He had no time for small talk or small minds and the look on his face betrayed his dread of frivolity. As we have seen in his earliest letters home from Göttingen, he was critical of his fellow students for not giving more time and attention to their studies; he never lost this attitude throughout his life at the bar or in politics, which made for an overly serious companion, a tad too serious for the average person to abide.

Haldane's Gifford Lectures were so unrelievedly dense that his audience found them exceedingly difficult to endure; and they are even more difficult for future generations to read. He began his lectures by taking aim at his Gifford predecessor, William James, who had published his lectures in book form as *The Varieties of Religious Experience*. Haldane dismissed the James lectures as an attempt to solve a rational problem on the basis of 'feelings.' It came as a surprise to no one to hear him announce that in 'these lectures, I shall place no reliance upon feelings as such.'[7] Sentiments or feelings, this German-trained rationalist philosopher went on to say, 'become valuable only after it has been justified by thought and not before.'[8] Of feeling as a foundation 'upon which to build a theory, there is unfortunately room for much doubt.' He looked upon James's ruminations on the subject as a departure from Lord Gifford's invitation. He noted this and promised in his lectures to hew more closely to the terms of Lord Gifford's initial invitation by first reminding his audience that 'in the twentieth century in which we are living, it must be recognised that apart from the sanction of Science the foundation of a faith is impossible.' Having thrown down the gauntlet with his dismissal of James, Haldane proceeded throughout a series of twenty lectures to lead his audience through the tangled labyrinth of metaphysical writings of the leading modern philosophers in an attempt to establish the 'pathway to reality.' 'We have, therefore, to return,' he told his audience, 'to a thinking consideration of the nature of God in the spirit of Lord Gifford. If we are to find such a foundation, and would see the truth we must not fear whither the pathway may lead us.' Put starkly, he announced, 'the task of these lectures will be to answer the question: how, in the commencement of the Twentieth Century, ought we to conceive of God?'[9] In light of his personal theological doubts, the choice of topic appeared strange to some of his friends. But he had studied the terms set down for the lectures and obviously thought that he could bring a certain rigorous perspective to bear upon the central concern underlying them. Above all, he appeared determined to take up the cudgels thrown down the previous year by William James, who, in *The Varieties of Religious Experience*, tended to question the historical efficacy of the Bible.

After showing how Aristotle had improved upon Plato and how Hegel 'first taught people to understand Aristotle' correctly, Haldane commended John Stuart Mill but with the caution that even Mill had led thinkers astray. Haldane next laboured to rescue philosophy from the limitations of the categories employed in the various sciences. Unlike ancient philosophers, who understood philosophy as the never-ending quest for the truth about the whole of reality, Richard Haldane was a thoroughgoing modern philosopher who – since reading René Descartes's *Discourse on Method* – had sought 'final truth.'[10] This led him to a critical examination of the procedures of the various sciences, especially mathematics and physics.

With the aid of Hegel, Haldane confidently proceeded by clearing away the tangled underbrush of metaphysical confusion concerning the nature of God allegedly accumulated since the time of Aristotle. In the process he attempted to correct 'the images and metaphors' of Christian theology, which, he said are 'inadequate in an inquiry of the character prescribed by Lord Gifford' – which would have come as a shock to Lord Gifford, whose own theological musings were replete with metaphors. At the end of this process we are not surprised to learn that 'by the word "God" is nothing short of the Highest and most Real.'[11] And, while it would appear from that assertion that God, thus understood, is not the personal God of Christian salvation history, Haldane attempted later to show that in 'some sense ... God is a Person, and we have to inquire in what sense!' The quest, he affirmed, must be nothing less than an articulation of the 'world as it must appear in the mind of God.' This led him to understand God as Hegel had taught: as 'Absolute Mind.' Human consciousness, he insisted, is a defining characteristic of man and points unmistakeably in the direction of an Absolute Mind, or God. At this point he paused to rescue Hegel from a misconception, that is, that 'he indentified the Absolute Mind with mind as it appears in History.' Mind as it appears in history is never less than finite, he explained. What Hegel was pointing to was an understanding of the relationship of the human mind and the Absolute Mind, or God. 'Man is at once in separation from and in union with God, because the foundation of his existence is Intelligence, the essential characteristic of which is Dialectic, difference in unity and unity in difference.'[12]

Man, said Haldane, has a double nature out of which arises the consciousness of separation from God, which is the grounds of the concept of sin, and, on the other hand, the consciousness of union with God, or religion. This led him to the conclusion that 'finite spirit man is nonetheless spirit, consequently he is essentially free, and therefore *responsible*.'[13] With God, Haldane insisted, 'to create must mean to think, and to think to create.' Earlier he had demonstrated that 'self-consciousness turns out to be the highest of all categories and to be the basis of all intelligence and therefore the presupposition of our reasoning about the nature of ultimate reality, God must be self-conscious.'[14] It is for this reason, he continued, that philosophical discussions of God's reality must avoid anthropomorphisms or presenting God in the image of man, however natural and harmless such a practice was in other spheres of inquiry. There is a natural tendency among men, he noted, to express themselves in philosophical discourse in terms of time and space – natural because all men live in time and space. But God does not live within time and space, he insisted. 'For the scope of the Divine Intelligence is not contracted by finite ends as is ours.'[15] And it is through religion that man passes 'beyond his finiteness' to comprehend God, comprehension that he, in turn, expresses in human terms. Echoing Aristotle as Hegel had done, Haldane acknowledged that all men live in the world of the senses: 'It is the consciousness of a direct relation to God, but in forms that belong to the region of feeling, and are consequently describable only symbolically. Under its own forms it grasps the presence of God as here and now in the object world; it is the sense that He is immediately manifested, and this feeling is expressed in the symbols and pictorial manifestations of the creeds.'

From here Haldane announced that Christianity gave expression to the metaphysical theory of the philosophers, especially Aristotle as refined by Hegel. 'This Christianity expresses in the well-known symbolical form of a Father who sends His Only Begotten Son into otherness, the world, to return to Him with the otherness overcome and the redemption of the world accomplished.'[16] As for the Christian doctrine of the Trinity, 'it is an analysis in symbolical form of the three aspects or moments in the self-consciousness of God, in Hegelian terminology, Logic, Finite Intelligence (including Nature and Finite Spirit), and Absolute Spirit; the realisation of the Universal and the Particular in the Individual.'

Haldane concluded his excursus into the 'pathway to reality' by allowing that a religious faith that 'characterizes the self-surrender of the will in Religion is a sense of reality above and beyond what is seen. In its doctrines of the eternal nature of the self and of degrees in reality Metaphysics teaches the same truth in scientific form.' While somewhat compatible with Christian natural theology, Haldane's Absolute Spirit is far from being the God of Abraham, Isaac, and Jacob. His examination gave no ground to either faith or the biblical grounds of faith in God. To this extent he did not propound the philosophical basis of a Hebrew or Christian theodicy.

These lectures also gave a clear account of how far he had migrated from his Göttingen professor Hermann Lotze into the embrace of Hegelian abstractions. Where Haldane found the sufficiency of reason, Lotze did not. Lotze clearly left open the possibility that there were ultimate questions that 'only the new and special faculty of Faith is competent to answer.'[17] For Lotze, what passed for science was itself based on faith.[18] Haldane's beloved German teacher wrapped the issues in a quandary: 'If religion were a pure product of human reason, philosophy would be the only competent organ of its discovery and interpretation. If reason is not of itself capable of finding the highest truth, but on the contrary stands in need of a revelation which is either contained in some divine act of historic occurrence, or is continually repeated in men's hearts, still reason must be able to understand the revealed truth at least so far as to recognise in it the satisfying and convincing conclusion of those up-ward-soaring trains of thought which reason itself began, led by its own needs, but was not able to bring to an end.'[19] As Lotze concluded, 'religious faith is comparable not to this immediate evidence of ultimate principles but to another element that co-operates in the construction of knowledge – namely to the *intuition* by which content is given to those principles, and by which those universal laws are supplied with cases to which they may be applied.'[20]

For Richard Haldane, there was no place for intuition. Only the cold rationalism of natural reason guided by Hegel would assist the philosopher in his quest for truth. It stands as a mystery why Haldane did not respond to his teacher's thoughtful ruminations on the very subject he had undertaken to expound in his Gifford Lectures. He must surely have known that, in the second volume of his *Microcosmos*, Lotze had explored in great detail many of the same themes. He must have known that Lotze explicitly discussed the rational basis of the Christian faith in chapter 1 of book 8 of the *Microcosmos* and how the ancients unaided by revelation had 'ended in scepticism.'[21] In many respects, the master was not bested by his student. Only by ignoring Lotze's great work could Richard Haldane undertake his Gifford Lectures. But to that extent they remain unsatisfying. This failure to engage Lotze in a friendly dialogue on these major philosophical issues with which Lotze himself had laboured so deeply was not uncharacteristic of Haldane. Throughout his life he rarely confronted an opponent directly, preferring to outflank him by challenging parallel arguments. He clearly had Lotze in mind throughout these lectures but never mentioned him by name.

Haldane's Gifford Lectures were well received by most – the exception being a few perceptive divines who could not find the God of revelation in his lectures – and even understood by a few; they were not easy to follow at times but they did present a good account of the workings of this truly philosophic mind.[22] They also demonstrated beyond dispute how his mind was struggling with the Hegelian influences he had absorbed over so many years.

Hegel and the Shaping of Haldane's Thought

The response to Haldane's writings and public philosophical musings have run the gamut from puzzled admiration to outright dismissal. His first biographer, Sir Frederick Maurice, tended to be somewhat perplexed by Haldane's interest in philosophy and, as a result, relegated it to the minor reaches of his life. The latest biography, by Jean Graham Hall and Douglas F. Martin, nods in the direction of the philosophic but then gives it a pass. Dudley Sommer's biography attempts a more robust account in a separate chapter dedicated to the subject but with mixed results. All four biographers, however, retain a respect for the man's philosophical mind. On the other hand, John Saywell's account of Haldane's contribution to Canadian constitutional jurisprudence culminates, as we have seen, in an outright dismissal of Haldane's philosophical preoccupations as so much 'Teutonic metaphysics.'[23] Saywell's clear intention is to confine the understanding of Haldane's judgments to the sociological or historical context. As a result, he never ventures into Haldane's preoccupation with Hegelian philosophy generally or with his specific determination to uncover the importance of the Hegelian *Sittlichkeit* in the law of the constitution. He views Haldane the philosopher as uninteresting and uninformative. This attitude stands in contrast with Asquith's contemporary assessment that 'Richard Haldane is the greatest philosopher and the greatest politician now alive.'[24] It is unfortunate that Saywell's book, otherwise so good, fails to appreciate the importance of Hegelian philosophy in the life and work of Viscount Haldane.

But where does one begin to uncover evidence of Hegel's influence in shaping Haldane's mind and how did that influence shape his views of law and state? The question leads to, of all places, Montreal, Quebec. In 1913 Viscount Haldane as lord chancellor had accepted an invitation to speak to the Canadian and American bar associations at a meeting in Montreal at the beginning of September of that year. The Montreal meeting was the thirty-sixth annual meeting of the American Bar Association and the first joint meeting of the American and Canadian bar associations. It was also the first time that the American Bar Association had met outside the United States. The joint conference was designed to celebrate the centenary of the Treaty of Ghent which had brought the War of 1812 to a conclusion. It was highly unusual – in fact, unprecedented – for the lord chancellor to leave the United Kingdom since he was by his office custodian of the Privy Seal and, by strict tradition, the seal must never be left unattended. Haldane's visit to Montreal required the explicit permission of the king, which the sovereign readily granted. The lord chancellor was given leave to go to Montreal on the understanding that he would do so as quickly as the available means of transportation allowed. Haldane undertook the trip and kept to a very strict schedule upon arrival. It was so tight that he felt obliged to turn down an invitation from President Woodrow Wilson to visit the White House while he was in the United States on his way to Canada. But why did he undertake this arduous five-day journey across the Atlantic to address an assembly of American and Canadian lawyers and judges? What did he have to say that he considered so important as to leave the Privy Seal in the hands of a special commission? The answers are contained in the speech to the convention to which he gave the curious title: 'Higher Nationality: A Study in Law and Ethics.'

Haldane, accompanied by his sister, Elizabeth, and his secretary, Sir Kenneth Muir-Mackenzie, left Liverpool on the *Lusitania* on the morning of 25 August 1913 and arrived early Friday afternoon, 29 August, in New York, where he was greeted by a group of lawyers led by Attorney General James McReynolds, former U.S. secretary of war Jacob H. Dickinson, and Francis Rowle, chairman of the bar association reception committee. Upon boarding the ship, the reception committee had difficulty finding their distinguished guest; he was not in his stateroom or in the first-class lounge where they had anticipated meeting him. They knew for certain that he was on board so they kept looking. At length the committee found the lord chancellor on the upper deck where he was leaning over the railings calmly watching the other passengers disembarking. After exchanging greetings, the relieved reception committee led their guest to a press conference with American reporters.

Members of the press met the lord chancellor in the ship's saloon where – to their surprise – they found him conversing with Justice Oliver Wendell Holmes of the United States Supreme Court; quite by coincidence Holmes had been visiting Britain in August and was returning to the United States on the same ship. He and Haldane enjoyed frequent long conversations during their voyage from Liverpool. The lord chancellor enjoyed discussing Canadian constitutional cases with the American judge; he found Holmes's thoughts on federal constitutions especially instructive.[25] Harold Laski became a messenger between Haldane and Holmes for many years; he reported to Holmes in 1920 that Haldane had a wish 'to talk with you on some Canadian cases he's handling just now.'[26] In 1913 Haldane compared his five-day seminar with Holmes on the federal character of the American constitution and the role played by judges since Marshall in the famous *Marbury v. Madison* case of 1803[27] to his own involvement in the emerging debate over judge-made constitutional law.[28] We will never know what they discussed in detail but it is difficult to imagine that they did not discuss their roles as judges. And, whereas Haldane was a very good listener, Holmes was a very good talker with a unique epigrammatic style for which he became famous.

Haldane welcomed the reporters and escorted them to a room off his suite and opened himself to a full battery of questions ranging from the U.S. policy towards Mexico – on which the lord chancellor declined to express an opinion – to what he thought of the campaign then raging in England in support of women's suffrage. He expressed support for the women's cause but deplored their rough tactics. He went on to comment on the state of affairs in Germany and the contentious issue of Irish Home Rule which he had long supported. The *New York Times* featured Haldane's arrival on the first page with a follow-up story on page three complete with a photo showing the lord chancellor in morning coat and a tall hat.[29] His sister appeared alongside him looking severe and uncomfortable wrapped in a fur collar though the temperature that day in New York was mild and the winds light.

The party was taken by car to the Hotel Plaza, where a suite of rooms on the tenth floor had been booked. The *New York Times* described the lord chancellor as a man 'of medium height, stocky build, smooth shaven and his forehead is high ... There is a twinkle in his eye and this is not the only indication that beneath the grave exterior which the dignity of his place forces upon him, he has a keen sense of humor.'[30] This was a fair portrait of the man with the exception of the 'keen sense of humor.' Richard Haldane, according to the testimony of his closest friends, was virtually humourless.

Next to the front-page story of his arrival appeared a short box story received by the *New York Times* by cable from England. The caption read: 'Criticizes Lord Haldane.' The brief piece reported that the *Law Journal* back in London criticized the lord chancellor for leaving the Great Seal in the hands of a commission of three persons. This, the journal complained, constituted the creation of 'an entirely new precedent by retaining the office of Lord Chancellor while three commissioners are appointed to its duties. Hitherto, in modern times the Seal has been placed in commission only when a vacancy occurred in the office.' None of the reporters appeared to have been aware of the issue for not one of them questioned the lord chancellor about the matter. News of Haldane's trip to Montreal was widely disseminated throughout Britain, as was the fact that he had been encouraged to go by the king. But not a few British lawyers criticized the voyage as unnecessary.

After spending the night in New York, the lord chancellor and his entourage were ferried up the Hudson River by the industrialist J. Pierpont Morgan on his yacht, *The Corsair*. The party arrived in the early afternoon at the United States Military Academy at West Point where the lord chancellor was met by a delegation headed by the Canadian minister of justice, J.C. Doherty. After reviewing an honour guard of West Point cadets, Haldane and his greeters proceeded up the Hudson to Albany where he was feted at a formal dinner sponsored by Doherty. At midnight, Viscount Haldane and his party left on a special Pullman train for Montreal where he arrived the next morning at ten minutes to eight. The *Montreal Gazette* announced the lord chancellor's visit under the banner: 'Great Gathering of Notable Men.' The lead editorial proclaimed that 'no men more notable in the realm of law have ever gathered in any city of Canada or America.'[31] Twenty-five hundred delegates attended the bar association meetings, straining available hotel accommodations beyond the limits; some delegates had to be billeted in private homes throughout the city.[32]

In an interview with the press upon arrival in Montreal, Haldane acknowledged that it was 'his first visit to the shores of your beautiful Dominion.'[33] Turning to legal matters, Canadian reporters pressed the lord chancellor for his views on the continuation of appeals to the Judicial Committee of the Privy Council. Before answering that question, Haldane launched into an account of his deep interest in the constitutional affairs of Canada and claimed that, as a barrister, he had been retained by Ontario Premier Sir Oliver Mowat in several cases before the Judicial Committee. 'Now as head of the Judicial Committee of the Privy Council,' he went on to say, 'I hear all the appeals on your big questions every year in the month of July, which we call Canadian month.'[34] As for the termination of appeals, the lord chancellor replied: 'I do not think that further limitations than those already existing are necessary ...There are big questions, as instance the marriage question, which we heard a year or so ago, around which surged so keen controversies, that it would be hard to get a thoroughly detached opinion in the country affected and it is convenient for you to be able to get such a detached opinion from the Privy Council.'[35] He went on to concede that there were 'a few appeals of a trifling nature' that ought never to reach the Privy Council, 'but Canada transgresses no more in this respect than England, Ireland or Scotland.' 'Most of your appeals,' he repeated, 'are of great importance and interest.'[36]

Haldane's press interview contained several puzzling answers which no one of the reporters appeared to pick up. For example, why would one expect that a matrimonial or divorce case could not be heard fairly in the home country where, presumably, the law and context would be better known than in distant London and before judges of the Privy Council? As well, his comment on 'trifling' appeals to the Judicial Committee was curious because neither England nor Ireland nor Scotland has ever had the right of appeal to the Privy Council. The House of Lords, not the Judicial Committee, was and remains to this day the highest court of appeal for all three component parts of the United Kingdom. The Judicial Committee of the Privy Council has domestic jurisdiction in two areas only: ecclesiastical causes involving the established Church of England and, recently, appeals from the General Medical Council. Perhaps politeness or the lack of legal training on the part of reporters prevented them from pursuing the issues further. Nevertheless, it was a gaff of the first order on the part of the distinguished lord chancellor. But no one appeared to notice.

The convention assembled at the Princess Theatre in Montreal to hear the lord chancellor, the keynote speaker, at the afternoon session on Monday, 1 September. The assembled notables included the Canadian prime minister, Robert Borden, the former president of the United States, William Howard Taft, Canadian Chief Justice Sir Charles Fitzpatrick as well as the Canadian minister of justice, J.C. Doherty, and delegates from all forty-eight states as well as lawyers and judges from every province of Canada. Viscount Haldane was introduced to the convention by the chief justice of the Supreme Court of the United States, Edward D. White. After acknowledging the chief justice's introduction, the lord chancellor thanked Frank B. Kellogg, president of the American Bar Association, for coming to London to extend the invitation to him personally. After reading greetings from King George, in which the king noted that the keeper of the Great Seal was not normally granted permission to leave the United Kingdom during his tenure as keeper but was granted special leave in light of the importance he attached to the assembled lawyers and judges on this occasion, Haldane turned to his prepared text. The speech was long and very dense.

The learned lord chancellor had come the distance to deliver an important message to this assembly of judges and lawyers and he took no hostages. The speech was reported in the Montreal newspapers as well as in the *Canadian Law Times*. The *Law Times* ran an editorial stating that 'the address itself was delivered without stay or hesitation, in the voice of the cultivated English gentleman – in print it is literature, and epoch-making in its importance to the nations most vitally concerned, and worthy of the theme, worthy of the occasion, and worthy of the Lord Chancellor of England.'[37] But it became clear that the speech was not an easy one to summarize, replete as it was with German and Latin phrases which the speaker did not condescend to translate. The heart of Haldane's message was, he told his audience, contained in the German word *Sittlichkeit*, which, he admitted, 'is a word impossible to render into English.' The brave *Gazette* reporter who attempted to rise to the bait gave the following account of the speech:

The speech was delivered in a voice which probably carried further than might be expected for its strength, on account of its fine timber and clear articulation.

It was of such a nature that the closest attention was necessary in order to follow the argument developed step by step and the mental efforts of the hearers was responsible for a certain lack of applause, but here and there some popular appeal such as the recital of the King's message authorizing the visit of the Lord High Chancellor or some expression of opinion in the direction of the strengthening of amicable relations between the nations, evoked instant and enthusiastic applause from the audience.[38]

One doesn't have to read between the lines of this report too carefully to understand that the speech, which lasted over two hours, was almost impenetrable. And it was spoken by a man who was not a gifted orator or graced with a good voice. Everyone who ever heard Haldane speak agreed that he possessed a weak, high-pitched voice which did not carry very far. One can only imagine in these days before electronic public-speaking technology how difficult it was for this large audience to hear him beyond the first few rows.

The speech itself was nothing less than a learned philosophical discourse which would have challenged an assembly of professional philosophers well versed in modern German philosophy; many in the audience must have found sleep a welcome escape. The *Gazette* editorial, after making a noble effort to summarize the address, concluded that it was 'meat for strong men.'[39] The speech, reprinted in many places since it was delivered, was an Hegelian defence of the common law lawyer's and judge's obligation to make law, not merely to enforce it. Lawyers and judges, Haldane told his audience, have a privileged role in seeking out and implementing the *Sittlichkeit* of nations, both domestically and internationally. He spoke of 'the power of our lawyers in creating and developing the law as well as in changing it, a power which has been more exercised outside the legislature than within it.'[40] He urged members of the audience to understand their role as society's 'skilled advisers,' as those who, by understanding the '*General Will* of Society' (found in the *Sittlichkeit* of every nation), were better equipped than anyone else to play this important role. Because of their legal training, they were destined to guide nations schooled in the Anglo-Saxon legal traditions towards greater progress. It was a message that appealed to his audience and it was punctuated by repeated recourse to the authority of Hegel.

As Jonathan Robinson has explained in his account of Haldane's Hegelianism: 'The non-legal source of Haldane's judgments can be found in his philosophical views on the nature of the state. Simply put, these views were that the constitution of a state was the expression of the *general will*, and this will could only find expression in a state in which the personal willing of individuals and groups could will the positive laws of the state as their own subjective willing.'[41] Hegel owed his understanding of the *general will* to his great predecessor, Jean-Jacques Rousseau, who introduced the notion to modern philosophy. For Rousseau, as for Hegel, the *general will* is not simply the majority will of the community. It is much more than that and even at times is in conflict with the majority will. The *general will* is that will which members of the community as a whole *ought* to will after setting aside their private wills and interests. It is not simply synonymous with public opinion, as John Saywell appears to believe. Above all, it is the role of statesmen – especially lawyers and judges – to uncover this *general will* and craft it into a concrete constitutional way of life. The state constitution must, accordingly, be 'objective and independent of caprice, arbitrariness and idiosyncratic interest.'[42] It is this discovery of the *general will* which constituted for Hegel the highest responsibility of the modern statesman. At root and branch is Hegel's view that the unfolding of the modern state is both rational and ethical. It was for this reason that Haldane acknowledged in his speech that his comments had more in common with ethics than with strict law. Under the tutelage of Hegel, Haldane outlined the special role of lawyers and judges as the advisers of world historic figures charged with the responsibility to guide the course of progress, especially in the area of the constitutional law of the modern state.

His clear preference for German sources must have come as a shock to many in the audience not trained in continental philosophy. 'German writers have ... marked out the system to which I refer and have given it the name of "*Sittlichkeit*,"' he announced to his audience. 'In his book, *Der Zweck im Recht*, Rudolph von Jhering, a famous professor at Gottingen, with whose figure I was familiar when I was a student there nearly forty years ago, pointed out, in the part which he devoted to the subject of "*Sittlichkeit*," that it was the merit of the German language to have been the only one to find a really distinctive and scientific expression for it. "*Sittlichkeit*" is the system of habitual or customary conduct, ethical rather than legal, which embraces all those obligations of the citizen which it is "bad form" or "not the thing" to disregard.'[43] This was the negative part of *Sittlichkeit*, the part that marked out what a community ought *not* to do. The fuller, more positive, part of *Sittlichkeit* contained the notion of the progress of the World Spirit or *Weltgeist*, the spirit of world history that was moving nations towards a greater and greater freedom. It was the role of philosophy, Hegel insisted, to uncover this progressive spirit and to give it full force in law. For unlike Karl Marx and other like-minded philosophers, Hegel believed that the role of philosophy was not to change the world from without but to implement the given rationality of the world historic process or *Weltgeist* from within.

This speech, which Haldane had come all the way from England to deliver, was an unapologetic expression of admiration for the German language and habits of thought as well as a plea to enrich Anglo-Saxon law with the insights provided by Hegelian philosophy. To suggest that the 'Anglo-Saxon' legal tradition could be improved by the German philosophic advancements must have come as a surprise, not to say as a shock, to this Montreal audience, comprised principally of American judges and lawyers. And, given that the speech was delivered at a time when events in the kaiser's Germany were beginning to take on a distinctly bellicose tone, it must have seemed curious. Less than a year later, Great Britain was at war with Germany. Haldane's pro-German posture, however philosophically defensible in his own mind, was destined to rouse in due course the ire of the Northcliffe press and lead to Haldane's dismissal from the British war cabinet in 1915, just two years after delivering his speech in Montreal.

Undeterred by what must have been a puzzled if not restrained reception, Haldane pressed on, drawing on the writings of Jean-Jacques Rousseau and Johann Fichte and adeptly sprinkling his remarks with references to the Greek classical writings of Plutarch, Plato, and others, all pressed into the service of a 'full international *Sittlichkeit*.'[44] At no point in this long speech did he abandon the lofty theme or tone. If he succeeded in anything, it was in giving credence to the widely held view that Viscount Haldane had an imperious contempt for all but the highest of the philosophically minded. This view was burnished by his inclination to associate with Albert Einstein and other leading intellectuals of the day and not helped by his book *The Reign of Relativity*, which presumed to make the complexities of Einstein's theories available in extended form to the public at large.

Those who thought the lord chancellor might have become sensitive to his audience were to be disappointed. If he was aware of their discomfort – and there is every reason to doubt that he was – he certainly was not about to grant relief. For he concluded his speech with the remark: 'I do not apologize for having transgressed on the time and attention of this remarkable meeting for so long, or for urging what may seem to belong more to ethics than to law. We are bound to search after fresh principles if we desire to find firm foundations for a progressive practical life.'[45] There it was plainly spelled out: the lawyer's and judge's professional obligation was 'to find firm foundations for a progressive practical life.' A 'progressive practical life' demanded the active participation of the legal profession, without dispute the high priests of the new 'progressive' era which was opening up to the Western world. However dense at times, the message was an intoxicating brew to this audience of lawyers and judges; to be told by the highest-ranking member of the British bar and bench that they were at the centre of the unfolding of the historic process by virtue of their legal calling must have pleased them greatly, if they heard and understood it.

Addressing his audience directly, Haldane brought the speech to a close with the hope that 'we can draw into closest harmony the nations of a race in which all of us have a common pride.'[46] One can only guess at the relief this audience must have felt when the distinguished lord chancellor took his seat amidst loud and prolonged applause. It was not the first time Haldane had left his audience stimulated yet bewildered. One of his biographers tells the story that, at a dinner party one evening at 28 Queen Anne's Gate not long before leaving for Montreal, someone made the unfortunate suggestion that the host explain Einstein's theory of relativity. Haldane launched into an explanation that was appropriately obscure, with the result that 'gradually a cloud descended until at last even the candles lost their lighting power in the complexity of Haldane's explanations.'[47] His sister, Elizabeth, liked to tell the story of a woman who had attended her brother's Gifford Lectures in 1903. 'On going out of a concluding lecture a lady was heard to reproach another lady who had not ventured to attend. "But what was it about?" asked the latter, very naturally. "I haven't the slightest idea" said the first, "but it was perfectly delightful."'[48]

The lord chancellor's speech received perfunctory notice in the British press in addition to the disapproval expressed earlier by those who believed that the keeper of the Great Seal should not have left the country for such an event. But Haldane did not go to Montreal in order to reap personal acclaim. He went because he was on a mission and it mattered little to him how much it brought him into the limelight of public approval or disapproval. He never brooded over the comments of his political enemies; he simply ignored them. In this respect he stood out among his political and professional peers as an oddity. He was almost the ever-present but invisible man in the counsels of state. He was not, like Churchill, a long-winded self-promoter in cabinet meetings; in fact, he rarely spoke at all. Lloyd-George called him a 'baffling personality. In private he talked incessantly – in public he talked volubly and at interminable length on any subject ... There was one gathering at which he hardly ever spoke, and that was the Cabinet.'[49] But when he did he was 'dry as dust' and, according to the House Leader, Sir William Harcourt, the prospect of listening to Haldane was painful. Harcourt noted on one occasion when Haldane gave the army estimates in 1907: 'The House is too hot or is it my inflammation of blood at the prospect of three hours from Schopenhauer.'[50] And John Morley noted with exasperation on one occasion after listening to one of his speeches that '[Haldane] was very hard to follow ... His speeches have no paragraphs. There are full stops here and there, faintly marked, but no paragraphs.'[51]

One of those in the audience in Montreal was Felix Frankfurter, a future justice of the Supreme Court of the United States. At the time Frankfurter was a law officer in the Bureau of Insular Affairs in Washington. In a letter following the Montreal meetings, he wrote of the event to Justice Oliver Wendell Holmes. 'Christie [a Canadian and Harvard Law classmate of Frankfurter's] and I went to Montreal. I can't say that the Bar Association proceedings fired us. Oh, if there were only a tax on words! Two talks *did* stand out – the Lord Chancellor spoke in an attractively impressive way though with some unnecessary verbiage and the central theme had more of an air than the reality of novelty. Still it is something to be remembered.'[52] The other speech that impressed the young lawyers was that of Maître Fernand Labori, the elegant French lawyer and chief counsel for Alfred Dreyfus and Émile Zola: 'He spoke with the pace and flavor and felicity of France itself speaking,' Frankfurter reported.[53]

Many of the themes Haldane touched upon in his Montreal speech were revisited in his subsequent writings. In *The Reign of Relativity*, for example, he elaborated on the nature of law, taking direct aim at Jeremy Bentham and John Austin, the reigning founders of legal positivism: 'Law is more than a command. It is this indeed, but it has a significance which cannot be understood apart from the history and spirit of the nation whose law it is.'[54] A nation's law must be conceived as an instrument of the spirit moving peoples higher and higher up the steps of history towards a greater political freedom. The task of the 'skilled advisers' was to uncover, with the aid of moralists and sociologists, the 'history and spirit' of the nation. 'Without these we are sometimes unable to determine what is and what is not part of the law.'[55] But law for Haldane, following Hegel, was not an abstraction; it was the soul of the nation 'the chief foundation of freedom within a civilized community.'[56] 'It is this sense of obligation towards others, not merely subjective, like that of conscience, and not external, like the law'; it is the ever elusive but powerfully important *Sittlichkeit*. 'Different nations excel in their *Sittlichkeit* in different fashions,' he went on to explain. 'The spirit of a great community and its ideals may vary from those of other communities. Moreover, nations sometimes present the spectacle of having degenerated in this respect. The world is always changing, and the nations within it change their levels, and not invariably for the better.'[57]

The lord chancellor took his judicial responsibilities very seriously and sought out the company of lawyers, judges, and politicians from the Empire in order to learn from them directly what the sentiments and progressive aspirations – the *Sittlichkeit* – of their people were. He cultivated the friendship of Oliver Mowat, premier of Ontario, very early in his career and kept abreast of the growing tensions that were beginning to mount in Canada following the passage of the British North America Act, 1867. As early as 1884, he became involved, as we have seen, with Canadian constitutional cases. His first occasion came in a Quebec case in which his performance had so pleased Freshfields solicitors, as well as the lawyers from Quebec, that they recommended him to Oliver Mowat and Edward Blake. After this initial case from Quebec, Haldane claimed that 'I had a very large business as a Junior in the constitutional cases from Canada in the Privy Council. Ontario gave me its general retainer, and I appeared for the Prime Minister [Mowat], through the long series of his struggles with Sir John MacDonald, the Prime Minister of Canada, for the right of the province to pass its own legislation.'[58] This was the most precise statement of his view on the character of the constitutional conflict between the Canadian provinces and the central Parliament he ever made. He viewed the tension between the national government and the provinces as nothing less than a battle in which the provinces sought to pass their own legislation without being overridden by the central Parliament or government. He took pride in the claim that he was considered in Canada as an expert on the constitution, which must have annoyed his growing body of critics back in Canada. But he was not unaware of the criticism of legal authorities in Canada. His letters during his active years on the Privy Council are replete with comments that he had dined with lawyers from Canada: 'Last night we had the first of our Canadian dinner parties. The guests made me feel as if I were one of the Fathers of Canada.'[59] He appears to have dismissed his Canadian critics with relative ease for he never dwelt on their comments. He was content simply to record his involvement in Canadian cases: 'I spent Saturday and much of Sunday in preparing the judgment in an important case on the constitution of Canada, where I am now as well known as here.'[60]

8

In the High Court of Hegel

We need a new order of statesmen in the world to-day – for our nation, for our international league – those who understand federalism.
– Mary P. Follett, *The New State*

Richard Burdon Haldane, now Viscount Haldane of Cloan, in one important sense picked up where Lord Watson had left off: during his tenure on the Judicial Committee, he continued to favour the legislative aspirations of the Canadian provinces. But it is a mistake to view Haldane's judicial contributions as simply the continuation of Watson's decentralization of the Canadian constitution, however formally he was bound by the decisions of his predecessor. The story is more complicated than that, and Haldane was a far more complicated man than his predecessor. And just as Watson had found ways around inconvenient precedents, so too would Haldane, as, indeed, do most judges. But Richard Haldane brought a degree of learning to the bench unequalled by most of his predecessors. It might even be said that no one since Lord Chancellor Francis Bacon in the sixteenth century brought as much learning to the high bench as did Haldane. He was a man who wore his learning heavily and brought it to bear upon everything he undertook: from military organization through education for workers, the law, and, above all, philosophy itself. As John Saywell remarks at the beginning of his reflections on Viscount Haldane: 'From 1911 until his death in 1928, at least in Canadian appeals, Haldane dominated the Judicial Committee as no one had *before* or would afterwards.'[1] Saywell is correct, for there is nothing in Haldane's Judicial Committee judgments to suggest that his jurisprudence owed anything to Lord Watson's pragmatic jurisprudence. There is simply no evidence to support the claim that 'Lord Watson [was] Haldane's ideal statesman-jurist.'[2] Richard Burdon Haldane was his own man with his own philosophical jurisprudence that took him far beyond the reaches of his Scottish predecessor. He was a man driven by a mission that went beyond the narrow confines of the Canadian constitution, however gratuitous he was in assuming the mantel of 'expert in Canadian constitutional cases.' His vision encompassed the extension of the English respect for the rule of law – as it had been refined through the senior judiciary of the House of Lords and the Judicial Committee – throughout the Anglo-Saxon world, which included the United States and the far corners of the British Empire.

The Role of the Judiciary

At the heart of this story of the role these two Scottish law lords played in shaping the Canadian federal constitution is the issue of judicial review and the nature of the judicial function. Saywell's book on the judicial interpretation of the Canadian constitution bears the subtitle: 'Judicial Power and the Shaping of Canadian Federalism.' Our earlier review of the decisions of the law lords during Watson's years on the bench passed over in silence the central issue of what a judge does when he or she interprets a constitutional document. Should judges have *power*? Ought they to be engaged in 'shaping Canadian federalism?' Is not 'power' the function of the executive arm of government representing the people? Is it not the proper function of the legislative arm of government to give 'shape' to the Canadian federal system?

At first the lords on the Judicial Committee viewed the British North America Act, 1867 as an act of the imperial Parliament and subject to the normal rules of statutory construction. In *Bank of Toronto v. Lambe*, Lord Hobhouse enunciated the basic rules of construction for interpreting 'the Federation Act.' In doing so he dismissed, out of hand, the invitation to apply constitutional principles derived from non-British sources such as the federalism decisions of the Supreme Court of the United States; he resisted the 'guidance of that great judge [Chief Justice John Marshall].'[3] Hobhouse also rejected the invitation to learn from French law 'dating from a time anterior to the [Canadian] Federation Act.'[4] The lords of the Judicial Committee made it clear that they were bound to interpret the terms of the British North America Act according to the settled tenets of statutory construction handed down to them over many centuries; this approach was viewed as sufficient to guide them. But, in fact, the law lords of the Judicial Committee, especially under the direction of Haldane, departed from the established way of interpreting statutes as Hobhouse had enunciated it when they served notice that they would never allow themselves to become unduly bound by the terms of the parchment; the written document was to be respected but never allowed to prevent them from 'shaping' the course of the law. This meant that the study of the new constitution for Canada was to focus, not on the legislative history of the constitutional provisions, but on what previous judges had said about the constitution. In such an approach, constitutional law becomes the accumulated wisdom of what previous judges have said about the constitution without regard for constitutional or legislative history.

What Judicial Committee law lords laid down about the federal legislative authority under the 'Peace, Order, and good Government' clause of the Canadian constitution was done in disregard of the legislative history of the clause. As we have seen, however, in recent years the Supreme Court of Canada has tended to back away from the 'emergency doctrine' and cover conditions beyond emergency. But there remains a reluctance to consult the legislative history of constitutional provision; the intention of the legislature of Parliament continues to play little role in constitutional judging. The intentions of the Canadian draftsmen of the act, that is, the legislative history of the act, is placed beyond the reach of the court.[5] To the extent that Haldane adopted this approach to judging, he was linking arms with what Watson had begun, but he took a slightly different tack. Haldane sought out, by direct contact with Canadian lawyers and politicians, information on the tensions between the provincial and national governments over legislative jurisdiction. He was on friendly terms with central political figures, such as Oliver Mowat.[6] Watson never was. Haldane's stamp covering his long years on the Judicial Committee is clearly evident today in the *practice* of the Canadian constitution. The judgments of the Judicial Committee, as the final court of appeal for Canada until 1949, constituted directives to the courts of Canada on how judges were to interpret the terms of the constitution.

When confronted with the obligation to interpret the Canadian constitution, which is both written and federal, Canadian lawyers thought that British jurists were entering uncharted territory since the English constitution is neither. As well, the British constitution does not change through judicial pronouncements; it continues to evolve through the political interplay of the three functions of government. Haldane himself attempted to shed light on the issue by lauding the unwritten character of the English constitution. 'In the first place our constitution is unwritten,' he announced on one occasion. 'It can be studied adequately only in practice, and not in books which describe it from documents which are never adequate to the reality with its varying shades.'[7] The implication from what he said was that British jurists were to treat the Canadian constitution as if it were unwritten; to adjudicate its terms as they were accustomed to do in British constitutional cases, alive to the practice of the unwritten constitution. The unwritten character of the British constitution was one of its dominant virtues. Haldane went on to say: 'In the second place, just because the Constitution is unwritten, it is continuously altering while national policies and purposes are being developed. What was true ten years ago may not be true today, and changes are often almost impossible to ascertain merely from written records. New principles are, according to national habit, clothed in old forms, which are preserved, although the significance of the language that describes them has really altered.'[8] His point was that written documents, including constitutional documents, become of secondary importance in the mind of judges in such circumstances seeking those 'new principles.' For a judge guided by this approach, it was no difficult step to rule in favour of a provincial request for greater legislative power even when the request challenged an article of written authority. Viscount Haldane lived by this philosophy and his rulings as a judge become more readily understood when we understand his mind.

On the other hand, the judges of the Judicial Committee did not think that they were placed in a new position with the passage of the British North America Act, 1867: they were required to judge the terms of a statute of the imperial Parliament and they did that every day. The fact that it was an instrument of constitutional self-government for a colony did not require them to alter their approach to interpreting the act of Parliament. That the act had a constitutional history back in Canada meant very little to them.[9] Nor did it matter to them that Canadians viewed the constitutional statute as more than an ordinary one. Colonial lawyers liked to think that the new constitution placed judges of the Judicial Committee in a unique position. But the law lords did not see it that way. Members of the Judicial Committee believed that the principal challenge before them was to elucidate the terms of an act of the imperial Parliament which purported to provide, in some sense, a 'federal' constitution for Canada. The Canadian act stated that the parties to the agreement wished to be 'federally united into One Dominion under the Crown of the United Kingdom of Great Britain and Ireland, with a Constitution similar in Principle to that of the United Kingdom.' This is the only place in the act that 'federalism' is mentioned. Both Watson and Haldane attempted to follow the judgments of the previous Judicial Committee boards in Canadian cases and distinguished those precedents that gave them trouble, just as they would have done in any other non-constitutional case that came before them. Canadian judges and lawyers saw the matter more in the light of American constitutional jurisprudence; they watched as the Supreme Court of the United States wrestled with the provisions of their constitution relating to the 'commerce clause' and other 'federalism questions.' They watched and admired the way the great American judges such as Marshall had worked out the conflicting claims of the two levels of legislative authority in the early years of the republic's history.[10] Any attempt on their part to have the lords of the Judicial Committee consider their appeals in similar terms was rebuffed as impertinent and inappropriate.

Prior to the passage of the British North America Act, 1867, constitutional history was the study of the constitution of the United Kingdom. It included, in addition to a few notable common law judgments, the study of the legislative record in order to uncover the intention of Parliament. The chief obligation of English judges under this older order was to find the intention of Parliament and to give effect to that intention. Meanwhile, the new approach that was fast emerging in the United States placed emphasis on the understanding of the constitution as it was revealed in the judgments of past courts and not on the intention of the framers of the constitution. The distinction between the two approaches is critical. The new jurisprudence tended to exclude constitutional history and rely exclusively on the reasoning of judges in previous cases. It is the difference between studying the constitution and studying what judges say about the constitution. As Gary McDowell has written of the American experience: 'This older view of the Constitution as paramount to the ordinary law and to the branches of the government has become undermined to a great degree by a new judicial view of the Constitution. This view is made up of two distinct but related lines of judicial logic. The first is that the opinions of the Supreme Court – constitutional law – have the same status as the Constitution itself: the second is that the Constitution is not bound by any particular theory, is not permanent and fixed, but is instead free to move amoeba-like through history.'[11]

An examination of the leading constitutional texts in Canadian and American law schools will confirm that this new approach of focusing exclusively on court judgments – an approach made famous by the celebrated Christopher Columbus Langdell at Harvard Law School in the nineteenth century – has taken firm hold in the education of both Canadian and American lawyers and future judges. It is no coincidence that the Judicial Committee would eventually come to devise principles of judicial construction based on a view of the constitution of Canada as a 'living tree,' requiring pruning and tending as circumstances emerged. It is a view perfectly consistent with Haldane's previously stated views on the virtues of an unwritten constitution. The new constitutional law, the 'living tree' ethos, views judges as the custodians of a constitutional arboretum where their proper function is to prune and trim. Neither is it a coincidence that constitutional history has been virtually expunged from the education of constitutional lawyers in Canada and the United States. While some American law schools give attention to the American founding debates and the *Federalist Papers*, almost no one in Canadian law schools studies the debates on the Quebec Resolutions that took place in all the colonial legislatures in 1865. Constitutional history has been replaced by the study of the constitutional opinions of judges who eschew the appeal to the 'intention of the fathers of Confederation,' or other references to the history of the constitution.

The 'living tree' school of constitutional jurisprudence enunciated by Lord Sankey[12] gave formal endorsement to a kind of judging that encouraged judges to roam throughout the constitutional arboretum with a vision of what it should look like without regard to the intentions of the landscape architect. As Lord Sankey observed in the *Edwards* case, 'the question is not what may be supposed to have been intended, but what has been said.'[13] This curious observation obscured the fact that most people – including legislators – express in words what they intend. What is said cannot be separated from what was intended. By contrast, Oliver Wendell Holmes, writing on the theory of legal interpretation, noted two decades before Sankey's comments that 'the purpose of written instruments is to express some intention or state of mind of those who write them, and it is desirable to make that purpose effectual, so far as may be, if instruments are to be used. The question is how far the law ought to go in aid of the writers.'[14]

Under the 'living tree, approach, judges were obliged to bring the constitution into tune with the shifting *mores* of the times. And no one contributed more to this school of constitutional jurisprudence than Richard Burdon Haldane, who, under the guidance of G.W.F. Hegel, refined the role of judges as searchers-out and defenders of the *Sittlichkeit*: that 'instinctive sense of what to do and what not to do in daily life and behaviour that is the source of liberty and ease.'[15] The quest for *Sittlichkeit* was the abiding central thread that permeated all Haldane's reasoning in Canadian constitutional cases. It is no coincidence that he was the author of a book titled *The Reign of Relativity*, for as the times change so, too, must the public acceptance of the latest 'progressive' social standard which judges are called upon to weave into the fabric of the law. All of this would have numbed into oblivion the noble Lord Watson; sufficient for him was the task of weakening the centralizing forces of the constitution. But to secure the benefits of the 'progressive temper of the times' was the very grist to Haldane's philosophic mill. That is also why he embraced Hegel: it was the historically dynamic character of Hegelianism that caught his attention and captivated him for the remainder of his life. Law was the life of the state and it was ever changing under the influence of the *Weltgeist*, the World Spirit of freedom as 'progress.' It is for this reason that Haldane's story is not simply a continuation of Lord Watson's and why that story is so much more complicated and more interesting.

Reimagining Canada

Viscount Haldane knew that he had stepped into a cauldron of controversy when he presided over Canadian cases. Having appeared as a barrister in a number of Canadian appeals, he also knew that he was inheriting a body of precedent set down, principally by Lord Watson, which favoured the provinces, and he welcomed these precedents. He was also aware that he was inheriting a fractious colonial history; he knew from his own inquiries and from informal association with Canadian politicians and lawyers that several of the provincial governments were pitted against an intransigent central government supported by a constitutional document which paid lip service to federalism and which armed the central government with legislative powers over the provinces. But he was confident that he was equal to the task of untangling the knotted terms of the Canadian constitution. It was a task he embraced with enthusiasm, guided as he was by his understanding of the Hegelian philosophy of state.

It has become customary in recent years to denigrate the Canadian fathers of Confederation and their constitution of 1867. Paul Romney, for example, has written that their efforts – combined with the incompetence of the British parliamentary draughtsmen – conspired to produce a document that went one better than the 'apocryphal committee that set out to design a horse and achieved a camel.'[16] However gratuitous this comment may appear, there is no doubting that the plan of Confederation was a barely disguised attempt to form a constitution whose principal feature was a strong central Parliament and government with weak component provinces. This presented a critical problem: How could a constitution that gave the national government the power to disallow provincial acts of legislation, for up to two years from the passage of the act, even acts that were in every respect validly enacted, be called *federal*? Romney has written: 'The earliest strains between Ontario and Ottawa occurred over disallowance, but the first of the primary legal issues to flare up was that of executive power.'[17] Not only did Ontario begin to seek relief in the courts in order to find a way out from under the federal dominance, but other provinces, such as Quebec under Premier Mercier, also sought to restrain the intrusion of federal powers into their jurisdictions. The pesky threat of disallowance was resolved politically; the federal government simply stopped exercising it, but not before 122 provincial acts had been disallowed between 1867 and 1942.[18] The political process served to resolve a few of the jurisdictional issues dividing the two levels of power but the most important ones, dealing with the 'Peace, Order, and good Government' clause and the content of the 'property and civil rights in the province,' were settled by appeal to the Privy Council. And Viscount Haldane played a central role in these matters.

He knew from his many conversations with Canadian lawyers and judges when they visited London that the constitution designed by the fathers of Confederation seemed to have been seriously out of sympathy with the ambitions of the provincial politicians and the people of the times. It is difficult to imagine that Haldane was not aware of Joseph Howe's public repudiation of Confederation as 'The Botheration Scheme' or his mission to London begging the government to refuse to adopt the scheme.[19] There is no evidence to show that Haldane conversed with Howe or sought his advice. Such a conversation would have confirmed Haldane in his view of the provincial cause. Yet he must have known that so widely was Confederation repudiated in Nova Scotia, for example, that eighteen of the nineteen members of Parliament sent to the first session in Ottawa under the new constitution were elected on a platform calling for its repeal.[20]

There is no question that the constitutional interpretations of Watson and Haldane – however seriously offensive to many Canadian legal and historical scholars at the time – constituted a repudiation of the work of our framers.[21] 'Blame Hegel' might in part be true; but only in part. Watson was not indebted to Hegel. But surely one cannot envisage that Scottish jurist ever validating a constitution for Canada where provincial laws could be disallowed up to two years after their passage, on virtually any subject regardless of the constitutional authority to pass them. It is too much to say that Hegel saved us from the Quebec Conference plot, which had, in fact, been hatched in George Brown's constitutional committee before the delegates met in Quebec City in 1865. The Confederation act was a product of the ambitions of leading Canadian political leaders: Macdonald, Brown, Cartier, and Alexander Galt, assisted by Tupper of Nova Scotia and Samuel Leonard Tilley of New Brunswick. They designed a constitution that was 'similar in principle to that of the United Kingdom,' with all the overbearing powers of the central administration, and then they tried to impose it on the provinces. In the United States the draft constitution of the Philadelphia convention of 1787 was sent to the various states for ratification by conventions held for that purpose. The Quebec Resolutions were debated in the legislature of Canada in 1865 and favourably adopted by a majority vote. It is often forgotten, however, that a majority of *francophone* members in the legislature of the United Canadas from Quebec voted against the Quebec plan of Confederation.[22] And those who did not support the plan – even Quebec anglophones such as Christopher Dunkin – spoke against it precisely on the grounds that it ran roughshod over the legitimate aspirations of the people of the provinces. Not surprisingly, then, the new constitution found its way into the courts soon after its adoption in 1867. The conflicting claims to exclusive legislative authority in large matters, such as taxation, made litigation inevitable.

Mowat is entitled to a special place in this constitutional saga because he was the one who was to emerge as an important influence on the thinking of Viscount Haldane in Canadian constitutional affairs.[23] Mowat had been appointed to the Ontario Court of Chancery three years before Confederation but was coaxed to return to politics in 1872 by Edward Blake, Alexander Mackenzie, and the indomitable George Brown of the *Globe*. Mowat became premier and had the Ontario legislature pass two acts dealing with the office of the lieutenant governor. These two acts *declared* that the lieutenant governor had the power to appoint Queen's Counsel and to establish the order of precedence in the provincial courts.[24] They went unchallenged for almost a decade because the Macdonald government was defeated in 1873 and replaced by the Liberal government of Alexander Mackenzie. Yet these seemingly innocuous acts contained a constitutional time bomb. If they were allowed to stand, they would have constituted a powerful legal challenge to the office of the governor general, who, at least in the minds of the framers of the Confederation act, provided the only formal link with the imperial crown. It was the expectation and wish of the fathers of Confederation that the lieutenant governors of the provinces would be 'agents of the federal government.' The sleeper issue remained dormant until Lord Watson, as we have seen, ruled in *Liquidators of the Maritime Bank* (1892) that 'it would require very express language, such as is not to be found in the Act of 1867, to warrant the inference that the Imperial Legislature meant to vest in the provinces of Canada the right of exercising supreme legislative powers in which the British Sovereign was to have no share.'[25] This important decision, by locating the queen in the right of the province, became the solid legal foundation for the later claims to provincial 'autonomy' which the Haldane board enthusiastically championed.

Canada's Constitutional Expert

Haldane frequently claimed to be an expert in Canadian constitutional affairs and not without some reason. Between 1912 and 1929, there were forty-one appeals from Canada, principally involving disputes over federal and provincial legislative jurisdiction. And Viscount Haldane took part in many of those cases, both as a barrister and later as a judge of the Judicial Committee. His place in Canadian constitutional affairs led him to take offence at those who presumed, as Joseph Chamberlain did on one occasion, to speak with authority in the House of Commons on Canadian constitutional affairs. Haldane could not resist a riposte to Chamberlain's comments: 'As one of the standing counsel for the province of Canada which has of late years been engaged in the most frequent conflicts with the Dominion on the bloodless battlefield of the Privy Council offices in Downing Street, I had come to imagine that the provisions of the British North America Act, 1867, as interpreted over and over again by the Judicial Committee, could not be misunderstood, at least in their most general terms. This illusion was dispelled by Mr Chamberlain's speech.'[26] Considering that during the early 1880s the young barrister was still a junior member of the bar, this was a rather testy correction. Then again, many found the pretentious Chamberlain a target not to be resisted.

Haldane was eventually to sit on thirty-two Canadian appeals and delivered nineteen judgments for the board. His claim to expertise in Canadian cases was repeated upon arrival in Montreal in 1914, when he explained that he made it a rule to give over the entire month of July to Canadian appeals. In one letter to his mother he boasted that 'yesterday I have disposed of a heavy Canadian appeal and I am up to my elbows in writing the judgement. I have to write practically all the judgements in the [Canadian] constitutional cases for since Lord Watson's time there has been no other who knew this branch of learning.'[27] He could not resist saying in the same letter that 'the Canadians now call me their "father of the Privy Council," they want my portrait hung up there.'[28] However much this was an exaggerated view of his importance in Canadian cases, there is little doubt that he attempted to keep in touch with Canadian legal and political affairs by inviting lawyers from Canada – either those who were in town on other business or those who appeared before him – to dinner at 28 Queen Anne's Gate. In 1924 he related how '[Lyman Poore] Duff of the Supreme Court of Canada and his wife dined here last night. He and I are the repositories – so his Prime Minister of Canada says – of the learning about the Canadian Constitution.'[29] One frequently finds among his correspondence notes such as this: 'I had an eminent Canadian at dinner last night, I spent the evening going into Canadian affairs.'[30] On another occasion we find him writing: 'Last night the Canadian lawyers entertained me at dinner and treated me with reverence like a father.'[31] The very next evening, he wrote: 'Last night we had the first of our Canadian dinner parties. The guests made me feel as if I were one of the Fathers of Canada.'[32] These references to contacts with Canadian lawyers and Supreme Court judges lends support to Alan Cairns's view that the law lords of the Judicial Committee took into account the political and legal developments in Canada during those early years while litigating Canadian cases.[33] Whether that was true of Watson or other members of the Judicial Committee is doubtful, but it was certainly true of Haldane. Still, Haldane was also aware that back in Canada he was not universally well received. 'I am being much abused from Canada,' he once noted, 'over the constitutional judgement disallowing the Lemieux Act.

But we have no one of us the least doubt about the judgement, and we remain, of course silent.'[34]

Much has been written about Richard Haldane's work ethic. He would frequently study briefs far into the night and appear in court the next morning fresh and ready. He brought these habits with him to the bench. In one letter he gave an account of a day in his life in the Privy Council. 'Yesterday I had a great day in the Presidential chair at the Privy Council. I drove through six hearings of petitions and gave judgement in all of them. Then a full appeal, and half of a second appeal. I was not tired and was able to have an hour's conversation with Col. House the American who wished to see me. And in the evening I made a speech to lawyers at the Holborn Restaurant, and then I hosted a reception at the Lord Chancellor's and afterwards to do some reading here. Not bad for aged 65.'[35] His sister, Elizabeth, related that her brother 'sat 5 days a week straight on. Had Canadian lawyers at dinner. Nesbitt and Newcombe.'[36]

Shortly after his return to England from Montreal, Haldane had an exchange of letters with Chief Justice Sir Charles Fitzpatrick. Apparently the chief justice had written to Haldane complaining that the lord chancellor did not give sufficient attention to Canadian cases. Haldane was not pleased by Fitzpatrick's admonition, which touched a sensitive chord in the hardworking lord chancellor. He replied immediately to set the record straight: 'You speak of myself as not giving personal attention to Canadian cases. I have sat on every case of importance since I became Chancellor and have instituted the Canadian July ... I have bent the whole strength of our tribunal in cases from Canada even to the sacrifice of English work in the House of Lords of two Judges – which was what the Imperial Conference asked for ... And it certainly never gave more time or pains as Canadian cases. If we do not fall below the level reached in the Alberta, Fishery and Cotton cases, I shall be well content. But no lower standards will suffice.'[37] It is difficult to guess what prompted Fitzpatrick's complaint because Richard Haldane was widely known to be a conscientious judge with a genuine interest in Canadian cases. He concluded his letter to the chief justice rather testily with the remark that 'you must take us or else do what you are quite within your rights in doing by abolishing the Appeal. You must not mind my writing thus freely but when I have been making some of the hardest efforts of my life I do not like to have them misunderstood.'[38] Having felt the sting of the lord chancellor's reply, Fitzpatrick responded with a letter the next month in which he more or less apologized. As for termination of appeals, well: 'As a Catholic and native of Quebec I would deplore any change in our Constitutional relations.'[39] What did the fact of his Catholicism have to do with appeals to the Judicial Committee? Quebec had almost always enjoyed success before the Judicial Committee and was in no hurry to terminate appeals. In any event, the matter did not develop further and Sir Charles Fitzpatrick was himself invited to sit as a member of the board, the second Canadian judge to do so.[40]

There is little doubt that Viscount Haldane did not think very highly of the British North America Act. He especially did not like the kind of federal system it proposed for the country. He made it clear very early in his judicial career that he was not overly impressed with and never inclined to accede to the Supreme Court of Canada's early favourable attitude towards the central government at the expense of the provinces.[41] There is no question that, after appearing before the Judicial Committee seven times for the provinces between 1894 and 1904, Haldane became convinced that the people of the provinces – not merely their governments – were chafing under the centralizing forces of the new Canadian constitution. He was in close contact with leading provincial lawyers and politicians, several of whom, such as Edward Blake, appeared in his court as advocates. Haldane, clearly, as a Scot by temperament, resisted the dominance of a central legislative authority. His mind recoiled at the conflicting claims to exclusivity contained in sections 91 and 92. How could both levels of government have 'exclusive' jurisdiction over the same areas of legislation, such as taxation? And what did the act mean by the sweeping legislative authority in the name of 'Peace, Order, and good Government?' How was this compatible with the 'exclusive' provincial powers over 'property and civil rights?'

Like his contemporaries on the bench, Viscount Haldane struggled with the concept of federalism and, hence, was uncomfortable with the federal pretensions of the Canadian constitution. His most explicit treatment of federalism appeared in an address he delivered before the Royal Colonial Institute in London, in May 1900, titled 'Federal Constitutions within the Empire.' In that address he sought to discover 'the nature of the unwritten relations of the Imperial Government to the derivative constitutions which have grown out of the parent stem.'[42] He showed special interest in the constitutions of Canada and Australia, both of which he said possessed 'derivative constitutions upon so-called federal principles.' Here, once again, we are told that the constitutions of Canada and Australia were 'but skeletons' and that 'the practice of governors, ministers, parliaments, and judges have to endow with flesh and blood before the dry bones can live.'[43] Such language from the very man who eschewed the use of metaphorical language in both philosophy and law was puzzling. How 'dry bones' could come to life by the application of 'flesh and blood' remains both an anatomical and a constitutional mystery. But there it was: the colonial draughtsmen in both Canada and Australia, by implication from Haldane's remarks, were incompetent to provide for themselves a constitution worthy of the name. But those colonial politicians who sought assistance from the defects of their founding statesmen were told not to expect immediate relief, for 'the process of endowment may be gradual.'[44] The learned viscount went on to assure his audience that the 'essence of the British constitution is ... neither rigid nor even written.' Hence those colonial constitutions purporting to be based on the imperial model – such as the Canadian desire for 'a constitution similar in principle to that of the United Kingdom' – invited a 'process of silent approximation to the parent example.'[45] This portion of his address was pure muddle. Having got himself trapped in the fleshless bones of the skeletal imagery, he clawed his way up to the more secure grounds of constitutional history by talking about the essential characteristics of the British constitution, which must have been well known to the members of the Colonial Institute. One can only imagine the relief experienced by this audience to leave the constitutional boneyard and to find themselves in the more comfortable lounges of the constitutional history and practice of the Empire.

To make matters worse, in the case of Canada, Haldane proceeded to observe that Canadians had not been served well by their own nascent Supreme Court, which began to show, he announced, 'a tendency in its judgements which caused suspicion and friction in the Provinces.' As a result, he continued, 'a series of questions emerged sharply, of such delicacy that it was essential that they should be decided by an arbiter holding an absolutely even hand between the contending parties, and simply interpreting the words of the Dominion Act in the light of that British Constitution which its object was to reproduce.'[46] How the unitary British unwritten constitution could provide guidance to judges faced with a constitutional document that aspired to meet the aspirations of the parties to be 'federally united,' he did not say. There is no doubt, however, that the arbiters were to be the law lords sitting as the Judicial Committee. That august body, he went on to observe, 'settled that the true view of the [Canadian] Act was that it established a federal distribution of not only legislative but executive powers and that in the matters delegated to them the Provincial governments had an authority as high as that of the Central Government. The relationship was, in other words, held to be one of strict coordination and that in executive as well as legislative matters.'[47] 'On this principle,' Haldane concluded grandly, 'one burning conflict after another was stilled.' The overriding ambition of the Judicial Committee, he insisted, was not to interfere with the right of colonial governments to enjoy autonomy in their own concerns, but only to keep the Empire together and 'to pervade its institutions with a spirit that is imperial in the noblest sense.'[48] It became clear that the true Hegelian philosopher-judge would always aspire to infuse the derivative constitutions and the Empire as a whole with the 'noblest spirit' – the respect for law and parliamentary responsible government – which lies at the heart of the unwritten British constitution.

It comes as no surprise that Haldane's judicial tactic was to insist on the 'absolute coordinate power of the provincial legislatures' with the federal Parliament. He deplored, he said, the use of the term 'federal' in the act as an 'inaccurate and inappropriate term, and how it came to be used in this statute it is difficult to conceive.'[49] One of the first obstacles in the way of a 'genuine federal system' for Canada was the head of section 91. That provision outlining the legislative powers of the central government contained the troublesome 'Peace, Order and good Government' clause. The section reads as follows: 'It shall be lawful for the Queen, by and with the Advice and Consent of the Senate and House of Commons, to make Laws for the Peace, Order, and good Government of Canada, in Relation to all Matters not coming within the classes of Subjects by this Act assigned exclusively to the Legislatures of the Provinces.' The provision does not end there, as we have seen. It concludes: 'and for greater Certainty, *but not so as to restrict the Generality of the foregoing Terms of this section* [i.e., 'Peace, Order, and good Government'], it is hereby declared that (*notwithstanding anything in this Act*) the exclusive Legislative Authority of the Parliament of Canada extends to all Matters coming within the Classes of Subjects next hereinafter enumerated.'

The explicit words of the provision make it very difficult to avoid the point that the central Parliament was intended to have under 'Peace, Order, and good Government' a broad legislative power, 'notwithstanding anything in this Act.' Clearly, this provision, in the minds of the Judicial Committee, had to be cut back or redefined so as to restrict the intruding reach of federal jurisdiction. Watson and Haldane both agreed that the provision was simply not compatible with the minimal conditions of a federal constitution. Unfortunately, a previous decision of the board stood in the way. The Judicial Committee had decided in *Russell v. The Queen* (1881–2)[50] that the Canada Temperance Act, 1878 was a valid exercise of federal legislative power under the 'Peace, Order, and good Government' clause. Judah Benjamin had argued on the basis of *Citizens Insurance v. Parson* (1881–2)[51] that the central Parliament had no power to pass the act in question. He contended in *Russell* that the act was not for the 'Peace, Order, and good Government' of Canada because the law provided for local option. If it had applied to the whole Dominion, Benjamin argued, then it would be within the power of the Dominion Parliament.

Sir Montague Smith viewed the issue in the context of a case that arose in the courts of New Brunswick. In the *City of Fredericton v. The Queen*, the Supreme Court of Canada reversed a judgment of the Supreme Court of New Brunswick which had held that the Canada Temperance Act, 1878 was ultra vires the power of the Dominion government.[52] Smith noted at the opening of his judgment in *Russell* that 'the present appeal to Her Majesty is brought in effect to review the last-mentioned decision [*City of Fredericton*].' After citing the 'Peace, Order, and good Government' clause at the head of section 91, he then proceeded to say that the issue of legislative competence must be decided by first asking whether the matter of the legislation was covered in section 92 outlining the powers of the provincial legislatures. 'It is evident,' he concluded, 'that the matter of the Act is not within the class of subject No.9 [92] and consequently that it could not have been passed by the Provincial Legislature by virtue of any authority conferred upon it by the sub-section.'[53] He went on to say that what 'Parliament is dealing with in legislation of this kind is not a matter in relation to property and its rights, but one relating to public order and safety.'[54] The legislation controlling the consumption of liquor was analogous, he reasoned, to protecting the public from 'exposure of cattle having a contagious disease.'[55] Laws of this sort were clearly designed for 'the promotion of public order, safety or morals' and as such 'fall within the general authority of Parliament to make laws for the order and good government of Canada.'[56] Taking aim at Judah Benjamin's argument that the act trenched upon the provincial powers over 'property and civil rights in the province,' Sir Montague noted: 'Few, if any, laws could be made by Parliament for the peace, order and good government of Canada which did not in some incidental way affect property and civil rights.'[57]

The important point to note in this case is that Sir Montague treated the scope of the 'Peace, Order, and good Government' clause on its own merits and its relationship to property civil rights in the provinces. His analysis was, in short, a thorough examination of the scope of the general power and its relationship to the enumerated powers under section 92 governing the provincial legislatures. This judgment, however, became an obstacle to the ambitions of both Lord Watson and Viscount Haldane to expand the legislative powers of the provinces. Watson paid lip service to it and skirted it whenever convenient. Both Scottish jurists took encouragement from Sir Barnes Peacock, who announced in *Hodge v. The Queen* the very next year that *Russell v. The Queen* had to be 'properly understood.' The proper understanding, he explained – absorbing into the explanation *Citizens Insurance v. Parsons* as well – was 'that subjects which in one aspect and for one purpose fall within section 92 may in another aspect and for another purpose fall within section 91.'[58] John Saywell cites Haldane's comments that 'Lord Watson did not believe in the judgments of this Board in *Russell v. The Queen*,' as if that somehow solved the problem.[59] Haldane explicitly acknowledged that it became a 'tacit rule, a convention between judges and counsel that *Russell v. The Queen* was not to be cited.'[60] They lacked the power to overrule previous judgments of the board, so they simply ignored them. This was, in fact, the only way that the Judicial Committee could treat previous judgments which stood in the way of new directions, a state of affairs that endured until 1966. Convention prohibited it from reversing previous judgments because that would be tantamount to saying that the board had given wrong advice to the queen on a previous occasion.

But Haldane's determination to restrict the 'Peace, Order, and good Government' clause narrowly as possible also ran into Watson's rulings that it was validly invoked in matters of 'national concern.' Watson, it will be recalled, had ruled in *Local Prohibition* that federal legislation 'must not trench on any of the subjects in s. 92 ... unless they have attained such dimensions as to affect the body politic of the Dominion.'[61] Haldane argued that, Watson notwithstanding, the federal Parliament could not exercise its authority under 'Peace, Order, and good Government' even in times of great public importance if it trenched on provincial jurisdiction. He ruled that 'highly exceptional circumstances,' such 'as those of a great war,' would justify the federal intrusion into matters covered in section 92. But he was determined to restrict the application of the 'Peace, Order, and good Government' clause to times of national emergency. And so it came as no surprise that he served notice in the *Insurance Reference* (1916)[62] that the federal Parliament, neither by the 'regulation of trade and commerce' clause nor by the 'Peace, Order, and good Government' clause, could invade areas of provincial jurisdiction. In the *Board of Commerce Case*[63] he took off the gloves and ruled that conditions like 'war and famine' would be required before the federal Parliament could invoke its authority under 'Peace, Order, and good Government' to invade the provincial areas of jurisdiction.

In *Toronto Electric Commissioners v. Snider* (1925), Haldane overturned federal legislation that was designed to settle industrial disputes. He did so on the grounds that the federal legislation invaded the provincial jurisdiction over civil rights in the provinces. He said that the 'Peace, Order, and good Government' clause could be invoked only in 'cases arising out of some extraordinary peril to the national life of Canada, such as the cases arising out of a war.'[64] As Peter Hogg has noted: 'In neither of these two important cases did the Privy Council make any reference to the "national dimensions"' test of Lord Watson.[65] It simply ignored the Watson's ruling in *Local Prohibition*.

Haldane did not win any plaudits throughout Canadian legal circles when he explained in *Snider* that the decision of the board in *Russell* had to be understood as validating the use of 'Peace, Order, and good Government' because the 'evil of intemperance at that time amounted in Canada to one so great and so general that at least for the period it was a menace to the national life of Canada so serious and pressing that the National Parliament was called on to intervene to protect the nation from disaster.'[66] And, as if this were not sufficient to explain *Russell*, Haldane added: 'An epidemic of pestilence might conceivably have been regarded as analogous.' As for Sir Montague Smith, the author of *Russell*, Haldane explained: 'Their Lordships find it difficult to explain the decision in *Russell v. The Queen* as more than a decision of this order upon fact, considered to have been established at its date rather than upon general law.'[67] The facts in *Snider* did not, he calculated, amount to 'an emergency putting the national life of Canada in unanticipated peril such as the Board which decided *Russell v. The Queen* may be considered to have had before their minds.'[68]

It is difficult to conclude whether this judgment perpetrated a greater calumny upon Sir Montague Smith or upon the Canadian people. However considered, the judgment must be ranked among the most outrageous judicial opinions ever penned in the annals of Canadian public law. It showed indelibly what Haldane meant when he wrote in *Rodriquez v. Speyer Bros* (1919) that 'I think there are many things of which the judges are bound to take judicial notice of which lie outside the law properly so called, and among those things are what is called public policy and the changes which take place in it. The law itself may become modified by this obligation of the judges.'[69]

The calumny is in no way mitigated by the fact that Haldane would finally come to the conclusion that the 'Peace, Order, and good Government' clause should be restricted to times of national emergency. His decision in *Snider* simply made explicit and stated boldly what he had already noted in softer terms in the *Re Board of Commerce*[70] and *Fort Francis*[71] cases. But this was only the beginning of his efforts to restrict the reach of the central Parliament and to expand the legislative powers of the provincial governments. Having achieved the first objective by neutering the head of section 91, he then proceeded to extend the powers of the provincial legislatures by expanding provincial authority over 'property and civil rights in the provinces.' Section 92(13) of the Canadian constitution states that the provincial legislatures have 'exclusive' legislative jurisdiction over 'property and civil rights in the province.' Haldane soon emerged as an inflexible defender of provincial ambitions to revise what Saywell calls the 'misshapen federal system.'[72] In so doing he became, indeed, in the words of Senator Eugene Forsey, 'the wicked step-father of the Canadian constitution.'[73] Wicked, however, only in the minds of those who sided with the fathers of Confederation and a strong centralized constitution; not wicked to those provincial politicians who chafed under the centralizing terms of the constitution. For a clear statement of how Haldane understood the Canadian constitution, we can cite *Attorney General for Australia v. Colonial Sugar Co.*,[74] where he said that 'in Canada there is no federal system.'

As we have seen, during his years on the Judicial Committee, Haldane wrote nineteen judgments on cases from Canada, fifteen of which involved the division of legislative powers under the terms of sections 91 and 92. He consistently championed the cause of the provinces against the claims of the federal government in trade and commerce cases where he expanded the provincial authority over property and civil rights. His disposition to take into account the conditions of the provinces in the teeth of a strong claim for federal dominance was first evident in *In re Marriage Legislation in Canada* (1912).[75] Lawyers for the federal government claimed that provincial authority permitted it to deal with the solemnization of marriage, an argument that on its true construction meant the regulation of the evidentiary or religious formalities by which the contract was to be authenticated or sanctified. They also argued that the terms of the constitution act of 1867 must be interpreted widely as meaning the whole contract of marriage independent of formalities which are separable therefrom. In that sense, solemnization followed on a completed contract declared by the Dominion to be valid, and the jurisdiction assigned to the province was not intended to carry with it the power of impairing or destroying the validity of the contract. Lawyers for the province of Quebec argued strenuously that the federal authority over 'marriage and divorce' must have the same meaning that it had in all previous pre-Confederation enactments flowing from French law. Haldane, ruling in favour of the provinces, noted: 'The common law of England and the law of Quebec before confederation are conspicuous examples, which would naturally have been in the minds of those who inserted the words about solemnization into the statute. Prima facie these words appear to their Lordships to import that the whole of what solemnization ordinarily meant in the system of law of the provinces of Canada at the time of confederation is intended to come within them, including conditions which affect validity.'[76] This was the case to which Haldane alluded, when he spoke to reporters in Montreal in 1913, as an example of the impartial role the Judicial Committee played in the life of the Empire.

The next important decision in which Haldane spoke for the Judicial Committee was *John Deere Plow v. Wharton* (1915).[77] The question in that case was whether British Columbia could compel Dominion companies to register under a provincial registration law. Haldane observed that the provincial authority over property and civil rights had to be subject to some limitations. The Judicial Committee decided, accordingly, that the Dominion powers arising out of its authority over the regulation of trade and commerce prevented the provinces from legislating so as to deprive Dominion companies of their status and powers. Those Canadians who hoped that the Judicial Committee was swinging back towards the Dominion took delight in the *John Deere* ruling. Their enthusiasm was to be irrevocably destroyed, however, in the next case. In *Attorney General for Canada v. Attorney General for Alberta* (1916),[78] the question was whether the federal government could prevent insurance companies from operating without its consent. The big hurdle was Lord Watson's 'refinement' of *Russell v. The Queen* (1881–2) in 1894.[79] Haldane was unable to find a way of upholding the federal legislation at issue in this case. According to the Watson refinement, the federal government could enter such areas of provincial concern or jurisdiction only where the province had no power under section 92 or where the subject was of paramount national importance. Haldane could scarcely argue that the regulation of insurance companies was of national importance or constituted an emergency. The federal legislation in question was accordingly held to be ultra vires.

The next major cases came to the Judicial Committee as requests for advisory opinions. In the cases *In re Board of Commerce Act* (1920)[80] and *In re Combines and Fair Prices Act* (1922),[81] the board was asked whether the federal government could regulate retail prices. The federal government rested its arguments on both the 'Peace, Order, and good Government' clause and the 'regulation of trade and commerce.' As in other cases, Haldane and the Judicial Committee were guided by the principles laid down by Lord Watson. As already noted, Watson had limited the power of the federal government to interfere in provincial matters involving property and civil rights to 'highly exceptionally circumstances.' Haldane did not believe that the federal act in question was justified by any highly exceptional circumstances, not even the First World War. This is not to imply that Haldane was a reluctant follower of Watson's efforts to diminish the federal power and to increase the provincial powers. Far from it; he welcomed the direction set down by his predecessor. He was, indeed, an enthusiastic defender of provincial powers and exerted a considerable influence in broadening the provincial legislative authority under the terms of property and civil rights. In *Bonanza Creek Gold Mining Co.* (1916),[82] Haldane decided that, although the provinces were given the power to incorporate only companies 'with provincial purposes ... actual powers and rights are one thing and capacity to accept extra-provincial powers and rights is quite another. In the case of a company created by charter the doctrine of ultra-vires has no real application in the absence of statutory restriction added to what is written in the charter. Such a company has the capacity of a natural person to acquire powers and rights.' This had the effect of conferring power on provincial companies to conduct business beyond the limits of the province. It did much to expand the commercial power of provincially incorporated companies and, by implication, reduce the federal power to control them.

At this point it is important to ask the question asked of Lord Watson: Why did Viscount Haldane go to such lengths to reshape the Canadian constitution? The ambition took on the form of a crusade or obsession. Why did he find this matter so compelling? To whom was he talking? There is no question that he was on intimate terms with Ontario Premier Oliver Mowat and that he entertained him along with Edward Blake and a long list of other Canadian lawyers.[83] He became fully aware of the struggle between the federal government in Ottawa and the aspirations of the various provinces from the very moment Confederation took root. The message he kept getting from his Canadian sources was that the provinces wanted greater freedom to legislate for their own purposes; that they chafed under a constitution that contained the central authority to disallow provincial legislation for up to two years after the passage of legislation.

Haldane studiously avoided legislative history; he rarely ever alluded to the Canadian fathers of Confederation or to the many lengthy legislative debates that took place at Confederation throughout the four principal colonies over the terms of union. History and the intention of the framers were irrelevant for him, except, as we shall see in a moment, on one occasion. The focus of his attention was the Confederation document and its defect as a 'federal' constitution. He set out to correct what Saywell calls the 'misshapen federal system.' The more Haldane read the constitution and the more he talked with members of the Canadian bar who visited London, the more he became the champion of the cause of provincial autonomy, the more sensitive he became to the struggling provincial *Sittlichkeit*.

In one of his last Canadian cases, *John Deere Plow v. Wharton* (1915),[84] Haldane broke with his earlier reluctance to consult history and studied the process leading up to Confederation; here he acknowledged that the Confederation act was based on 'the resolutions passed at Quebec in October, 1864'; but he went on to suggest that the act was a 'political agreement' and that 'the obscurity of language' was due to the fact that the resolutions were the work of a 'large assemblage.' The duty of the judge working with such a document, he suggested, was to sort out the conflicting matters and make up for the shoddy work of the politicians and the legislative draughtsmen. 'It may be added that the form in which provisions in terms overlapping each other have been placed side by side shows that those who passed the Confederation Act intended to leave the working out of and interpretation of these provisions to practice and to judicial decision.'[85] Indeed, he went on to state that it would be 'unwise on this or any other occasion to attempt exhaustive definitions of the meaning and scope of these expressions.'[86] True to his Hegelianism, he was suggesting that the meaning of words and the scope of their expression could not be defined once and for all;

succeeding generations would determine for themselves their meaning and scope. Throughout this judgment, Haldane noted repeatedly that it would be wise for the courts to avoid any attempt 'to decide each case which arises without entering more largely upon an interpretation of the statute than is necessary for the decision of the particular question in hand.' This long-established and wise rule was intended, he averred, to prevent 'injustice to future suitors.' And, faithful to his provincial bias, he said that the proper procedure was to enquire first 'if the subject-matter falls within any of the heads of s. 92 [and if so] it becomes necessary to see whether it also falls within any of the enumerated heads of s. 91.'[87] Besides, the learned lord continued, 'the language of these section and of the various heads which they contain obviously cannot be construed as having been intended to embody the exact disjunctions of a perfect logical scheme.'[88] After all, the entire Confederation act was the work of politicians and legislative draughtsmen, individuals who lacked the intelligence to envision and enact 'a perfectly logical scheme' – something only the philosophical judge could be expected to do.

All of this was perfectly consistent with his Hegelian sensitivity to the prevailing *Sittlichkeit*, which was nothing less than the plea for broader provincial legislative powers; provincial politicians were pleading for the right to give shape and direction to life in the provinces. They were being hampered from doing so by the terms of a constitutional document that paid lip service to federalism while exercising the centralizing power of a unitary state. However much Haldane – following Hegel – allows for the role of public opinion, the 'general will' and majority public opinion are not the same thing; public opinion must always be subservient to the general will. Under the inspiration of Hegel, who drew upon Rousseau and Montesquieu in this matter, Haldane articulated a doctrine of the central importance of the 'general will.' The general will, or 'the common will' as Haldane called it, was 'nothing apart from our own wills. It is just our own will at their social level.'[89] It is that will, as Rousseau had previously articulated it, which the entire community ought to will, having set aside the natural attachment of each citizen's private or selfish will. In this sense it is the will of the community that expresses the genuine common good of all members of the state. This is what Hegel meant when he wrote that if 'the state is to realize *Sittlichkeit*, then it must constitute a common life in which all find their identity.'[90]

9

The State and the Reign of Relativity

We know now that there are no immutable goals – there is only a way, a process, by which we shall, like gods, create our own ends at any moment – crystallize just enough to be of use and then flow on again.
– Mary P. Follett, *The New State*

No matter how one likes to cut it, Haldane's jurisprudence in Canadian constitutional cases was tortuous. Despite David Schneiderman's efforts to explain it by placing it in the context of the emerging debate at the time over 'corporate personality,' a debate influenced by the ideas of Frederic William Maitland and Harold Laski, it remains, as Saywell pointedly remarks, 'bizarre.'[1]

Haldane's jurisprudence can be understood from his own writings alone; it does not require the support of external forces such as the writings of Maitland or others. One of the principal resources available for an understanding of Haldane's jurisprudence is his major philosophical work, *The Reign of Relativity*, which he published in 1921.

Haldane and Relativity

In *The Reign of Relativity*, Haldane attempted to give a concise account of the 'general principle of the relativity of knowledge.'[2] It is an important notion, he contended, which is of ancient lineage but had been lost for many centuries. He located it in the thought of Plato and Aristotle but claimed that what 'seems to be needed in our own day is not merely its statement in a form adapted to our times, but its rescue from obscurity, arising from unconscious assumptions and distorting metaphors.'[3] Leibnitz and Kant came close to rescuing the concept but never quite succeeded. Success came when 'science has begun to scrutinise its own foundations, and to apply its own methods in the investigation.' Einstein and 'most modern mathematicians and physicists' have shown the way towards a final rescue of the principle of relativity. This quest of the scientists led them into 'a domain which for long they did not think of entering.' It also led them to cross over into a new domain where they met the metaphysician.[4] This great modern discovery 'does not apply only in physical science, or only in philosophy in relation to that kind of science ... but to art and religion and knowledge generally.'[5]

Because the principle of relativity of knowledge does not 'belong to any single domain,' Haldane stated, Einstein's teaching should be regarded only as an illustration of its application to a special subject. 'Relativity in its widest sense is an old and familiar idea. It sometimes only means that our view of things in the world varies with our personal circumstances. The hills look as if on fire. But if I change my position I see that what I took to be fire was really an appearance due to my position and produced by the light of the sunset. A book seems obscure and dull; with fuller knowledge it becomes both lucid and engrossing. A neighbour seems objectionable. I have not appreciated his character. When I come to do so I believe in him, and take an altogether different view of his nature.'[6] Relativity of knowledge also implies, as Sir William Hamilton and Kant taught, that what we think is direct knowledge of objects is little more than a knowledge of the *phenomenon*, the outer appearance of things, meaning that the 'thing in itself,' the *noumenon*, is beyond the reach of our knowledge. But, Haldane insisted, 'relativity may have yet a third meaning. It is alleged that, however much we exclude speculation about the metaphysical character of reality, and however earnestly we refuse to go behind actual experience, that experience is dependent on conditions, inasmuch, as the observer employs, and is compelled by the constitution of his mind to employ, standard conceptions which exclude from him all but certain aspects of what appears. These conceptions may belong to the domain of physical science, or of biology, or of morals, or of religion. The task of the inquirer is in each case to discover what they are, and to define their characters and their relations to each other.'[7]

Having set down the conditions for the exploration of the relativity of knowledge, Haldane proceeded to give an enthusiastic summary of Einstein's general theory of relativity as it applies to physical science. In this summary he drew on his many conversations with the great mathematical physicist, who had introduced him to exciting realms beyond mere physics. 'The outcome of Einstein's doctrine is a new and more searching set of generalisations about space and time, and the objects in them ... If he is well founded in what he says, we have now to accept certain consequences of the principle that we can only describe with accuracy the positions of objects in nature if we bear in mind that their relations in space and time are relative to the special co-ordinates or systems of reference of the observer and vary accordingly.'[8] Haldane's embrace of Einstein's theory of relativity was breathtaking at times; he raced forward like a child who has just discovered the meaning of a riddle and is anxious to share the secret with others. He was led with equal enthusiasm to abandon the old order of knowledge which, he said, held sway in the past. With great enthusiasm, Haldane recounts the challenge to modern British astronomy that Einstein's rejection of Newtonian absolute space constituted. 'The English Astronomer Royal took up this challenge in 1917, when, the war notwithstanding, the details of Einstein's calculations had reached this country. In 1919 two English expeditions were sent out to West Africa and Brazil respectively. Successful observations were made. In November the Astronomer Royal announced the results to the Royal Society. Einstein's calculations had proved to be substantially the true one, and something like a revolution in a great department of scientific thought was the result.'[9] 'Stated generally,' he concluded, 'the teaching of Einstein is that absolute rest and motion are meaningless for physical science, and that motion can signify only the changing positions of bodies relatively to each other.'[10] But Haldane was insistent that Einstein's great discovery had far-reaching 'importance for any theory of the ultimate character of reality.'[11] It didn't matter that Einstein's theory was adapted by A.S. Eddington or A.N. Whitehead or by Moritz Schlick in Germany; 'there is a broad feature which all the different views exhibit in common.'[12] And, after explaining the application of the theory of relativity to the various branches of physical science, Haldane turned in part two of *The Reign of Relativity* to the metaphysical foundations of relativity.

He announced that the world of human beings, not simply the world of mathematical physics, was a world in a constant flux and in need of understanding. 'How the world we experience seems to us, and what it really is for us, thus depends in the event on interpretation, and the meaning which is the result of that interpretation. Knowledge is a process, an activity. It is what we have called dynamic and never static, in the nature of subject rather than substance.'[13]

The most significant contribution Hegel made to Haldane's appreciation of relativity was the principle of the historical process where the World Spirit, *Weltgeist* as freedom, gradually produces a universal *Sittlichkeit*. Hegel attempted a grand synthesis, a synthesis that combined 'the rational, self-legislating freedom of the Kantian subject with the expressive unity within man and with nature for which the age longed.'[14] Freedom became the essence of man and his new history was the record of the unfolding and extension of the universal spirit of freedom over time from one person to some people and then to all people. He attempted to demonstrate the working of the historic process in his philosophy of history from east to west, culminating in the German Protestant state. 'Only the Germanic nations have in Christianity come to the consciousness that man as man is free, that spiritual freedom truly constitutes his nature.'[15]

Haldane was captivated by the invitation to apply this to the affairs of the world, especially the affairs of the British Empire. He became convinced of the importance of contributing to the extension of freedom in the modern British state by guiding the development of rational law through the progressive constitutional development of the state. The Hegelian state required the guidance of those who understood that history constituted not only a progressive unfolding of freedom but also an ordered freedom. For this reason, Hegel criticized the Reform Bill of 1830; it had the right intention of doing away with rotten boroughs and extending the franchise progressively, but he criticized it for contributing to the weakening of an already weak parliamentary system. He lamented the decline of Hobbes's strong monarch. Clearly, he was no modern democrat. In these matters, Haldane went part way with his mentor; he accepted the need for the guidance of prudent national leaders who would direct the affairs of state towards ordered liberty. But he drew back from the concept of the powerful monarch so much admired by Hegel.

Haldane understood that his function as a philosopher imposed on him the duty to understand the dynamics of the historic process as well as the obligation to provide guidance in the unfolding of that process, a task that few of his contemporaries were equipped to perform. This is why there was a sense of urgency in his writings and in his judicial judgments. Hegel, he wrote in *The Reign of Relativity*, did not believe in 'any absolute, outside and apart from human knowledge.'[16] Historical relativism, the belief that all standards of right and justice evolved with the progressive unfolding of the *Weltgeit*, was attractive to Haldane. It meant that constitutional documents that purported to set down for future generations laws and 'values' were to be distrusted. The prevailing *Sittlichkeit* determined the common 'values' and the role of the lawyer and judge was to keep abreast with the currents of this motive force. The state is in a condition of constant becoming and must resist the efforts of legislators to arrest the process by imposing the dead demands of parchment law.

This was the conviction that prompted Haldane to undertake his trip to Montreal in 1913. He was clearly driven to enunciate it to the leading legal minds of North America assembled there for the American and Canadian bar association meetings. He understood that the democratic spirit of freedom was evolving in North America and he wanted to make sure that the legal fraternity understood their mission. The invitation to the Anglo-Saxon legal world was to understand its role in guiding the particular state *Sittlichkeit* as well as the 'new kind of international *Sittlichkeit* based on more than the letter of any agreement.'[17] He spoke emphatically that 'each nation should broaden progressively.' 'Within a state and apart from all legal sanction there exist ... systems of morality and of the habitual good behaviour which the Germans call *Sittlichkeit*. These systems vary with the standards of different nations, but their essential features are common. All good people, of whatever nationality, recognise analogous obligations of truth and justice, and in the main they resemble in their sense of what is and what is not good form in social life.'[18] He was convinced that, despite the setback of the Great War, 'there are already some indications that higher than merely national purposes are moving mankind, and that it is struggling to express them in institutions that may in the end prove to have dominating influence.'[19] True to his Hegelianism, Haldane believed that the constitution of a country must continue to evolve to keep abreast of the felt necessities of the times. This belief was based on the Hegelian premise that the past contains no permanent wisdom; that the work of the fathers of Canadian Confederation, for example, contained no permanent guidelines which future generations would be wise to follow, since their 'wisdom' has been superseded by the wisdom of the historic process. As Haldane had written about the state: 'The state is made, not by external acts, but by the continuous thought and action of the people who live its life. In this sense it is never perfect for it is a process that remains always unbroken in creative activity.'[20]

In Hegel the law of the constitution is forever pointing towards an horizon that is constantly moving further into the distance; the just political order does not exist as a final obtainable objective. As Mary Follett observed: 'Progress is an infinite advance towards the infinitely receding goal of infinite perfection.'[21] Haldane found much in Follett's book to applaud. He especially liked what she said about democracy. Follett wrote that 'the essence of democracy is not in institutions, it is not even in "brotherhood": it is in that organizing of men which makes most sure, most perfect, the bringing forth of the common idea. Democracy has one act only – to free the creative spirit of man.'[22] At the forefront of this movement, however, Haldane, departing from Follett, saw the legal profession and the institution of the judiciary as the critical 'aristocratic' element in the new Hegelian democracy. Follett had no corresponding role for the judiciary; in her philosophy of state, the social engineer takes the place of judges and lawyers.

For Hegel, human nature is constantly evolving towards a higher wisdom; there is no natural right or natural law, no natural virtue; it is replaced by an ever changing political landscape which culminates only at the end of history (which he thought had arrived with the establishment of the Prussian state). There are no 'inalienable rights,' no rights that inhere in the very nature of human beings which transcend all times; there are only those rights that citizens enjoy as the gift of the state at any given time and they can change from time to time as the state power determines.[23] Hegel's political philosophy leads, accordingly, to statism, a statism that declares all the highest public and private moral standards and enforces them by state power.

Not nature, as in the Platonic-Aristotelian philosophy, but the state is the source or fount of all rights and privileges. Neither nature nor God – as in the Judeo-Christian traditions – provides the conditions for human moral sufficiency. The state alone is supreme in that it provides the moral and ethical standards of each successive epoch; all moral standards are historically relative. Hegel's most enduring contribution to modern public philosophy was his central thesis that the inner core of the ever expanding *Weltgeist* is the notion that ethical or moral standards change over time; what was wrong in one generation becomes right in a succeeding generation. Above all, it means that there is no permanent notion of what constitutes justice. Justice becomes whatever the state says it is at any given historic epoch. There is no transcendent or transpolitical standard of appeal. Verification of the ongoing spiral of expansive freedom – the path of the *Weltgeist* – lies solely in history. This is why Hegel spent so much of his time reinterpreting the received accounts of past history in an attempt to demonstrate that recorded history is the account of the unfolding of the *Weltgeist*. His revisions portrayed the course of past history not as the accomplishments of men and arms but as the working of the World Spirit propelling the course of nations – through the unknowing complicity of 'world historical figures' such as Alexander the Great, Caesar, and Napoleon – towards a greater moral and political freedom.

Haldane's intellectual power provided Hegel with a hearing beyond the reach of other men. His critics might accuse him of many things – and they did – but lack of enthusiasm for the future of the British Empire led by the Anglo-Saxon jurisprudence was not one of them. *The Reign of Relativity* was published in May 1921 to great critical acclaim; it went immediately through several editions and was widely praised by the philosophical fraternity. The subject matter of this book was a long time aborning; he had been thinking about the issues for many years before finally putting pen to paper following his dismissal – he called it his 'liberation' – from the government in 1915.

Unlike other politicians who have been sent into exile for one reason or another, Richard Haldane went happily back to Scotland and cheerfully to his study where – in the company of his beloved dog, Bruce – he turned his mind to writing *The Reign of Relativity*. 'The truth never stands still,' he wrote. 'It is always changing its form as our categories change. Relativity thus acquires a new meaning for us ... What is fundamental and essential is the development of fresh results of utility in application. For the sake of this progress must always be taking place in the correction and evolution of our conception.'[24] The ever inquiring mind at work, never content to simply apply old forms to new issues, Haldane brought all this to the law. He eschewed the pretence to finality in all branches of human life: 'That supposed finality must be actual falsehood, whether we are dealing with daily affairs, or with literature and art, or with philosophy or with science. It is not faith in final truth so called, because for us human beings there is no such thing as absolute and final truth, but the quality of strenuousness and progress in the search after it that alone can give us a sense of finality attained in which we can rest.'[25]

For Hegel, there were three forms of common life: the family, civil society, and the state. 'The state came to complete the trio. For it offers once more a deeper unity, an inward unity, like the family. But it will not be just an immediate one based on feeling. Rather unity here is mediated by reason. The state is a community in which universal subjectives can be bound together while being recognized as such.'[26] The role played by the law in this process was critical to Haldane. In *John Deere v. Wharton* (1915),[27] for example, he ruled for the board that the province of British Columbia did not have the authority to interfere with the carrying on of the business of the John Deere Plow Company, which had been incorporated by the federal Parliament. But he acknowledged in *John Deere* that federally incorporated companies would continue to be subject to provincial laws of general application.[28] The point is clear: the local *Sittlichkeit* of British Columbia was formally acknowledged and set free to develop.

Mary Follett Teaches Federalism

The question arises at this point: Why did Haldane not acknowledge a *national* Canadian *Sittlichkeit* rather than the fragmented *Sittlichkeiten* of the provinces? Were not the German principalities united under Bismarck to form a single pan-German nationality with a unifying national *Sittlichkeit*? Yes, but, as Mary P. Follett wrote in 1918, the emergence of the militaristic German state was a result of the misapplication of 'true Hegelianism.' One must distinguish, she insisted, between 'the real Hegel and the Hegel who misapplied his own doctrine, who preached the absolutism of a Prussian State.'[29] She urged her readers to ignore Germany and, instead, turn to the English philosophers Thomas Hill Green and Bernard Bosanquet – both well known to Richard Haldane – for an understanding of 'the true Hegelian doctrine.'[30] There can be little doubt that Haldane's view of the appropriateness of the federal form of government for Canada was confirmed by Follett's chapter on the proper understanding of federalism.

Until the time he read Follett's book, Haldane's understanding of federalism was imperfectly conceived. He was confident in the belief that the aspirations of the Canadian provinces ought to be supported. But it was not until he had read *The New State* that he understood more clearly how compatible his instincts were with Hegelianism. Follett extolled the virtues of federalism as the 'unifying state.' 'The federal state is the unifying state. Our goal must always be the unified state – the unified state to be attained through the federal form.'[31] How must Haldane have warmed to her argument when she insisted that 'true Hegelianism finds its actualized form in federalism.'[32] Haldane believed that his Canadian critics who charged him with fracturing the country were wrong. He viewed the provincial chafing under the centralizing terms of the British North America Act, 1867 as the *Sittlichkeiten* of the provinces working their way up towards a national *Sittlichkeit*. It was a perfect example of the Hegelian dialectic at work. True Hegelianism rejects the imposition of unity from the top; the aspirations for unity must come from the people, from the bottom up. The emerging and inevitable clashing of the provincial *Sittlichkeiten* at the national level was to be resolved by the highest national court of appeal, the Judicial Committee of the Privy Council. The result, in due course, would be a national *Sittlichkeit*.

The Limits of Sovereignty

In *The Reign of Relativity*, Haldane expanded on the concepts of the state and sovereignty. It is of paramount importance to note that he remarks on the limitations of power entrusted to legislatures. He says that 'there has always to take place a careful balancing of considerations, in order to determine the extent of the mandate that has been entrusted to the legislature.'[33] There must be a balancing, he contended, because the 'legislature does not really represent sovereign power. Sovereignty has its definite source, and even the highest institutions in the state may not be able to claim it.'[34] Confusion arises, he wrote, from the assumption that the state and sovereignty are the same and indivisible. 'For some purposes' – he does not say which ones – 'the state is always single and sovereignty not broken up.'[35] This is especially true, he continued, when one nation deals with another nation. 'Even where there is a federal constitution, and the executive is by the constitution independent of the legislature' – as in the United States – 'the state is still one and indivisible so far as other nations are concerned.'[36] But the same is not true within states. Within the federal state, where the executive is constitutionally separated from the legislative branch of government, 'sovereignty is divided and can be exercised unitedly only if there is concurrence of purpose on the part of the separate institutions which compose it.'[37] He then added the note: 'The Dominion of Canada and the Commonwealth of Australia illustrate the same principle in other forms.'

By this Haldane appeared to mean that the federal constitutions of Canada and Australia are characterized by the fusion of the legislature and the executive as in the United Kingdom. But he insisted that the state was subject to more than formal legal restraints, that 'the general will of the people' counts for a great deal. Passing beyond the region of jurisprudence, he says, leads to the conclusion that within 'a state and apart from all legal sanction there exist ... systems of morality and of the habitual good behaviour which the Germans call *Sittlichkeit*.'[38] They are not the same for all nations – *Sittlichkeit* is relative to nations according to the 'standards of different nations' – 'but their essential features are common.'[39] 'Different nations excel in their *Sittlichkeit* in different fashions.'[40] This belief in the common character of the various national *Sittlichkeiten* led him to take up the cause of the League of Nations. The sentiment born of the exhaustion of war has led, he noted, to the emergence of a 'new kind of international *Sittlichkeit*.' Granted, he admitted, the new international *Sittlichkeit* is not yet sufficiently strong to overcome the clash of *Sittlichkeiten* among nations: 'Still, the desire is there, and bears witness to its real foundation.'[41] Haldane may have expressed a genuine sympathy for a world united in peace against the forces of war, but he was not naive. He hoped that each nation of the world would 'broaden progressively' by coming to realize that 'higher than merely national purposes are moving mankind.'[42] But, given history's long record of war upon war, he was not overly optimistic.

As a good Hegelian, Haldane concluded that 'there always has been a reality of a nature outside and beyond that of the state. However shadowy it is there, and it shows itself to be at least capable of development into stable forms ... For the source of this reality is the same as the source of that of the state itself. Both are due to the character of mind, which works and creates general opinion at levels that transcend the ends, not only of the particular self, but of the mere citizen of any particular nation.' Returning to the earlier theme of the importance of mind, Haldane concluded that 'the mind is ... inadequately described as a thing among other things. It is what can be adequately spoken of only in terms that belong to its own character. It is that within which all that is particular as well as all that is universal fall, and is that which by its overreaching intellectual activity establishes distinctions between true and false and real and unreal, that have meaning and validity only for itself ... It is what exists at no single degree or level either in actuality or in knowledge. It is the dynamic principle to which is referred back all that falls within experience, and not only all that falls within it but all that gives it significance.'[43]

The only true reality is the human mind and the fully thinking person is one being who understands this and bends his every effort to shape the course of nations by giving formal legal shape to the latent *Sittlichkeit* found in every nation. The task of the intellectual is to give concrete shape and form to that progressive principle which gives life to the general will of the people, who, for the most part, are ignorant of the existence of this motive force for national or state progress. It was just such a task Viscount Richard Haldane set for himself. And that could only be achieved by the rule of law. 'Morality, properly so called, is not enough for citizenship. Society requires binding rules of a positive character, and institutions by means of which these can be made effective. Such rules must restrain effectively arbitrariness in individual conduct, in the interest of the community.'[44] The judicial tribunals have a special role to play and it is the responsibility of judges to ensure that the principles of law are fairly applied. 'The laws contain general rules of conduct, expressed in objective form, and enforced by sanctions applied by the state. But they are not always to be found expressed in definite and unchanging form, and the tribunal which enforces them often has to consider a context of a far-reaching character, a context which may have varied from generation to generation, and which may render even a written rule obsolete, or make it necessary to apply one that is unwritten and about which ethical judgments are at variance.'[45]

As he attempted to demonstrate in Canadian cases, the role of the judge, sitting in the Judicial Committee, was to listen to the rumblings of discontent coming on appeal from the colonies and to assess how they revealed the progressive ambitions of the nation. The obligation of the law lord was to give legal effect to those ambitions. He must act more than as a judge in equity who seeks to apply the general terms of the law to a specific case. The judge of the Committee of the Privy Council, as Haldane viewed it, was charged with the responsibility of interpreting the provisions of a whole range of national constitutions – from Malta and India to New Zealand and Canada – where a given people is attempting to work out their lives together in a peaceful community. In many cases, the written provision, the parchment, has to be interpreted even in open defiance of its explicit terms. But Richard Burdon Haldane saw the future role of the Judicial Committee in even grander terms than that. His dream was to reform the structure of the British judiciary in domestic matters by creating a ministry of justice and by strengthening the role of the Judicial Committee of the Privy Council as the supreme appellate court of the Empire. The accumulated genius of the Anglo-Saxon law would serve as the 'silken bonds of the Empire.'[46]

10

Supreme Tribunal of the Empire

We are far away from the continental conception of a Judge as a mere interpreter of rigid codes.
> – R.B. Haldane, 'Address to the University Law Society,' 1921

There is no disputing that Richard Burdon Haldane had his full share of successes at the War Office and on the Judicial Committee. But he was singularly unsuccessful in his efforts to transform the Judicial Committee and the House of Lords into a 'supreme tribunal of the Empire.' Nor was he successful in his attempts at reorganizing the office of the lord chancellor or instituting a ministry of justice responsible to the House of Commons. Indeed, his life's story would be seriously incomplete if it were not to reveal how central to his ambitions were these failed causes. By reconstituting the Judicial Committee through a combination of elements of the House of Lords, Haldane believed that the great body of British law would bind the member states into a coherent and effective judicial body, a body infused with the benefits of Hegelian philosophy of state and presided over by judges who understood their role in the unfolding of the Hegelian *Weltgeist*. It would ensure the survival of the great body of British jurisprudence – one of the enduring achievements of the civilized world – and serve as a beacon to other nations.

Weaving the Silken Bonds of Empire

As early as 1900 Richard Haldane spoke to the Scottish Law Society in Edinburgh in glowing terms of the value of appeals to the Judicial Committee as a 'real and most important portion of the silken bonds which with so little friction hold our great Empire together.'[1] But the bonds were not simply institutional in nature; they were substantive. The glue that bound the colonies at the apex of the judicial process in the Judicial Committee was the inherited spirit of the Anglo-Saxon legal tradition embedded in the judgments of a long list of decided cases. 'For the spirit is everything with a tribunal of a nature so anomalous from a modern point of view as is the Judicial Committee of the Privy Council. It is hopeless to search for the secret of such success as it has had merely in printed documents. For it is not in the written letter that the description of the real nature of the Court is to be found. The true description can only be given by those who, living here, or coming from afar have been in daily contact with the working of this extraordinary organization, and have experienced the extent to which it is continuously seeking to adapt its life to the needs which it has to fulfil as a link between the parts of this Empire.'[2] He insisted that the 'printed documents' did not contain a record of the success of this extraordinary judicial body. The virtue of the body resided in an understanding of the 'King as supreme judiciar of the Empire.'[3] He went on to explain that the Judicial Committee itself did not, in fact, render judgment: 'It simply makes a recommendation which is carried out by a formal Order made by the Sovereign at a subsequent stage in a full meeting of the Privy Council.' In this way, the 'King as supreme judiciar' remained intact 'but only for the Empire beyond the limits of Great Britain and Northern Ireland. For within these limits the jurisdiction of the Sovereign as the supreme tribunal of appeal has long ago been absorbed by Parliament, and taken over by the House of Lords. Throughout the rest of the Empire the old prerogative jurisdiction of the King-Emperor remains, but remains constitutionally limited by the necessity of advice, not from his Ministers, but from a Judicial Committee of the Privy Council, consisting of judges.'[4]

Haldane had visions of greater things for the 'King as supreme judiciar of the Empire.' He had an ambition to bind the Empire by amalgamating the House of Lords and the Judicial Committee into one great imperial appellate tribunal. In order to put this matter along with other reform proposals on the parliamentary agenda, he had persuaded the government to appoint a committee to study the whole 'machinery of government.' The committee was struck in July 1917 to 'enquire into the responsibilities of the various Departments of the central executive Government, and to advise in what manner the exercise and distribution by the Government of its functions should be improved.'[5] This committee, which included, at Haldane's insistence, Beatrice Webb among others, sat until December 1918. The final report outlined a long list of reforms by which the process of governing Great Britain – from proposals for cabinet reforms to recommendations touching several major departments of government – might be improved.[6] The tenth chapter, entitled 'Justice,' was written by Haldane almost unassisted by anyone else. In this chapter Haldane issued a formal plea for the establishment of a ministry of justice responsible to the House of Commons through a minister of justice and a major restructuring of the Judicial Committee of the Privy Council.[7]

Before outlining his proposals for a ministry of justice, Haldane expatiated at length upon the duties imposed upon the lord chancellor as a way of showing how over a series of centuries the office had become monstrous and inefficient. After noting that 'there is no functionary at present who can properly be called a Minister responsible for the subject of Justice,'[8] Haldane simply began by enumerating the responsibilities that went with the office of lord chancellor. The list of duties imposed on the occupant of the office, as set out by Haldane, is nothing less than staggering: the lord chancellor is responsible in the House for all bills in any way touching legal practice or procedure, and for all bills when he is appealed to on points of law or interpretation. He is, as well, head of appeals as 'President of the Supreme Appellate Court of Great Britain and Ireland' and president of the Judicial Committee of the Privy Council. And, of course, he is, by virtue of occupying the woolsack, Speaker of the House of Lords. Here is how Haldane described a typical week in the life of a lord chancellor:

The House of Lords sits judicially on four days of the week during the period of the year which corresponds roughly with, but is a little shorter than, the time of the legal sittings of the Supreme Court. During all this time, therefore, the Lord Chancellor on four days of the week is sitting from 10:30 to 3:45 or 4 o'clock with an interval of half an hour for lunch. The work while it lasts is extremely laborious, and it is easy to imagine that on those days on which the House sits as a Court of Appeal from 10:30 to 3:45 and when he has to deal with ordinary Parliamentary business from 4:15 to 7:30 or 8 only a man of very exceptional physical vigour can find either leisure or strength to cope with the many duties of his high office.[9]

The lament continued: 'The mere enumeration of the number of hours consumed in judicial business, however, does not exhaust the matter, for especially in recent years, the judgements of the House of Lords have been put into legal form.' And, of course, the lord chancellor must write his judgments, read the judgments of his colleagues, and frequently discuss with them the points of law or matters of fact which arise in the course of the case. There are no law clerks to assist with the thinking through of cases and the mining of precedents. In Haldane's time the lord chancellor had the services of a low-level clerk who fetched 'references or books.' Other than that, he had at his disposal the services only of a permanent secretary, who was until 1915 Kenneth Muir Mackenzie.

The list of responsibilities assumed by the lord chancellor does not end there. For in Haldane's era he was obliged to preside as president of the Judicial Committee and supervise the lords of appeal as well as oversee 'the constitution of the Court and the appointment of Lords in the Judicial Committee of the Privy Council.'[10] In addition, Haldane explained, the lord chancellor is responsible for the appointment of judges and tribunals throughout the realm. Even civil servants of the judicial departments come under his jurisdiction, with minor exceptions. When not performing one of these functions, the lord chancellor chairs the Rule Committee of the Supreme Court, which comprises the lord chief justice, the master of the rolls, the president of the Probate, Divorce and Admiralty Division, four other judges of the Supreme Court, two barristers who are members of the General Council of the Bar, and two solicitors, one a member of the Law Society and also of the Provincial Law Society. This committee is charged with the responsibility of revising the Annual Practice, which contains 720 orders. The lord chancellor is also responsible for the county court system of the country. 'There are 55 County Court Judges and 600 courts. All the judges are appointed by the Lord Chancellor alone, and are removable by him. The Registrars, who are themselves minor judges, besides being responsible for the finance of their Courts, are appointed by these Judges, subject to the approval of the Lord Chancellor and are removable by the latter.'[11]

It should come as no surprise that Haldane concluded: 'It will readily be understood that the administrative work connected with the appointment of so many judges, their conduct when appointed, and the innumerable complaints which arise in the course of administration, constitute a gigantic task.'[12] 'Gigantic' is hardly the word to describe the towering burdens imposed on the luckless occupant of this high office. The reader approaches exhaustion just from reading the list of responsibilities. But the list continues unabated. Recent legislation, Haldane observed, continued to heap more work upon the lord chancellor's department. Registration of title of land as well as the Public Trustees Act, 1907 imposed the duty to supervise all public trustees. At this point a *cri de coeur* arises from the pages: 'Notwithstanding the passing of the Mental Deficiency Act, 1913, the Lord Chancellor still retains duties in relation to lunatics.'[13] And, yes, the appointment of all justices of the peace – except those in the Duchy of Lancaster – fell within his department. One would have thought that war would provide a respite for the lord chancellor. Far from it. At the outbreak of the First World War, the government imposed further burdens on the lord chancellor in matters arising from legislation pertaining to the war effort. For example, the lord chancellor was designated to oversee the implementation of the Courts Emergency Powers Act, the Defence of the Realm Act – one of the most controversial pieces of legislation to come out of the war – the Trading with the Enemy Act, and a host of other wartime regulations.

Haldane's lament was not exhausted with the listing of the lord chancellor's duties. He turned at this point to the lord chancellor's office itself and reminded his readers that the Office of Permanent Secretary is of very recent creation. Until 1885, the lord chancellor was assisted by a principal secretary and certain other secretaries with assigned duties. These officials were personal to the lord chancellor of the day and went in and out of office with him. 'When the Lord Chancellor went out, his Secretaries destroyed or took with them any official records which they had kept, presumably on the ground that they were too confidential to be entrusted to the Secretaries about to enter upon office.'[14] The tradition of regarding the office records as the personal property of the lord chancellor of the day has since been corrected, he noted in passing. It is difficult to miss the undercurrent of sarcasm in Haldane's observation on this practice: 'It was probably thought that a succeeding Lord Chancellor might feel embarrassed by a detailed knowledge of the proceedings of his predecessor.'[15] Small wonder that Haldane, at the conclusion of his long recitation, called for 'a readjustment of the duties of the Lord Chancellor's Department.'

His principal recommendations relating to the restructuring of the Judicial Committee of the Privy Council and the establishment of a ministry of justice to be located in the House of Commons were not adopted. Nor was the recommendation that the House of Lords choose its own Speaker, thereby lessening the load on the lord chancellor. The report had urged that the Judicial Committee be reconstituted to become 'the Supreme Tribunal, not only for the Empire outside the United Kingdom, but for England, Scotland, and Ireland as well.'[16] All appeals would go to this new expanded body. 'The [new] Judicial Committee of the Privy Council would sit in as many divisions as were required, and these division would have their appropriate procedure and forms, etc.'[17] This recommendation along with his strong case for the establishment of a ministry of justice to be located in the House of Commons fell on deaf ears. The Judicial Committee has never been reconstituted into the Supreme Court of the Empire, but Haldane's proposal to establish a ministry of justice is still being *talked* about to this day. It has yet to become a reality.

The lack of enthusiasm for the Machinery of Government Committee report has been attributed, in part, to the times. As Frederick Maurice stated: 'The Report appeared at an unfortunate time. A General Election was in progress when it was published, and the General Election was followed by the complicated business of demobilization, by unrest and strikes at home, by disturbances in Ireland, and by the preoccupation of the Prime Minister and those in his immediate circle with the Treaties of Peace. So it failed to command the attention it deserved; the opportunity for a general reconstruction was there, but the time for it was lacking.'[18] The times, indeed, were awash in tears. The country had just emerged from the bloodiest war in its history. The blood-drenched battlefields of France were still fresh in the memories of millions of people. Among those who had perished in the great offensives of 1916 and 1917 were several notables, such as Raymond Asquith and Rupert Brooke, who had gathered at Mells and other country houses before and during the early years of the war. As Dudley Sommer has written: 'Mells, their beautiful Somerset home which held so many memories for Haldane, was burnt down and a few weeks later Edward Horner died of wounds received in the Battle of Cambrai.'[19] In a letter to his mother, Haldane lamented the loss of the brightest of the younger generation but, true to his character, had his eye on the future post-war problems: 'The terrible thing for the future of the country is that when peace comes we shall be found with problems, more difficult, more pregnant of good or evil than any with which this horrible war confronts us, and the men who could succeed us, and bring back with them from their trial by fire, new inspiration and fresh ideals are being swept away by the hurricane. Raymond Asquith, "Bron" Lucas, and Edward Horner have gone from our own circle, and the gaps in the number of those to whom we could hand on our task grows wider daily.'[20] Never one to brood, Haldane quickly concluded his letter: 'After moments of despair, I return with new zeal to my thesis, better education, greater opportunities for those who are left to us.' Once again, the reign of reason prevailed over emotion.

Despite his failure to transform the Judicial Committee into a Supreme Court of the Empire in 1919, Richard Haldane never ceased preaching its merits whenever the occasion arose. In *Education and Empire*, which he wrote in 1902, he had mused at great length in an essay entitled 'The Appellate Courts of the Empire' on the virtues of the 'two great tribunals of our empire,' the Judicial Committee and the House of Lords as the final court of appeal. He made it abundantly clear that these two judicial bodies were not the products of 'merely abstract minds'; they emerged out of the spirit of the unwritten constitution 'our people live under at home and abroad.' These two legal institutions are the direct product of the genius of the forces that have always operated 'from within rather than from without.'[21] He was convinced that the two judicial institutions were 'the silken bonds which, with so little friction, hold our great empire together' and ought to be more formally constituted so as to ensure the preservation and extension of the benefits of the quality of justice they dispense. Unblushingly, he told a story of a mythical traveller 'who had penetrated into a remote part of India where he found the natives offering up a sacrifice to a far-off but all-powerful god who had just restored to the tribe the land which the Government of the day had taken from it. He asked the name of the god. The reply was: "we know nothing of him but that he is a good god, and that his name is the Judicial Committee of the Privy Council."'[22] Needless to say, the 'spirit of fearless justice is the outcome of the calibre of the men who have sat in the tribunal.' This anecdote led Haldane into a lengthy panegyric on the merits of his illustrious Scottish predecessor, Lord Watson, who, he claimed, 'had rendered more services to the empire than many a distinguished statesman.'[23] It was this great jurist, he averred, who rescued the Canadian constitutional framers from their own folly, a sentiment not well received in Canadian legal circles. He then noted that Canada had established its own Supreme Court under the influence of a few Canadian politicians 'who were suspicious of interference from Downing Street.' This court, he said, was intended to 'get rid as far as possible of the Privy Council as a Canadian Court of Appeal.'[24]

There is no truth to this assertion. The provision for a 'general court of appeal' was in the constitution of Canada from the very beginning.[25] And everyone involved in the Canadian constitutional debates leading to Confederation knew that appeals to the foot of the throne were secure. But no matter. Haldane believed that, through Lord Watson's efforts, nefarious intentions to replace the Privy Council with the Supreme Court of Canada were frustrated. The great Lord Watson, Haldane boasted, 'worked out a different view of the Canadian Constitution from that which had been foreshadowed by the Canadian Courts.' In sum, as we have seen, Watson allegedly rescued Canadians from themselves. Haldane, in an attempt to show the importance of the Judicial Committee's work for the Empire, and departing from his abhorrence of metaphors, proclaimed that Lord Watson had 'filled in the skeleton which the Constitution Act had established, and in large measure shaped the growth of the fibre which grew round it.'[26] This was another occasion when Haldane might well have avoided the lapse into metaphor. How does one 'fill in' a skeleton or 'shape the growth of the fibre which grew round it?' Perhaps this speech was what triggered the Oxford Aristotle scholar A.E. Taylor to rail against Haldane's abuse of the English language. In one place, Taylor referred to Haldane's 'violent and unnatural inversion of the English order of words.'[27] 'Worse than all,' he continued, 'there seems to run through nearly every argument a perplexing strain of verbal ambiguity which raises a suspicion of confusion of thought.' However harsh that judgment, there is no question that the grotesquery of the imagery is exceeded only by the gratuity of Haldane's description of how Watson resolved single-handed the nagging tensions between the federal and provincial governments by stopping the federal intrusions into legitimate provincial preserves. Haldane's fulsome language prompted the image of the great law lord standing defiantly before the courts of Canada with his hand held high and, in a thundering Scottish accent, announcing that the skeleton shall not pass 'unless garbed in the proper fibre!'

But Haldane's real purpose on this occasion was not to praise Watson. It was to recommend the fusion of the two great judicial bodies into one great 'Imperial Court of Appeal.'[28] And it would be housed in more appropriate grand circumstances befitting its dignity. 'It would cause it to sit always in the House of Lords, instead of letting its members sit, as they now do when they represent the Privy Council, in a shabby room up a dirty staircase off Downing Street.'[29] Warming to his theme, Haldane enthused that such a 'reform would make possible a really great tribunal, worthy of the glories of the greatest empire the world has ever seen.'[30] But, unfortunately for Haldane's ambitions, there was little enthusiasm throughout the nations of the Empire. On two occasions, imperial conferences were held – one in 1901–2 and another in 1911 – where the idea was bandied about but without resolution to proceed. The idea was never popular in those dominions – except briefly in Australia[31] – which Haldane alleged would benefit the most from such a grand court. Strange that this man who spoke so enthusiastically about the spirit of the colonies or dominions should have been so blind to the strength of the spirit of those dominions for self-government, including the right and privilege of deciding their own destinies at the hands of their own judges. To be fair, Haldane did hint that 'the Judicial Committee would take notice of the growth of autonomy in the Dominions and would govern its attitude towards appeals in light of the new political developments.'[32] Fail the idea might and did, but it was not for want of Richard Burdon Haldane's efforts. Tenacious to the end, he returned to the subject in his Machinery of Government report some twenty years later. Like a dog with a bone, he was not prepared to surrender it up.

But his other great recommendation for judicial reform enjoyed better success although it was a long time in gestation. In the Machinery of Government report, Haldane, after listing the enormous responsibilities that were placed on the shoulders of the lord chancellor and his department, recommended the establishment of a ministry of justice. This new ministry was designed to bring the administration of justice under one central government department. 'By justice,' the report noted, 'is here meant the machinery by which the rights and obligations of citizens are defined, protected and enforced.' This meant that both the civil and criminal courts, the police, and the prevention of crime as well as punishment for crimes would be centralized and come under the control of a minister of the crown answerable to the House of Commons. The new ministry would also be responsible for recommending reforms to the law and for protecting the legal status of citizens. Many of these functions were at the time under the responsibility of the Home Office. Major functions such as overseeing the national police force, including the operation of prisons, as well as the appointment of justice clerks and clerks of the peace in addition to children's courts would be transferred to the new ministry of justice.

The Haldane report also recommended that responsibility for the

Metropolitan Police as well as local police forces in addition to Military Service Tribunals and courts martial should be brought under the direct administration of the lord chancellor. At the time of writing, these functions were scattered throughout several existing ministries, including, in a major way, the Home Office. Needless to say, the Home Office was not pleased with the recommendations; the immediate response from a full spectrum of vested interests was not favourable. As a result, the government did not act on the recommendations. When Haldane resumed his place on the woolsack as the first Labour lord chancellor in 1924, he sent for the permanent secretary of the Home Office, Lord Waverley. In the course of the conversation about the relation of the Home Office and the lord chancellor, Haldane remarked that 'I think we had better quietly forget what was in the Report.'[33] And so this reform, so dear to the heart of the lord chancellor, never came to pass. The idea, however, continues to emerge and continues to be proffered as a much-needed reform.[34]

A careful study of Haldane's recommendations for reforms of the judicial process in Great Britain contained in the Machinery of Government report suggests that the recommendations would certainly have improved the public service of the country. What Haldane had offered was nothing less than a thorough overhaul of the public-service departments beginning with the size and composition of the cabinet. As one friendly critic put it, 'the Committee, deeply impressed by War Cabinet experience, expressed the confident view that future peacetime Cabinets would continue to be small and to be served by a Cabinet Secretariat.'[35] No question about it, the Haldane report envisaged a 'massive redistribution of the work of existing departments.' However efficient the British public service was, and its reputation for efficiency was very high, there can be little doubt that the entire maze of departments and agencies of government had increased over many centuries in response to demands of the day; as a result, by the time Haldane and his committee undertook their study, the public departments and agencies constituted a rabbit's warren of overlapping jurisdictions and functions.

To no one's surprise, the 'turf war' that erupted in response to the proposals was explosive. And no one played a greater role in the efforts to prevent the new ministry from seeing the light of day than Sir Claud Schuster (1869–1956). At the time of the release of the Machinery of Government report, Schuster was permanent secretary to the lord chancellor; Haldane had recruited him from the Home Office in 1915 and he was destined to remain in the position until his retirement in

1944. Schuster replaced Kenneth Muir Mackenzie when Mackenzie was appointed to the House of Lords in 1915.

There appears little doubt that Schuster could have served as the real-life model for the fictional 'Sir Humphrey Appleby' of the BBC series *Yes Minister!* and *Yes, Prime Minister!*. As Gavin Drewry has shown, Schuster worked his considerable skills behind the scenes in concert with like-minded bureaucrats who were opposed to the idea of a ministry of justice.[36] He engaged in clandestine intrigues despite the fact that new ministry was the child of his lord chancellor and much desired by him. Schuster had a considerable reputation in Whitehall, not all of it favourable. He seemed, especially, to have ruffled the feathers of some senior judges. As his successor as permanent secretary to the lord chancellor, Sir Albert Napier, wrote in the *Oxford Dictionary of National Biography*, 'Schuster's decisive and directive style was not always popular with the judges who resented the contemporary decline in their real power relative to the civil service. As author in 1932 of the report of the committee on ministers' powers, he [Schuster] helped to narrow the judiciary's scope in administrative matters, allowing civil servants to retain wide decision-making powers.'[37] Similarly, Sir Claud was clearly one of the targets of Lord Hewart, the lord chief justice and author of *The New Despotism*, a book renowned in its day for its often intemperate criticism of the power that was accumulated in the offices of a few senior public servants. When Lord Hewart unleashed a salvo at the lord chancellor's permanent secretary in December 1934, Sir Claud returned the invective but more discreetly, behind the scenes.

Schuster explained his view of Haldane in a private memorandum in 1943, a year before his retirement, in the following way:

Lord Haldane came to the office after having served for years as a Secretary of State in a highly organised department with a proper allowance of Private secretaries and with all such conveniences as are naturally attached to a modern office, such as shorthand, typewriting, a properly organised registry and an established course of business. It was, therefore, not unnatural that he should have felt himself overwhelmed when he ascended the Woolsack and should have been struck not only with the lack of method for the discharge of the ordinary business of the Department, but with the complete absence of any organisation for a continuous examination of the function which the Department supervised and for laying plans for the future.[38]

Schuster's statement is an interesting reflection on how the permanent secretary saw both the office and the lord chancellor. The fault was not with the chaotic procedures and practices of the lord chancellor's office but with the newcomer who had been unduly influenced by past experience 'in a highly organised department.' It almost seems as if Schuster blamed Haldane for becoming 'overwhelmed' when he entered into the administrative nightmare. Haldane gets no credit for putting order into a department that was admittedly devoid of the conveniences 'naturally attached to a modern office,' where there was a 'lack of method for the discharge of the ordinary business' and a 'complete absence of any organisation for a continuous examination of the function which the Department supervised and for laying plans for the future.' It is difficult to imagine a government department in greater disarray.

And what did all this say about the administrative capacities of the previous permanent secretary? Schuster gave the impression that it was he who righted the affairs of the lord chancellor's office – and to a large measure that was true – but certainly the lord chancellor himself gave direction and insisted on administrative reforms, as he had when he went to the War Office. There is no doubt that Sir Claud Schuster was highly protective of his departmental prerogatives and was suspicious of anyone who presumed to interfere with his administration. On one occasion in 1917, for example, when the secretary of the Reconstruction Committee, Vaughan Nash, requested that Schuster provide the committee with documents about the organization of his department, Schuster replied that the department was too busy to prepare a memorandum but would do so if Nash would 'clarify' what was required.[39] It was 'Sir Humphrey Appleby' at his very best. This skilful bureaucrat knew exactly how to deal with meddlesome outsiders. In due course, Schuster provided the committee with a sketch of the history of the lord chancellor's office. It was hardly what Nash and his committee were asking for and when Nash drew this to the permanent under-secretary's attention, he received no reply.

This enterprising schemer worked on several fronts. Not content to resist the efforts within the ministries of government, Schuster lobbied the governing bodies of both the barristers and the solicitors. It was there that he showed his manipulative skills in having the Bar Council speak out publicly against the plan for a ministry of justice, thereby muting the enthusiasm for the plan shown initially by the Law Society. The society's president, Samuel Garrett, on 25 January 1918, delivered an address entitled 'A Ministry of Justice and Its Tasks.' The speech was summarized in the *Law Times*, in February 1918, and was linked with the call for a National School of Law. By statute the permanent secretary to the lord chancellor must be a barrister of ten years' standing before being appointed to the position. Schuster had been a member of the Inner Temple since 1895, six years after Haldane had been called to the bar. He was prominent within the profession, becoming a bencher in 1925 and treasurer of the Inn in 1947. He therefore had connections with his senior colleagues throughout the profession. He wrote in February 1918 to Master Willes Chitty deploring the idea of a ministry of justice and pointed out that the proposal would absorb into the Home Office certain powers of appointment and non-judicial functions which were currently exercised by the lord chancellor's office. The audacity of the proposal meant that, if implemented, judicial appointments would be made by politicians 'out of touch with the Bar.'[40]

Given this kind of 'fifth column' activity within the lord chancellor's department and the fact that the focus of the government was on post-war reconstruction, there is little wonder that 'the official files disclose very little evidence of official reaction or response' to Haldane's recommendation for a ministry of justice.[41] Thus consigned to gather dust in the depths of public-service files, the idea of a ministry of justice disappeared from sight. It would be small consolation to Viscount Haldane to know that, though never implemented, it continues to surface from time to time. Schuster's successor, Sir Albert Napier, provided an account of the role played by Lord Schuster – as he was to become in the last years of his life – in the demise of the proposed ministry of justice that is interesting for many reasons, not the least of which is the comment that Viscount Haldane saw Schuster as 'the very man to create the new Ministry [Justice] when the time came.'[42] How could this shrewd judge of men not have seen that he had invited into the bosom of his department the very viper who would poison all efforts to bring about the ministry of justice so central to his ambitions?

The Dying Days of Canadian Appeals to the Judicial Committee

While these machinations were proceeding in London, back in Canada the movement to terminate appeals to the Judicial Committee began to grow slowly, fuelled by the reluctance of the board to uphold federal legislation in industrial disputes, popularly called New Deal legislation. The insensitivity shown by the Judicial Committee in striking down Prime Minister R.B. Bennett's design to pull the country out of the Great Depression appeared to be the last straw. Even provincial voices were being heard calling for termination of appeals.

But the fundamental question is, despite the setbacks in the New Deal cases, why did Canada – a country that had long cherished its monarchical ties with Great Britain – sever the right of appeal to the foot of the throne by terminating appeals in 1949? In Britain, appeal to the Judicial Committee was viewed as integral to the concept of Empire; in Canada it had been viewed as a critical means of strengthening the ties with the mother country. As Chief Justice Charles Fitzpatrick wrote in a letter to Viscount Haldane in 1914, 'whatever view may obtain in other parts of the Empire, so far as Canada is concerned, I think I may safely say that, amongst lawyers and judges competent to speak on the subject, there is but one opinion, that where constitutional questions are concerned an appeal to the Judicial Committee must always be retained.'[43] Yet the right of appeal was severed a little more than four decades later without the blare of trumpets and without a glance of disapproval from the average citizen.

This is not to say that some Canadian law societies did not resist termination. The Law Society of Upper Canada, one of the most influential law bodies in Canada, objected in a formal resolution of convocation in 1938. A blue-ribbon committee was struck under the chairmanship of the Honourable G.R. Geary to study the proposals for abolition of appeals and to come forward with a recommendation. In a unanimous recommendation – which was approved by convocation – the committee rejected the movement to abolish appeals. The report stated that appeals to the Judicial Committee of the Privy Council 'tends to keep our jurisprudence in harmony with the jurisprudence of Great Britain and the Empire.' It also warned that 'to sever the connection that exists between our judicial system and the British judiciary would increase the tendency to be so affected and so would be detrimental to the maintenance of those British traditions in the administration of justice which have had so large a part in building up the world over for respect for British institutions.'[44] Despite such opposition from the bar, the movement to abolish appeals to the Judicial Committee proceeded apace.

When the issue of legal appeal had been raised back in 1876, the imperial Privy Council said in a memorandum written for the benefit of Edward Blake: 'The Supreme Appellate authority of the Empire or the realm is unquestionably one of the highest functions and duties of sovereignty. The power of construing, determining, and enforcing the law in the last resort is, in truth, a power which overrides all other powers.'[45] The report concluded that 'to abolish this controlling power, and to abandon each Colonial dependency to a separate Final Court of Appeal of its own, is obviously to destroy one of the most important ties which still connect all parts of the Empire in common obedience to the source of law, and to renounce the last and most essential mode of exercising the authority of the Crown over its possessions abroad.'[46] For Great Britain to terminate appeals to the Judicial Committee was viewed as tantamount to abandonment of the colonies. Richard Haldane thought so strongly about these 'silken bonds of Empire' that he wanted to reinforce the status of the Judicial Committee as the final court of appeal for all the colonies and crown possessions.

While there was considerable support throughout the Canadian legal community for retaining appeals in constitutional matters, in criminal appeals the view was different. In 1888 – just two decades after the passage of the British North America Act, 1867 – the federal Parliament amended the Criminal Code so as to abolish appeals to the Judicial Committee in criminal cases. This statute operated successfully for almost forty years. It was not challenged in the Judicial Committee until 1926 in *Nadan v. The Queen*,[47] when the law lords declared the amendment invalid because it conflicted with two imperial statutes. The conflict of laws between Britain and the colonies was, in no small part, responsible for the imperial conference of 1926. The work of the conference resulted in the Statute of Westminster, which conferred on the dominions the capacity to amend or repeal imperial statutes, whereupon Canada moved to re-enact the 1888 statute and upon appeal to the Judicial Committee it was held to be valid.[48]

As one observer at the time recalled, when the Judicial Committee struck down the Industrial Disputes Investigation Act, the creation of William Lyon Mackenzie King, at the time deputy minister of labour and a future prime minister of Canada, the judgment drew 'bitter criticism from parliamentarians.'[49] The act had been in successful operation for almost twenty years. But some members of the judiciary, such as Justice Lyman Poore Duff, had a more sympathetic view of the matter. Duff quickly came to the defence of the Judicial Committee by reminding provincial politicians that, as far as he was concerned, 'if the Supreme Court of Canada of the 70's and 80's had had its way, the legislatures of the provinces would have been reduced to a status which would have made them little better than municipal councils.'[50] The law lords did little more than protect the provinces from 'judicial assault,' he announced. The line of reasoning followed by the early Supreme Court of Canada would have 'thrown our constitutional law into a state of chaos,' he declared. 'This was averted by the Privy Council.'[51] As well, Duff was not confident that the government of the day was appointing men to the federal bench who would inspire confidence. Given the low quality of some Canadian judges, he was prepared to leave appeal to the Judicial Committee alone, this despite his preference for seeing 'questions touching our constitution determined in Canada.'[52]

The enthusiasm of politicians for termination of appeals met, however, a major setback in 1928 when, in the *Edwards* case, the Supreme Court of Canada ruled that the terms of the British North America Act, 1867 authorizing the appointment of 'qualified persons' to the Senate did not include women. The judgment was greeted throughout Canada with editorial outrage. It was the first time in its history that the court was subjected to public ridicule. The *Ottawa Evening Journal* ran an editorial mocking the judges for their decision. 'What? Women "Not Persons?"'... The Supreme Court has made a terrible guess. How they came to make it, and they all married, only themselves and the Lord can know; and perhaps only the Lord ... Shame upon you gentlemen of the Supreme Court! Where is your gallantry, your chivalry? ... we're in the absurd position that a woman can sit in the House of Commons, where laws are really made and cannot sit in the Senate where they are merely reviewed.'[53]

No judicial decision has been more inaccurately reported or more wilfully distorted in the annals of Supreme Court of Canada history than the decision in the *Edwards* case to exclude women from the Senate.[54] According to some feminist scholars, the court's decision in *Edwards* purported to decide a metaphysical issue as to the personhood of women. This is incorrect. However inadequate the decision may have been – and it is difficult not to notice its inadequacy – it did not pronounce on the metaphysics of personhood. The five justices of the Supreme Court came unanimously to the conclusion that the words in section 24 of the British North America Act, 1867 had to be interpreted narrowly to mean that – at the time the provision was enacted – Parliament intended that only men who met the other qualifications of the section could be called to the Senate. The court said that the terms *when written* intended men only. If the imperial Parliament wished to rewrite the terms, it was perfectly within its jurisdiction to do so. It was not, the judges unanimously implied, their duty to amend the terms of the constitution. The line of reasoning is not very persuasive but, to be fair to the Supreme Court of

Canada judges, it was perfectly consistent with the established judicial tradition and anchored in the appropriate precedents.

It is often overlooked that many *men* in Canada were not considered 'qualified persons' under the terms of the constitutional provision. No man or woman can – to this day – be appointed to the Senate who does not have $4,000 over and above all encumbrances. A very sizeable body of men in 1928 in Canada who could not meet this requirement were, therefore, denied the status of 'qualified person' by the terms of the constitution. Needless to say, all children throughout Canada cannot be considered 'persons' for several reasons in addition to the monetary deficiency. Nevertheless, the ruling left the anomaly hanging: a man of wealth was by definition a 'qualified person' while a millionaire woman was not. On its face, the judgment was an absurdity.

The five prominent Alberta women who had initiated the proceedings – Henrietta Muir Edwards, Nellie L. McClung, Louise C. McKinney, Emily F. Murphy, and Irene Parlby – appealed the Supreme Court of Canada ruling to the Judicial Committee where Lord Sankey, who had succeeded to the lord chancellorship upon the death of his friend Viscount Haldane in 1928, presided over the board. For four days in July 1929, the law lords heard counsel for both sides argue the case. On 18 October the Judicial Committee announced, in a decision written by the lord chancellor, that the judgment of the Supreme Court of Canada was reversed; that the words 'qualified persons' included women and that women could be called to the Senate.[55] After reviewing the reasons for judgment given in the Supreme Court, Lord Sankey observed that the 'exclusion of women from all public offices is a relic of days more barbarous than ours.'[56] He then went on to say that 'the British North America Act planted in Canada a living tree capable of growth and expansion within its natural limits.'[57] The reversal of the Supreme Court judgment was warmly received throughout Canada – except at the Supreme Court, where the five justices, and especially Chief Justice Francis Alexander Anglin, brooded in embarrassment;[58] they were prepared neither for the public outrage nor for the reversal, so sure were they that the prevailing precedents sustained their conclusions. Among other authorities they had consulted was *Bebb v. The Law Society*,[59] a 1914 case decided unanimously in the House of Lords which ruled that Parliament had intended to exclude women from becoming solicitors. Each of the three law lords regretted that they were obliged under the authority of past judicial precedents to rule against Bebb's petition. All three lords of appeal ruled that it was up to Parliament to change the law, not the law courts. This was exactly the line of reasoning adopted by the Supreme Court of Canada in the *Edwards* case.[60] We will return to this case in the Postscript for a discussion of Lord Sankey's introduction of the 'living tree' metaphor and its impact on the course of Canadian constitutional interpretation, especially since the adoption of the Charter.

Apart from permitting the appointment of women to the Senate – Cairine Reay Wilson was called on 15 February 1930 to be the first woman to sit in the Senate of Canada – the judgment gave credence to those voices that were demanding the retention of appeals to the Judicial Committee. The Privy Council decision in *Edwards* proved to those in Canada who continued to champion the Judicial Committee appeals what Viscount Haldane had long proclaimed: the dominions required a more detached and impartial tribunal of final appeal in order to make up for the deficiencies of the colonial bench. Not a few judges and lawyers in Canada thought that the quality of the Canadian bench was low and that Canada was not yet ready for termination of appeals.

The desire for full self-government, for full nation status, became so strong throughout Canada, however, that termination of appeals became an object too difficult, politically, to resist. After the elimination of appeals in criminal cases – made easy by the rarity with which the Judicial Committee granted leave to appeal and after several earlier attempts to do so had failed[61] – it became only a matter of time before the termination of appeals in other cases would be achieved. The initial parliamentary move to end appeals came in 1947. Stuart Garson, the minister of justice, asserted in his remarks on the second reading of the bill in 1948 that termination of appeal to the Judicial Committee would remove 'one of the two badges of colonialism.'[62]

Ironically, it was an opinion of the Judicial Committee itself that had provided the final impetus towards termination of appeals. The Great Depression presented both the federal and provincial levels of government with unprecedented challenges. The provinces sought the financial assistance of the federal government and Parliament to lift them out of the dreadful political and social morass caused by extensive economic collapse. Unemployment soared with the widespread failure of business. The absence of social agencies by which to assist the hungry and hundreds of thousands of unemployed made the provincial governments turn to the federal government for assistance. The federal government and Parliament began to listen. In January 1935 Prime Minister Bennett acknowledged that 'the old order' had gone and in its stead he promised a 'New Deal' for Canadians, one that would see government enter into the economic life of the nation and come to the relief of the hungry and unemployed. Little did he know at the time that the Judicial Committee, armed with volumes of past judgments, would negate his efforts to bring the economy out of the doldrums. And nothing stood in the way more formidably than the judgments of Viscount Haldane, especially his interpretation of the criminal law power of Parliament and his narrow rulings on the federal government's authority over trade and commerce.

John T. Saywell cannot resist referring to Haldane's 'bizarre *dicta* which had strangled the federal power over criminal law and trade and commerce.'[63] Haldane's judgments, he says, were 'constitutional absurdities.'[64] Although expressed many years after the fact, these sentiments dominated the discourse of Canadian constitutional experts at the time and resulted in the call for termination of appeals to the Judicial Committee. It was clear that the opposition of Watson and Haldane, deeply entrenched in the record, stood squarely in the way of Parliament's – and the Supreme Court's – efforts to come to the relief of the provinces. The Watson-Haldane legacy was a huge barrier preventing Parliament's use of the 'Peace, Order, and good Government' clause in matters that did not constitute a 'national emergency' and forbad federal authority to grant relief in economic matters under provincial areas of jurisdiction, a doctrine that the Supreme Court of Canada reinforced in the Anti-Inflation reference case years later in 1976.[65]

The demands on the two levels of government in Canada during the Great Depression showed the constitutional jurisprudence of the Judicial Committee to be a tangled nightmare which prevented the country from responding to the needs of its people and their governments. Despite the momentary setback to the pressure for termination of appeals caused by the *Edwards* decision, Prime Minister Louis St Laurent served notice that his Liberal government would begin the steps to eliminate appeals to the Judicial Committee. When the bill to terminate appeals was first introduced into the Canadian House of Commons in 1947, St Laurent rejected the not-unreasonable suggestion of George Drew, leader of the opposition, that the government consult the provinces before doing so; after all, such consultation was the preferred legal means for the resolution of federal-provincial disputes. The suggestion, St

Laurent said, was unnecessary. The bill to terminate was debated in 1948 and received royal assent and came into effect in 1949.[66] Neither St Laurent nor his minister of justice, Ernest Lapointe, was prepared to dilute the federal prerogative to recommend constitutional amendments to the imperial Parliament, despite Justice William Charles Crockett's strongly worded dissent in the reference to the Supreme Court which validated Parliament's right to terminate. Crocket had argued that termination affected the cherished relationship between the provinces and the crown. The right to appeal to the 'foot of the Throne' could not, he reasoned, be breached by a simple act of Parliament. And no province cherished that right more than the province of Quebec. It should be remembered that the provincial governments enjoyed the privilege of direct appeal to the Judicial Committee from their courts of appeal and, thus, could bypass the Supreme Court of Canada. A few muffled voices were heard throughout the country in protest on the occasion of termination of appeals, noticeably from the Law Society of Upper Canada, but to no avail; the issue had become a political one and appealed to the rising tide of nationalism. Appeal to the Judicial Committee of the Privy Council was formally terminated in 1949 and the Supreme Court of Canada became the country's final court of appeal.

Haldane as First Labour Lord Chancellor

The last major event in the life of Viscount Haldane occurred in 1924 when he returned to the woolsack at the request of Ramsay MacDonald, the first Labour Party prime minister. MacDonald was under pressure to show that the new political force, a party founded as the champion of the working classes, could produce a competent administration. He knew that, as prime minister in a minority Parliament, he would have to skate on thin ice. He needed all the help he could get from those who were sympathetic to the labour cause but not card-carrying members of the movement. He liked the progressive sentiments he heard from Viscount Haldane over the years and wanted to bring him into the administration. Labour was effectively shut out of the House of Lords and Haldane had publicly expressed his sympathies for the reform program of the new Labour Party. Lord Sankey, who had long coveted the position, blamed the scheming Lord Haldane when he was himself passed over for the woolsack. He claimed that Haldane 'put a pistol' at MacDonald's head to become the first Labour government's first lord chancellor.[67] But Sankey's claim lacks credibility.

Haldane's version of his appointment recounts how the new Labour prime minister came begging to 28 Queen Anne's Gate. As early as 1923, MacDonald had sounded out Haldane for a post in his cabinet. According to Haldane, MacDonald offered him a choice between president of the Board of Education or the lord chancellorship. Haldane demurred and in a lengthy letter to the prime minister said that he 'had no personal wish to return' to the cabinet.[68] He concluded his letter with an invitation to MacDonald to visit him at Cloan. MacDonald accepted Haldane's invitation and soon made the trip to Perthshire. By the time he left to return to London, he had secured Haldane's agreement to join in the first Labour cabinet as lord chancellor. This version of events contains no gun to the future prime minister's head. In any event, when the Conservatives, under Stanley Baldwin, were defeated in the House of Commons on 21 January 1924, Ramsay MacDonald was summoned by the king and asked to form the first Labour ministry, which he did the following day with Viscount Haldane as lord chancellor. Labour's triumph was, however, to be short lived. MacDonald's Labour government, amidst a medley of petty parliamentary scandals and policy missteps, was sent packing after ten months in office. MacDonald and his cabinet resigned on 3 November 1924, to be replaced in the election later that month by Stanley Baldwin's second administration following a bitter contest at the polls.

Few members of Parliament were more active in the short time this first Labour government was in power than Viscount Haldane. He piloted through the House of Lords several important bills such as the Land Law Reform Bill and the Housing Bill (which became the Housing Act in 1925). The latter measure proposed to supply two and a half million houses for the working classes over a period of fifteen years. In speaking on the bill in the Lords, Haldane was hooted down when he attempted to meet Conservative charges that it constituted the devil's tail of socialism. 'In a sense, it is a Bill,' he conceded, 'which is coloured by Socialism, but,' he dared to suggest, 'we are all Socialists now!'[69] The Fleet Street press delighted in reporting how Haldane's effrontery produced long and boisterous booing by Conservative members of the House of Lords. It was an unusual and unseemly occasion for the normally sedate, not to say somnolent, Upper House. Yet, however much Haldane's leadership in the House of Lords pleased MacDonald, his relationship with the prime minister began to sour quickly when it became evident that the Scottish lord was not to toe the party line as MacDonald wished. Haldane's native non-partisanship got him into

hot water with the government when he insisted on speaking with opposition members and keeping them informed of legislative initiatives.
He simply could not robe himself in the kind of partisanship required
by the ideologically driven Labour Party any more than he was able to
become a card-carrying Fabian socialist. He sat his vast frame upon the
political fence and it drove his friends on the political left to distraction.

Much to his satisfaction, Viscount Haldane's brief return to the woolsack provided him with the opportunity to participate in several more
Canadian cases in the Judicial Committee. He believed he had made an
indelible mark in the legal record by setting important precedents in
Canadian constitutional cases. What he left behind in the form of precedents was meant to serve as a barrier to any future meddling with the
division of powers in the Canadian constitution. He genuinely thought
that he had settled the major controversies, that he had made up for the
deficiencies of the original constitution which had contained too much
ambiguity with respect to the division of legislative powers between
the two levels of government. He was persuaded that he had championed the *Sittlichkeit* of the Canadian provinces and had sorted out the
main reasons for conflict between the federal and provincial levels of
government. He felt that the country could now get on with making the
constitution work for the people of Canada.

But the new generation of law lords who succeeded him on his death
in 1928, led initially by Lord Atkin more than by Lord Sankey, saw
matters differently. They soon came to view the large body of Haldane
jurisprudence as an obstacle to be dealt with. It quickly became apparent to observers of the Judicial Committee that the new law lords were
not simply going to bow to the past precedents of their predecessors
although formally obliged to do so. Viscount Haldane, for example,
had ruled in *Board of Commerce*, and confirmed in *Snider*, that the federal government under 91(2), the trade and commerce clause, could not
interfere with property and civil rights in the provinces. The new board
found this ruling too restrictive and sought a way around the barrier
by distinguishing Haldane's past judgments. This soon became the
preferred way of overruling previous judgments of the Privy Council.
In *Attorney General of Canada v. Attorney General of British Columbia*,[70]
which came on appeal to the Judicial Committee in October 1929, a
year after Haldane's death, the law lords gave the impression that they
would stay the course set by Watson and Haldane. The case came on
appeal from a decision of the Supreme Court of Canada rendered in
May 1928. British Columbia had challenged the federal Fisheries Act,

1914, which provided that no one shall operate for commercial purposes a fish cannery, or, in British Columbia a salmon cannery, without a licence from the federal minister of marine and fisheries. The province argued that the federal legislation invaded the exclusive legislative authority over 'property and civil rights in the province' (section 92[13]). The provinces of Quebec and Ontario joined in the reference as interveners; so too did the fishermen of Japanese descent. The Supreme Court of Canada, relying on the past judgments of the Judicial Committee which under Watson and Haldane had jealously guarded provincial powers over 'property and civil rights,' ruled the federal act ultra vires the power of the federal Parliament. To no one's surprise, the Judicial Committee affirmed the ruling.

What made this of special interest to Canadians was that the Judicial Committee judgment, written by Lord Tomlin, took upon itself to summarize in four propositions the accumulated wisdom of the board relating to 'questions of conflict between the jurisdiction of the Parliament of the Dominion and provincial jurisdiction.'[71] But danger always lurks behind attempts to summarize a long and less-than-coherent body of constitutional jurisprudence. Tomlin's first proposition fairly but only partially summarized the line of reasoning that 'legislation of the Parliament of the Dominion so long as it strictly relates to subjects of legislation expressly enumerated in s. 91, is of paramount authority, even though it trenches upon matters assigned to the provincial legislatures by s. 92.' But the second proposition tended to say a lot less than the line of previous jurisprudence would suggest. Tomlin stated: 'The general power of legislation conferred upon the Parliament of the Dominion by s. 91 of the Act in supplement of the power to legislate upon the subjects expressly enumerated must be strictly confined to such matters as are unquestionably of national interest and importance and must not trench on any of the subjects enumerated in s. 92 as within the scope of provincial legislation, unless these matters have attained such dimensions as to affect the body politic of the Dominion.'[72] This summary tended to signal that the board was moving back from the more restrictive previous rulings of the Judicial Committee. It appeared to wave off without a nod in his direction the rigid emergency doctrine enunciated by Viscount Haldane. Canadian court observers tended to take courage that the pendulum was beginning to swing back in the direction of those who favoured a more energetic federal presence in Canadian domestic affairs. Yet this initial trend was to be short lived inasmuch as the Supreme Court of Canada began to embrace the

Haldane emergency doctrine. As recently as 1976, the Supreme Court reaffirmed the emergency doctrine in the *Anti-Inflation* reference.[73] Subsequent bancs of Supreme Court judges have moved, as we have seen in *Crown Zellerbach*, back to a more flexible use of the 'Peace, Order, and good Government' clause.

11

Recollections and Last Days

'I had the reputation,' said Haldane, 'of persuading my friends to take courses which they might not have taken apart from me. I was looked upon by the official group as an intriguer.'

– André Maurois, *The Edwardian Era*

Richard Burdon Haldane stood out among his friends for one small thing among others: he remained throughout his life clean-shaven in the midst of friends who were wrapped in facial whiskers. To say nothing of George Bernard Shaw, whose great beard has become legendary, Haldane's older friend Edward Caird – successor to Benjamin Jowett as master of Balliol College, Oxford – sported the grandest mutton chops in an effort to distract attention from his complete baldness. Another friend of Haldane's, Andrew Seth Pringle-Pattison, prided himself on a great white beard that balanced his full head of equally white hair, making him look every inch like Father Christmas. Even his Welsh friend Henry Jones allowed himself a neatly trimmed moustache. But not Richard Haldane. Only once in his life – when as a young student he returned from Göttingen sporting a moustache – did he indulge this common male vanity. He was truly the Jacob to his many Esau friends.

His principal secretary at the War Office, John Buchan, described his old friend in his memoirs. 'To the ordinary man he was a reputation rather than a person. His large smooth face, with the kindly wrinkles round the eyes, suggested a benevolent sphinx; his manner of speech was that of an oracle declaiming wisdom from some cloudy tripod, an impression enhanced by his small toneless voice.'[1] Writing while governor general of Canada, Buchan went on to comment that Haldane 'was so unlike those of other public figures that he became the centre of myth. The impression got abroad that his methods were of a subtlety which was almost devious. It was wholly false. He was a practical man, and was always prepared "by indirections to find direction out." What he had in a full degree was the gift of persuasion, the power of wearing down opposition by sheer patience and reasonableness; and he had also that chief of diplomatic talents, the ability to read an opponent's mind and shape his argument accordingly.'[2] This talent, we are told, 'made him a tremendous figure at the Bar. He was a learned lawyer, but there were many legal pundits. Where he differed from his rivals was in his power of getting back to principles and presenting his argument as an inevitable deduction from any sane conception of the universe ... He could dignify the most prosaic case by giving it a philosophic background.'[3] Buchan retained a deep affection for his former superior throughout the remainder of his life.

But no one gave a fuller account of Richard Burdon Haldane than his Fabian friend Beatrice Webb, who spent hours recording in her diaries her impressions of notable people of her generation, especially those with whom she associated in a variety of social causes. This was her description of Haldane:

His bulky awkward form and pompous way, his absolute lack of masculine vices and 'manly' tastes (beyond a good dinner), his intense superiority and constant attitude of a teacher, his curiously wooly mind would make him an unattractive figure if it were not for the beaming kindliness of his nature, warmly appreciative of friends and a certain pawky humour with which he surveys the world. And there is pathos in his personality. In spite of the successful professional life, the interest and entertainment of constantly mixing with the most powerful minds and in the most stirring affairs, the enjoyment of luxurious living to a man with a first-rate digestion, he is a restless lonely man – in his heart still worshiping the woman who jilted him seven years ago ... When we are together we are constantly discussing hotly. He has been converted in a sort of vague metaphysical way to the principles of collectivism. But whether it is that his best brains are given to his professional work or whether it is that he is incapable of working out or even fully comprehending concrete principles, he never sees the right side of the question until you have spent hours dinning it into him ... all the same, we two [she and Sidney] and he remain genuinely fond of each other.[4]

Beatrice, who served with Haldane on the Machinery of Government committee and knew him for his work in education for the working class, said that he took 'incurable delight in mental mistiness,'[5] adding that he 'finds his relaxation in bad metaphysics and in political intrigue.'[6] Poor Beatrice, she who would never know metaphysics good or bad, nevertheless found him a 'generous-hearted man, affectionate to his friends and genuinely enthusiastic about the advancement of knowledge.' Then, as if it were necessary to rescue him from any semblance of virtue, she hastened to observe: 'His ideal has no connexion with the ugly rough and tumble of work-a-day world of the average sensual man, who is compelled to earn his livelihood by routine work and bringing up a family of children on narrow means.'[7] This is a rather odd comment from one who never had children of her own, was born into riches, and was far removed from 'bringing up a family of children on narrow means.'

Unfortunately, we have no corresponding comments of Haldane on Beatrice Webb. His good friend Herbert Henry Asquith, moved to comment on Beatrice Webb on one occasion, said of her: 'To me hers is, *au fond*, a tiresome type of mind.'[8] It was not unlike Asquith to find her tiresome but Richard Haldane never did so. He enjoyed the stimulation of her company and dined with her and her husband, Sidney, frequently. Indeed, he conspired over a long period with Sidney Webb to bring about the establishment of the University of London. But, as much as he liked Sidney, Haldane was taken by Beatrice. She possessed two qualities that appealed to the Scot: she was intelligent and she was beautiful. And perhaps more to the point, she remained beyond his reach despite his alleged unsuccessful efforts to woo her. Beatrice Webb's repeated efforts in the campaign of national reform made little impact on the man and it frustrated her to no end; the meeting of minds was simply too unequal.

Osbert Sitwell saw Haldane as a ponderous figure who tended to enter a room 'with the air of a whole procession.' On the one hand, he appeared to some as 'more akin to that of a butler of a great house than a Minister of the Crown.'[9] On the other, those who knew him from within the confraternity of philosophy spoke very highly of him. This man who consorted with Albert Einstein was remarkably free of arrogance, however much he was accused of it. Yet others claimed that his philosophical mind led him to be contemptuous of the average person. On one occasion after he joined the Labour government in 1924, a member of the party with strong academic ties asked him with a tinge of sarcasm whether he found his interest in philosophy of any practical use. Haldane replied: 'Well, I find it quite useful in dealing with ignorance with which I have to contend a great deal in these days.'[10] This exchange, unexplained, reveals the man as one who was impatient with his adversaries. It is a thoroughly inaccurate picture of him. He did not respond spitefully to those who pressed him for commitment, such as the proponents of Fabian socialism who were impatient with his need as a philosopher to examine the issues at the level of first principles. They were deeply committed social engineers for whom the principles of political and social action were clearly available and required only the hard work of committed statistical enthusiasts, such as the Webbs. Haldane frustrated them because he was a philosopher who was constantly learning, constantly thinking. As Beatrice Webb said of Arthur Balfour, a keen philosopher in his own right, 'he is delightfully responsive intellectually, a man with ever-open mind, too open perhaps, seeing that on no question has it been sufficiently closed by study and thought to have developed principles. There comes a time in life when surely the mind should be "made up" conclusively as to the particular questions with which it is mainly concerned; man's work in life is action and not enquiry.'[11] These words could have been said of Richard Haldane with equal validity.

Socialist partisans, such as the Webbs, were sure in their conviction that socialist equality was the ultimate moral principle and the ground of all human good; having reached that conclusion, they felt that further enquiry was unnecessary; now was the time to press on with a program of reform. This was the difference between the Webbs and Richard Haldane. When Beatrice was once chided by her elder sisters – she had eight, all of whom eventually married into comfort – for her efforts to educate herself in sociology and psychology, all with a view 'to make a show ... before old and young philosophers,'[12] Beatrice responded testily: 'What sensible woman wants a philosopher for a husband?'[13] Then she promptly returned to her study of Herbert Spencer's *Social Statics*. Little wonder that she chose Sidney Webb rather than Richard Haldane for her life's partner. Beatrice lived for many years a life of unfulfilled enthusiasms. In 1884 she confided her frustrations to her diary: 'Why should a mortal be born with so much aspiration, so much courage and patience in the pursuit of an ideal, and with such a beg-

garly allowance of power wherewith to do it?' She was convinced that
the new social sciences inspired by Auguste Comte and Herbert Spencer had provided the principles of social action. And, since the 'impulse
of self-subordinating service was transferred, consciously and overtly,
from God to man,' it was time to get on with the task of reforming society.[14] The church had missed its opportunity to provide the way; the
time was now for the social scientist in the service of socialism. 'The
memory of the low, cunning, brutal faces of the loafers and cadgers
who hang about the Mint haunts me when I feel inclined to put down
the Trade Union reports and take up a bit of good literature,' she wrote
to her beloved Sidney. She was now totally committed to the 'the religion of Humanity.'

What lingering respect she had for religious efforts at social reform
was restricted to Cardinal Henry Manning, who had taken practical
steps to alleviate the miserable conditions among the poor of London
and championed the rights of labour. She cited his report on the housing conditions of the poor. 'The state of the houses,' declared Manning,
'families living in single rooms, sometimes many families in one room,
a corner apiece – these things cannot go on. The accumulation of wealth
in the land, the piling up of wealth like mountains in the possession
of classes or of individual, cannot go on if these moral conditions of
our people are not healed. No commonwealth can rest on such foundations.'[15]

The Webbs had attempted for several years to enlist the 'Young Radicals' in the Liberal Party – Asquith, Haldane, Grey, Sydney Buxton, and
Arthur Acland – to the cause of socialism but without success. They
saw the 'Young Radicals,' especially Richard Haldane, as lukewarm in
their commitment to socialism; but Haldane was never a socialist, as
John Buchan was quick to note.[16] 'He seemed more open-minded than
the others [in the Fabian movement] and readier to kindle to a new vision.'[17] 'Where he differed from his rivals,' Buchan continued, 'was in
his power of getting back to principles and presenting his argument as
an inevitable deduction from any sane conception of the universe. To
differ from him seemed to be deny the existence of God. He could dignify the most prosaic case by giving it a philosophic background. This
was no mere forensic trick; it was the consequence of sincere a conviction, of a habit of mind which saw everything in organic relations.'[18] As
Dudley Sommer has summed up the impression Haldane made on the
general public: 'Haldane was more attracted by ideas than by people,'
which did not match the public's idea of what a politician should be.[19]

But even to his youthful friends, such as Raymond Asquith, Haldane was a serious intellectual presence. As the young Asquith wrote in 1898: 'Old Haldane is staying here [at Cloan] amongst others, and coming upon me as I read Lucretius' *De rerum natura*, took up the English and declaimed 30 lines or so of the corresponding Latin with the greatest accuracy and vigour. I was delighted, for he is a man of no classical attainment. I had a long and interesting talk with him afterwards on the subject of scholarship in general: he has a profound contempt for the English Aristotelians, Platonists, and more particularly for Jowett, and a corresponding admiration of the Germans, amongst whom he was bred.'[20] It is unquestionably true that Haldane had little regard for the celebrated Jowett, whose permanent achievement has been a translation of Plato's *Republic* which did much to extinguish interest or enthusiasm for the great Greek philosopher throughout succeeding generations. This famous translation, having wrung out of the *Republic* every ounce of philosophical rigour and manly virtue, achieved the questionable result of reducing the great ancient philosopher to the level of a quaint English gentleman.

Haldane himself was in many respects the cause of the unflattering assessments that haunted him throughout his life. Yet this life-long bachelor – one who, it was frequently claimed, tended to look down on lesser mortals – was especially good to children. Herbert Asquith, the prime minister's second son, recalled years after meeting Richard Haldane many times as a young boy that 'Haldane was a magnificent and generous host, lavish to his guests and very courteous to children, treating them as though they were his contemporaries.'[21] It was this habit of treating children as adults or as being interesting in their own right that endeared him to them. Young people appeared to like him while finding him amusing, especially when they caught him off-guard in the midst of a most unphilosophic pursuit, like swimming. Raymond Asquith related how, when on a visit to Mells to see his fiancée Katherine Horner in July 1900, he became temporarily transfixed when he caught sight of 'R.B. Haldane swimming in the large rush-filled and island lake below the broad terrace – a vast white mass with the brain of Socrates and the shape of Nero executing his absurd antics from a thin plank which bent double under his weight and sporting fantastically in the water.'[22] We have no way of knowing whether Haldane was aware that he was providing such mirth to spying young eyes. But we do know that he would have been mortified. This episode in the life of R.B. Haldane is one of the very rarest kind where the man is not engaged in a serious pursuit. Apart from long walks – he once walked from Brighton to London – he seldom took part in any sport; he did not fish, nor did he hunt, though most of his friends, such as Edward Grey, enjoyed both. He was in every sense 'un homme serieuse.'

Upon word of his death on 19 August 1928, tributes flooded in. People from all walks of life and from the four corners of the Empire wrote expressing their grief. His old friend and political colleague going back many years, Edward Grey, wrote in *The Scotsman* that Haldane was 'a man of deep and constant affection ... his intimate friends knew that if anyone of them was in perplexity and trouble Haldane would give unsparingly, not merely sympathy, but precious time, practical advice and earnest thought.'[23] G.P. Gooch, writing in the *Contemporary Review*, summed up the contribution to the state this Scot had made over so many years. 'His supreme ambition was to apply ideas to life, and hence a purely political or a purely academic career would have failed to satisfy him. Democracy without leadership, he used to say, is a mob, and leaders without intellectual training, we may add, are apt to be very treacherous guides. No man of our time had a fuller, richer or more useful life, and few have left a larger number of friends and causes to mourn their loss.'[24]

Not to forget what Dr Johnson said – 'In lapidary inscriptions a man is not upon oath'[25] – those who knew him personally said that he 'was the soul of courtesy.'[26] As one former colleague stated, he 'never heard Haldane say an unkind word about anyone.' His private papers confirm this remark; his rare comments on his political enemies, such as Lord Northcliffe, never descended into bitterness or unfairness – much to the annoyance of his friends such as Sir Edmund Gosse, who was enraged at the treatment his friend had suffered at the hands of the press for his German sympathies. He was sensitive in the little things that meant a great deal to people. 'When Haldane became Lord Chancellor,' a barrister who had appeared before him recalled, 'there were no facilities for lunch on the premises of the Privy Council. Haldane arranged with Oddenino's to provide lunch on the premises for the Bar. Alas, Haldane has gone; Oddenino's is gone – and the facilities for lunch have gone as well.'[27]

He was sensitive in large measures as well, as the visits he paid to the imprisoned Oscar Wilde amply demonstrate. Haldane related in his *Autobiography* how he had known Oscar Wilde 'in the days of his social success' and how he had been 'haunted by the idea of what this highly sensitive man was probably suffering under ordinary prison treatment.'[28] Haldane had met Wilde many times through the Webbs and George Bernard Shaw and was fully aware of his trial and tribulations. Unfortunately, he does not reveal his thoughts on the conviction of Wilde on the charge of 'indecent behaviour with men.' But we do know that he took pity on this poor broken Irish literary genius and visited him at Holloway Gaol. He saw Wilde alone in his cell; at first, the prisoner refused to speak. Haldane gives an account of that visit: 'I put my hand on his prison-dress-clad shoulder and said that I used to know him and that I had come to say something about himself. He had not fully used his great literary gift, and the reason was that he had lived a life of pleasure and had not made any great subject his own. Now misfortune might prove a blessing for his career, for he had got a great subject.'[29]

It is difficult to believe that anyone – even the philosophic Haldane – would address another man imprisoned and broken in spirit in this way. From what we know of Haldane's personality, it strikes a discordant note; he was a warm and generous man and must surely have presented himself as such to the celebrated prisoner. But we have only Haldane's account of the incident and that written late in life. In any event, during the interview Haldane suggested that he would get books for the prisoner as well as pen and ink. 'He burst into tears,' Haldane recorded, 'and promised to make the attempt.'[30] In addition to Pascal's *Provincial Letters* and *Pensées* and Walter Pater's *The Renaissance*, Wilde requested the *De Civitate Dei* and *Confessions* of St Augustine and Mommsen's *History of Rome*. He also requested and was provided with the major works of Cardinal John Henry Newman, his *Essays on Miracles* as well as *The Grammar of Assent*, *Apologia pro Vita Sua*, and *The Idea of a University*. These works were procured for the prison library and Wilde had access to them 'under the usual regulations.'

As Wilde's biographer, Richard Ellmann, has written: 'Haldane continued to urge the Home Office to provide him with more books and with writing materials, but the Home Office did not want to be accused of preferential treatment.'[31] Despite these bureaucratic roadblocks, Haldane continued his assistance to Wilde. He visited him later in Wandsworth Prison and kept himself informed of Wilde's condition through his contacts in the Home Office. Word reached him one day that the prisoner was not faring well under the regimen at Wandsworth – 'some of the warders were brutes' – and in due course Haldane persuaded the home secretary to have the prisoner transferred to Reading Gaol. It appears that Haldane was never aware of the humiliation Wilde suffered in that transfer to Reading. 'The move took place on 21 November, and proved to be the single most humiliating experience of Wilde's prison life.' As Ellmann reports, 'handcuffed and in prison clothing, [Wilde] had to wait on the platform at Clapham Junction from 2.00 to 2.30 on a rainy afternoon. A crowd formed, first laughing and then jeering at the manacled prisoner. One man recognized that this was Oscar Wilde, and spat at him. "For a year after that was done to me," Wilde wrote in *De Profundis*, I wept every day at the same hour and for the same space of time."'[32] Wilde did not forget his promise to the solicitous Haldane. In his *Autobiography*, Haldane reported: 'On his release there came to me anonymously a volume, *The Ballad of Reading Gaol*. It was the redemption of his promise to me.'[33] Once again, the comment appears cold and self-indulgent. But he wrote it about a year before his death in 1928.

Haldane never met Wilde after his release; the poet departed for France immediately upon leaving prison. He died in Paris not long afterwards, on 30 November 1900, amidst squalor and disease. Unfortunately, he did not leave behind any comments on the kindness Haldane had paid to him, which must surely have given him some measure of relief during his imprisonment. Yet his biographer makes it clear that Wilde was deeply grateful to Haldane for his generosity and continued support throughout those horrible two years in prison. Wilde left behind, as well, *The Ballad of Reading Gaol*, one of the great poems of the period which could also be seen as a memorial to Richard Haldane's generosity. What comes through in the details of this sordid episode is that the prison conditions of Britain were monstrous, approaching what we today would associate with the dreadful conditions of prisons in some other parts of the world. The prison guards and the uncompromising bureaucratic procedures of the Home Office regulations were revolting when exposed to light. 'The horror of prison-life,' Wilde wrote after leaving prison, 'is the contrast between the grotesqueness of one's aspect and the tragedy in one's soul.'[34] Any decent person would have been appalled at the treatment prisoners such as Wilde received during their incarceration. The urbane Richard Haldane went out of his way – and it took a great deal of courage, in the face of widespread public disapproval of Wilde, for him to do so – to ease the pain of a gentle soul who ran afoul of a draconian law. His was the one expression of decency that can be found in this affair.

The Case of the 'Very Voluble Baptist'

Most of the cases Richard Haldane heard as a law lord had to do with .

constitutional matters. He rarely sat on a criminal appeal. On one occasion, however, in 1921, he sat in the House of Lords in a case involving 'a young and very voluble Baptist who says he was falsely put into a lunatic asylum.'[35] Haldane assured his mother that he was 'treating him in a gentle fashion, but he will be a great trial before he is done.' The poor man insisted on arguing his own appeal and was constantly finding himself in a tangle of legal procedures. The affable judge tried his best to assist him. After the second day of the trial, Haldane related in a letter home: 'I am having a hard time on the Woolsack with my young Baptist appellant in person. He is very excitable and was put in the Asylum for, among other things, assaulting his mother. He is very clever, but very vain and loquacious. He is having a fair and polished hearing and we show him courtesy.'[36] In time, however, the court's patience with the young appellant began to wear thin. 'The young man's case goes on,' Haldane reported a few days later. 'But we are very gentle with him. But he is tiring and addresses us as if we were jurymen.'[37] Haldane was personally tried by the young fellow. 'I am just off to shepherd my young Baptist. I do not bark or bite at him but wag my tail gently. However, he is not easy to keep to his point.'[38] Four days later we read that 'I begin to groan under the young Baptist.' On 8 February he wrote to his mother: 'I hope to finish this case of the young Baptist today.'[39] Still, two days later he is still writing: 'Today will, I hope, prove the final day of the young Baptist. I have been as kind and polite to him as the necessity of guarding the public purse permitted.'[40] Finally, he was able to report to his mother that 'Yesterday we finished with the young Baptist. He delivered a peroration composed of texts from Job and elsewhere. I am writing the judgement.'[41] Two days afterwards, Haldane is still writing the judgment. Finally, on 7 March, he wrote: 'I am going to deliver judgement in the lunatic's case – against him – I hope he will not make a disturbance.'[42] Surely to no one's surprise, the young fellow did, indeed, create a disturbance. *The Times* gave an account of how Lord Haldane had the appellant ejected from the court for interrupting him as he was delivering his judgment.[43] And so ended the case of the 'lunatic Baptist,' much to the relief of the lord chancellor and his mother.

'My Dear Edmund'

Perhaps the closest personal friend Richard Haldane ever had – apart from his sister, Elizabeth – was Sir Edmund Gosse, librarian of the

House of Lords. Gosse, as we saw earlier, was enraged at the press assault upon the reputation of Haldane in 1915 and wrote to *The Times* in
defence of his friend. But he was more than a good friend to Haldane;
he saw to it that Haldane's writings – at the instigation of the man himself – were sent to the right people both in Britain and in the United
States.

The voluminous correspondence between the two men, housed at
the Brotherton Library at Leeds University, reveals an intimacy out of
the ordinary. In one sense the two constituted an odd couple: Haldane
and his love of Goethe and Heine and Gosse with his devotion to Ibsen
and his distrust of the Germanic. On one occasion, Gosse had written
disparagingly of Goethe and Heine. Haldane upbraided him: 'How
naughty of you to say what you did about Goethe and Heine! But I say
nothing.'[44] Apparently stung by the rebuke, Gosse did not reply right
away, which prompted a response from Haldane: 'My dear Edmund,
Why have I no word from you! Can you have been revolted at my gentle reproach about the Great Goethe? If so, let his spirit depart, for he
must not separate you and me.'[45] The letters to Gosse from Cloan in
Scotland are especially revealing. They show a man completely at ease
with himself after being driven from office by the scurrilous treatment
of the Fleet Street press. He positively exudes with enthusiasm from
his Scottish retreat, reading philosophy and comforted by his beloved
dog, Bruce: 'Even as late as September, 1917, Haldane refused to defend himself against the pro-German charges.[46]

From these letters to and from Gosse we learn that Richard Haldane's brother, John, was involved in the war effort by attempting to
break down the sulphur chlorine gas used by the Germans. He hoped
'to succeed in breaking into the molecule sufficiently fast to make it
innocuous.'[47] One has to wonder whether Haldane was aware that he
was breaking the Official Secrets Act by writing openly about such matters. Then again, H.H. Asquith while prime minister during the early
years of the war used frequently to write about military tactics and manoeuvres to his friend Venetia Stanley,[48] also in contravention of the
Official Secrets Act.

Gosse was also a useful friend inasmuch as he was a go-between for
Haldane and influential Americans. He frequently forwarded to Elihu
Root, the former secretary of state, William Howard Taft, the former
president, and Abbott Lawrence Lowell, the president of Harvard University, Haldane's accounts of the British government's efforts to avoid
war during the run-up to August 1914. At Haldane's private request,

Gosse sent Taft a copy of the White Paper containing correspondence between Great Britain and the European powers.[49] The correspondence showed that Haldane used Gosse as a means of keeping key American political figures informed of the state of affairs between Britain and other European powers; one gets the impression that the lord chancellor was doing this in ignorance of his political superiors, such as Asquith. It strikes the reader as a serious breach of propriety, but to skirt official restrictions seems to have been common practice at the time. These letters to Gosse reveal, also, that Haldane consulted regularly with his friend the librarian on a wide range of matters, not excluding cases actively before the court. On several occasions, the lord chancellor sent draft copies of his judgments to Gosse and requested his comments. And Gosse was always ready with his advice.

The Wider Circle of Friends

Richard Haldane had a select circle of friends, beyond those in the law, mainly in the area of education. One such friend was Harold Laski, the political science professor at the London School of Economics and Political Science and a moving force behind the Labour Party. Laski kept up a long correspondence with Justice Oliver Wendell Holmes of the United States Supreme Court. That correspondence reveals that both Laski and Holmes had a very high regard for Haldane's legal and philosophic mind. But the letters also show a human side to Haldane that many people never saw. On one occasion, Laski wrote to Holmes about a small dinner party he attended at 28 Queen Anne's Gate:

And while I'm telling tales, let me record one delightful anecdote of Haldane's. Frida and he and I dined here *a trois* the other night and we got talking of Margot Asquith. Years ago, he [Haldane] said, he went bail for John Burns after the Trafalgar Square Riots and when prison had made Burns eminent Miss Tennant expressed a desire to meet him. So Haldane arranged a dinner – Margot Tennant, Miss Beatrice Potter, (Mrs. Webb), Mrs J.R. Green, Asquith and Grey. When Burns arrived Miss Potter seized upon him and began to discuss the technique of trade union organisation. Miss Tennant waited a moment strolled across and remarked casually, Mr. Burns, what beautiful eyes you have! Thenceforward, said Haldane, Burns talked to no one else. Miss Potter sulked, Mrs Green went home early, Asquith tried to get in a word, but Margot Tennant and Burns sat on the sofa by themselves with complete aplomb and he saw her home. Isn't that the definition of triumph?[50]

This anecdote reveals a man who loved to gossip with his friends and share his table with them, as he did frequently over many years, acquiring a sterling reputation as a host in the process. He served not only the best wine but 'the best cigarettes in London.'[51] The Laski letter is by no means representative, however, of the meals at Queen Anne's Gate. Most of the time his guests were men of eminence such as Albert Einstein or other philosophers such as Andrew Seth Pringle-Pattison and Edward Cairns and the conversation was very serious. And there were many meals prepared for visiting Canadian judges and lawyers through whom Haldane kept himself informed of events in Canada.

The Man in the Rear-View Mirror

At the end of this work of prying into the corners of a man's life, I have come to view Richard Haldane as an image in the rear-view mirror. Having listened to numerous commendations of the man and to even more condemnations of him, I see Haldane as a gentle, enquiring person who allowed few people or few events to interfere with his philosophic approach to life in all the aspects in which he was involved: from education reforms to military reorganization to judicial reforms of Canada's constitution. He was a superb administrator and his name still appears favourably in the journals of public administration; he continues to command the respect of public servants throughout Britain long after his death. The Empire is no more and has been replaced by the weaker Commonwealth and several countries like Canada have terminated all legal appeals beyond their own Supreme Courts. He, of course, did not live to see the dissolution of the Empire but his legacy has lived on in some countries of the Commonwealth, such as Canada, where his judicial judgments on the *Sittlichkeit* as the aspiration of nations remain firmly in place.

Despite his wide circle of acquaintances, which included professional philosophers at Oxford and Cambridge as well as the University of London and judges throughout the Empire and in the United States, he had few real close personal friends. Neither his professional and political friends, such as H.H. Asquith and Edward Grey, nor his acquaintances, such as George Bernard Shaw and the Webbs and educators such as Harold Laski, were intimate with him. In his many letters to these friends, he would invariably address them by their family name, as was the custom of the day. The sole exception to this practice was his letters to Sir Edmund Gosse. In no other correspondence does the cool philosopher reveal the warmth that he does in these letters. As we have seen, the letters to Gosse always begin with 'My dear Edmund' or 'My dearest friend' and the like. And they frequently expose a man seeking affection from the recipient. 'My dear Edmund, why have I no word from you?' Haldane went into details about the cases he was trying at the moment and sought Gosse's advice. And throughout all of this long correspondence, in which he exposed his deepest thoughts, he never spoke unfavourably of other people, not even his inveterate enemies in the Northcliffe press. The closest he came was when discussing an emerging philosopher. 'I am deep in Bergson – with whom I am more and more dissatisfied.'[52] A judgment of philosophic detachment, nothing personal. Of Bertrand Russell, he wrote that he was 'the greatest mathematical genius we have produced for a long time.'[53] Haldane's sister, Elizabeth, wrote Gosse on one occasion and expanded on her brother's affection for the great librarian.[54]

He was clearly a curious man, kind and generous and warm to his friends yet, to many, aloof and even cold. His home at 28 Queen Anne's Gate was open to a series of visitors and a good meal. He exulted, especially, in the intellectual efforts of young philosophers. In December 1914, for example, while preoccupied with details at the War Office, Haldane wrote to Walter Cunningham, a young professor at Middlebury College, Vermont, saying that he had read the young scholar's book, *Thought and Reality in Hegel's System*, and how much he enjoyed it.[55] He liked it so much, in fact, that he lent it to F.H. Bradley after praising the Oxford scholar for his own philosophical writings. The praise meant a lot to Bradley, who wrote in return: 'The approval or disapproval of the greater number of those who read books on philosophy, is I am afraid, not worth very much. But a word of praise from men who, like yourself, have worked at the subject successfully and know it from the inside is a real encouragement.'[56]

He never appeared to feel threatened by others but was rather genuinely interested in learning from them. And he possessed a keen interest and affection for Canada, especially its constitutional development. As we have seen, he frequently held dinner parties for visiting Canadian lawyers and politicians. The letters to his mother are replete with comments on Canada and Canadian affairs; he constantly sought out from his Canadian visitors news about developments in Canada. Whether he was, as Eugene Forsey once called him, a 'wicked step-father of the Canadian Constitution,' there is little doubt that he was most certainly a step-father. Deep in the dust of Canadian legal history, however, is a lingering resentment of Viscount Haldane. Several powerful writers on the constitution have harboured a deep resentment of this Scottish law lord for emasculating the 'Peace, Order, and good Government' clause of the constitution of Canada and thereby weakening the central authority of Parliament.[57] In addition to Forsey, Bora Laskin, who became chief justice of the Supreme Court of Canada, called Haldane 'a constitutional Houdini' who twisted the federal general power out of all proportion in an effort to grant 'autonomy' to the provinces.[58] Frank Scott, dean of law at McGill University, and a chorus of others joined in the fray.[59]

Whatever his legacy in the histories of the period, Viscount Haldane's influence endures today in the Supreme Court of Canada in ways, perhaps, he would never have imagined but might have hoped for. And that would have pleased him to know. It may come as a surprise to many Canadians to learn that G.W.F. Hegel has long had a place in the intellectual life of Canada and continues to do so to the present day. As David MacGregor has written, 'Hegel looms large in Canada.'[60] Those who would pursue this matter will find especially helpful Robert C. Sibley's recently published book *Northern Spirits: John Watson, George Grant and Charles Taylor: Appropriations of Hegelian Political Thought.* It remains for us, however, to explore briefly how and in what form Hegelianism has penetrated into the judicial life of Canada, especially with the adoption of the Charter of Rights and Freedoms.

Postscript

The Haldane Legacy and the Modern Court

This notion of a 'living' constitution – a pillar of modern liberalism – comes out of the doctrine of progress and, as the more honest Progressives admitted, the historicism of German political philosophy.

– Ronald J. Pestritto, *American Progressivism*

Most Canadians outside the narrow confines of university philosophy departments will be surprised to learn that G.W.F. Hegel has sunk deep roots in our culture and continues to exercise a considerable influence. As Robert Fulford noted in his review of Robert C. Sibley's *Northern Spirits: John Watson, George Grant and Charles Taylor: Appropriations of Hegelian Political Thought*, 'Canada has Hegelian feminists, Hegelian constitutionalists, Hegelian sociologists, Hegelian political scientists.'[1] Fulford continued: 'Sibley ... suggests that even Canadians who don't actually read Hegel are intuitively Hegelian.' Hegel's Canadian presence is so pervasive that it led David MacGregor to conclude in 'Canada's Hegel,' almost two decades before Sibley's book appeared, that 'Canada is awash in Hegel.'[2] Adding great weight to Hegel's Canadian presence is, of course, Charles Taylor, a native son of Montreal and acknowledged as one of the world's leading Hegel scholars. But there was a long line of Canadian philosophers who introduced students to Hegel's teachings before Taylor appeared on the scene. Scholars such as John Watson at Queen's University, H.S. Harris at York University

(known for decades as 'the dean of Canadian Hegelians'), Emil Facken-
heim at the University of Toronto, and John Burbidge at Trent, to name
only four, prepared the foundations for the pervasive reach of Hegelianism throughout Canada over the course of many years.[3] Given the
depth of Hegel's presence in Canadian intellectual culture, it would be
strange if one did not find his influence in Canadian law schools where
all our judges are educated.[4]

Hegel in Canada

The challenge at this point in concluding our account of Viscount Haldane's life is to identify the character of his enduring Hegelian influence on the law of Canada, especially since the adoption of the Charter
of Rights and Freedoms in 1982. It is relatively easy to demonstrate his
impact on the federal structure of Canada but it is quite another matter
to show how his abstract philosophical influences have come to shape
the *moral* life of the Canadian polity through the judgments of judges.
But judges are no less susceptible to the influence of philosophers and
prominent scientists, such as Hegel, Charles Darwin, and Max Weber,
than the rest of us; it would be remarkable if it were otherwise. They
receive the same education and draw from the same well of influences
as the general educated population.[5]

It is a constant source of wonder to listen to the language of public
discourse – including court judgments – and hear allusions, implied
and explicit, to Darwin's 'natural selection' and to Weber's 'fact-value'
distinction without formal acknowledgment of the source. There appears to be no need to announce the source, so deeply have such ideas
become embedded in Western thinking, giving credence to John Maynard Keynes's observation that 'the ideas of economists and political
philosophers, both when they are right and when they are wrong, are
more powerful than is commonly understood. Indeed, the world is
ruled by little else.'[6] As well, Justice Oliver Wendell Holmes, writing
on the 'Law in Science and the Science in Law' during the period when
Haldane was active on the Judicial Committee and in touch with him,
said: 'I am immensely struck with the blind imitativeness of man when
I see how a doctrine, a discrimination, even a phrase, will run in a year
or two over the whole English-speaking world.'[7]

No serious student of Canadian law or history doubts that Viscount
Haldane had a profound influence on the course of the constitutional
jurisprudence in Canada; as noted frequently throughout this book,

Haldane's legacy endures in the emergence of stronger provinces and a weaker federal government than intended by our dominant constitutional framers.[8] But what was not made explicit in the previous discussion of Haldane's impact on the Canadian constitution was the *moral* character of the Hegelian historicism which lies at the root of his constitutionalism. It is precisely the historical relativism at the core of Hegel's thought – the internal dynamic moral force – that continues to have the greatest impact on the life of Canada. Hegel's great and most enduring contribution to modern Western thought has been historical relativism and it has spread like a virus throughout the Western world.[9]

Since Hegelianism almost never appears in our midst without a mask, it is frequently difficult to recognize its presence; it appears under a variety of forms as 'modern liberalism,' 'modernism,' or 'progressivism.' But at the core of these various forms lies Hegelian historical relativism, more frequently than not in tandem with social Darwinism. Darwin was frequently associated with Hegel in the writings of Haldane's contemporaries, such as David George Ritchie, who wrote *Darwin and Hegel and Other Philosophical Studies* in 1893.[10] We should not be surprised to find an amalgam of Hegel and Darwin in Canada's legal progressivism. Darwin more than anyone else prepared the general public throughout the West to accept the philosophical sophistications of Hegelianism as its new social and political orthodoxy.[11]

Hegelian historical relativism affirms that all values are relative to their times, that there are no enduring or permanent trans-historical values. Following Rousseau, Hegel taught that human nature is historically determined and continually being transformed, that it changes essentially with each succeeding epoch and with each new epoch, new values replacing old ones. In his *Philosophy of History*, Hegel presented a new account of world history purporting to show that what we call freedom was little more than the 'spirit of freedom' which, he claimed, began in the East and made its way westward through a process called dialectic. The dialectical process advanced, he wrote, by a series of conflicts or wars. Simply stated, this means that every historical period or epoch produces for a time a prevailing thesis (a temporarily settled orthodoxy) but within that thesis itself resides a restless countervailing force or anti-thesis which in time begins the struggle to oust the prevailing thesis with the promise to expand the enjoyment of a greater political and moral freedom. Out of the struggle of these inherent forces within each epoch a new synthesis emerges and prevails, claiming for the moment the role of thesis. But within this new synthesis (which is now the prevailing new thesis) there resides a challenging liberating force which emerges in time – as a butterfly out of its chrysalis – to challenge the prevailing new thesis. The process continues, he confidently affirmed, until the 'end of history' when everyone will be free. 'Progress,' Hegel wrote, 'appears as an advancing from the imperfect to the more perfect; but the former must not be understood abstractly as *only* the imperfect, but as something which involves the very opposite of itself – the so-called perfect – as a *germ* or impulse.'[12] Thus, Hegelian historicism appears among us in common parlance in the form of progressivism, the ambition to extend freedom and equality to every human indulgence under the imprimatur of progress.

In the course of the nineteenth century and into the twentieth, disciples of Hegel introduced historicism by transforming natural rights into historical rights. As Justice Holmes said in his characteristically dismissive way, there 'was no meaning in the rights of man except what the crowd will fight for.'[13] The war against natural rights in the name of history became the prevailing doctrine of liberals no less than of conservatives. As Harry Jaffa has noted: 'There were left-wing as well as right-wing Hegelians, the most famous of the former being Karl Marx and the most famous of the latter, certainly for [American] purposes, being John C. Calhoun. Historic rights were held by Hegel to be rational, and each successive, "synthesis" of the antecedent "thesis" and 'antithesis" was believed to move mankind to a higher level of rationality.'[14] Hegel was the first to promote the notion of the course of history as the record of human rationality in the cause of freedom. That is what he meant when he insisted that 'history is rational.' What we call history, he taught, is the record of 'mind' or 'consciousness' evolving over the course of time. This means that all previous epochs are inherently imperfect and awaiting the corrections provided by succeeding epochs. And, paradoxically, he understood that this process was driven by men's passions, not their reason. It was the passions of such men as Napoleon that unknowingly gave direction to the Mind of history. As Jaffa, once again, summarizes the matter: 'The conflicts in the historical process were driven entirely by men's passions, not their reason. Philosophers did not arrive at the truth by abstract reasoning, as Plato and Aristotle had mistakenly believed, but by discovering, through long and exacting historical study, the design in events caused by the great non-philosophical agents of historical change, such as Napoleon, Bismarck, and Lincoln [and Churchill]. The victors in great wars were instruments of "the cunning of history," which used them for rational ends that formed no necessary part of the victor's own conscious intentions.'[15]

The principal 'prophet and patriarch of the new judicial power' in the United States was Oliver Wendell Holmes, the only justice of the Supreme Court of the United States with whom Haldane maintained serious contact over many years.[16] Haldane admired Holmes greatly and wrote a laudatory account of the man in 1921.[17] Holmes had secured a place among serious American and British students of law with the publication in 1881 of *The Common Law*. In this work Holmes sought to elicit experience as superior to logic in the life of the law as well as to affirm the legislative character of judging. In this matter Holmes was echoing the thoughts of John Austin, the principal proponent of the new legal positivism in nineteenth-century Britain. In *The Province of Jurisprudence Determined* (1832), Austin had written: 'I cannot understand how any person who has considered the subject can suppose that society could possibly have gone on if judges had not legislated, or that there is any danger whatever in allowing them that power which they have in fact exercised, to make up for the negligence or the incapacity of the avowed legislator.' He concluded magisterially: 'That part of the law of every country which was made by judges has been far better made than that part which consists of statutes enacted by the legislative.'[18]

No one has exercised greater influence over American law than O.W. Holmes. 'Holmes' influence,' writes Michael Ulhmann, 'over contemporary law and law teaching has no rival. He has been claimed, to one degree or another and however implausibly, by virtually every important sect of modern jurisprudence. Thanks chiefly to the enthusiasm of Felix Frankfurter and Harold Laski, he was even more implausibly claimed by the Progressives as a champion of social reform.'[19] Above all, Holmes wished nothing more than to expunge morals from the law: 'For my own part, I often doubt whether it would not be a gain if every word of moral significance could be banished from the law altogether ... We should lose the fossil records of a good deal of history and the majesty got from ethical associations, but by ridding ourselves of an unnecessary confusion we should gain very much in the clearness of our thought.'[20] We will never know the extent of Holmes's influence on Viscount Haldane but one thing is certain: his thinking was consistent with the Hegelian philosophy to which Haldane was attached. Holmes was no philosopher but his power of rhetoric has won for him and his moral nihilism a solid place in the teaching of law in the United States and beyond.

Truth in History

Is there any evidence that Haldane sowed the seeds of Hegelian historicism in the minds of Canadian judges through his non-judicial writings and speeches? In his Creighton Lecture, Haldane addressed the question of 'Truth in History' and in so doing gave the fullest account of his understanding of historicism than at any other time. On that occasion he said that 'no event in history of any kind can be judged without full knowledge of its context and of the spirit of its particular age.'[21] He added: 'The test of relevancy is the standard of what is necessary, not merely for exactness, but for the adequate portraiture of the spirit of the time. And this test necessitates great insight into the characteristics of that spirit.'[22] The 'spirit of the times' was the dominant factor in judging for Viscount Haldane. Since all truth is historically conditioned and relative to the given period, past claims to truth are easily discarded in favour of the 'spirit of the [present] time.' Accordingly, the task of the judge was, for Haldane, to seek out that spirit and to be sympathetic to the expanding demands of the spirit. In the Canadian context today, judges are meant, under the Charter of Rights and Freedoms, to be sympathetic to the spirit that is currently driving social policy. The approach adopted by Justice Bertha Wilson embodied the Haldane approach when she insisted that the terms of the Charter must be 'contextualized.'[23] Clearly, Wilson's approach meant going beyond the wording of the parchment, even one called a Charter. That is precisely what Viscount Haldane bequeathed to the Canadian courts, especially the Supreme Court of Canada.

Bertha Wilson deserves more than a passing glance here in light of her own explicit acknowledgment of the influence of the Scottish Enlightenment upon her thinking. She was educated in the humanities at the University of Aberdeen, especially in philosophy and psychology. Ellen Anderson, Wilson's biographer, has written of how Wilson's Charter jurisprudence of 'contextual balancing of competing rights' was rooted in the Scottish Enlightenment: 'These were attitudes engrained in her long before law school through immersion in a culture shaped by Scottish enlightenment philosophy, and then further reinforced by her deep religious values and by her interdisciplinary program of studies at the University of Aberdeen.'[24]

Given her background in philosophy and psychology, it is not surprising that Bertha Wilson would think deeply about the nature of judging and the development of the judicial function.[25] Her Goodman

Lectures, given at the University of Toronto in the fall of 1985, reveal a mind comfortable with the deeper issues of constitutional judging, especially with the advent of the Charter. Justice Wilson made it clear on this occasion that she was not captive of an 'embalmed legal tradition' or a victim of the view that *stare decisis* was a 'form of ancestor worship.'[26] She inferred that she was not tied to the traditional view of deference to the legislature and that she understood that the Canadian Charter of Rights and Freedoms represented 'a fundamental re-ordering of the political balance of power' in Canadian law and politics; that the courts were given important new powers to chart new directions in social policy in Canada. She recognized that the Charter obliged judges to 'put the law into a larger social perspective and to relate it to the reality of every-day life.'[27] She was committed to 'contextualizing the law' by going beyond the words of the constitutional text and broadening the base of the admissible evidence in Charter cases.

'Contextualizing' the law is little more than taking into account the dominant social forces of the times, an approach in which, Wilson insisted, 'relevant social science information' would become critical in assisting the judge to come to a decision.[28] On one extrajudicial occasion, Justice Wilson returned to this theme and asserted that 'all constitutional guarantees must be expounded in a way that is responsive to contemporary reality.'[29] Not surprisingly, she embraced the 'living tree' doctrine made famous in *Edwards* and rejected as 'necessarily restrictive' the 'textual approach' to judging because it placed too much emphasis 'on the words of the constitutional document as signifiers of legislative intent.'[30] Legislative intent, she insisted, was 'largely fictional.' The Charter, she argued, changed everything: the legislative bodies in Canada, Parliament and the provincial legislatures, must now answer to the courts because that constitutional document 'explicitly designated the Court as the forum for choosing from among a variety of policy options.'[31] In this instance, in relying on the *intention* of the Charter, Justice Wilson embraced a paradox: whereas the intention of Parliament in any given legislation was to be set aside as 'largely fictional,' the intention of Parliament contained in the Charter was obvious and to be embraced and applied by judges with enthusiasm.[32]

The message was clear: policy choices over which Canadians will inevitably contend are no longer to be resolved in the legislative arena, that is, in Parliament and in the provincial legislatures, but in the Supreme Court of Canada by nine judges unaffected by the 'majoritarian machinery of the legislatures and the Parliament.'[33] Our judges, now armed with the sword of the Charter, stand vigilant to thwart policy decisions made by elected representatives who are, apparently, held captive by the 'majoritarian machinery.' This anti-majoritarian component of the new way of judging came in whispers; hardly anyone has taken notice of it. The literature is virtually silent on this astonishing innovation.

Wilson's suspicion of majoritarian democracy is perfectly consistent with Hegel's distrust of the majority, whether she was aware of this or not. It was precisely the threat of majoritarianism that led him to intrude himself, we recall, into British politics with his opposition to the Reform Bill of 1831. By extending the franchise in the Reform Bill, the general will would become diluted, he argued, by the selfish desires of the masses. He championed a higher wisdom, of learned philosophers who could divine the general will – the will the people ought to pursue – and enact laws that furthered the aims of that general will. As we have seen earlier, for Hegel, the majority will was not often in harmony with the general will because it was almost always blinded by narrow partisan self-interest. By embracing the Charter mandate, as expounded by Bertha Wilson, the Supreme Court of Canada has been reconstituted as a body of sages capable of keeping Canadian society in harmony with the liberal-progressive polity enunciated in the Charter, that is, the new national *Sittlichkeit*, as Haldane would have understood it. Neither Hegel nor Haldane would be displeased by these recent changes in our constitutional life.

Wilson's distrust of the majority is shared by other justices of the Supreme Court of Canada, who have warned us about the limitations of the 'majority' and the necessity for judges to go beyond the words of the Charter by appealing to 'unwritten principles' which provide them with access to a higher wisdom not available to ordinary citizens. All of this leads us to the current Supreme Court of Canada and to its leading intellectual force, Chief Justice Beverley McLachlin.

In a certain sense, Chief Justice McLachlin has taken up where retired justice Bertha Wilson left off. In her 2005 Lord Cooke Lecture, entitled 'Unwritten Constitutional Principles: What is Going On?' and delivered before the Faculty of Law at Victoria University of Wellington, Wellington, New Zealand, the chief justice explored the duty of judges in constitutional cases to have recourse to 'unwritten principles.' McLachlin argued on this occasion that it is frequently the obligation of the judge to go beyond the written constitutional text to find 'fundamental norms of justice so basic that they form part of the legal structure of governance and must be upheld by the courts, whether or not they find expression in constitutional texts.'[34] This obligation is especially important, she insisted, where the written constitution is silent, as in the federal government's reference to the Supreme Court regarding the Clarity Act. In that case, she said, 'the Supreme Court turned to Canada's history and convention, as well as the values that Canadians through their governments had enacted in their written constitution. It examined these in the light of a long-recognized treatment of Canada's evolving constitution as a "living tree."'[35] As a result 'the Court ensured that an important legal gap was filled.'[36]

There is very little in this speech with which Viscount Haldane would disagree. When McLachlin spoke about the duty of judges 'to give content to unwritten constitutional principles,'[37] she was singing from Haldane's hymn book. It is precisely this kind of 'judicial statesmanship' that Haldane espoused as a central part of the judicial function and emboldened him in Canadian cases. As well, he frequently appealed to the virtues of the unwritten character of the English constitution. Haldane, as we have seen, rejected the notion of a permanent human nature governing the world of men and women. With Harold Laski of the London School of Economics, he believed that 'laws, governments, customs are not truths absolute and universal, but relative to the time of their origin and the country from which they derive.'[38]

The basic tenet of the new modern constitutional jurisprudence expressed by Chief Justice McLachlin – that judges are obliged to seek out and apply the 'higher,' 'deeper' principles of justice – places Canada's highest court in the tradition of modern jurisprudence which accords a primacy to judges within an intellectual context marked by Hegel's historicism. In saying that the 'unwritten principles that transcend the exercise of state power ... [are] derived from the history, values and culture of the nation, viewed in its constitutional context,' the chief justice is paraphrasing the sentiments of Viscount Haldane. And so, too, would he have agreed with her comments that 'while the *Charter* is no longer in its infancy, these are still early years in its life. The *Charter* is still a work in progress, an unfinished project. Perhaps it will always be. Future generations will have a great role to play in shaping it.'[39] But, as we shall see, there is an important substantive character to the unfinished project and the role to be played by judges. For McLachlin and a majority of judges on the Supreme Court of Canada, the 'unwritten principles' – discernible by their reflective wisdom – must serve the cause of Canada as a progressive, liberal state.

All of this stands in contrast to the ambitions of the Canadian statesmen in the nineteenth century. John A. Macdonald, George-Étienne Cartier, George Brown, Alexander Galt, Thomas D'Arcy McGee, and the other framers of our constitution strove to establish a country with a constitution 'similar in principle to that of the United Kingdom.' The ambition was to establish a regime entirely different from that of the United States where the judiciary occupies a constitutionally entrenched position of importance. Traditionally, the British judicial approach has been to accord a firm deference to the legislature; this tradition was expected to serve as a guide to Canadian judges. The 'living tree' doctrine – the product of a single Judicial Committee judgment – has never been adopted by the British judiciary. In Canada it has the effect of detaching courts from the ancestral judicial function and the broader legislative process while making them captives of the social trends of the moment. The arrival of the Charter has apparently settled the matter in the minds of our judges. The prevailing view is that the constitutional amendment of 1982 entrenched the court as well as the 'living tree' interpretation of judging. This idea is highly debatable. For one thing, is it constitutionally legal for an act of the imperial Parliament, even in the form of a constitutional amendment, to confer such extraordinary powers on the judiciary? The whole of British constitutional history repeatedly demonstrates that neither the crown nor the Parliament should be without limitations on its powers. For another thing, the prevailing view tends to overlook an essential aspect of the English constitution: the obligation of all institutions of government to be wary of the concentration of power in the hands of unaccountable bodies.

Viscount Haldane and the Charter Court

The current Supreme Court of Canada believes that Canadian judges since the Charter are obliged to extend the 'equal benefit' of the law to all persons who reside in Canada – not merely to all citizens but to all persons, including landed immigrants. The Supreme Court acknowledged from the very first encounter with the Charter that it was assuming a new role in judging and that it would actively embrace the new mandate as it itself defined that mandate. Led by then Chief Justice Brian Dickson, the Supreme Court in the earliest Charter decisions declared that it would be the advocate of a progressive new political order in Canada. The court claimed that this was its obligation under the

Charter. It is important to recognize that, for the first time in its history, the court itself defined the scope of its new role. And, by the nature of the judicial function, those who question the expansiveness of the self-definition have no recourse.

Chief Justice Dickson had signalled long before the *Big M Drug Mart* case that he endorsed Lord Sankey's 'living tree' metaphor. In *British Columbia v. Ellett Estate*, 1980,[40] he wrote: 'If the Canadian Constitution is to be regarded as a "living tree" and legislative competence as "essentially dynamic" then the determination of categories existing in 1867 becomes of little, other than historic, concern.'[41] One would have thought that, if the metaphor is to be embraced in all its richness – and it was an improvement over Haldane's fleshless skeletons –Dickson would have noted that every good tree depends on the health of its trunk and the richness of the soil, that is, literally, on its 'historic' roots; rather than separate the living constitution from its historic roots, the metaphor should prompt reflection on the historic conditions which gave rise to the tree, not simply indulge the spread of the new branches. But Dickson and subsequent judges have failed to do this.

The court in *Big M Drug Mart* not only struck down a federal act but also set down general rules for interpreting the terms of the Charter. In a lengthy judgment, Chief Justice Dickson ruled that the duty of judges under the Charter was to seek out the purpose of the item protected, not to seek the intention of the Charter draughtsmen.[42] Judges armed with the Charter were now obliged, he argued, to seek out the evolving traditions and principles of the Canadian liberal-democratic society. As Peter Russell has observed with approval: 'Not only were the results of these early Charter cases in marked contrast to the Court's treatment of the Bill of Rights, but the methods the judges used to interpret the Charter also went well beyond the traditional legalistic approach. Chief Justice Dickson took the lead in expounding a purposive approach to the Charter. This method of interpretation calls upon judges to consider the broad historical and philosophical reasons which have made the right or freedom a cherished value in our society.'[43] But this is precisely the opposite of what the purposive approach demands. As the court has shown, it leads to contemporary social-science musings, not historical or philosophical groundings. As well, Russell never explains what was wrong with the 'traditional legalistic' approach. It would have been helpful if he had explained how the 'purposive' approach differs from the intent of the legislature.

In fact, the new method of interpretation introduced by Dickson offered judges the freedom to roam throughout the pages of the emerging body of social-activist literature and expand the application of a given law to areas of public and private life where the legislation was never intended to apply.[44] It is no coincidence that, in its reasons for judgment, the Supreme Court of Canada has begun to identify its reliance upon this literature. The new approach to judging permits judges to reach out on their own initiative and bring in as aids to interpretation articles and books that treat the social issue in dispute, as the judgments of Justice Bertha Wilson have demonstrated.[45] For Wilson, the 'starting point in Canadian law for a discussion of constitutional interpretation is, of course, the "living tree" metaphor formulated by Lord Sankey in the *Edwards* case.'[46] But this is exactly how an Hegelian would reason: what the parliamentary draughtsmen intended was not determinative. Justice Wilson went on to question whether 'the largely fictional notion of legislative intent is an appropriate solution when the *Charter* has explicitly designated the Court as the forum for choosing from among a variety of policy options.'[47] But does the Charter really demand this? What the judges of the moment see as a desirable extension of the law, alone, appears to justify the extension, as we see in the Ontario Court of Appeal's same-sex marriage decision. To proceed in this manner is to proceed as Haldane would have our judges proceed.[48] To do so is to seek out the *Sittlichkeit* of the Canadian nation, devoid of all moral content, at a given moment with minimum regard for legislative intent or tradition.

This new approach to judging was mandated, Chief Justice Dickson and the court majority in *Big M Drug Mart* reasoned, by the new responsibilities placed on the shoulders of the court by the new constitutionally entrenched Charter.[49] This understanding placed the court in the forefront of social and political reforms, not at the rear where it had traditionally been positioned, endorsing but not charting new social initiatives or moral standards. Prevailing 'community standards' are no longer sufficient to justify a prohibition by the Parliament of Canada or the provincial legislatures.[50] Under the terms of the Charter, Supreme Court justices appear to have adopted Viscount Haldane's invitation that judges be guided by the 'progressive spirit of the times,' the general will imperfectly understood by the people. The burden for Canadian judges imposed by the Charter now requires them to see to what extent the Charter list of rights and freedoms can be extended to provide a greater freedom from government restrictions and traditional social mores. Chief Justice Dickson argued forcefully that, with the Charter, Canadian judges were placed in the forefront of an expansive liberal social-reform agenda.

The court itself, however, quickly became embroiled in disagreement over the 'discovery' within the Charter of such 'implied rights' as the right of employees to strike under the terms of 'freedom of association' and 'the right to life, liberty and security of the person.'[51] For the first time, members of the court began to take serious aim at the jurisprudence of their colleagues. Justice William McIntyre pointedly stated that 'the *Charter* should not be regarded as an empty vessel to be filled with whatever meaning we might wish from time to time.' In the highly contentious case involving abortion, McIntyre went further to remind his colleagues that 'the courts must confine themselves to such democratic values as are clearly found and expressed in the Charter and refrain from imposing or creating other values not so based.'[52] Yet such cautions were to fall on deaf ears, for the Supreme Court of Canada soon began to adopt the 'purposive' approach enunciated by Chief Justice Brian Dickson and enthusiastically espoused by Justice Bertha Wilson and subsequent courts. And in so doing it was linking arms with Viscount Haldane's instruction to judges to seek out the *Sittlichkeit* of the times and to give it judicial force, the intention of the legislature notwithstanding.

No better example of the new emerging *Sittlichkeit* can be found in Canada than the efforts of the gay and lesbian community to seek legislative validation for its objectives. This community has consistently sought relief by way of the courts, which, in turn, have given instructions to Parliament and the legislatures. The Supreme Court of Canada has been at the forefront of this movement. Gays and lesbians have been quietly challenging prevailing community standards for some decades, starting in the 1960s. Initially, gay and lesbian public demonstrations were looked upon as intriguing but not threatening to the prevailing public standards of decency. At this point, the gay movement was primarily underground or in the closet. In Hegelian terms, the movement at this early stage constituted, beneath the surface, the antithesis to the prevailing and dominant moral and religious thesis. Public reactions started to change, however, with the emergence of bathhouses where men could meet for sexual purposes. It soon became evident that gay activists were seeking 'equal benefit of the laws' as promised by the Canadian Charter of Rights and Freedoms. The closeted antithesis began to challenge publicly the traditional – anti-homosexual – thesis by claiming the full range of privileges and rights enjoyed by the old thesis as enshrined in the Charter. The aim of the gay-rights movement was to construct a new thesis, one that would grant full Charter rights to all citizens regardless of sexual orientation. It was a perfect unfolding of the Hegelian dialectic.

In order to achieve this objective, the gay movement had to convince others to abandon a traditional condemnation of homosexuality that was both philosophically and religiously based. The proponents were able to find sympathetic politicians within the ranks of the Liberal Party, the New Democratic Party, and the Bloc Québécois. All three of these parliamentary forces were quick to reject both the argument from nature as well as the biblical foundations of the prohibition against homosexuality. Once this objective was achieved, the gay-rights movement mounted a campaign based on the Charter to have its social agenda fully endorsed by law, though it then ran into vocal public opposition in its bid to achieve same-sex marriage. The new thesis that emerged out of this success based on the Charter sowed the seeds of the new *Sittlichkeit* which now validates the extension of full social benefits to the gay community.

It is important to note that the success of the gay-rights movement did not come about as a result of the Canadian legislative process, where it continued to run into opposition; it came about through a series of judgments of Canadian courts. The Supreme Court of Canada in the *Vriend* decision (1998) captured the issue in a nutshell. The Alberta Court of Appeal had explicitly rejected 'judicial legislation,' ruling that it was the proper province of the Alberta legislature to make or amend the law, not the court's. The Supreme Court of Canada reversed the Alberta decision and ruled that, despite the repeated legislative debates on the issue, the Charter of Rights and Freedoms trumps the Alberta Human Rights Protection Act. In this the court was enunciating a new pan-Canadian *Sittlichkeit*. It should not be overlooked that the Canadian courts, with the benefit of the Charter, have begun to extend the provincial *Sittlichkeiten* that Haldane and the Judicial Committee had enunciated. In the nineteenth century, Haldane and the Judicial Committee were intent on discovering and giving full force to the provincial *Sittlichkeit*, not a national *Sittlichkeit*. Armed with the Charter, which applies to all of Canada and all levels of government in the country, the Canadian courts see themselves as obliged to seek out and give effect to *pan-Canadian* standards even at the expense of provincial standards formally announced after lengthy legislative debate. For the first time in our history, owing exclusively to the Charter, the national *Sittlichkeit* has trumped provincial *Sittlichkeiten*.

Since under the Hegelian view there is no permanent human nature, and hence no permanent trans-historical morality – only the evolving moral standards that come with the unfolding of the historic process – there can never be stable or permanent moral or social values. Those intellectuals in the vanguard of history teach that all values change with the times; what was once forbidden now becomes acceptable simply by force of the historical process under the impetus provided by the twin demands of freedom and equality. Reinforcing this development in Canada is the emerging secularist ethos that has embraced the notion that neither nature nor traditional religious values can provide permanent standards for the modern Canadian state. Since human nature is historically changeable, it cannot be the source of permanent social and moral values. The old *Sittlichkeit* founded in the classical philosophy of natural right, Judeo-Christian revelation, and the Koran has been replaced by the new *Sittlichkeit* which is a direct legacy of Hobbes and Rousseau by way of Hegel.[53]

What is especially intriguing about this judicial development in Canada is that it is more evident in the United States and Canada than even in Britain. But in the United States the issue has occasioned serious debate.[54] With the passage of the Human Rights Act by the United Kingdom Parliament in 1998, British courts are simply authorized to point out any inconsistency with an act of Parliament and the European Convention for the Protection of Human Rights and Fundamental Freedoms.[55] Canadian constitutional jurisprudence since the Charter shares much with recent American jurisprudence where Hegelian historicism has taken firm root under the 'living constitution' infatuation.[56] It is curious to note that the 'living tree' ethos does not appear to have taken root in the United Kingdom. Our judges and our courts share a greater affinity with American judges and courts than they do with our historic British counterparts.[57] This is intriguing because Canadian popular culture has become increasingly anti-American while at the same time importing into Canada an Hegelian-based jurisprudence of historical relativism.

The Majority as Obstacle

What some find troubling about the recent trends in the Supreme

Court of Canada is the underlying distrust of democratic politics which would appear to be a direct legacy of Hegelian anti-democratic sentiment. Chief Justice McLachlin stated the point clearly in 1999 at a conference in Ottawa on public policy when she referred in her remarks to 'the tyranny of the majority which led to World War II.' Her point was that Western nations following the war had begun to take steps to incorporate into their constitutions a bill of rights in order to prevent the emergence of tyrants such as Hitler. It would appear from her remarks that Hitler's monstrous regime was an example of 'tyranny of the majority.' This statement – deleted from the published version of her address – raised not a few eyebrows, for very good reasons. Can one locate in McLachlin's anti-majoritarianism an Hegelian anti-majoritarianism coupled with the German philosopher's trust only in the 'general will'? We will never know how Hegel would have viewed Hitler; we do know that he approved of Napoleon as a 'world historic figure.' In any case, McLachlin's remarks about Hitler and the tide of democracy mask several errors. First, Hitler did not come to power on the wave of a democratic majority. His brown shirts bludgeoned voters into submission and perverted the democratic process. He took over a democratic but weak Weimar regime and turned it into a police state. Second, the distrust of majority sentiment in a democracy is very dangerous. The move away from 'community standards' test is a move away from the legitimacy of majority sentiment. Certainly at times the majority must be protected from itself. That is why we have a Charter of Rights. But it is a short step from distrust of tyrannical majority sentiment to distrust of all democratic majority sentiment.

The distrust of the majority runs deep in the Chief Justice McLachlin's thinking. Eight years before her Cooke speech, in defending a strong judiciary, she told members of the Lawyers Club in Toronto that 'the judicial function is, at its heart, anti-majoritarian.' She seemed to imply that the court ought to resist all majority wishes; that the duty of the Supreme Court of Canada, armed with the Charter of Rights and Freedoms, is to uncover the *general will* (though she never uses the term) and to be its agent in the name of progress. But what replaces majority will in a democracy? McLachlin's answer appears to be: the majority consensus of members of the Supreme Court of Canada, who are obviously more in touch with the liberal social and political agenda (the general will) of Canada than our elected politicians.[58] Here, she overreached. Surely, she did not intend to say that all majority sentiment was to be resisted. There is no question that the judiciary has an obligation to protect the minority from a tyrannical majority. But that obligation is a far cry from asserting that the majority can never be right.

Judges of the Supreme Court of Canada have, under the Charter, become a body privileged by virtue of their position as judges charged with the responsibility of expanding the application of liberal-progressive standards in our national life. The Charter did not enact neutral principles; it is a document with a definite liberal or progressive ideological bias which allegedly gives the courts the duty to expand its reach. Viscount Haldane would approve. An ethos is emerging in the Supreme Court which is profoundly suspicious of the democratic majority; in this the court shares much in common with Mary P. Follett, for whose book, *The New State*, Viscount Haldane volunteered to write the introduction in 1920. In that work Follett called for a 'new conception of politics,' a reconstituted democracy that encourages the organization of 'men in small, local groups.'[59] Above all, she rejected the common understanding of democracy as rule of the majority. 'Democracy means,' she insisted, 'the will of the whole, but the will of the whole is not necessarily represented by the majority, nor by a two-thirds or three-quarters vote, nor even by a unanimous vote; majority rule is democratic when it is approaching not a unanimous but an integrated will.'[60] This sounds very much like Chief Justice McLachlin. Hegel could not have put the definition of the general will more succinctly. This 'all-will,' Follett proceeded to affirm, 'gives us a new idea of aristocracy' and indicates the role to be played by the wise.[61] The new aristocracy is based on the acknowledgment of 'the ignorance of the average man, his satisfaction in his ignorance.'[62] Under the guidance of the new aristocracy, democracy becomes committed to freeing 'the creative spirit of man.' But the new democracy aided by the new aristocracy emerges from the bottom up. It emerges from 'neighbourhood organization movements,' not waiting for ideal institutions or perfect men; it finds whatever creative forces there are within a community and builds the future with them.[63] Just as for Hegel, national constitutions for Follett cannot be the product of wise men sitting in conclaves and drafting the terms of a document. They must arise out of the cunning of history under the influence of warrior men who command the currents of the historic process. This was one of the features that Haldane admired so much about the English constitution; it was not a written parchment born out of the wisdom of a founding convention; it was a product of long years of struggle, including civil war. Follett joined forces with Hegel when she wrote that people, 'like gods,' create their 'own ends at any moment.'[64]

There is no question that the Canadian Charter of Rights and Freedoms opens the door for judicial activism unlike any previous statutory instrument in Canadian history. The critical question is: To what extent does the Charter introduce into Canada the Hegelian virus of historicism leading to the soft despotism of an aristocratic judiciary? And, since the Charter is entrenched in the constitution and hence a part of the fundamental law of the country, judges armed with it wield enormous power. No court in the British Commonwealth is robed with an equivalent power. The Charter sets down a full panoply of rights and privileges which courts are mandated to enforce. But, its supporters quickly note, the document explicitly provides for restrictions on the courts by way of section 33. That section provides that the Parliament of Canada and the provincial legislatures have power to legislate notwithstanding rights and privileges enunciated in several sections of the Charter. Unfortunately, a succession of federal prime ministers have publicly repudiated the use of the 'notwithstanding clause.' The general consensus throughout the country is that the override provision provided by section 33 is dead.[65] Furthermore, alas, every available opinion poll indicates that the Canadian people have greater faith in their judges than in their elected representatives. The people of Canada are being led by the courts closer to John Austin's view that those laws made by judges are better than those made by the elected members of Parliament or the legislatures. If this is true, it bodes poorly for Canadian democracy.

At first, the Canadian courts moved cautiously into the new territory. But lately they have begun to extend and apply the terms of the Charter to areas never envisaged by the Parliament that enacted it, seeking, instead, 'the spirit' of the values contained in the document. Without reference to a specific provision of the Charter, the Supreme Court of Canada, drawing on Dickson's judgment in *Big M Drug Mart*, revised the definition of marriage to include same-sex relationships.[66] Despite the objections to this ruling by many Canadians, there is a growing body of opinion, especially among judges, that the Charter constitutionalizes liberal or progressive social values and places them beyond the reach of Canadian democratic institutions by making the courts the final *formulators* as well as the final arbiters of Canadian social mores.[67] Such a transformation constitutes nothing less than a seismic shift of political power from the elected representatives of the people to the unelected judiciary. Some constitutional authorities counter with the argument, however, that the transformation was initiated by the elected representatives of the people, not by judges, and to that extent it is in keeping with the democratic character of the Canadian constitution.[68] There is nothing inherently undemocratic, however, for elective legislative bodies to adopt the rulings of unelected judges.

Conclusion

Now that we have followed his life from his earliest days in Scotland and Germany to his years on the highest bench of the realm in London and to his death in 1928, it is difficult not to say that Richard Burdon Haldane would be pleased with what has taken place in Canada since the adoption of the Charter. Clearly, Canadian judges are functioning in a manner that would not displease him inasmuch as they are giving voice to what they believe to be the progressive *Sittlichkeit* of the nation armed with the 'equal benefit of the laws' clause of the Canadian Charter of Rights and Freedoms.

But the prevailing Canadian *Sittlichkeit*, as understood by the Supreme Court of Canada, is captive of the Hegelian historicism where traditional standards or mores are jettisoned for more 'progressive' social standards. Those Canadians who oppose this development in the law of the land have no recourse to a countervailing authority. The new Charter-based Canadian *Sittlichkeit* stands in defiance of the hopes and ambitions of the fathers of our nation at Confederation. The dominant role now played by judges renders appeals to our founding principles irrelevant, devoid of all legal authority. Our country was founded in the hope of perpetuating a country with a 'constitution similar in principle to that of the United Kingdom.' Central to the constitution of the United Kingdom is the notion of deference to the legislature as an instrument of perpetuating the central democratic principle of responsible democratic government. It would be difficult to find a Canadian authority today to say of Canada what Harry Jaffa said recently about the United States: 'The principles upon which this nation was founded are those upon which its survival, no less than its prosperity, depend.'[69]

The power and promise of Hegelian historicism lies in the conviction that the past, with its standards of right and wrong and its grounding in a trans-historical conception of human nature, is as dead as Hegel's successor, Nietzsche, announced at the close of the nineteenth century; only the beckoning future with ever expanding social and moral 'freedoms' matter to the government or the courts. The compass provided to Canadians by the Charter of Rights and Freedoms is an instrument without a magnetic north. Just exactly as Hegel would have it. The Hegelian state provides a fence around a vacant lot where there are no noble causes, where liberty unrestricted by nature becomes licence. Above all, the Hegelian state leads to statism, where the government – aided by an ideologically complicit judiciary – assumes a dominant role in enforcing a social and political order that is prompted by a 'progressive' understanding of liberty and equality. It doesn't matter whether the new expressions of liberty and equality conflict with traditional community standards. Modern progressivism understands itself as in full control of its unswerving commitment to 'progress' precisely by overcoming traditional standards. It is for this reason that the modern Hegelian state appears intolerant when it demands an end to public discussion of the issues once the government has made its decision to support a given objective. The traditional understanding of marriage, for example, must give way to accommodate the demands of a vocal segment of the community under the twin 'progressive' imperatives of liberty and equality.

Haldane's eclectic Hegelianism, by contrast, attempted to hold fast to a core ancestral wisdom contained in Anglo-Saxon jurisprudence and thereby provide a magnetic north to the nations of the British Empire. To this extent, he urged a looking back for guidance. He failed to appreciate, perhaps, that once on board the Hegelian train of history the engineer has no access to a rear-view mirror. Indeed, he has no need for one; the past is dead as a guide and can provide no sense of future direction, especially in central moral and political issues.[70] History is not viewed in the Hegelian lexicon as a fulfilment of human nature towards a greater moral wholeness; it is a sequence of overcomings, from a lower to a higher order of freedom, with no looking back to brake the progress of history. In this way, Hegel prepared the way for Darwin and is the reason Darwin was first embraced in Germany rather than in any other modern nation.

The last words go to Hanna Arendt, who once wrote: 'To think, with Hegel, that truth resides and reveals itself in the time-process itself is characteristic of all modern historical consciousness, however it expresses itself, in specifically Hegelian terms or not.'[71]

Notes

Preface

1 Heuston, *Lives of the Lord Chancellors*, 228.
2 When I attended a Rotary Club of Edinburgh meeting in October 2005, I was asked by a retired general surgeon what I was doing in Edinburgh. When I told him I was writing a book about Viscount Haldane, he immediately exclaimed: 'The best Secretary of State for War this country ever had.' Other members at the table nodded in agreement. A full ninety years after leaving the War Office, Hadane is still remembered this way.
3 Saywell, *The Lawmakers*.
4 Robinson, 'Lord Haldane and the British North America Act.'

Introduction

1 *Canadian Bar Review*, 25 (1947): 1054.
2 Girard, *Bora Laskin*, 365.
3 For an earlier version of this view, see Laskin, 'The Supreme Court of Canada,' 1038.
4 *Reference re Anti-Inflation Act*, 1975. See also *R. v. Crown Zellerbach Canada Ltd.*, [1988] 1 S.C.R., 401.
5 A contrary view of Confederation is offered by Paul Romney, who, in *Getting It Wrong*, argues that the traditional centralist interpretation of

Confederation is a 'vast fabric of myth.' For a discussion of this issue, see Saywell, *The Lawmakers*, 116.

6 Sommer, *Haldane of Cloan*, 110.

7 Haldane, 'Oliver Wendell Holmes,' 36.

8 Ibid.

1: Home and School for the Mind

1 Mary Elizabeth Haldane left an extensive account of her youthful days for the edification of her children and grandchildren. These were edited and later published by her daughter Elizabeth under the title: *Mary Elizabeth Haldane: A Record of a Hundred Years (1825–1925)*.

2 Ibid., 16.

3 Ibid.

4 Ibid., 35–6.

5 Ibid., 41.

6 Ibid., 45–6.

7 Ibid., 44.

8 Ibid.

9 Ibid., 20.

10 Ibid., 56–7.

11 Ibid., 53.

12 Ibid., 62–3.

13 Ibid., 75–6.

14 Ibid., 123–4.

15 Ibid.

16 Ibid., 157.

17 Ibid., 100.

18 Ibid., 101.

19 Ibid., 164.

20 Ibid., 168.

21 For information relating to the office of writer to the signet, I am grateful to Elaine Bird, director of information services and librarian, the WS Society, Edinburgh. I am also indebted to Neville Schaffer, QC, of Glasgow and Edinburgh for assisting me in this and related matters.

22 Cruikshank, *Charles Dickens and Early Victorian England*, 6.

23 Ibid., 8.

24 Ibid., 5.

25 Wood, *Nineteenth Century Britain*, 174.

26 Cited by Briggs, *Victorian People*, 60.

27 Wood, *Nineteenth Century Britain*, 174–5.
28 Ibid., 176.
29 Cited by White, *London in the Nineteenth Century*, 457.
30 Mary Elizabeth Haldane, *A Record of A Hundred Years*, 68.
31 For an extensive account of living conditions in Scotland during Haldane's lifetime, see Smout, *History of the Scottish People, 1830–1950*.
32 For a history of Edinburgh, see Edwards and Paul, eds., *Edinburgh: The Making of a Capital City*.
33 See Buchan, *Crowded with Genius*.
34 Ibid., 107.
35 Haldane, *Autobiography*, 4.
36 Elizabeth Haldane, *From One Century to Another*, 93.
37 Ibid.
38 Ibid., 93–4.
39 For a full account of Elizabeth Haldane's involvement in the education of women in the professions, see ibid., 50–60.
40 Ibid., 5.
41 Sommer, *Haldane of Cloan*, 43.

2: The University of Edinburgh and the Seeds of German Philosophy

1 Bradley, 'Hegel in Britain,' 4, 163.
2 Ibid., 8.
3 Ibid.
4 Kennedy, *Professor Blackie: Sayings and Doings*, 63.
5 Ibid., 64.
6 Ibid., 35–6.
7 Sommer, *Haldane of Cloan*, 44.
8 Richard Haldane, *Universities and National Life*, 'Great Britain and Germany: A Study in National Characteristics,' 114–15.
9 Ibid., 'The Dedicated Life,' 77.
10 Ibid., 83.
11 Ibid., 'Great Britain and Germany: A Study in National Characteristics,' 149.
12 Ibid.
13 Kojeve, *Introduction to the Reading of Hegel*, 33.
14 Quoted in Merz, *A History of European Thought in the Nineteenth Century*, 1: 159.
15 See Stern, *The Politics of Cultural Despair*, chapter 5, 'The Corruption of German Education,' 102.

16 Crankshaw, *Bismarck*, 238.

17 Berlin, *Vico and Herder*, 147.

18 Stern, *The Politics of Cultural Despair*, 344.

19 Willis, 'Stirling, James Hutchinson.'

20 Ibid., 3.

21 See William, *The Whig Supremacy, 1714–1760*, 40–1.

22 For a fuller discussion of this matter, see Pinson, *Modern Germany*, 59–65.

23 Haldane to his mother, 21 April 1874, Haldane Papers, National Library of Scotland (NLS), MS5927.

24 Haldane, *Autobiography*, 13.

25 Haldane to his mother, 24 April 1874, Haldane Papers, NLS, MS5927.

26 Ibid.

27 Ibid.

28 Ibid.

29 Ibid.

30 Ibid.

31 Ibid.

32 Haldane to his mother, 2 May 1874, ibid.

33 Ibid.

34 Ibid.

35 Schwegler, *Handbook of the History of Philosophy*, 340.

36 Ibid., 341.

37 For a general overview of Lotze's philosophy and his place in the philosophical debates of his time, see William R. Woodward, 'Inner Migration or Disguised Reform: Political Interests of Hermann Lotze's Philosophical Anthropology,' *History of the Human Sciences*, 19, no. 1 (1996): 1. See also Santayana, *Lotze's System of Philosophy*.

38 Haldane to his mother, 12 May 1874, Haldane Papers, NLS, MS5927.

39 Ibid.

40 Ibid.

41 Haldane to his mother, 6 July 1874, ibid.

42 Lotze, *Microcosmus*, 2: 548.

43 Ibid.

44 Haldane to his mother, 16 June 1874, Haldane Papers, NLS, MS5927.

45 Elizabeth Haldane, 'My Own Recollections,' NLS, MS 20229.

46 Lecture Notes, Edinburgh, 1875, NLS, MS20213. These notes consist of seventy-eight handwritten pages of notes.

47 Ibid., 13.

48 Ibid., 33.

49 Ibid., 62–3.

50 Cited in Maurice, *Haldane: 1856–1915*, 24.
51 Haldane, *Autobiography*, 22–3.
52 Ibid., 23–4.
53 Maurice, *Haldane: 1856–1915*, 24.
54 James, *The Rise and Fall of the British Empire*, 198.
55 Ibid.
56 Morton, *The Kingdom of Canada*, 468.
57 For an extensive discussion of this matter, see Vaughan, *The Canadian Federalist Experiment*.

3: The Practice of Law and Life in Parliament

 1 Haldane, *Autobiography*, 25.
 2 As mentioned earlier, Haldane's maternal great-grandfather stipulated in his will that the name 'Sanderson' be added to the family name from his death forward.
 3 Ibid.
 4 Ibid., 26.
 5 Ibid.
 6 Ibid., 36.
 7 Holbrook Jackson, *The Eighteen Nineties*, cited in Havighurst, *Twentieth/Century Britain*, 30.
 8 For a recent graphic account of life in London during the nineteenth century, see White, *London in the Nineteenth Century*.
 9 Ibid., 453.
10 Ibid., 107.
11 Ibid.
12 Beatrice Webb, *My Apprenticeship*, 113.
13 Ibid., 115.
14 See a discussion of *Bebb v. The Law Society* (1914) in *Canadian Law Times*, 34 (1914): 621–34.
15 *The Law Times*, 54 (1872–3), 16 November 1872, 'The New Scheme of Education for the Bar,' 33.
16 Haldane Papers, NLS, MS5930, 119.
17 Haldane, *Autobiography*, 31.
18 Ibid.
19 Ibid., 33.
20 By all accounts, Elizabeth Garrett Anderson was an extraordinary woman. Not only was she active in the social life of London but she became the first woman medical doctor. See Anderson, *Elizabeth Garrett Anderson*.

21 Ibid.
22 Ibid.
23 Cited in White, *London in the Nineteenth Century*, 290.
24 Haldane, *Autobiography*, 27–8.
25 Mary Elizabeth Haldane, *A Record of a Hundred Years*, 'Note by Her Eldest Son,' 123–4.
26 Ibid., 125.
27 Ibid.
28 Elizabeth Haldane, *From One Century to Another*, 64.
29 Ibid., 65.
30 Ibid., 71.
31 I am grateful to Sydney Demarsq, a Halifax architect, for this description of the Cloan house.
32 Ibid., 92.
33 Haldane Papers, NLS, MS5928, 25 June 1878, 226.
34 Ibid.
35 Ibid., 27 June 1878, 227.
36 Ibid., 28 June 1878.
37 Ibid.
38 Ibid.
39 Ibid., 2 July 1878, 281.
40 Ibid., 28 June 1878, 260.
41 Ibid., 13 July 1878, 290.
42 Sommer, *Haldane of Cloan*, 51.
43 Haldane, *Autobiography*, 34.
44 Ibid.
45 White, *London in the Nineteenth Century*, 171.
46 The best account of Benjamin's life is Evans, *Judah P. Benjamin*. Unfortunately, the author does not treat at length Benjamin's legal career at the English bar. He does, however, give an account of the elaborate dinner organized in Benjamin's honour by the leading members of the English bar upon his retirement at the Inner Temple in 1882 (397).
47 Ibid., 236–7.
48 For a wonderful account of Scott and the Scottish Enlightenment, see Bertha Wilson, 'The Scottish Enlightenment: The Third Schumiatcher Lecture in "The Law as Literature,"' *Saskatchewan Law Review*, 51 (1978): 258.
49 'Memories' (Christmas 1917), Haldane Papers, NLS MS5920, 16.
50 Ibid.
51 Ibid., 35.

52 'Davey of Fernhurst,' *LoveToKnow 1911 Online Encyclopedia*, copyright 2003, 2004 Love To Know.

53 Ibid., 37.

54 Ibid.

55 Ibid., 38.

56 Ibid.

57 Ibid.; Horace Davey was to reappear for Quebec when the case was heard in November 1884. See *A.G. Quebec v. Reed*, (1884) 10 A.C. 141; 1 Olmsted 216.

58 Haldane Papers, NLS MS6004, 2 August 1921, 37.

59 Ibid., 39.

60 *In re Scottish Petroleum Company*, [1883] 23 Ch.D. 413.

61 Haldane, *Autobiography*, 39.

62 Ibid., 40.

63 Ibid.

64 Hall and Martin, *Haldane: Statesman, Lawyer, Philosopher*, 80.

65 Hall and Martin speculate that the unnamed woman was Mrs Elizabeth Garrett Anderson, the first woman doctor, at whose home, as related earlier, Haldane had attended dances. But there is little to support this speculation. Hall and Martin, *Haldane: Statesman, Lawyer, Philosopher*, 56–7. 'It must be emphasized,' these authors say, 'that there is no evidence to suggest that any infatuation with Elizabeth Garrett Anderson was reciprocated.' Ibid., 57.

66 Haldane Papers, NLS, MS5914, 1 March 1881, 176.

67 Haldane Papers, NLS MS5944, 23.

68 Ibid.

69 Maurice, *Haldane: 1856–1915*.

70 See, Cooper, *Old Men Forget*: '[Haldane] is intolerant of the people whom he describes as uneducated' (57). He appeared to include both Kitchener and Churchill in this category.

71 Sommer, *Haldane of Cloan*, 154.

72 Hall and Martin, *Haldane: Statesman, Lawyer, Philosopher*, 37.

73 Haldane Papers, NLS MS5928, 30 June 1878, 280.

74 Kant, *Critique of Pure Reason*, 312.

75 Hegel, *Philosophy of Right*, para 258.

76 Hall and Martin, *Haldane: Statesman, Lawyer, Philosopher*, 87.

77 Maurice, *Haldane: 1856–1915*, 38.

78 Ibid., 39.

79 Ibid.

80 Ibid.

81 Trevelyan, *Grey of Fallodon*, 138.
82 Sommer, *Haldane of Cloan*, 68.
83 Clifford, *The Asquiths*, 15.
84 Ibid., chapter 4, 'An Abyss of Domesticity,' 54.
85 Ibid., 70.
86 Wood, *Nineteenth Century Britain*, 345.
87 Elizabeth Haldane, *From One Century to Another*, 243.
88 Sommer, *Haldane of Cloan*, 71.
89 Hall and Martin, *Haldane: Statesman, Lawyer, Philosopher*, 96.
90 Sommer, *Haldane of Cloan*, 76.
91 Ibid., 77.
92 Kennedy, *Professor Blackie*, 36.
93 Haldane, *Autobiography*, 294–5.
94 See Ashby and Anderson, *Portrait of Haldane at Work on Education*.
95 Haldane, *Autobiography*, 295.
96 Ibid, 127.
97 The best discussion of Haldane's educational reforms can be found in Ashby and Anderson, *Portrait of Haldane at Work on Education*, especially chapter 4, 'Above the Snow-line,' 59.
98 Ibid., 298.
99 Hall and Martin, *Haldane: Statesman, Lawyer, Philosopher*, 317.

4: From the Inns of Court to the War Office

1 Maurice, *Haldane, 1856–1928*, 1: 38.
2 Elizabeth Haldane, *From One Century to Another*, 60.
3 Ibid.
4 Haldane Papers, NLS, MS5944, 94.
5 Ibid., 51.
6 Haldane, *Autobiography*, 118.
7 Ibid., 119.
8 Cited by Sommer, *Haldane of Cloan*, 84. John Haldane wrote one of the essays in this collection; Richard Haldane and Andrew Seth Pringle-Pattison edited the collection and contributed essays to it.
9 Ibid.
10 Ibid., 85.
11 Ibid.
12 Ibid.
13 Haldane, *Autobiography*, 352.
14 Sommer, *Haldane of Cloan*, 88.

15 Ibid.

16 Ibid.

17 Ibid.

18 Ibid., 89.

19 Haldane, *Autobiography*, 348.

20 Hegel, *The Philosophy of History*, 161.

21 Haldane, 'Memories,' Haldane Papers, NLS, MS5920, 32.

22 Ibid.

23 Sommer, *Haldane of Cloan*, 93.

24 *Nobels' Explosives Co. Ltd. v. Anderson*, 11 TLR 266. House of Lords (1894).

25 Sir John and Frances Horner were close friends of H.H. Asquith. Their daughter Katherine married Asquith's eldest son, Raymond.

26 Elizabeth Haldane, *From One Century to Another*, 191.

27 Haldane, *Autobiography*, 182.

28 Elizabeth Haldane, *From One Century to Another*, 214.

29 Beatrice Webb, *Our Partnership*, 325.

30 Haldane, *Autobiography*, 182–3.

31 Maurice, *Haldane: 1856–1915*, ix.

32 Spiers, *Haldane: An Army Reformer*, 38.

33 Haldane, *Autobiography*, 184.

34 The practice of purchasing commissions in the army had long been the subject of dispute. As Field Marshal Lord Carver has written: 'Of all the reforms, the abolition of purchase as a method of obtaining commissions and promotions was to arouse the greatest controversy. The method was indefensible that allowed men like Cardigan and Lucan with no military experience to rise to high command, because they were ready to spend large sums on buying their way up the military ladder for reasons of social prestige.' *The Seven Ages of the British Army*, 156.

35 Ibid.

36 Ibid.

37 Haldane, *Autobiography*, 326.

38 Haldane Papers, NLS, MS5974, 196.

39 French, *Field Marshal, 1914*, 305.

40 Ibid., 306.

41 Lord Riddell, *War Diary, 1914–1918*, 138, cited in Williams, *The Other Battleground*, 49.

42 See Williams, *The Other Battleground*, 51–5.

43 Sommer, *Haldane of Cloan*, 163.

44 Haldane to Lord Milner, 6 July 1901, Milner, *Milner Papers*, 2: 162.

45 Haldane, *Autobiography*, 231.

46 Cited by Sommer, *Haldane of Cloan*, 166–7.

47 Haldane, *Autobiography*, 185.

48 Ibid.

49 Haldane Papers, 'Memorandum by the Secretary of State for War on Army Organization,' NLS, MS5418, 38.

50 Haldane, *Autobiography*, 200.

51 Haldane, *Universities and National Life: Four Addresses to Students*, 4.

52 *Report of His Majesty's Commissioners Appointed to Inquire into the Military Preparations and Other Matters Connected with the War in South Africa*, Cd. 1,789 (1904), xl. Lord Esher's minority report appears at 114.

53 *The Scotsman*, 5 October 1900, 10.

54 Ibid., 109.

55 For a good overview of Fisher's reforms of the Royal Navy, see Maurois, *The Edwardian Era*, 'Fisher and the Navy,' 271–7.

56 Cited by Barnett, *The Swordbearers*, 110.

57 Cited by Epstein, *Modern Germany*, 313.

58 For an intriguing account of events leading up to the proclamation, see Taylor, *English History*, 3–6.

59 Blake, ed., *The Private Papers of Douglas Haig*, 22.

60 Swinton, *Eyewitness*.

61 Robertson, *Soldiers and Statesmen*, 38.

62 Ibid.

63 *London Daily Chronicle*, 12 January 1914.

64 Lord Carver, *The Seven Ages of the British Army*, 162

65 Haldane, *Autobiography*, 231.

66 Ibid., 231–2.

67 Barnett, *The Swordbearers*, 117.

68 Ibid., 119.

69 Ibid.

70 Cited by Maurice, *Haldane: 1856–1915*, 162.

71 Ibid.

72 Haldane, *Autobiography*, 189.

73 Ibid., 288.

74 This episode remains to this day steeped in mystery. Who knew what and when and who approved what is still a matter of historical confusion and disagreement. See Sommer, *Haldane of Cloan*, 257n.1.

75 Ibid., 256.

76 See, Koss, *Lord Haldane: Scapegoat for Liberalism*.

77 Maurice, *Haldane: 1856–1915*, 163.

78 Sir Winston Churchill, *Great Destiny*, ed. F.W. Heath (New York: G.P. Putnam's and Sons 1965), 260.

79 Maxse Papers, West Sussex Record Office, f.470.7. Cited by Hall and Martin, *Haldane: Statesman, Lawyer, Philosopher*, 254–5.

80 Ibid., 255.

81 Sommer, *Haldane of Cloan*, 326. See also in the same work, and on the same page, the lengthy letter from Earl Grey to Prime Minister Asquith deploring the charges being levelled against Haldane 'in certain quarters.'

82 Sommer, *Haldane of Cloan*, 254.

83 Haldane, *Autobiography*, 285–6.

84 Asquith, *Moments of Memory*, 240.

85 Spiers, *Haldane: An Army Reformer*, 12.

86 Harold Laski to Oliver Wendell Holmes, 6 June 1921, Howe, ed., *Holmes-Laski Letters*, 235.

87 Gosse Papers, Brotherton Library, Special Collections, Leeds University, Letters to Edmund Gosse, Haldane to Gosse, 9 September 1917. The letters between Gosse and Haldane in this collection, which number more than 600, reveal an intimacy between the two men that does not appear any where else in the Haldane Papers. Haldane refers to Gosse as 'my dearest Edmund' and says 'you are my wonderful friend.'

88 Gosse Papers, Brotherton Library, Special Collections, Leeds University, vol. 3, newspaper clippings, letter to *Morning Post*, January 1915.

89 Ibid., Haldane to Gosse, 23 August 1917.

90 Ibid., 16 August 1917.

91 Ibid., 23 August 1917.

5: Haldane in the School of the Master

1 See Lotze, *Microcosmus*, 2: 154–6.

2 Ibid., 552.

3 Ibid., 370.

4 Haldane, 'Introduction' to Follett, *The New State*, vi.

5 Cited in Avineri, *Hegel's Theory of the Modern State*, 239.

6 Haldane, 'Hegel,' *Contemporary Review*, 233.

7 Ibid.

8 Ibid., 234.

9 Ibid.

10 Ibid., 239.

11 Ibid.

12 Ibid., 240.

13 Ibid., 244.
14 Ibid.
15 Ibid., 245.
16 Nietzsche, *On the Advantage and Disadvantage of History for Life*, 'Introduction,' 1.
17 Rosen, *Nihilism: A Philosophical Essay*, 89.
18 Ibid., 103.
19 Hegel, *Philosophy of History*, 25.
20 Rosen, *Nihilism: A Philosophical Essay*, 64.
21 See Vaughan, *The Political Philosophy of Giambattista Vico*.
22 Hegel, *The Phenomenology of Spirit*, trans. A.V. Miller (Oxon, U.K.: Clarendon Press 1977), 460.
23 Haldane, *The Conduct of Life and Other Addresses*, 37.
24 Patten, *Hegel's Idea of Freedom*, 23.
25 Friedrich, *The Philosophy of Hegel*, 226.
26 Ibid., 291.
27 Haldane, 'Introduction' to Follett, *The New State*, vi.
28 Ibid., 'Philosophy of Right and Law,' 291.
29 Ibid., 292.
30 Ibid., 293.
31 Ibid., 291.
32 Hegel died of typhus in 1831 and as a result did not live to see the Reform Bill become law in 1832.
33 Hegel, *Philosophy of History*, 453–4.
34 Ibid., 454.
35 Ibid.
36 Follett, *The New State*, 267.
37 Friedrich, *The Philosophy of Hegel*, 540–1.
38 See Hegel, *Philosophy of Right*, para 277, for a fuller account of his objections to the separation of powers.
39 Ibid., para 273.
40 See Pangle, *The Political Philosophy of Montesquieu*.
41 Hegel, *Philosophy of Right*, para 257.
42 Ibid., para 209.
43 Ibid., 'Introduction,' vi.
44 Ibid., v.
45 Ibid., viii.
46 Ibid.
47 Ibid., ix.
48 Ibid., xii.

49 Ibid., xxv.
50 Haldane, 'The Meaning of Truth in History,' 24.

6: Haldane in the Shadow of Lord Watson

1 Writing to his wife, Margot, Asquith said: 'I have just done what I never in this life expected to do – sent a submission to the King that the dignity of a Viscount of the United Kingdom be conferred on the Rt. Hon. R.B. Haldane, Secretary of State for War, with the title of Viscount Haldane of Cloan in the County of Perth.' Cited in Sommer, *Haldane of Cloan*, 242.

2 See his letters home recounting his enthusiastic participation in these debates: Haldane Papers, NLS, MS5986, especially 26 October 1911, 241.

3 Sommer, *Haldane of Cloan*, 242.

4 Haldane, *Autobiography*, 238.

5 Cited in Sommer, *Haldane of Cloan*, 242.

6 See Lovell, *English Constitutional and Legal History*, 274–6.

7 One other domestic jurisdiction was acquired in 1998 when by legislation the General Medical Council was granted right of appeal.

8 Hall and Martin, *Haldane: Statesman, Lawyer, Philosopher*, 172–3.

9 Ibid., 175.

10 Ibid.

11 See Swinfen, *Imperial Appeal*.

12 Canada attempted to terminate appeals to the Judicial Committee as early as 1888 but the act was ruled invalid in 1926 in *Nadan v. The King*, [1926] A.C. 482; after the passage of the Statute of Westminster, 1926, the 1888 statute was re-enacted and was ruled valid by the Judicial Committee in *British Coal Corporation v. The King*, [1935] A.C. 500.

13 See Snell and Vaughan, *The Supreme Court of Canada*.

14 Saywell, *The Lawmakers*, 155.

15 We shall return to the inefficiencies of this high office in a later discussion of Haldane's Machinery of Government Committee report.

16 House of Lords Debates, 26 July 1966, col. 677. See Scarman, *English Law*, 5.

17 For an account of the participation of justices of the Supreme Court of Canada on the Judicial Committee, see Snell and Vaughan, *The Supreme Court of Canada*, 181–3.

18 For an extensive discussion of David Schneiderman's view that the roots of Watson's jurisprudence can best be found in 'the ideological presuppositions of the constitutional lawyer of the nineteenth century' rather than in 'the text of the constitution,' see Saywell, *The Lawmakers*, 143–4 and 185–6. I am in agreement with Saywell that there is no plausible evidence to sup-

port Schneiderman's speculations. Indeed, they fly in the face of Haldane's own musings on the subject of Hegel and the law of the state, especially in his preface to Follett's book.

19 Lord Denning, *Borrowing from Scotland* (Glasgow: Jackson, Son 1963), 279.
20 'Lord Watson,' *Scottish Law Review*, 15 (1899): 229.
21 Ibid., 237.
22 Ibid., 238.
23 Ibid., 240.
24 Saywell, *The Lawmakers*, 120.
25 Cited in ibid., 366.
26 *Delgamuukw v. British Columbia*, [1997] 3 S.C.R., 1010 at 1081.
27 Ibid.
28 'Lord Watson,' *Juridical Review*, 11 (1899): 279.
29 Cited in Saywell, *The Lawmakers*, 121.
30 Risk, 'The Scholars and the Constitution,' 496 at 497.
31 See Hewitt Bernard, 'Minutes of the Quebec Conference,' Macdonald Papers, vol. 46, Library and Archives Canada. See also Pope, *Confederation Documents*.
32 Dawson, *The Government of Canada*, 107.
33 Ibid.
34 Ibid., 106.
35 See, for a strong defence of what the Privy Council did under Watson and Haldane, Cairns, 'The Judicial Committee and Its Critics.' See also Frederick Vaughan, 'Critics of the Judicial Committee of the Privy Council: The New Orthodoxy and an Alternative Explanation,' *Canadian Journal of Political Science*, 19 (1986): 495.
36 See *The Federalist Papers*, especially Alexander Hamilton in Federalists nos. 15 to 22 on the 'insufficiency of the present Constitution' and Federalist no. 23 on executive energy.
37 For a discussion of the federal authorities considered by the Canadian fathers of Confederation, see this author's *The Canadian Federalist Experiment*, especially chapter 5, 'The Ambiguous Embrace of Federalism,' 91.
38 Saywell, *The Lawmakers*, 114.
39 On the use of language, such as 'classes of subjects,' etc., see Vaughan, *The Canadian Federalist Experiment*, chapter 5, 'The Ambiguous Embrace of Federalism,' 91.
40 *Parliamentary Debates on Confederation of British North American Provinces*, 3rd Session, 8th Provincial Parliament of Canada (Quebec: L. Hunter, Rose and Co. 1865), 33.
41 Ibid.

42 For an account of the establishment of the Supreme Court of Canada, see Snell and Vaughan, *The Supreme Court of Canada*.

43 II S.C.R., (1877), 70.

44 Ibid., 87.

45 Ibid., 88.

46 Ibid., 93.

47 Ibid., 95.

48 III S.C.R., (1879), 1.

49 Ibid., 575.

50 Saywell, *The Lawmakers*, 146.

51 The best account of Lord Watson's constitutional jurisprudence relating to Canada can be found in ibid.

52 *Attorney General for Ontario v. Attorney General for the Dominion*, A.C. 348; Olmsted, ed., *Canadian Constitutional Decisions of the Judicial Committee*, 3 vols., 1: 343 (hereafter 'Olmsted'). Unless otherwise noted, all references to Judicial Committee judgments are from Olmsted.

53 *The Citizens' Insurance v Parsons*, A.C. 7; Olmsted, 1: 94.

54 Ibid., 345.

55 See Pope, *Confederation Documents*, 55–88.

56 Viscount Haldane, 'The Work for the Empire of the Judicial Committee of the Privy Council,' *Cambridge Law Review*, 1 (1923): 48.

57 Those cases were: *L'Union St. Jacques de Montreal v. Dame Julie Belisle*, (1874) 6 A.C. 31; *Dow v. Black*, (1874–5) 6 A.C. 272; *Attorney General for Quebec v. Queen Insurance Co*, (1878) 3 A.C. 1090; *Valin v. Langlois*, (1879) 5 A.C. 115; *Bourgoin v. La Compagnie du Chemin de Fer de Montreal*, (1879–80) 5 A.C. 381; *Citizens Insurance v. Parsons*, (1881–2) 7 A.C.; *Dobie v. The Temporalities Board*, (1881–2) 7 A.C. 736; *Russell v. The Queen*, (1881–2) 7 A.C. 829; *The Queen v. Boileau*, (1881–2) 7 A.C. 46.

58 *Dobie*, Olmsted, 1: 128.

59 Ibid., 136–7.

60 Ibid., 138.

61 See, for example, *Earl of Zetland v. Hislop*, HL 7 (1882) 427 [Scotland].

62 The most recent biography of Benjamin is Evans, *Judah P. Benjamin*.

63 For a fuller discussion of this issue, see Vaughan, *The Canadian Federalist Experiment*, chapter 5, 'The Ambiguous Embrace of Federalism.'

64 *Bank of Toronto v. Lambe*, (1887) A.C. 222.

65 Ibid., 226.

66 Saywell, *The Lawmakers*, 117.

67 *Liquidators of the Maritime Bank v. The Receiver General of New Brunswick*, (1892) A.C. 437.

68 Ibid., Olmsted, 1: 270.
69 See Watson's judgment where he talks of 'each province retaining its independence and autonomy,' ibid., 268.
70 Ibid., 269.
71 Haldane to Gosse, 25 May 1915, Gosse Papers, Brotherton Library, Leeds University.
72 Haldane to Gosse, 5 August 1920, Gosse Papers, Brotherton Library, Leeds University.
73 *Attorney-General for Ontario v. Attorney General for the Dominion*, Olmsted, 1: 345. Emphasis added.
74 Ibid., 355–6.
75 Ibid., 144.
76 'Canada: Prohibitory Liquor Laws Case,' a transcript from the Shorthand Notes of Messers Martin and Meredith, 13 New Inn, Strand, London, WC. This is a handwritten transcript of the proceedings before the Judicial Committee, 1895. A printed version is available as *The Liquor Prohibition Appeal, 1895, An Appeal from the Supreme Court of Canada to Her Majesty the Queen in Council* (London: William Brown and Co. 1895).
77 *Hodge v. The Queen*, 9 A.C., 1883–4, 117; Olmsted, 1: 184.
78 Kennedy, *Professor Blackie: His Sayings and Doings*, 212–13.
79 Ibid., 215.
80 Ibid., 214.
81 Ibid., 216.
82 Saywell, *The Lawmakers*, 145.

7: Haldane and the Reign of *Sittlichkeit*

1 Laski to Holmes, 12 January 1921, in De Wolfe Howe, ed., *Holmes-Laski Letters*, 1: 241.
2 All references will be to the Gifford Lectures online, at www.giffordlectures.org.
3 Churchill, *My Early Life*, 129.
4 Winwood Reade's book was originally published in London by Watts and Co. in 1872; it is available on-line at www.exclassics.com/martyrdom.
5 Ibid.
6 Cooper, *Duff Cooper Diaries*, 19.
7 Ibid., 2.
8 Ibid.
9 Ibid., 5.
10 Ibid., end of lecture 1, 6.

11 Ibid., 8.

12 Ibid., lecture 5, 10.

13 Ibid.

14 Ibid., 12.

15 Ibid.

16 Ibid., 14.

17 Lotze, *Microcosmos*, 2: 660.

18 Ibid., 661.

19 Ibid., 660.

20 Ibid., 661–2.

21 Ibid., 336.

22 For critical reviews of *The Pathway to Reality*, see *Mind*, 1903, 527–35; *International Journal of Ethics*, 9 (1904): 253–7; *Philosophical Review*, 13, no. 1 (1904): 55.

23 Saywell, *The Lawmakers*, 186.

24 Maurice, *Haldane: 1856–1915*, 112.

25 See Laski to Holmes, 14 December 1920, in De Wolfe Howe, ed., *Holmes-Laski Letters*, 2: 235.

26 Ibid.,

27 1 Cranch 137 (1803).

28 See Wolfe, *The Rise of Modern Judicial Review*.

29 *New York Times*, 30 August 1913, 1.

30 Ibid., 3.

31 *Montreal Gazette*, 1 September 1913, Editorial, 8.

32 Ibid., 2 September 1913, 10.

33 Ibid. 1 September 1913, 5.

34 Ibid.

35 Ibid. The case he was referring to was *In re the Matter of a Reference to the Supreme Court of Canada of Certain Questions concerning Marriage*, (1912) A.C. 880; Olmsted, 1: 650.

36 Ibid.

37 *Canadian Law Times*, 33 (1913): 790.

38 *Montreal Gazette*, 2 September 1913, 5.

39 Ibid., 10.

40 Haldane, 'Higher Nationality,' in Boucher, ed., *Scottish Idealists*, 186.

41 Robinson, 'Lord Haldane and the BNA Act,' 61.

42 Mitias, 'Law as the Basis of the State: Hegel,' 291.

43 Haldane, 'Higher Nationality,' 188.

44 Ibid., 197.

45 Ibid., 200.

46 Ibid., 201.
47 Sommer, *Haldane of Cloan*, 381.
48 Elizabeth Haldane, *From One Century to Another*, 208.
49 Lloyd-George, *War Memoirs*, 2: 1010.
50 Chamberlain, *Politics from Inside*, 69.
51 Ibid.
52 Frankfurter to Holmes, 6 September 1913, in Mennel and Compston, eds., *Holmes and Frankfurter*, 15.
53 Ibid.
54 Haldane, *The Reign of Relativity*, 351.
55 Ibid.
56 Ibid.
57 Ibid., 351.
58 Haldane Papers, NLS, MS5920, 'Memoirs,' 28.
59 Haldane to his mother, 19 May 1924, NLS, Haldane Papers, MS6007, 83.
60 Haldane to his mother, 1 December 1924, ibid.

8: In the High Court of Hegel

1 Saywell, *The Lawmakers*, 150. Emphasis added.
2 Ibid.,183.
3 *Bank of Toronto v. Lambe*, (1887); Olmsted, 1: 234.
4 Ibid., 235.
5 See Binnie, 'Constitutional Interpretation and Original Intent' (2004).
6 See Romney, *Mr Attorney*, 242.
7 Haldane, *Selected Addresses and Essays*, 220.
8 Ibid.
9 On occasion, the law lords did in fact allude to Canadian history. Lord Sankey, for example, in *Edwards*, after noting that 'the appeal to history ... in this particular matter is not conclusive,' went on to remark that the political compromise contained in the London Resolutions was 'a compromise which will remain a lasting monument to the political genius of Canadian statesmen.' Olmsted, 2: 641.
10 See Frederick Vaughan, 'Precedent and Nationalism in the Supreme Court of Canada,' *American Review of Canadian Studies*, 6 (1987): 2.
11 McDowell, *Equity and the Constitution*, 128.
12 See Lord Sankey, *Edwards v. Canada*, [1930] A.C. 124; Olmsted, 2: 641.
13 Ibid., Olmsted, 2: 642.
14 Holmes, 'The Theory of Legal Interpretation,' 417, 419. Holmes went on to note that, if 'supreme power resided in the person of a despot who would

cut off your hand or head if you went wrong, probably one would take every available means to find out what was wanted.'

15 Haldane, 'Higher Nationality,' in Boucher, ed., *The Scottish Idealists*, 189.

16 Romney, *Mr Attorney*, 241. See Saywell, *The Lawmakers*, for similar sentiments.

17 Romney, *Mr Attorney*, 242.

18 See Varcoe, *The Distribution of Legislative Power in Canada*.

19 Ibid., 39–40.

20 Ibid., chapter 5, 'The Repeal Movement,' 61–79.'

21 See Risk, 'The Scholars and the Constitution,' 496.

22 See the vote count in *Parliamentary Debates on Confederation of British North American Provinces* (Quebec, 1865), 962.

23 For a good discussion of the role played by Oliver Mowat, see Romney, *Mr Attorney*, chapter 6, 'In Right of Ontario,' 240–81.

24 36 Vict. c. 3, c. 4.

25 Lord Watson, *Liquidators of the Maritime Bank of Canada v. Receiver-General of New Brunswick*, (1892) A.C. 437 at 443; Olmsted, 1: 269.

26 *The Times*, 25 January 1887.

27 Haldane to his mother, 9 July 1921, Haldane Papers. NLS, MS6004, 73. The case he referred to was: *Attorney General of Canada v. Attorney General for Quebec*, (1921) A.C. 413; Olmsted, 2: 174.

28 Ibid., 132 overleaf. Viscount Haldane's portrait is one of the few that hang in the Judicial Committee chambers in 11 Downing Street to this day.

29 Haldane to his mother, 9 July 1921, Haldane Papers, NLS, MS6004.

30 Haldane to his mother, 21 April 1921, Haldane Papers, NLS, MS6004.

31 Haldane to his mother, 18 May 1924, Haldane Papers, NLS, MS6007.

32 Haldane to his mother, 19 May 1924, Haldane Papers, NLS, MS6007.

33 See Cairns, 'The Judicial Committee and Its Critics,' 301.

34 Haldane to his mother, 7 February 1925, Haldane Papers, NLS, MS6007.

35 Haldane to his mother, 29 July 1921, Haldane Papers, NLS, MS6004.

36 Elizabeth Haldane to her mother, 20 December 1915, Haldane Papers, NLS, MS20230.

37 Haldane to Chief Justice Sir Charles Fitzpatrick, 29 December 1913, Haldane Papers, NLS, MS5910.

38 Ibid.

39 Fitzpatrick to Haldane, ibid., 9 January 1914.

40 With the Judicial Committee Amendment Act, 1895, the queen was authorized to appoint judges to the Judicial Committee; Chief Justice Henry Strong was the first Canadian judge to be appointed. See Snell and Vaughan, *The Supreme Court of Canada*, 68–9 and passim.

41 Haldane, *Education and Empire*, 'Appellate Courts of the Empire,' 32.
42 Ibid., 89.
43 Ibid., 99.
44 Ibid.
45 Ibid.
46 Ibid., 111.
47 Ibid.
48 Ibid., 112.
49 Canada, Sessional Papers, 1895, no. 20, 'Judicial Committee of the Privy Council,' *Brophy v. Attorney General of Manitoba*, oral argument, 302.
50 *Russell v. The Queen*, (1881–2) 7 A.C., 829; Olmsted, 1: 145.
51 *Citizens Insurance v. Parsons*, (1881–2) 7 A.C. 96; Olmsted, 1: 94.
52 *City of Fredericton v. The Queen*, 3 Supreme Court Reports, 505.
53 *Russell v. The Queen*; Olmsted, 1: 153.
54 Ibid., 155.
55 Ibid.
56 Ibid., 156.
57 Ibid.
58 *Hodge v. The Queen*; Olmsted, 1: 197.
59 Saywell, *The Lawmakers*, 162.
60 Ibid.
61 *Attorney General for Ontario v. Attorney General for Canada*, (1896) A.C. 348; Olmsted, 1: 356.
62 *Attorney General of Canada v. Attorney General of Alberta*, [1916] 1 A.C. 588.
63 *Board of Commerce*, (1922) 1 A.C. 191.
64 *Toronto Electric Commissioners v. Snider*, [1925] A.C. 396 at 413; Olmsted, 2: 409.
65 Hogg, *Constitutional Law of Canada*, 453.
66 *Toronto Electric Commissioners v. Snider*, (1925) A.C. 412; Olmsted, 2: 409.
67 Ibid.
68 Ibid., 412.
69 *Rodriquez v. Speyer Bros*, [1919] A.C. 59, at 79.
70 *In re Board of Commerce and Combines and Fair Prices Act*, (1922) A.C. 381.
71 *Fort Frances Pulp and Power Co. v. Manitoba Free Press*, (1923) A.C. 695.
72 Saywell, *The Lawmakers*, 183.
73 Forsey, 'In Defence of Macdonald's Constitution,' 23.
74 *Times Law Report*, 30 (1914): 207.
75 *In re Marriage Legislation in Canada*, (1912) A.C. 880; Olmsted, 1: 650.
76 Ibid., Olmsted, 658.
77 *John Deere Plow v. Wharton*, [1915] A.C. 330.

78 *Attorney General of Canada v. Attorney General of Alberta*, (1916) A.C. 588; Olmsted, 2: 1.
79 *Attorney General of Ontario v. Attorney General of Canada*, (1894) A.C. 189; Olmsted, 1: 304.
80 *In re The Board of Commerce Act*, [1922] A.C. 191; Olmsted, 2: 245.
81 *In re Combines and Fair Prices Act*, [1922] A.C. 191; Olmsted, 2: 245.
82 *Bonanza Creek Gold Mining Co. v. The King*, [1916] A.C. 566.; Olmsted, 2: 16.
83 See Romney, *Mr Attorney*, especially chapter 6, 'In Right of Ontario,' 240–81.
84 *John Deere Plow v. Wharton*, [1915] A.C. 330; Olmsted, 1: 717.
85 Ibid.
86 Ibid., 338; Olmsted, 1: 725.
87 Ibid., 724.
88 Ibid., 725.
89 Haldane, *The Reign of Relativity*, 365.
90 Taylor, *Hegel*, 444.

9: The State and the Reign of Relativity

1 Schneiderman, 'Harold Laski, Viscount Haldane and the Law of the Canadian Constitution in the Early Twentieth Century,' 551.
2 Haldane, *The Reign of Relativity*, 32.
3 Ibid., 33.
4 Ibid., 33–4.
5 Ibid.
6 Ibid., 34–5.
7 Ibid., 35.
8 Ibid., 44.
9 Ibid., 52.
10 Ibid., 55.
11 Ibid., 59.
12 Ibid., 119.
13 Ibid., 163.
14 Taylor, *Hegel*, 539.
15 Hegel, *Lectures on the Philosophy of History*, 18.
16 Haldane, *The Reign of Relativity*, 330.
17 Ibid., 375.
18 Ibid., 374.
19 Ibid., 376.
20 Haldane, 'Introduction' to Follett, *The New State*, xii.

21 Follett, *The New State*, 51.
22 Ibid., 159.
23 It was for this very reason that the late professor Donald Smiley opposed the Canadian Charter of Rights and Freedoms. See Donald V. Smiley, 'Canadian Federalism and the Resolution of Federal-Provincial Conflict,' in Frederick Vaughan, Patrick Kyba, and O.P. Dwivedi, eds., *Contemporary Issues in Canadian Politics* (Scarborough, Ont.: Prentice-Hall 1970), 49.
24 Haldane, *The Reign of Relativity*, 268.
25 Ibid.
26 Taylor, *Hegel*, 431.
27 [1915] A.C. 300; Olmsted, 1: 717.
28 Ibid., 730. The ruling struck down the British Columbia legislation 'in its present form.' Haldane went on to note that the legislation 'might have been competent' under certain general requirements; and again, 'it might also have been competent' if it had been a 'statute of general application.' He virtually showed the B.C. draftsmen how to rewrite their legislation so as to meet the court's objections.
29 Follett, *The New State*, 267.
30 Ibid.
31 Ibid., 301–2.
32 Ibid., 267.
33 Haldane, *The Reign of Relativity*, 373.
34 Ibid.
35 Ibid.
36 Ibid.
37 Ibid.
38 Ibid., 374.
39 Ibid.
40 Ibid., 353.
41 Ibid., 375.
42 Ibid., 376.
43 Ibid., 377.
44 Ibid., 350.
45 Ibid., 352.
46 Haldane's grand perception of the Judicial Committee's role in nation building prompted Frank Scott at McGill to object that that august body was 'too remote, too little trained in our law, too casually selected' to perform such a task better than our own courts. See Frank Scott, 'The Consequences of the Privy Council Decisions,' *Canadian Bar Review*, 15 (1937): 485 at 494.

10: Supreme Tribunal of the Empire

1 *The Times*, 9 January 1900.
2 Haldane, *Selected Addresses and Essays*, 226.
3 Ibid., 220.
4 Ibid., 223.
5 See Lord Bridges, 'Haldane and the Machinery of Government,' 254.
6 *Report of the Machinery of Government Committee*, 1918, Parliamentary Papers, NLS, HMSO, CD9230.
7 Ibid., para 31 at 72.
8 Ibid., 63.
9 Ibid., 65.
10 Ibid., 66.
11 Ibid., 68.
12 Ibid.
13 Ibid.
14 Ibid., 71.
15 Ibid.
16 Ibid., 72.
17 Ibid.
18 Maurice, *Haldane: 1915–1928*, 64.
19 Sommer, *Haldane of Cloan*, 347–8.
20 Cited in ibid., 348. See MacKenzie, *The Children of the Souls*.
21 Haldane, 'The Appellate Courts of the Empire,' *Education and Empire*, 132.
22 Ibid., 135.
23 Ibid., 136.
24 Ibid., 137.
25 British North America Act, 1867, s. 101.
26 Haldane, 'The Appellate Courts of the Empire,' 139.
27 Taylor is cited in 'Lord Haldane: Philosophy and Lucidity of Language,' *Canadian Law Times*, 42 (1922): 645. This article is simply signed: 'B.T.'
28 Haldane, 'The Appellate Courts of the Empire,' 146.
29 Ibid.
30 Ibid.
31 See E.R. Cameron, 'The House of Lords and the Judicial Committee,' *Canadian Bar Review*, 1 (1931): 223, where the author discusses this issue.
32 Ibid., 224.
33 Viscount Waverely, 'Haldane the Man,' 217.
34 See, for example, the press release from the Legal Action Group, 'Ministry of Justice Would Help Judicial Reforms,' 11 November, 2003, Lag.org.uk.

35 Charles H. Wilson, principal of the University College of Leicester, in the Haldane Lecture at Birkbeck College, London, 5 December 1956. Reprinted in Sommer, *Haldane of Cloan*, 346.

36 See Drewry, 'Lord Haldane's Ministry of Justice,' 396.

37 Sir Albert Napier, 'Schuster, Claud,' *Oxford Dictionary of National Biography*, 284.

38 Cited in Drewry, 'Lord Haldane's Ministry of Justice,' 401.

39 Ibid., 402.

40 Ibid., 404.

41 Ibid.

42 Ibid., 411.

43 Fitzpatrick to Haldane, cited by L.A. Cannon, Address to Canadian Bar Association, tenth annual meeting, August 1925, *Canadian Bar Review*, 1 (1925): 480.

44 'Extracts from the Minutes of Convocation of the Law Society of Upper Canada in 1938,' Appendix 'D,' 49. I am grateful to Justice Horace Krever for making this document available to me.

45 Cited in Cannon, Address to the Canadian Bar Association, 460–1.

46 Ibid.

47 *Nadan v. The Queen*, (1926) A.C. 482; Olmsted, 2: 447.

48 See *British Coal Corp. v. The King*, (1935) A.C. 500; Olmsted, 3: 121.

49 Williams, *Duff: A Life in the Law*, 124.

50 Ibid., 126.

51 Ibid.

52 Ibid., 127.

53 *Ottawa Evening Journal*, 25 April 1928, 8.

54 In this matter the author is in fundamental disagreement with the recent study of the 'Persons case' by Robert J. Sharpe and Patricia I. McMahon: *The Persons Case: The Origins and Legacy of the Fight for Legal Personhood*. The Judicial Committee did not settle an abstract issue with regard to 'legal personhood.' It ruled that women could be validly appointed to the Senate of Canada under the 'qualified persons' provision of the British North America Act, 1867.

55 *Henrietta Muir Edwards v. Attorney General for Canada*, (1930) A.C. 124; Olmsted, 3: 630.

56 Ibid., Olmsted, 2: 633.

57 Ibid., 641.

58 See Sharpe and McMahon, *The Persons Case*, chapter 10, 'The Political, Cultural and Legal Legacy of the Persons Case,' 189, for an interesting account of Chief Justice Anglin's continued resentment at being overruled in this

case and his efforts to discredit the Judicial Committee's 'living tree juris-prudence.'

59 *Bebb v. Law Society*, Court of Appeal judgment, *Canadian Law Times*, 34 (1914): 621.

60 For a more complete study of the *Edwards* case, see Sharpe and McMahon, *The Persons Case*.

61 For an account of the parliamentary and judicial efforts to terminate ap-peals to the Judicial Committee, see Snell and Vaughan, *The Supreme Court of Canada*, 185–95. The reluctance of the Judicial Committee to hear appeals in criminal cases appears to have been premised on the belief that, since convictions in criminal cases were the products of juries, it was wise not to interfere with those collective judgments. The sanctity of the jury system lay at the root of the committee's refusal to hear criminal appeals, even in the case of *Riel*, whose appeal was denied.

62 Ibid.

63 Saywell, *The Lawmakers*, 190.

64 Ibid., 191.

65 *Re Anti-Inflation Act*, [1976] 2 S.C.R. 373.

66 For a discussion of the parliamentary manoeuvres relating to termination, see Snell and Vaughan, *The Supreme Court of Canada*, 182–92.

67 Cited in Ward, *James Ramsay MacDonald*, 124.

68 Sommer, *Haldane of Cloan*, 393–5.

69 House of Lords, Debates, 29 July 1924, cols. 22–3.

70 *Attorney General of Canada v. Attorney General of British Columbia*, [1930] A.C.; Olmsted, 3: 617.

71 *A.G. for Canada v. A.G. for British Columbia*, 1930 A.C. 111; Olmsted, 2: 623.

72 Ibid., 623–4.

73 *Re Anti-Inflation Act*, [1976] 2 S.C.R. 373.

11: Recollections and Last Days

1 John Buchan, *Memory Hold the Door*, 128.

2 Ibid., 129.

3 Ibid.

4 Beatrice Webb, *Our Partnership*, 226.

5 Cited in Lord Bridges, 'Haldane and the Machinery of Government,' 254.

6 Beatrice Webb, *Our Partnership*, 227.

7 Ibid.

8 MacCarthy, ed., *H.H.A.: Letters to a Friend*, 4 March 1926, 159.

9 Sommer, *Haldane of Cloan*, 426.

10 Viscount Waverley, 'Haldane the Man,' 220.
11 Norman and Jeanne MacKenzie, *The Diary of Beatrice Webb*, 2: 261.
12 Beatrice Webb, *My Apprenticeship*, 93.
13 Ibid.
14 Ibid., 123.
15 Ibid., from Cardinal Manning's *The Rights of Labour*, 157.
16 Buchan, *Pilgrim's Way*, 131.
17 Ibid.
18 Ibid., 128.
19 Sommer, *Haldane of Cloan*, 54.
20 Jolliffe, ed., *Raymond Asquith: Life and Letters*, 45.
21 Asquith, *Moments of Memory*, 27.
22 MacKenzie, *The Children of the Souls*, 20.
23 Earl Grey, *The Scotsman*, 24 August 1928, 4.
24 G.P. Gooch, *The Contemporary Review*, 1928, 424.
25 Boswell's *Life of Johnson*, 1776.
26 Earl Jowett, 'Haldane and the Law,' 230.
27 Ibid., 231.
28 Haldane, *Autobiography*, 166.
29 Ibid.
30 Ibid.
31 Ellmann, *Oscar Wilde*, 475.
32 Ibid., 465.
33 Haldane, *Autobiography*, 167.
34 Ellman, *Oscar Wilde*, 465.
35 Letter to his mother, 28 January 1921, Haldane Papers, NLS, MS6004, 86.
36 Ibid., 29 January 1921, 87.
37 Ibid., 2 February 1921, 88.
38 Ibid., 4 February 1921, 89.
39 Ibid., 8 February 1921, 90.
40 Ibid., 10 February 1921, 91.
41 Ibid., 11 February 1921, 92.
42 Ibid., 7 March 1921, 93.
43 'Court Disturbance Leads to Ejection,' *The Times*, 9 February 1921, 1.
44 Haldane to Gosse, Gosse Papers, Brotherton Library, Leeds University, Special Collections, vol. 3, 28 November 1916.
45 Ibid., 6 December 1916.
46 See ibid., 9 September 1917.
47 Ibid., 8 September 1917.
48 See Mackenzie, *The Children of the Souls*, 116.

49 Gosse Papers, 4 September 1914.
50 Laski to Holmes, 14 March 1921, in De Wolfe Howe, ed., *Holmes-Laski Letters*, 1: 251.
51 Ibid., 11 February 1921, 248.
52 Gosse Papers, Haldane to Gosse, 18 August 1916.
53 Ibid., Haldane to Gosse, 5 September 1916.
54 Ibid., Elizabeth Haldane to Gosse, 26 August 1917.
55 Cunningham to Haldane, 10 January 1914, Haldane Papers, NLS, MS5910, 165.
56 Ibid., Bradley to Haldane, 17 February 1914, 172.
57 See Laskin, '"Peace, Order and Good Government" Re-Examined,' 1054. See also Risk, 'The Scholars and the Constitution,' 496.
58 See Schneiderman, 'Harold Laski, Viscount Haldane, and the Law of the Canadian Constitution in the Early Twentieth Century,' 521.
59 See Risk, 'The Scholars and the Constitution,' 496.
60 David MacGregor, 'Canada's Hegel,' *Canadian Literary Review*, 2, no. 2 (1993): 18.

Postscript: The Haldane Legacy and the Modern Court

1 Robert Fulford, 'What Divides Us Makes Us Hegel,' *National Post*, 29 July 2000, C1.
2 David MacGregor, 'Canada's Hegel,' *Canadian Literary Review*, 2, no. 2 (1993).
3 See H.S. Harris, 'The Hegel Renaissance in the Anglo-Saxon World since 1945,' *The Owl Of Minerva*, 15 (fall 1983): 77.
4 I am not unaware of the more recent debate taking place in some of our law schools over 'contextualism'; fortunately, this subject lies well beyond the scope of this book. See Shalin Sugunasiri, 'Contextualism: The Supreme Court's New Standards of Judicial Analysis and Accountability,' *Dalhousie Law Journal*, 1 (1999): 126. But also see the symposium on 'The Myth of Context in Politics and Law,' *Harvard Law Review*, 110, no. 2 (1997): 1292.
5 For an account of Darwin's extensive influence, see Ruse, *The Darwinian Revolution*.
6 Keynes, *The General Theory of Employment Interest and Money*, 383.
7 Holmes, 'Law in Science – Science in Law,' 455.
8 I am fully aware of recent revisionist attempts to knock John A. Macdonald, George Brown, George-Étienne Cartier, and the other dominant authors of Confederation off their pedestals by such scholars as Paul Romney.

But I remain unpersuaded. See the author's *The Canadian Federalist Experiment*.

9 I am borrowing the word 'virus' in this context from the writings of George Grant. See *English-speaking Justice*, 55.

10 David George Ritchie, *Darwin and Hegel with Other Philosophical Studies* (London: Swan Sonnenschein 1893). For a discussion of Ritchie, see Boucher, ed., *The Scottish Idealists*.

11 See Kelly, *The Descent of Darwin*.

12 Hegel, *Philosophy of History*, 57.

13 Holmes to Laski, 28 July 1916, in De Wolfe Howe, ed., *Holmes-Laski Letters*, 1: 8.

14 Jaffa, *A New Birth of Freedom*, 84.

15 Ibid., 85.

16 For an account of Holmes's judicial philosophy, see Walter Berns, 'Oliver Wendell Holmes, Jr,' in Frisch and Stevens, *American Political Thought*, 167–90.

17 Viscount Haldane, 'Oliver Wendell Holmes,' *New Republic*, 34 (1921): 46.

18 Austin, *The Province of Jurisprudence Determined*, 191.

19 Ulhmann, 'The Darwinian Mind and Faith of Justice Holmes,' 22.

20 Ibid.

21 Haldane, *The Conduct of Life and Other Addresses*, 41.

22 Ibid., 42.

23 See Anderson, *Judging Bertha Wilson*, chapter 6, 'A Canadian Philosophy of Judicial Analysis,' 132–48. See also Sugunasiri, 'Contextualism,' 128. Given Wilson's important contribution to Charter jurisprudence, it is a curious oversight on the part of John Saywell to exclude her from his account of the early Charter years.

24 Anderson, *Judging Bertha Wilson*, 134.

25 See, for example, Wilson, 'The Making of a Constitution,' 370.

26 Bertha Wilson, 'The David B. Goodman Memorial Lectures,' University of Toronto, 26–27 November 1985, mimeo, Lecture no. 2, 1.

27 Ibid., 10.

28 Ibid., 14.

29 Bertha Wilson, 'Women, the Family and the Constitutional Protection of Privacy,' *Queen's Law Journal*, 17 (1992): 11.

30 Ibid., 18.

31 Ibid., 20.

32 For a good discussion of the implications of Wilson's approach to the Charter, see Grant Huscroft, 'A Constitutional "Work in Progress"? The *Charter* and the Limits of Progressive Interpretation,' in Huscroft and Brodie, eds., *Constitutionalism in the Charter Era*, 413.

33 Ibid., 3.

34 McLachlin, 'Unwritten Constitutional Principles,' 1.

35 Ibid., 20.

36 Ibid., 21

37 Ibid., 23.

38 Harold J. Laski, *Political Thought in England*, 109.

39 Chief Justice Beverley McLachlin, 'Coming of Age: Canadian Nation-hood and the *Charter of Rights*,' a speech delivered at the Association of Canadian Studies Conference, Ottawa, 17 April 2002.

40 *British Columbia v. Ellett Estate*, [1908] 2 S.C.R. 145.

41 Ibid., 478.

42 For a discussion of this matter and its relation to the American debate over 'original intent,' see Robert J. Sharpe and Kent Roach, *Brian Dickson: A Judge's Journey* (Toronto: Osgoode Society for Canadian Legal History / University of Toronto Press 2003), 318–19.

43 Russell, *The Judiciary in Canada* 360.

44 See Knopff and Morton, *Charter Politics*, 'Interest Groups and the Charter,' 27; see also Leishman, *Against Judicial Activism*.

45 See Anderson, *Judging Bertha Wilson*.

46 Wilson, 'The David B. Goodman Memorial Lectures,' Lecture no. 2, 16.

47 Ibid., 20.

48 Haldane relates how on one occasion, when arguing before the Court of Appeal, he referred to the 'mind' of the legislature as a guide to the interpretation of a statute. Lord Esher cried out from the bench: 'Mind of the legislature? And you, Mr. Haldane, have been twenty years in the House of Commons and yet speak of it.' Haldane, *Autobiography*, 70.

49 For a discussion of how 'contextualism' emerged out of Dickson's *Big M Drug Mart* decision and shaped the course of modern Supreme Court jurisprudence, see Sugunasiri, 'Contextualism.' See also Ellen Anderson, 'Enlightened Postmodernism: Scottish Influences on Canada's Legal Pluralism,' LLM thesis, University of Toronto, Faculty of Law, 1998. Anderson writes: 'Out of its Scottish heritage, Canada (the world's first postmodern state) has evolved a largely unconscious and common sense postmodern legal ethics which is revealed in contemporary Canadian legal theory and epitomized by our contextual Charter jurisprudence' (7).

50 See *R. v. Labaye* [2006] 260 D.L.R. (4th) 595.

51 See the judgments of Justices Gérard La Forest, Jean Beetz, and Gerald Le Dain in *Alberta Labour Reference*, [1987] 1 S.C.R. 313.

52 *Regina v. Morgentaler*, [1988] 1 S.C.R. 30.

53 Almost fifty years ago, at the height of the Cold War, an American author, George Feifer, interviewed a Soviet judge about the purpose of Soviet

courts. When Feifer said that crime in the West is viewed as a part of human nature, as inherent in the human condition, the Soviet judge replied:
'Nonsense, I must say. There is no such thing as human nature. Man is
the product of his surroundings, of the social and economic system which
molds him. Change the mold and you change the man. And that is what
we are doing ... Don't damn us because we haven't yet succeeded. We
know that. But you aren't even trying. You laugh at our goals and let your-
selves slide deeper into crime in the name of a theory of man – and then
call us dogmatic.' Cited by Russell in *The Judiciary in Canada*, 86–7.

54 See Wolfe, *The Rise of Modern Judicial Review*.
55 See Kate Malleson, 'A British Bill of Rights: Incorporating the European
Convention on Human Rights,' in Howe and Russell, eds., *Judicial Power
and Canadian Democracy*, 27.
56 See Jaffa, *A New Birth of Freedom*, 86–8.
57 See Sharpe and Roach, *Brian Dickson*, 319, for an account of the relationship of the Dickson Court with American Supreme Court justices.
58 Chief Justice McLachlin was expressing a sentiment which is found in
Bertha Wilson's Goodman Lectures. In the second lecture, Wilson said that
'judicial protection of individual and minority rights vis-à-vis the majority
clearly requires a distinct segregation of the courts from the majoritarian
machinery of the legislatures and the Parliament' (3).
59 Follett, *The New State*, 142.
60 Ibid.
61 Ibid., 157.
62 Ibid., 159.
63 Ibid., 202.
64 Ibid., 100.
65 At a conference celebrating the twenty-fifth anniversary of the Charter
held at McGill University, March 2007, a panel of distinguished law professors and several of those who participated in the Trudeau government
at the time the Charter was being written, such as Tom Axworthy, unanimously agreed that the 'notwithstanding clause' would never be used by
the federal government. Eddie Goldenberg, principal adviser to former
Prime Minister Jean Chrétien, agreed with that assessment and so did
other members of the conference who worked in Prime Minister Paul
Martin's government.
66 *Reference re Same-Sex Marriage*, [2004] 3 S.C.R. 698.
67 This matter is not saved by virtue of the 'notwithstanding clause' of section 33 of the Charter. For all intents and purposes, this section remains
stillborn. Given the prevailing climate of support for the Charter and the

favourable image of judges armed with this document, no government is likely to invoke it.

68 The chief proponent of this position is Peter H. Russell. See his *Constitutional Odyssey*, 268–9.

69 Harry V. Jaffa, 'God Bless America,' *Claremont Review of Books*, spring 2008, 45.

70 For an account of how the United States is coping with many of these problems, see Diggins, *The Lost. Soul of American Politics*.

71 Arendt, *Between Past and Future*, 68.

Bibliography

Abel, Albert. 'Role of the Supreme Court of Canada in Privy Council Cases.' *Alberta Law Review*, 35, no. 3 (1965): 43.

Anderson, Ellen. *Judging Bertha Wilson: Law as Large as Life*. Toronto: Osgoode Society for Canadian Legal History / University of Toronto Press 2001.

Anderson, Louisa Garrett. *Elizabeth Garrett Anderson, 1837–1912*. London: Faber and Faber 1939.

Anderson, R.D. *Education an Opportunity in Victorian Scotland*. Oxford: Oxford University Press 1983.

Arendt, Hanna. *Between Past and Future*. New York: Penguin Press 1968.

Ashby, E., and M. Anderson. *Portrait of Haldane at Work on Education*. London: Macmillan 1974.

Asquith, H.H. *Memoirs and Reflections, 1852–1927*. 2 vols. London: Cassell 1928.

– *H. H. A. Letters of the Earl of Oxford and Asquith to a Friend, 1922–1927*. London: Geoffrey Bles 1934.

Asquith, Herbert. *Moments of Memory: Recollections and Impressions*. London: Hutchinson 1937.

Asquith, Margot. *An Autobiography*. 2 vols. in 1. New York: George H. Doran 1920.

Austin, John. *The Province of Jurisprudence Determined*. Ed. H.L.A. Hart. London: Weidenfeld and Nicolson 1954.

Avinveri, Shlomo. *Hegel's Theory of the Modern State*. Cambridge: Cambridge University Press 1976.

Bale, Gordon. *Chief Justice William Johnstone Ritchie: Responsible Government and*

Judicial Review. Ottawa: Carleton University Press for the Supreme Court of Canada Historical Society 1991.

Balfour, A.J. *The Foundation of Belief*. London: Longman, Green 1895.

Barker, Michael. *Gladstone and Radicalism: The Reconstruction of Liberal Policy in Britain, 1885–94*. London: Harvester Press 1975.

Barnett, Correlli. *The Swordbearers: Studies in Supreme Command in the First World War*. London: Eyre and Spottiswoode 1963.

Barton, D. Plunket, Charles Benham, and Francis Watt. *The Story of Our Inns of Court*. London: G.T. Foulis. N.d.

Becker, Carl L. *The Declaration of Independence: A Study in the History of Political Ideas*. New York: Vantage Books 1942.

Beiser, Frederick C. 'Hegel's Historicism.' In Frederick C. Beiser, ed., *The Cambridge Companion to Hegel*. Cambridge: Cambridge University Press 1993.

Berlin, Isaiah. *Vico and Herder: Two Studies in the History of Ideas*. New York: Viking Press 1976.

Best, Geoffrey. *Mid-Victorian Britain, 1851–75*. London: Fontana Paperbacks 1985.

Binnie, Ian. 'Constitutional Interpretation and Original Intent.' *Supreme Court Law Review*, 15 (2004).

Blake, Robert, ed. *The Private Papers of Douglas Haig, 1914–1919; Being Selections from the Private Diary and Correspondence of Field-Marshal the Earl Haig of Bemersyde*. London: Eyre and Spottiswoode 1952.

Bosanquet, Bernard. *The Philosophical Theory of the State*. 2nd ed. London: Macmillan 1910.

Boswell, James. *Life of Johnson*. Ed. R.W. Chapman. Oxford: Oxford University Press 1970.

Boucher, David, ed. *The Scottish Idealists: Selected Philosophical Writings*. Exeter, U.K.: Imprint Academic 2004.

Bradley, James, 'Hegel in Britain: A Brief History of British Commentary and Attitudes.' *Heythrop Journal*, 1, no. 20 (1979), Parts 1 and 2: 1, 163.

Brides, Lord, 'Haldane and the Machinery of Government.' *Public Administration*, 35 (1957): 254.

Briggs, Asa. *Victorian People*. Chicago: University of Chicago Press 1955.

British Broadcasting Corporation, ed. Foreword by Harman Grisewood. *Ideas and Beliefs of the Victorians: An Historic Evaluation of the Victorian Age*. London: Sylvan Press 1949.

Brown, Robert Craig, and Ramsay Cook. *Canada 1896–1921: A Nation Transformed*. Toronto: McClelland and Stewart 1974.

Browne, G.P. *The Judicial Committee and the British North America Act*. Toronto: University of Toronto Press 1967.

Brudner, Alan. *The Unity of the Common Law: Studies in Hegelian Jurisprudence.* Berkeley: University of California Press 1995.

Bryce, James. *William Ewart Gladstone: His Characteristics as Man and Statesman.* New York: Century 1898.

Buchan, John. *Memory Hold-the-Door.* Toronto: Musson Book 1940.

− *Pilgrim's Way: An Essay in Recollection.* Cambridge, Mass.: Riverside Press 1940.

Cairns, Alan C. 'The Judicial Committee and Its Critics.' *Canadian Journal of Political Science,* 4 (1971): 301.

Cannon, L.A. 'Some Data Relating to the Appeal to the Privy Council.' *Canadian Bar Review,* 8 (1925): 455.

Carver, Field Marshal Lord. *The Seven Ages of the British Army.* London: Weidenfeld and Nicolson 1984.

Chamberlain, Austen. *Politics from Inside.* London: Cassell 1936.

Charteris, Evan. *Life and Letters of Sir Edmund Gosse.* London: William Heinemann 1931.

Churchill, Winston S. *My Early Life.* London: Thornton Butterworth 1930.

Clapham, J.H. *An Economic History of Modern Britain: The Early Railway Age, 1820–1850.* Cambridge: Cambridge University Press 1926.

Clifford, Colin. *The Asquiths.* London: John Murray 2002.

Cooper, Duff. *Old Men Forget.* London: Rupert Hart-Davis 1953.

− *Duff Cooper Diaries.* London: Weidenfeld and Nicolson 2005.

Crankshaw, Edward. *Bismarck.* New York: Viking Press 1981.

Cruikshank, R.J. *Charles Dickens and Early Victorian England.* London: Sir Isaac Pitman and Sons 1949.

Dahrendorf, Ralf. *Society and Democracy in Germany.* New York: Doubleday Anchor 1967.

D'Arcy, Martin. *The Sense of History: Secular and Sacred.* London: Faber and Faber 1959.

Davie, G.E. *The Democratic Intellect: Scotland and Her Universities in the Nineteenth Century.* Edinburgh: University of Edinburgh Press 1961.

Dawson, Christopher. *Understanding Europe.* New York: Sheed and Ward 1952.

Dawson, R. MacGregor. *The Government of Canada.* Toronto: University of Toronto Press 1954.

Devaux, P. *Lotze et son influence sur la philosophie anglo-saxonne.* Brussels: Lamartin 1932.

Dicey, A.V. 'Teaching of English Law at Harvard.' *Harvard Law Review,* 13 (1889–1900): 423.

Diggins, John P. *The Lost Soul of American Politics: Virtue, Self-Interest and the Foundations of Liberalism.* New York: Basic Books 1984.

Drewry, Gavin. 'Lord Haldane's Ministry of Justice: Stillborn or Strangled at Birth?' *Public Administration*, 61 (1983): 396–414.

Dyzenhaus, David. 'The Unwritten Constitution and the Rule of Law.' In Grant Huscroft and Ian Brodie, eds., *Constitutionalism in the Charter Era*, 383.

Eidelberg, Paul. *The Philosophy of the American Constitution*. New York: Free Press 1968.

Ellis, C. Hamilton. *Railways: A Pictorial History of the First 150 Years*. New York: Peebles Press 1974.

Ellman, Richard. *Oscar Wilde*. London: Hamish Hamilton 1987.

Engels, Friedrich. *The German Revolutions: The Peasant War in Germany* and *Germany: Revolution and Counter-Revolution*. Edited with Introduction by Leonard Krieger. Chicago: University of Chicago Press 1967.

Epstein, Klaus. *Modern Germany: Its History and Civilization*. Princeton, N.J.: Princeton University Press 1968.

Evans, Eli. *Judah Benjamin: The Jewish Confederate*. New York: Free Press 1989.

Falls, Cyril. 'Haldane and Defence.' *Public Administration*, 35 (1957): 245.

Figgis, J.N. *Churches in the Modern State*. New York: Longman, Green 1913.

'The Final Appeal: Reform of the House of Lords and the Privy Council, 1867–1876.' *Law Quarterly Review*, 80 (1964): 343.

Follett, M.P. *The New State: Group Organization the Solution of Popular Government*. New York: Longman, Green 1926. Fifth Impression, with Introduction by Lord Haldane.

Forsey, Eugene. 'In Defence of Macdonald's Constitution.' *Dalhousie Law Journal*, 3 (1976): 529.

Frankfurter, Felix. *Mr. Justice Holmes and the Supreme Court*. Cambridge, Mass.: Harvard University Press 1939.

French, John. *Field Marshal, 1914*. London: Constable 1919.

Friedland, Martin. *Courts and Trials: A Multidisciplinarian Approach*. Toronto: University of Toronto Press 1975.

Friedrich, Carl J. *The Philosophy of Hegel*. New York: Modern Library 1954.

Frisch, Morton, and Richard G. Stevens. *American Political Thought*. Boston: Cangage Publishing 1983.

Gillespie, Michael A. *Hegel, Heidegger and the Ground of History*. Chicago: University of Chicago Press 1984.

Girard, Phillip. *Bora Laskin: Bringing Law to Life*. Toronto: University of Toronto Press / Osgoode Society for Canadian Legal History 2005.

Gosse, Edmund. *Father and Son: A Study of Two Temperaments*. London: William Heinemann 1907.

Grant, George. *English-speaking Justice*. Sackville, N.B.: Mount Allison University 1974.

Greenwood, Murray. 'Lord Watson, Institutional Self-Interest, and the Decentralization of Canadian Federalism in the 1890s.' *University of British
Columbia Law Review*, 9, no. 2 (1974): 244.

Haldane, Elizabeth S. *From One Century to Another*. London: Alexander
Maclehose 1937.

Haldane, Mary Elizabeth. *A Record of a Hundred Years (1825–1935)*. Edited by
her daughter. London: Hodder and Stoughton 1930.

Haldane, Richard Burdon. 'Hegel.' *Contemporary Review*, 68 (1895): 232.

– *Education and Empire: Addresses on Certain Topics of the Day*. London: John
Murray 1902. [This collection contains the essay 'Federal Constitutions
within the Empire.' It is incorrectly cited by Schneiderman as a separate
book. See David Schneiderman, 'Harold Laski, Viscount Haldane and the
Law of the Canadian Constitution.']

– *The Pathway to Reality*. 2 vols. London: John Murray 1903.

– *Army Reform and Other Addresses*. London: T. Fisher Unwin 1907.

– *Universities and National Life*. London: John Murray 1910.

– *Universities and National Life: Four Addresses to Students*. London: John
Murray 1912.

– 'The Nature of the State.' *Contemporary Review*, 117 (1920): 761.

– 'Address to the University Law Society.' *Cambridge University Law Journal*,
1, no. 2 (1921).

– 'Oliver Wendell Holmes.' *New Republic*, 34 (1921): 46.

– *Pathway to Reality*. London: John Murray 1921.

– *The Reign of Relativity*. London: John Murray 1921.

– *The Philosophy of Humanism*. London: John Murray 1922.

– 'Work of the Judicial Committee.' *Juridical Review*, 7, no. 3 (1922). Repr. in
Selected Speeches and Addresses.

– 'Meaning of Truth in History.' In *Selected Essays and Addresses*. London: John
Murray 1928.

– *Selected Addresses and Essays*. London: John Murray 1928.

– *An Autobiography*. London: Hodder and Stoughton 1929.

– *The Conduct of Life*. Freeport, N.Y.: Books for Libraries Press. Repr. 1968.

– *The Conduct of Life and Other Addresses*. New York: Books for Libraries Press
1968.

Hall, Jean Graham, and Douglas F. Martin. *Haldane: Statesman, Lawyer, Philosopher*. Chichester, U.K.: Barry Rose Law Publishers 1996.

Havighurst, Alfred. F. *Twentieth/Century Britain*. Evanston, Ill.: Row, Peterson
1962.

Hazelhurst, Cameron, Sally Whitehead, and Christine Woodland. *A Guide to
the Papers of British Cabinet Ministers, 1900–1964*. Cambridge: Cambridge
University Press for the Royal Historical Society 1996.

Hegel, Georg Wilhelm Friedrich. *Lectures on the Philosophy of History*. Trans. John Sibree. London: Henry G. Bohn 1956.
– *The Philosophy of History*. Translated with Introduction by Carl J. Friedrich. Cambridge, Mass.: Harvard University Press 1956.
– *Philosophy of Right*. Trans. T.M. Knox. Oxford: Oxford University Press 1957.
Herr, Richard. *Tocqueville and the Old Regime*. Princeton, N.J.: Princeton University Press 1962.
Heuston, R.V.F. *Lives of the Lord Chancellors, 1875–1940*. Oxford: Clarendon Press 1964.
Hogg, Peter W. *Constitutional Law of Canada*, 5th ed. Toronto: Carswell 2002.
Holmes, Oliver Wendell. 'The Theory of Legal Interpretation.' *Harvard Law Review*, 12 (1899): 417.
– 'Law in Science – Science in Law.' In *Collected Legal Papers*. New York: Houghton Mifflin 1930.
Holroyd, Michael. *Bernard Shaw*, 2 vols. London: Chatto and Windus 1988.
Howe, Mark De Wolfe, ed. *Holmes-Laski Letters: The Correspondence of Mr. Justice Holmes and Harold J. Laski, 1916–1935*. 2 vols. New York: Atheneum 1963.
Howe, Paul, and Peter H. Russell, eds. *Judicial Power and Canadian Democracy*. Montreal: McGill-Queen's University Press 2001.
Huscroft, Grant, and Ian Brodie, eds. *Constitutionalism in the Charter Era*. Toronto: University of Toronto Press 2004.
Jaffa, Harry V. *A New Birth of Freedom: Abraham Lincoln and the Coming of the Civil War*. Lanham, Md., Boulder, Colo., and New York: Rowman and Littlefield 2000.
James, Lawrence. *The Rise and Fall of the British Empire*. New York: St Martin's Press 1994.
Johnson, C.O. 'Did Judah Benjamin Plant the States Rights Doctrine in the Interpretation of the British North America Act? *University of Toronto Law Journal*, 20 (1970): 55.
Johnson, Steven. *The Ghost Map: The Story of London's Most Terrifying Epidemic and How It Changed Science, Cities and the Modern World*. New York: Riverhead Books 2006.
Jolliffe, John, ed. *Raymond Asquith: Life and Letters*. London: Century Hutchinson 1987.
Jowett, Earl. 'Haldane and the Law.' *Public Administration*, 35 (1957): 222.
Kant, Immanuel. *The Critique of Pure Reason*. New York: St Martin's Press 1965.
Kelly, Alfred. *The Descent of Darwin: The Popularization of Darwinism in Germany, 1860–1914*. Chapel Hill: University of North Carolina Press 1981.
Kennedy, Howard Angus. *Professor Blackie: His Sayings and Doings*. London: James Clarke 1896.

Kennedy, W.P.M. *The Constitution of Canada: An Introduction to Its Development and Law*. Oxford: Oxford University Press 1922.

- *Essays in Constitutional Law*. Oxford: Oxford University Press 1934.

Keynes, John Maynard. *General Theory of Employment, Interest and Money*. London: Macmillan 1936.

Klibansky, Raymond, and H.J. Paton, eds. *Philosophy and History: The Ernst Cassirer Festschrift*. New York: Harper Torchbook 1963.

Knopff, Rainer, and F.L. Morton. *Charter Politics*. Scarborough, Ont.: Nelson Canada 1992.

Kojeve, Alexandre. *Introduction to the Reading of Hegel*. Edited by Allan Bloom, translated by James H. Nichols, Jr. New York: Basic Books 1960.

Koss, Stephen E. *Lord Haldane: Scapegoat for Liberalism*. New York: Columbia University Press 1969.

Lampert, Laurence. *Nietzsche's Teaching*. New Haven, Conn., and London: Yale University Press 1986.

Langdell, Christopher Columbus. *Harvard College: A Record of the Commemoration, on the Two Hundred and Fiftieth Anniversary of the Founding*. Cambridge, Mass.: Harvard University Press 1886.

Lash, Joseph P. *From the Diaries of Felix Frankfurter*. New York: W.W. Norton 1975.

Laski, Harold J. *Authority in the Modern State*. New Haven, Conn.: Yale University Press 1919.

- 'Canada's Constitution.' *New Republic*, 35 (4 July 1923): 159.

- *Political Thought in England: Locke to Bentham*. Oxford: Oxford University Press 1961.

Laskin, Bora. 'Peace, Order and Good Government Re-Examined.' *Canadian Bar Review*, 25 (1947): 1054.

- 'The Supreme Court of Canada: A Final Court of and for Canadians.' *Canadian Bar Review*, 29, no. 2 (1951): 1038.

Leishman, Rory. *Against Judicial Activism*. Montreal: McGill-Queen's University Press 2006.

Lloyd-George, David. *War Memoirs*, 2 vols. London: Macmillan 1933–6.

Lockwood, John F. 'Haldane and Education.' *Public Administration*, 35 (1957): 232.

Logan, D. *Haldane and the University of London*. London: Birkbeck College 1960.

Lonergan, Bernard J.F. 'Topics in Education.' *Collected Works of Bernard Lonergan*. Toronto: University of Toronto Press 1993.

Lotze, Hermann. *Microcosmus*. 2 vols. Translated by E.E. Constance Jones. Edinburgh: T. and T. Clark 1888. [Originally published in German in 1856.]

Lovell, Colin, R. *English Constitutional and Legal History*. New York: Oxford University Press 1962.

Lowith, Karl. *Meaning in History*. Chicago: University of Chicago Press 1967.

MacCarthy, H.H.A., ed. *Letters to a Friend*. 2nd series. London: Geoffrey Bles 1934.

McClelland, V.A. 'Manning's Work for Social Justice.' *Chesterton Review*, 17, no. 4 (1992).

McConnell, H.W. 'The Privy Council and the New Deal Cases.' *Osgoode Hall Law Journal*, 9 (1971): 221.

McDowell, Gary L. *Equity and the Constitution: The Supreme Court, Equitable Relief, and Public Policy*. Chicago: University of Chicago Press 1982.

MacKenzie, Jeanne. *The Children of the Souls: A Tragedy of the First World War*. London: Chatto and Windus 1986.

Mackenzie, Norman and Jeanne. *The Diary of Beatrice Webb*. London: Virago Press 1983.

McLachlin, Chief Justice Beverley. 'Unwritten Constitutional Principles: What Is Going On?' A paper delivered at the 2005 Lord Cooke Lecture, Victoria University of Wellingon, Faculty of Law, Wellington, New Zealand, 1 December 2005 [unpublished at the time of writing].

MacMillan, Margaret. *Paris: 1919*. New York: Random House 2001.

Mallory, J.R. 'The Courts and the Sovereignty of the Canadian Parliament.' *Canadian Journal of Economics and Political Science*, 10 (1944): 165.

Maurice, Sir Frederick. *Haldane, 1856–1928*. 2 vols. London: Faber and Faber 1937.

Maurois, André. *The Edwardian Era*. New York: Appleton-Century 1933.

Mennel, Robert M., and Christine L. Compston. *Holmes and Frankfurter: Their Correspondence, 1912–1934*. Hanover, Mass., and London: University Press of New England 1996.

Milner, Roger. *Milner Papers*. 2 vols. London: Cassell 1931–3.

Mitias, Michael H. 'Law as the Basis of the State: Hegel.' *Interpretation*, 9, nos. 2 and 3 (1981): 279.

Morgan, J.H. 'The Riddle of Lord Haldane.' *Quarterly Review*, 252 (1929): 171.

Morrison, J.G. *Oliver Mowat and the Development of Provincial Rights in Ontario: A Study in Dominion-Provincial Relations, 1867–1896*. Toronto: Ontario Department of Public Records and Archives 1961.

Morton, W.L. *Kingdom of Canada*. Toronto: McClelland and Stewart 1969.

Muggeridge, Kitty, and Ruth Adam. *Beatrice Webb: A Life, 1858–1943*. London: Secker and Warburg 1967.

Nietzsche, Freidrich. *On the Advantages and Disadvantages of History for Life*. Trans. Peter Preuss. Indianapolis, Ind.: Hackett Publishing 1980.

Olmsted, Richard A. *Decisions of the Judicial Committee of the Privy Council*. 3 vols. Ottawa: Queen's Printer 1954.

Pangle, Thomas L. *Montesquieu's Philosophy of Liberalism: A Commentary on the Spirit of the Laws*. Chicago: University of Chicago Press 1973.

Parliamentary Debates on the Subject of the Confederation of the British North American Provinces, 3rd Session, 8th Provincial Parliament of Canada. Quebec: Hunter, Rose 1865. Photographic reproduction of the original publication, Ottawa: Edmond Cloutier, Printer to the King's Most Excellent Majesty, Controller of Stationery, 1951.

Patten, Alan. *Hegel's Idea of Freedom*. Oxford: Oxford University Press 2002.

Pearce, Robert, and Roger Stearn. *Government and Reform: 1815–1918*. London: Hodder and Stoughton 1998.

Pestritto, Ronald J. *American Progressivism: A Reader*. Lexington, Ky.: Lexington Books 2008.

Pinson, Koppel S. *Modern Germany: Its History and Civilization*. 2nd ed. New York: Macmillan 1966.

Pippin, Robert, B., and Otfried Hoffe, eds. Translation by Nicholas Walker. *Hegel on Ethics and Politics*. Cambridge: Cambridge University Press 2004.

Pope, Joseph. *Confederation Documents*. Toronto: Carswell 1895.

Pringle-Pattison, Andrew Seth, and R.B. Haldane, eds. *Essays in Philosophical Criticism*. New York: Burt Franklin 1971. [Originally published in 1883.]

Pryke, Kenneth G. *Nova Scotia and Confederation*. Toronto: University of Toronto Press 1979.

Radice, Lisanne. *Beatrice and Sidney Webb: Fabian Socialists*. London: Macmillan 1984.

Reader, W.J. *Life in Victorian England*. London: B.T. Batsford 1964.

Report of the Machinery of Government Committee, 1918. Parliamentary Papers, CD 9230 London HMSO, NLS. [Often called 'The Haldane Report.']

Risk, R.C.B. 'The Scholars and the Constitution: P.O.G.G. and the Privy Council.' *Manitoba Law Journal*, 23 (1996): 496.

Robertson, William. *Soldiers and Statesmen*. London: Constable 1921.

Robinson, Jonathan. 'Lord Haldane and the British North America Act.' *University of Toronto Law Journal*, 20 (1970): 55.

Romney, Paul. *Mr Attorney: The Attorney General for Ontario in Court, Cabinet, and Legislature, 1791–1899*. Toronto: Osgoode Society 1986.

– 'Why Lord Watson Was Right.' In Janet Ajzenstat, ed., *Canadian Constitutionalism*. Ottawa: Department of Justice 1992.

Rosen, Stanley. *Nihilism: A Philosophical Essay*. New Haven, Conn.: Yale University Press 1969.

Ruse, Michael. *The Darwinian Revolution*. Chicago: University of Chicago Press 1979.

Russell, Peter H. *The Judiciary in Canada: The Third Branch of Government*. Toronto: McGraw-Hill Ryerson 1987.

– *Constitutional Odyssey*. Rev. ed. Toronto: University of Toronto Press 2004.

Santayana, George. *Lotze's System of Philosophy*. New York: Scribner and Welford 1889.

Saywell, John T. *The Lawmakers: Judicial Power and the Shaping of Canadian Federalism*. Toronto: Osgoode Society for Canadian Legal History / University of Toronto Press 2002.

– and George Vegh. *Making the Law: The Courts and the Constitution*. Toronto: Copp Clark Pitman 1991.

Scarman, Sir Leslie. *English Law: The New Dimension*. London: Stevens and Sons 1974.

Schneiderman, David. 'Harold Laski, Viscount Haldane and the Law of the Canadian Constitution in the Early Twentieth Century.' *University of Toronto Law Journal*, 48 (1998): 521.

Scott, Frank R. *Essays on the Constitution: Aspects of Canadian Law and Politics*. Toronto: University of Toronto Press 1977.

Sharpe, Robert J., and Patricia McMahon. *The Persons Case: The Origins and Legacy of the Fight for Legal Personhood*. Toronto: Osgoode Society for Canadian Legal History / University of Toronto Press 2007.

Short, Edward. 'Winston Churchill and the Old Cause.' *Crisis*, 23, no. 11 (2005): 26.

Smith, Steven B. *Hegel's Critique of Liberalism*. Chicago: University of Chicago Press 1989.

Snell, James G., and Frederick Vaughan. *The Supreme Court of Canada: A History of the Institution*. Toronto: Osgoode Society for Canadian Legal History / University of Toronto Press 1985.

Sommer, Dudley. *Haldane of Cloan: His Life and Times, 1856–1928*. London: George Allen and Unwin 1960.

Sparrow, Gerald. *The Great Judges*. London: John Long 1974.

Spiers, Edward M. *Haldane: An Army Reformer*. Edinburgh: University of Edinburgh Press 1980.

Stern, Fritz. *The Politics of Cultural Despair: A Study of the Rise of the Germanic Ideology*. New York: Doubleday Anchor 1965.

Stevens, Robert. *Law and Politics: The House of Lords as Judicial Body, 1800–1976*. Chapel Hill: University of North Carolina Press 1978.

Stirling, James Hutchison. *The Secret of Hegel*. London: Longman, Green 1865.

Strauss, Leo. *Natural Right and History*. Chicago: University of Chicago Press 1953.

Strayer, Barry. *The Canadian Constitution and the Courts*. 3rd ed. Toronto: Butterworths 1988.

Swinfen, David B. *Imperial Appeal: The Debate on the Appeal to the Privy Council*. Manchester, U.K.: University of Manchester Press 1987.

Swinton, Ernest Dunlop. *Eyewitness: Being Personal Reminiscences of the Great War, including the Genesis of the Tank*. London: Hodder 1932.

Taylor, A.J.P. *English History: 1914–1945*. Oxford: Clarendon Press 1965.

Taylor, Charles. *Hegel*. Cambridge: Cambridge University Press 1975.

Teagarden, Ernest M. *Haldane at the War Office*. New York: Gordon Press 1976.

Thwaite, Ann. *Edmund Gosse: A Literary Landscape, 1849–1928*. London: Secker and Warburg 1984.

Trevelyan, G.M. *Grey of Falloden*. London: Longmans 1937.

Truscott, Bruce. *Red Brick University*. London: Faber and Faber 1943.

Ulhmann, Michael. 'The Darwinian Mind and Faith of Justice Holmes.' *Claremont Review of Books*, winter 2009, 26.

Underhill, Frank. 'Edward Blake, the Supreme Court of Canada and Appeal to the Judicial Committee.' *Canadian Historical Review*, 19 (1938): 257.

Varcoe, F.P. *The Distribution of Legislative Power in Canada*. Toronto: Carswell 1954.

Vaughan, Frederick. *The Political Philosophy of Giambattista Vico*. The Hague: Martinus Nijhoff 1972.

– *The Canadian Federalist Experiment: From Defiant Monarchy to Reluctant Republic*. Montreal and Kingston: McGill-Queen's University Press 2003.

Vipond, Robert. *Liberty and Community: Canadian Federalism and the Failure of the Constitution*. Albany: State University of New York Press 1991.

Ward, Stephen R. *James Ramsay MacDonald: Low Brow among the High*. Cincinnati, Ohio: Peter Lang Publishers 1990.

Waverley, Viscount. 'Haldane the Man.' *Public Administration*, 35 (1957): 217.

Webb, Beatrice. *My Apprenticeship*. London: Longmans Green 1926.

– *Our Partnership*, eds. Barbara Drake and Margaret Cole. Cambridge: University Press 1975.

Wellek, Rene. *Immanuel Kant in England, 1793–1838*. Princeton, N.J.: Princeton University Press 1931.

Wexler, Stephen. 'The Urge to Idealize: Viscount Haldane and the Constitution of Canada.' *McGill Law Journal*, 29 (1984): 609.

White, Jerry. *London in the Nineteenth Century*. London: Jonathan Cape 2007.

Wiley, Karen Boyett. 'Freedom in History: A Commentary on Hegel's Philosophy of History.' PhD thesis, University of Colorado, University Microfilms International, Ann Arbor, Mich., 1980.

Wilkins, Burleigh Taylor. *Hegel's Philosophy of History*. Ithaca, N.Y.: Cornell University Press 1974.

Williams, David Ricardo. *Duff: A Life in the Law*. Vancouver: University of British Columbia Press / Osgoode Society for Canadian Legal History 1984.

Williams, John. *The Other Battleground: The Home Fronts: Britain, France and Germany*. Chicago: Henry Regnery 1972.

Willis, Kirk. 'Stirling, James Hutchinson.' *Oxford Dictionary of National Biography*. Oxford: Oxford University Press 2004.

Wilson, Bertha. 'The Making of a Constitution: Approaches to Judicial Interpretation.' *Public Law*, 1 (1988): 370.

Wood, Anthony. *Nineteenth Century Britain*. London: Longmans, Green 1960.

Woodward, William R. 'Inner Migration or Disguised Reform: Political Interests of Hermann Lotze's Philosophical Anthropology.' *History of the Human Sciences*, 19, no. 1 (1996).

Wolfe, Christopher. *The Rise of Modern Judicial Review: From Constitutional Interpretation to Judge-Made Law*. New York: Basic Books 1986.

Woolf, James D. *Sir Edmund Gosse*. New York: Twayne Publishers 1972.

Young, Kenneth. *Arthur Balfour: The Happy Life of the Politician, 1848–1930*. London: George Bell and Son 1963.

Index

2010 Judy Fudge and Eric Tucker, eds., *Work on Trial: Canadian Labour Law Struggles*

Christopher Moore, *The British Columbia Court of Appeal: The First Hundred Years*

Frederick Vaughan, *Viscount Haldane: 'The Wicked Step-father of the Canadian Constitution'*

Barrington Walker, *Race on Trial: Black Defendants in Ontario's Criminal Courts, 1858–1958*

2009 William Kaplan, *Canadian Maverick: The Life and Times of Ivan C. Rand*

R. Blake Brown, *A Trying Question: The Jury in Nineteenth-Century Canada*

Barry Wright and Susan Binnie, eds., *Canadian State Trials, Volume III: Political Trials and Security Measures, 1840–1914*

Robert J. Sharpe, *The Last Day, the Last Hour: The Currie Libel Trial* (paperback edition with a new preface)

2008 Constance Backhouse, *Carnal Crimes: Sexual Assault Law in Canada, 1900–1975*

Jim Phillips, R. Roy McMurtry, and John T. Saywell, eds., *Essays in the History of Canadian Law, Volume X: A Tribute to Peter N. Oliver*

Greg Taylor, *The Law of the Land: The Advent of the Torrens System in Canada*

Hamar Foster, Benjamin Berger, and A.R. Buck, eds., *The Grand Experiment: Law and Legal Culture in British Settler Societies*

2007 Robert Sharpe and Patricia McMahon, *The Persons Case: The Origins and Legacy of the Fight for Legal Personhood*

Lori Chambers, *Misconceptions: Unmarried Motherhood and the Ontario Children of Unmarried Parents Act, 1921–1969*

Jonathan Swainger, ed., *A History of the Supreme Court of Alberta*

Martin Friedland, *My Life in Crime and Other Academic Adventures*

2006 Donald Fyson, *Magistrates, Police, and People: Everyday Criminal Justice in Quebec and Lower Canada, 1764–1837*

Dale Brawn, *The Court of Queen's Bench of Manitoba, 1870–1950: A Biographical History*

R.C.B. Risk, *A History of Canadian Legal Thought: Collected Essays*, edited and introduced by G. Blaine Baker and Jim Phillips

2005 Philip Girard, *Bora Laskin: Bringing Law to Life*

Christopher English, ed., *Essays in the History of Canadian Law: Volume IX – Two Islands: Newfoundland and Prince Edward Island*

Fred Kaufman, *Searching for Justice: An Autobiography*

2004 Philip Girard, Jim Phillips, and Barry Cahill, eds., *The Supreme Court of Nova Scotia, 1754–2004: From Imperial Bastion to Provincial Oracle*
Frederick Vaughan, *Aggressive in Pursuit: The Life of Justice Emmett Hall*
John D. Honsberger, *Osgoode Hall: An Illustrated History*
Constance Backhouse and Nancy Backhouse, *The Heiress versus the Establishment: Mrs Campbell's Campaign for Legal Justice*

2003 Robert Sharpe and Kent Roach, *Brian Dickson: A Judge's Journey*
Jerry Bannister, *The Rule of the Admirals: Law, Custom, and Naval Government in Newfoundland, 1699–1832*
George Finlayson, *John J. Robinette, Peerless Mentor: An Appreciation*
Peter Oliver, *The Conventional Man: The Diaries of Ontario Chief Justice Robert A. Harrison, 1856–1878*

2002 John T. Saywell, *The Lawmakers: Judicial Power and the Shaping of Canadian Federalism*
Patrick Brode, *Courted and Abandoned: Seduction in Canadian Law*
David Murray, *Colonial Justice: Justice, Morality, and Crime in the Niagara District, 1791–1849*
F. Murray Greenwood and Barry Wright, eds., *Canadian State Trials, Volume II: Rebellion and Invasion in the Canadas, 1837–1839*

2001 Ellen Anderson, *Judging Bertha Wilson: Law as Large as Life*
Judy Fudge and Eric Tucker, *Labour before the Law: The Regulation of Workers' Collective Action in Canada, 1900–1948*
Laurel Sefton MacDowell, *Renegade Lawyer: The Life of J.L. Cohen*

2000 Barry Cahill, 'The Thousandth Man': A Biography of James McGregor Stewart
A.B. McKillop, *The Spinster and the Prophet: Florence Deeks, H.G. Wells, and the Mystery of the Purloined Past*
Beverley Boissery and F. Murray Greenwood, *Uncertain Justice: Canadian Women and Capital Punishment*
Bruce Ziff, *Unforeseen Legacies: Reuben Wells Leonard and the Leonard Foundation Trust*

1999 Constance Backhouse, *Colour-Coded: A Legal History of Racism in Canada, 1900–1950*
G. Blaine Baker and Jim Phillips, eds., *Essays in the History of Canadian Law: Volume VIII – In Honour of R.C.B. Risk*
Richard W. Pound, *Chief Justice W.R. Jackett: By the Law of the Land*
David Vanek, *Fulfilment: Memoirs of a Criminal Court Judge*

1998 Sidney Harring, *White Man's Law: Native People in Nineteenth-Century Canadian Jurisprudence*